CONFEDERACY
OF
SILENCE

A True Tale
of the
New Old South

RICHARD RUBIN

ATRIA BOOKS

NEW YORK LONDON TORONTO SYDNEY SINGAPORE

ATRIA BOOKS

1230 Avenue of the Americas
New York, NY 10020

ISBN: 0-671-03666-1

First Atria Books hardcover printing July 2002

10 9 8 7 6 5 4 3 2 1

ATRIA BOOKS is a trademark of Simon & Schuster, Inc.

For information regarding special discounts for bulk purchases,
please contact Simon & Schuster Special Sales at 1-800-456-6798 or
business@simonandschuster.com

Cover design by Tom McKeveny

Printed in the U.S.A.

To the good people of Mississippi,
who treated me like one of their own.

Contents

PART III:
THE DEATH OF MY GREENWOOD

PROLOGUE

Thanksgiving, 1994

"Hey, you ol' Yankee Jew!" the voice boomed through the earpiece before I could say hello. Even if he had been able to disguise his thick Mississippi Delta accent, I would have known it was Jack Henderson. No one else in the world would ever address me that way. As always, it immediately lifted my spirits.

They needed it. Even though it was Thanksgiving Day, I wasn't feeling terribly festive or even thankful. A year had passed since I had returned to New York full of hope and promise, after having spent more than two years working as a freelance writer in Memphis, although to call what I did down there "freelancing" would be excessively romantic; in truth I had been a scavenger, hustling for any kind of writing work I could get, which meant taking jobs that none of the older, more established writers would touch: video scripts designed to sell prosthetic hips and knees; brochures for a woman who made her living tattooing makeup on other women; a safety manual for a slaughterhouse. All of that would change, though, in New York—or so I imagined when I moved back there, shortly before Thanksgiving, 1993. I was twenty-six years old, and absolutely certain that within weeks I would start publishing short stories and essays and articles in national magazines. Money and recognition could not possibly lie more than a few months in my future. But things didn't work out that way, not at all; and now, a year later, I had managed to land only one job—working on

I

a documentary that ran out of funding after a couple of months—and had yet to publish a single word anywhere. What I had done was revert to a bad habit I had picked up in Memphis—that of slowly starving to death. At least, I thought as I sat in my apartment that Thanksgiving morning in 1994, I'll get fed tonight. I *was* thankful for that much.

And then, as it always does at times like this in stories like this, the telephone rang.

Jack was calling to wish me a happy holiday, and because we hadn't spoken in several months. We went through our usual conversational routine, quickly dispatching the matter of what was new in our lives (not much on either side) before moving on to the subject of people we had both known when I'd lived in Greenwood, Mississippi—friends, coworkers, local bigshots and eccentrics and drunks, and, lastly, former high school athletes we had followed and covered for the newspaper. There was very little in any of these conversations to distinguish them from any other we'd had since I'd moved away; few people in Greenwood seemed to advance or change in any way, and no one ever seemed to leave, no matter how desperately they wanted or needed to do so. As much as hearing Jack's voice had cheered me up, after a few minutes on the phone with him I was starting to feel a certain depression creep over my consciousness. In an attempt to ward it off, I inquired about the one person whom I was certain had managed to move up and out of Greenwood to greater things. "How's Handy Campbell?" I asked. "I haven't been able to find him on TV yet. Who's he playing for these days?"

There was a pause. "You don't know?" Jack said.

"Know what?"

"He ain't playin' for anyone. He's sittin' in jail in the courthouse, waitin' on a trial."

"What?" I shouted. "What's the charge?"

"Oh, you'll like this one, Richit," Jack answered. *"Capital murder."*

An uncountable number of thoughts careered through my head, but none of them made any sense. Handy Campbell, a murderer?

I had always expected to see Handy playing in the NFL someday, not languishing in a cell in the county jail on his way to death row. This couldn't possibly be the same Handy Campbell I had known in Greenwood, an extraordinarily gifted athlete, a quarterback of exceptional and natural skill and grace who was also, nevertheless, a genuinely humble and soft-spoken person, the kind of kid who always looked at the ground and called me "Sir"—even though I was barely four years older than he—whenever he undertook to answer a question I had posed to him after a night of glory on the gridiron. It couldn't be.

"What did he do?" I asked Jack after I managed to regain the ability to speak. "Who did he kill?"

"Remember Freddie Williams? Drove a truck for UPS? Used to deliver to the *Commonwealth?*"

"Sure," I said. Freddie Williams was a flamboyant man not easily forgotten, especially in the context of a conservative town like Greenwood. "Handy Campbell killed *him?* Why?"

"What I heard was that him and this other guy, Myrick—you remember him?"

"I don't think so."

"Well, y'friend Handy and this Myrick wanted to borrow Freddie Williams's truck, and he told them, 'You can have it if you suck my dick.' So they did it and then they killed him."

"Get out of here!"

"I don't know, but it don't sound that far-fetched to me. I do know that when they found Freddie's body, he didn't have no pants on."

"This is crazy," I said. "Handy Campbell didn't kill anybody. Why would he do something like that? He couldn't. He's no more of a murderer than I am."

"Richit," Jack said, "when was the last time you saw your old friend Handy Campbell? You know he got kicked out of Ole Miss."

"No," I said. "I thought he went to Mississippi State."

"He did, but then he left and went to Ole Miss, and then he got hisself kicked outta there, and then a little later he come back to town and moved back in with his mama at Snowden Jones and I heard he was into drugs and that kind of thing. They said he and this Myrick wanted Freddie Williams's truck so they could rob dorm rooms at LSU. That's where they caught them, down there on the campus in Baton Rouge, with that truck all full of stuff."

"Jesus," I said, not knowing what else I could say. I was certain that Handy Campbell could not have murdered anyone, and equally certain that he would, nevertheless, be convicted of murder; I knew him and Greenwood and Mississippi too well to believe in the possibility of any other scenario playing out. I wanted to talk about it further with Jack, to run through the scant details again and search for a few shards of evidence that might point to some other conclusion. But I said nothing more; I knew that there was no point to it. Jack had clearly made up his mind about the whole thing already, and his opinion, expressed so succinctly to me, was obviously not his alone; it was, I understood, the judgment of the entire town. As far as Greenwood was concerned, Handy Campbell was guilty, and he was going to be convicted as a matter of course, and probably get the death penalty in the process. Never mind his athletic gifts, his cordiality and humility; never mind his exceptional promise. Those were all gone now. All that remained was a body in a jail cell, awaiting the inevitable. He was already dead.

And I took it personally.

෩ඁ෨

Handy Campbell and I had both barged into Greenwood's collective consciousness at the same time, he as the high school's star quarterback, I as the local newspaper's cub reporter. I had needed him for copy as much as he had needed me for coverage. But I got even more out of the bargain: Handy was my first big story in a strange new town at a strange new job. Writing about Handy Campbell, about his meteoric rise out of poverty and oblivion, about his weekly triumphs and the future that seemed to grow brighter with each successive Friday night, chased away my own loneliness and insecurity and alienation. When Handy Campbell did well on the football field, I did well in the newsroom. When Handy Campbell led the Greenwood High School Bulldogs to a victory no one but he had thought possible, Richard Rubin finally started to feel at home in Greenwood. And when he signed on with a big-time college football program, I took it as a harbinger of my own future glory. Handy and I had risen together. And now we were falling together.

Except I wasn't a black kid sitting in a Mississippi jail cell, awaiting trial for capital murder. I was a white kid, sitting in a Manhattan apartment, faced with no greater quandary than determining whether I was going to borrow next month's rent money from friends or take a cash advance on a credit card. I was a long way from Greenwood, Mississippi, so long that I could scarcely imagine that I had ever lived there at all. And yet, as my conversation with my friend Jack Henderson that afternoon drew toward a close, I realized that I had to go back again, and soon. I had to find out for myself what had kept Handy Campbell from a career in the National Football League, and what really had happened on the night that he and Lanardo Myrick—at least according to the State of Mississippi—murdered Freddie Williams in Greenwood. I had to know whether a jury would set him free or send him to the death house at Parchman Penitentiary. And I needed to be there when it happened.

I had borne witness to Handy Campbell's brightest nights. Now, I knew, I would have to bear witness to his darkest days. If I didn't, no one else would.

As noble as that sounded, though, I knew it wasn't the whole truth. I had other reasons for needing to return to Greenwood, reasons that were entirely my own. Greenwood, Mississippi had haunted me ever since I'd left it, silently slipping out before dawn one morning more than five years earlier. It dashed in and out of my essays, invaded my short stories, hijacked my dreams. Memories of Greenwood challenged everything I ever believed about right and wrong and human nature, waging such a good fight that at times they seemed poised to not only change my mind but to dismantle it. I had to make my peace with Greenwood, or expel it from my consciousness forever. This trip, I figured, would at last enable me to do one or the other.

It was an ambitious plan, and, I would discover, one that was exceedingly idealistic and naïve. It would take me a long time to figure out how much I had misjudged Greenwood, Mississippi.

But less than it had taken me the first time.

Part One

The High-Water Mark of My Confederacy

ONE

HOSPITALITY STATE

*T*he true wonder of hindsight lies not in its ability to clarify situations and events, but in its propensity to coat them with a glaze of dignity and glamour, even glory. Today, when people ask me why I moved to Mississippi in the summer of 1988, I tell them I did it for adventure, and to get a priceless education in the science of journalism, and because I wanted to see and experience and understand a place I had studied and written about extensively in college.

At the time, though, I was pretty sure I was going to Mississippi because I couldn't type.

❧❧

I was supposed to be a lawyer. In high school, I had excelled in the extracurricular activity known as Mock Trial, wherein young aspiring jurists pretend to be attorneys, jousting over fabricated criminal and civil suits in classrooms decked out to resemble courtrooms. My team and I were so good at it that we went all the way to the state championships in Albany my senior year.

In the fall of 1984 I enrolled at the University of Pennsylvania and, at the end of my freshman year, declared a major in American history, a major of choice for prospective lawyers. But during my sophomore year, something unthinkable and unconscionable happened: I began to develop a real passion for my major. The study of American history, I began to understand, concerned nothing less than the human condition, and I couldn't get my fill of it. I took enough history classes for two majors, many of them on subjects that could not possibly serve me in law school. And I always opted for term papers rather than exams—because, as I had discovered, I was also beginning to develop a real passion for writing.

In the winter of my junior year, I participated in a seminar on the subject of "Race in America" and watched, as part of the class, the PBS documentary *Eyes on the Prize.* Much of the first installment of that series dealt with the story of Emmett Till, a black fourteen-year-old boy who left his home in Chicago in the summer of 1955 to visit relatives in the tiny Delta town of Money, Mississippi. One afternoon, while playing with some cousins and their friends outside a small general store, Till removed from his wallet a photograph of a white girl and passed it around, explaining that the girl in the picture was actually his girlfriend. The other children were incredulous; they were, after all, black Mississippians, and in the Mississippi of 1955 black men didn't dare look at white women, much less date them. But Till was adamant, and the other children, looking to call his bluff, challenged him to walk into the store and ask the white woman behind the counter—twenty-one-year-old Carolyn Bryant—for a date. Perhaps no one, the film's narrator explained, will ever know for certain what happened next, but according to some of the other children present, Emmett Till strode into the store, bought some candy, and then, on his way out, turned to Carolyn Bryant and said "Bye, Baby."

Two nights later, young Till was awakened in his bed by two armed white men who were after "the boy who done all the talkin'." The two men— Carolyn Bryant's husband, Roy, and his half-brother, J. W. Milam—drove Till to a secluded bluff overlooking the Mississippi River and beat him savagely; then they drove him back to another spot, near Money, where they shot him in the head, tied a heavy cotton gin fan to his lifeless body (using barbed wire instead of rope), and dumped it into the Tallahatchie River.

Till's great-uncle, a sixty-four-year-old sharecropper named Mose Wright, reported the kidnapping to the Leflore County sheriff as soon as Bryant and Milam had driven off with his nephew. Local whites immediately claimed it was a hoax perpetrated by the NAACP to win sympathy for the burgeoning civil rights movement, which was just beginning to take hold in Mississippi following the Supreme Court's decision in *Brown v. Board of Education of Topeka, Kansas* the year before. But when Till's bloated, mutilated body surfaced in the Tallahatchie a few days later, the sheriff had no choice but to arrest Bryant and Milam and charge them with murder.

Almost immediately, the case made international headlines. Till's mother insisted on an open-casket funeral back in Chicago so that the world, she explained, could "see what they did to my son." *Jet* magazine printed photos of Till's mutilated body. And when the trial began, the following month, hundreds of reporters from all over the world jammed into the small courthouse in Sumner, Mississippi.

The trial itself was a mere formality. At one point, defense lawyer John Whitten told the jury of twelve white men that he was certain "every last Anglo-Saxon one of you will have the courage to free these men." And despite the great courage of Mose Wright, who dared to rise on the witness stand and point his finger at the two men who had kidnapped his nephew that night, Whitten was right: The jury acquitted Bryant and Milam after only forty-five minutes. Later, a juror confessed that the deliberation would not have lasted nearly so long had the jurors not also paused for a Coke in the interim. When it was all over, Bryant and Milam told their story to journalist William Bradford Huie, himself a Southerner. Yes, they had murdered Till, but he left them no choice because he had stuck to his story about having a white girlfriend and had refused to acknowledge that there might be anything wrong with that. "That's what this war is all about down here," Milam explained.

The documentary quickly moved on to a much longer segment about the Montgomery Bus Boycott of 1955, but I couldn't bring myself to leave Money, Mississippi. What kind of place was this? Was it possible that something like this could have happened in the same country in which I had been born, and only twelve years earlier? I had always known that things were different in the South, but my mind could not wrap itself around the notion that there might be room in my America for a place where two men could, with impunity, murder a fourteen-year-old boy for saying "Bye, Baby," or anything else. And yet, I also understood that I knew far less about Mississippi than I did any other state in the Union, and that for all I did know, even the laws of gravity might have been suspended there. In college I had met people from scores of foreign countries—some of which I'd never even heard of—but not a single soul from Mississippi. To me it remained a pure mystery, an abyss at the bottom of America. What was true for the South was true for Mississippi, I understood, but I perceived that there was also much about Mississippi that was untrue for the rest of the South—or even, for that matter, the rest of the world—things I couldn't even begin to fathom and could never learn at home in New York or in a classroom in Philadelphia.

A few segments later, *Eyes on the Prize* posed the rhetorical question "Mississippi—Is This America?" By that time, I had a burning desire to seek out my own answer to that question, to see that state and meet its people and try to discern who they all were and why and how they got that way—to explore this abyss, and understand it. So I dropped my old senior thesis topic (something about the Civil War, as I recall) and chose a new one—a study of James Meredith's integration of the University of Mississippi in 1962, an event that was preceded by years of lawsuits and venomous editorials and that precipitated a riot in which two people were killed and hundreds injured. I read through hundreds of Mississippi newspapers from the era, virtually memorized Meredith's autobiography, and managed somehow to get an interview with a former Mississippi state legislator named Karl Wiesenburg who had stood, virtually alone, in opposition to the governor's many attempts to prevent desegregation, and had been rewarded with ostracism and death threats. (Interestingly, Wiesenburg was himself a native New Yorker, a son of German Catholic immigrants, who enlisted in the Coast Guard in 1929 at the age of eighteen and was sent to their station at Pascagoula, Mississippi, where he promptly fell in love with a local girl.) "Mississippi," Wiesenburg told me, "was a state in agony. It was like a woman afraid she's about to be raped, and the federal government and James Meredith were the rapists." I submitted the thesis and won an award for it, but still I felt that I didn't understand Mississippi. I was starting to believe that I never would.

※※※

One day, early in my senior year, I was walking out of Stouffer Cafeteria when I experienced—quite possibly for the first time in my life—a genuine epiphany: I did not want to be a lawyer; I was not drawn to the law. Although becoming a lawyer meant that I would be assured of a good and steady income, that didn't seemed enough to me. I wasn't sure what I wanted to do, but I knew that practicing law in any form was not it, and I also knew that I, unlike most of my friends (who were much more mature and grounded than I was—at least according to my parents), would be miserable doing something that did not give me any personal sense of fulfillment. And so I took the law school applications that had been arriving in the mail and threw them in the garbage. Then I graduated from Penn and spent the summer of 1988 not relaxing and preparing for law school, as I had once anticipated, but trying to land a job.

Actually, I spent a good bit of that summer just trying to figure out what kind of job I wanted to land in the first place. I had come away from college with an impressive degree and some prestigious honors, but without, as I saw it, any discernible job skills, save the ability to compose solid sentences and proper paragraphs. I figured, though, that as job skills went, writing was among the more valuable of the lot, and that my presence would prove enticing to prospective bosses in any number of fields: advertising, marketing, public relations, television, radio, publishing. I didn't even allow myself to consider a career in journalism, which would have been my first choice, because I knew that no one started out as a reporter in New York; you either made your journalistic bones in some other city, or cajoled your way into a post at the *New York Times* as a deputy assistant wastebasket-emptier and prayed that you might find a way to slowly climb up the ladder to a position that involved some kind of writing. No, I thought, there are much better jobs in New York for a bright young man fresh out of the Ivy League and armed with a fistful of glowing references from prestigious professors.

I was mistaken. I perused the help wanted ads and responded to any I found even remotely alluring, sending out dozens of well-written, cheerful, confident cover letters, most of which elicited no response at all. A few drew form letters informing me that my letter and resumé would be kept on file; and a very few drew form letters inviting me to come down for an interview. Those very few were all for administrative assistant positions, and none of them paid enough to cover the rent on even the smallest of New York apartments; nevertheless, I was grateful for them and determined to succeed, convinced that it was just a matter of time before an opportunity to do good and creative and rewarding work presented itself to me.

Most of my interviews were at "employment agencies," dark little offices with unpainted walls and cracked, grimy linoleum floor tiles, where the person inspecting me was most often middle-aged and shabbily dressed and invariably chewing gum while spitting out questions in a tone of voice remarkably devoid of interest; the rest were at in-house personnel departments, slightly nicer offices occupied by slightly better-dressed, better-looking, and younger professionals who nevertheless showed no more interest in what I had to say. Wherever they occurred, though, they inevitably led to one paramount question, the answer to which determined whether you would go home that evening employed or disappointed: "How fast can you type?"

Not very, I always said. We'll call you, they always said. They never did.

Eventually, the whole thing started to make me angry. Here I am, I thought, interviewing for awful jobs that pay poverty wages and for which I am overqualified, and I'm not even getting them. Hell, I'm not even getting any second interviews. And all because I can't type. Why did I work so hard in high school in order to get into an Ivy League college? Why did I work so hard in college in order to make the Dean's List and win awards? For what did my parents shell out an obscene amount of money over the past four years? Was it all so that I could make a living using my fingers instead of my brain, and continue living at home?

And that's when I realized that if I was going to get a job in which I could learn and grow—a job I really wanted, for heaven's sake—I was going to have to leave New York.

That afternoon I went to the library and pored over recent issues of *Editor & Publisher*, a trade magazine for journalists. Flipping through the Help Wanted ads in the back, almost all of which demanded that the applicant possess years of experience and an archive full of clips—neither of which I had—I came across one, at the top right corner of the page, that both excited and frightened me:

SPORTS EDITOR

9,000-circulation six-day PM daily
in heart of the Mississippi Delta
seeks a sports editor. J-degree, experience preferred but not essential.
Call Emmerich, McNeill or Kalich,
at Greenwood, Miss., Commonwealth.

I made a copy of the ad and took it home. For several days I did nothing, unsure of whether I really had the nerve to answer it. Finally, one evening, I picked up the phone and dialed the number. As the line started to ring, I could feel my heart palpitating in my throat; I wondered if I'd be able to speak at all.

There was a click on the line, and then: "Commonwealth!" It was a male voice, crisp and high-pitched; the Southern accent was not terribly thick, but it was sharp as a razor blade. My face grew hot.

"Hello!" barked the voice. It was, I imagined, the voice of Mississippi.
I hung up.

The following night, having spent the previous twenty-four hours forti-
fying my resolve, I dialed the number again. The same voice answered:
"Commonwealth!"

"Uh, yes," I said, pausing to clear my throat. "May I speak to Emmerich,
McNeill or Kalich?"

"This is John Emmerich."

I cleared my throat again. "I was calling about the job? In *Editor &
Publisher*?"

The voice at the other end of the line suddenly grew warm and paternal. "And what's your name?" it asked.

I introduced myself and was immediately presented with a barrage of
questions about my education and experience. I confessed that I didn't
have much of the latter—a stint as editor of my high school newspaper,
during which time I produced two actual issues, and a few columns for
my college daily—and was surprised to hear that, as advertised, the position did not require any experience. "What do you know about sports?"
he asked.

"I know enough," I replied, a distinct confidence beginning to dawn
over me.

"Ever covered high school football?"

"Sure," I lied. The truth was that I hadn't even gone to any of my own
high school's football games, and had only attended football games at Penn
while inebriated to some degree or other. But I'd caught the Giants on television every Sunday, and I naively imagined that writing about high school
football was probably about as easy as watching the NFL on CBS.

"Good," he said, "because our high school football season's about to
begin, and that's going to take up most of your time." He explained that
his former sports editor, a Greenwood native named Jack Henderson who
knew everybody in town and had himself played varsity football when he'd
been in high school, had just up and quit to go sell insurance. "So I'm in a
bind, you see," he continued. "High school football's about the biggest
thing around here, and I'm gon' need somebody who can just jump right in
and cover it from day one. Y'understand?"

I told him I did; it seemed straightforward enough to me.

"Good," he spat, and immediately proceeded to explain that during football season, I would be working Tuesday through Saturday. The newspaper

came out every day but Saturday, and the daily deadline was 10:30 A.M., except for Sunday's paper, when it was around midnight Saturday. High school games were played on Friday nights; I would cover one myself—usually Greenwood High School—and have stringers cover the rest. After the game I would go back to the newsroom and write it up while fielding calls from the stringers and writing up their games, too. Saturday afternoons I would cover the local college—Mississippi Valley State University, a black school—when they were in town, then return to the newsroom to wait for other college scores. And all week, in addition to writing my own articles and editing others off the wire, I would be laying out the sports pages. "You've done layout before, I presume?" he asked. Again I said yes, even though I knew full well I never had, and was pretty sure I'd never even watched someone else do it; but it had already started to dawn on me that John Emmerich, my prospective employer, also knew I was lying, and didn't care.

He soon confirmed this. "Look," he said, "this is the way I see it: You don't have any experience, but you went to a good school. You need experience, and I need a reporter who's got a good brain in his head. It's a trade-off: I'm willing to train you if you're willing to work cheap. You come and work for a year or two here and you'll get enough experience to move on to a bigger paper somewhere. And in the meantime, I'll have a good reporter who fits into my budget. What do you think?"

It was my first job offer since college; I had no other prospects. And John Emmerich didn't seem to care whether or not I could type. "Sounds good," I said.

"How soon can you be here?"

"A couple of weeks," I said, suddenly aware of a great tumult in my stomach. "After Labor Day."

"All right, but don't make it any later. Our season is about to start."

And that was it. I had a job. I was on my way to Greenwood, Mississippi.

It didn't occur to me until after I hung up the phone that I had no idea what Greenwood, Mississippi was like, or what it looked like, or even where it was. Or, for that matter, what exactly John Emmerich had meant by "work cheap."

☙❧

A few days later I found out: two hundred and forty dollars a week. Even so, that was the least of my worries.

My parents were less than enthused when I told them of my plans and threatened, only half-facetiously, to have me committed if I even tried to go to Mississippi. Friends responded more enthusiastically, telling me at length how "cool" they thought the idea was. Nevertheless, every one of them ended the discussion with the question: "You're not actually going to *do* this, are you?" I myself wasn't sure; the main reason I'd told John Emmerich I needed two weeks before I came down was so that I could think things over at length, and see if, in the interim, I could come up with something better, or at least not in Mississippi.

But nothing better presented itself in that time, and a week after accepting the job, I finally started to accept the fact that I was actually going to take it. I bought myself a one-way plane ticket. I was still deeply conflicted—not to mention terrified—but I had no other options, and I found myself increasingly unable to present to myself a convincing case for reneging on my acceptance of the job in Greenwood. I began to feel as if I were in a car on a rickety old wooden roller coaster, ascending that first, sickeningly steep hill and not knowing what lay at the top; each click of the wheels on the track was another hour passing by, drawing me ever closer to God-only-knew-what. And yet, as my fear increased, so did my sense of resignation; and with each additional click, I knew better and better that there was no getting off this car. There was nothing to do but ride it out.

On the morning of September 8, 1988, I awoke early—actually, I had barely been asleep—stared out my bedroom window for a few minutes, and then shuffled downstairs for breakfast, a condemned man having his last meal. My parents didn't say much; by that time we were playing a game of chicken, waiting to see who would crack first. But they didn't, and I couldn't, my fear having risen to the level where it shut down all capacity for thought, leaving me without the ability to reconsider or reflect or do anything but proceed almost mutely to my doom. We loaded up the car and my mother drove me to LaGuardia Airport, and as we crossed over the Whitestone Bridge, I stuck my face through the open window and stared down at the East River as if it were the River Styx. When I hugged my mother good-bye at the airport curb, she reminded me that they would ship the rest of my things down to me in a few weeks—if I were still there.

❧

The only way to get from New York to Greenwood, Mississippi by public transportation is to fly into Memphis and catch a Greyhound bus for the final two hours of the trip. I did fine during the first leg, my fear-fraught mind, perhaps, relaxed somewhat by the thin stratospheric air. Even in Memphis International Airport I was all right, going so far as to chat up the porter who carried my bags out to the curb and helped me into a cab. As he directed my driver to take me to the bus station downtown, I handed him a generous tip and was comforted by my own largesse. This was going to be easy, I thought.

Then I got on the bus.

Already, my resolve had been softened somewhat by the sight of the Memphis Greyhound station, which was, like most bus stations, bleak and depressing. Years later, when I lived in Memphis, I went by this same station to see if it were, indeed, as I remembered it. It still had the same old ugly concrete walls and dingy floors, the same old tiny black-and-white coin-operated television sets attached to the same old cracked plastic seats occupied by the same old haggard and ragged people who appeared to have been left behind by life; but somehow, now, it looked different to me, less foreboding. Something had changed, I knew, but I couldn't quite spot it, and it took me a while before I realized that what had changed was me. Now I could afford to view the place as a mere curiosity, to regard it with a pure objectivity; I was neither departing nor arriving but only passing by, and I could see that it was hardly worse or better than any other bus station. But back on September 8, 1988, it was the gateway to Mississippi, the stepping-off point into the unknown. Back then, it was, for me, a place filled with an ominous gloom, and I thought it the worst I had ever seen.

Shortly after nine-thirty that night, the bus I was awaiting pulled into the station and an announcer called for boarders. I sprang to my feet, grabbed my bags and headed for the gate, relieved at the prospect of getting away from that awful waiting room. But as I settled into my seat and the doors closed and the bus began to back out of its space, it occurred to me that perhaps I had been a bit hasty in my eagerness to leave the station. Whatever it might have been, I thought, it was not Mississippi.

The bus wound its way through a few shabby south Memphis neighborhoods—I would visit them, too, years later, but like the bus terminal, they never looked quite as bad to me as they did that first time I saw them—and then, suddenly, the city seemed to end all at once, the house lights and streetlights disappearing abruptly into the road just behind me. I pressed my face against the window and glanced backward, trying to catch one last glimpse of them, some indication that there was still some kind of light out there, somewhere; but they were gone. All that remained were the two yellow cones that emanated from the headlights on the front of the bus, slicing through the darkness like needles through a pincushion for a few minutes before slamming into a huge billboard:

WELCOME TO MISSISSIPPI
THE HOSPITALITY STATE

The sign did not have the desired effect on me.

I suddenly became aware of just how dark it was outside the bus. I had never seen it so dark before. I was certain that it had never actually been so dark before. It was black—beyond black, really. This darkness was more than merely an absence of light; it was its own entity, and it was everywhere, all around me, seamless. It seemed to barge in through the windows of the bus and wrap itself around me like a moldy old comforter, blocking out everything else, even the thoughts in my head. I stopped looking out the window in search of some sign of human presence, already resigned to the understanding that I wouldn't spot one, couldn't. This place had to be entirely uninhabitable; who could survive amid such smothering darkness?

This bus, I thought, is the only thing standing in between me and the worst, most raw hostility that nature was capable of hurling against the kind of fools who might venture into a place where human beings obviously had no business being. This bus was a knife, plunging deep into some kind of beastly belly, from which there might indeed be no safe return.

O.K., so I was being a bit melodramatic. But what did I know of Mississippi? I knew about twisters and trailer parks, rednecks and the rebel yell, speaking in tongues and burning crosses. I knew about Goodman, Schwerner and Chaney, about James Meredith and Medgar Evers. I knew about the Reverend George Lee, shot to death in Belzoni, Mississippi for registering to vote. I knew about Lamar Smith, another black would-be voter, shot to death on the steps of a county courthouse in Brookhaven, Mississippi in front of twenty eyewitnesses, all of whom claimed afterward that they had seen nothing at all. And I knew about Emmett Till. I knew, too, that I was a New York Jew, a product of the Ivy League, a man—a kid, really—who had never worked with his hands or fired a pistol, or, for that matter, done much of anything except read and write. I knew a bit too much, and far too little.

The bus driver clicked on his microphone: "Clarksdale," he whispered, presumably to avoid awakening the majority of his passengers who were asleep.

"Clarksdale." Suddenly, as if on cue, a town appeared up ahead, or what I presumed to be a town; in any event, there were a few lights, and for those I was grateful. Clarksdale. Muddy Waters was from Clarksdale, I thought—that's all I know about the place, that Muddy Waters was from Clarksdale, and that when he got the chance to get out he grabbed it and headed up to Chicago and probably never looked back. The lights of Clarksdale were dimmer than I had hoped. They tried, halfheartedly, to beat back the darkness, and were scarcely successful. From what I could see, Clarksdale appeared to be nothing more than a series of deserted streets, dilapidated buildings and rusting old cars. There were no people to be seen, not a one; perhaps, I thought, they'd all moved up to Chicago with Muddy Waters.

At the Clarksdale Greyhound station, an old Depression-era building that looked to me to be abandoned, no one got off the bus or on it except for the driver, who stepped out for a second to stretch his legs; and soon we were back out on the highway ("Highway"? It was a narrow, two-lane road!), back into the black, the nothingness. Knowing it was hopeless, I glanced out the window, hoping to see something that might indicate that we on this bus were not the first people ever to venture over this terrain. But I couldn't see a thing, and then a man in his midthirties, who had been sitting since Memphis in the seat next to mine, decided to start talking to me. I hadn't paid much attention to him before—he looked a bit scruffy and tired, and had spent the entire trip until then either snoring lightly or popping peanut M&Ms into his mouth. Now, though, he began to speak; perhaps he sensed how anxious I was, or perhaps he was just bored, but for some reason he chose to start up a conversation with me just then.

"Pretty wild, huh?" he said, smiling and pointing out the window. "I ain't *never* seen anything like this before."

It wasn't exactly what I wanted to hear, but I needed some form of human contact by that point, and this was better than nothing. We chatted for a couple of minutes about the bus and the bus trip, and then he began to explain what he was doing there. "I'm seein' the country," he said. "I've been plannin' this for years and years, savin' up from all my jobs. I was working at a lumber mill at home, right, in Illinois, and then I went out to California to work on this construction crew that my brother-in-law was running, right? So I did that for a while, right, and then I went down to Texas, to West Texas, right, and I went to work for a buddy of mine who had this business painting houses . . ." He rattled off a half-dozen more jobs in as many states, and my mind drifted out the window again, returning just in time to hear him declare: "And now I'm takin' off and travelin' around and seein' the country, right, just like I always wanted to do." It sounded to me like he had already seen the country, more or less, but I kept my mouth shut. "So now I'm on my way down to New Orleans," he continued. "I always wanted to see New Orleans." He didn't think to ask me what I was doing on this same bus, or where I was headed, and I was glad not to have to discuss it with him or anyone else.

As he prattled on about his itinerary, though, the novelty of the conversation wore off and I began to grow annoyed and impatient with this man and his journey, although I could not at first discern why. I turned again toward the window. He didn't seem to notice.

Once again the driver's voice crackled over the P.A. "Tutwiler," he whispered. "Tutwiler." This time, though, there were no lights in the distance, and I was mystified at the thought that there might be even less to Tutwiler, Mississippi, than there had been to Clarksdale. The bus slowed down and pulled up alongside a lonely little white shack along the side of the highway. The old wooden benches outside were empty, and had been, I imagined, ever since they'd been built; they and a solitary light and a faded wooden sign—"Tutwiler" spelled out in plain black letters against a white background—were the only indication that people had ever had some kind of use for this shack. Once again, no one got on or off the bus—this time even the driver stayed put—and after a minute or so we were back on the highway, heading into the void once again. I turned to watch the shack of a bus stop grow smaller and smaller in the distance, and it occurred to me that I had so quickly grown resentful of the man in the next seat because I knew that in a few stops he would be doing the same thing, only this time the sign over the bus stop would read "Greenwood," and there, growing smaller alongside it, would be me.

☙❧

"Way-ebb," the bus driver whispered a few minutes later. "Way-ebb." Again the bus slowed down and pulled off the highway and up alongside another little white shack, this one even smaller than the last but with the same forlorn and forsaken benches. "Webb, Mississippi" read the sign, and of course no one got on or off the bus and I imagined no one ever had in Webb, Mississippi, and I started to wonder if the driver wasn't just toying with me by stopping in these tiny, deserted towns where no one could possibly ever want to board an interstate bus, much less disembark from one. Perhaps this is some sort of a game, I thought, the bus driver deliberately drawing the whole thing out, building the suspense, feeding my anxiety. But we didn't stop for long, and then we were back on the road again, and I knew the next stop was Greenwood. I looked at my watch: Eighteen minutes to midnight.

The estimated time of arrival for Greenwood was 12:04 A.M.

And it was then—sitting there and staring out the window at that black void with a little more than twenty minutes left to go—that I began to understand that what I was seeing outside the bus terrified me so much because it was just the same as what was inside me: absolutely nothing. I was an empty book; I had not done anything yet, had not really even lived yet. I had never been tested. But what bothered me most was the understanding that all of it was about to change forever. I didn't know what would happen when I got off that bus, or in the hours and days and weeks and months that would follow, but I knew that *something* would happen. It might not be traumatic or dramatic—hell, I might even like it—but it would change me forever. I was about to walk through a door, and I knew I would never be able to come back through it again. I would never be able to go home again, to sleep in the bed I had slept in the previous night, to eat at the table I had eaten at that very morning. There was no getting around it, either. Even if I stayed on this bus, paid the driver a few extra dollars and rode down to New Orleans, hopped a taxi to the airport and then a plane back to LaGuardia—even if I did all that, the person who arrived back home in New York would still be a different person than the one who had left the day before. He would be a person who had just faced his first big challenge and turned and fled. He would be a coward. A failure.

And just at that moment, as I realized that I had already walked through the door, that I had done it of my own free will and that I had better just accept it, and embrace it, and do the best I could—just then, as if to reassure me that I was finally starting to make some sense—I spotted a faint glow on the horizon, and the bus started to slow down.

This, I thought, could only be Greenwood. We passed a gas station, and then another, this one with a convenience store and bright, fluorescent tubes suspended over the pumps. Then a bar. A supermarket. A music shop with a neon sign in the shape of a clef note. The bus stopped: a *traffic light*. The first one since Memphis. O.K., I thought. That's a good sign.

The bus made a sharp left turn and suddenly it was in a parking lot. There was a building, too, larger than any I'd seen for hours, with a big dog painted on the wall and a few lights that flickered on and off in rhythm with each other. "Greenwood," the driver whispered, and I thought I saw his eyes in the mirror, looking at me. There was no one waiting at this station, either, and I was the only person getting up.

"Excuse me," I said, and the man in the next seat actually got up and stepped aside.

"Have fun," he said, without malice or sarcasm.

"Thanks," I said, and slid past him. I reached into the overhead shelf and grabbed the handles of my bag. I tugged at the straps, but it wouldn't give; it was jammed down in the crevice between the shelf and the ceiling. This is a sign, I thought. It's not time for me to get off this bus. Not yet. There's still time. I'll go back home, modify my career goals, lower my expectations. I'll learn how to type.

"Here," the man said. "Let me help you."

What was he doing? Why did he tamper with fate this way? "That's O.K.," I said, and tugged again, this time without any real resolve.

"No problem," he said. He slapped the top of his arm. "Sawmill biceps." He looped the straps around his fist and pulled the bag free with what seemed like no effort at all.

"Thanks," I said, as he held the bag out to me. I grabbed the straps myself; it was heavy, much heavier than it had felt just a few hours before.

"All right," he said, letting go. "You take care now."

I walked up the narrow aisle, looking out the window at the station. Where was my ride? I realized that I wasn't even sure who was supposed to be meeting me. I glanced at my watch: Eleven fifty-nine. Five minutes early! I walked slower.

All around me, people were sitting in big, cushy seats, feet up, backs tilted in full recline. A few turned and looked at me briefly, then went back to their books or crossword puzzles. The driver opened the door and stepped out. He stood there, perched on the little stairs, and smiled at me. Come on, I imagined him saying. This is it. This is you.

I made it to the door and was struck by a moist gust of wind. The driver stepped aside, onto the ground, revealing three tiny steps that led from the bus to the parking lot, each six inches high at the most. With each step, the air conditioning of the bus grew weaker and weaker. The wind came at me again. It smelled of earth and water. I relaxed my scowl and let it hit me square in the face.

Two

A FINE INTRODUCTION

September 9, 1988

Despite the fact that I couldn't spot him from the bus, my new boss, John Oliver Emmerich, Jr., was there at the station to meet me. His warm, moist hand grasped my chilled and clammy one and shook it firmly as he welcomed me to Greenwood; then he helped me load my bags into the trunk of his Cadillac and drove me back to his house, an unexpectedly modern ranch up in the hills a few miles east of town.

It was already well past midnight, but every light in the place was still on, and my new boss's wife, Celia, dressed with casual elegance, greeted us at the door as energetically as if I were the last guest arriving for a dinner party.

"Are you hungry?" she asked me, even before I'd had a chance to set down my bags. When I answered yes, a bit, she shot back, "Of course you are! What am I thinking? Come on, come on, we've got some bread and cheese and sausage. Can I fix you some tea? Come on, now, John, let's all sit down and have a bite and get to know Richard a little bit better!"

I had expected a hot cup of Lipton, but instead Celia brought me a glass of iced tea. Lesson number one: Down South, "tea" means the cold stuff. If you want the hot stuff, you'll have to be specific. I made a mental note and decided that this was almost certainly the last new piece of information my brain would be able to hold that day; I was tired and groggy and confused and, despite the warm welcome, still somewhat leery.

None of this, though, prevented my hosts from firing small-caliber

24

bullets of information at me, sometimes two at a time: I was welcome to stay there until I found a place, and of course they'd love for me to house-sit for them when they were traveling (which was fairly often), and John had a bunch of leads on apartments in town that I could check out starting tomorrow, and I could drive their son Wyatt's old Mustang until I found me a car, and Celia was a member and a big booster of the Greenwood Little Theater and they just did *Fiddler on the Roof* and it's too bad I missed it because I would have gotten a real kick out of it and I should be sure to get involved with their next production because they could sure use some-one like me in the cast and it was a great way to meet some very pretty girls besides. And I should be sure to come by the paper just as soon as I got settled so I could meet everybody, and everybody already knew all about me, and they were just as happy as all get-out to have me on board, and had I ever had grits and we'd be sure to have some at breakfast, and maybe they're an acquired taste but it's never too early to start acquiring it, and maybe we should all go have lunch at the Crystal Club, it's a real local trea-sure and just full of local color and I'd just get the biggest kick out of it, and of course I was used to fancier places but there were some very nice restaurants down in Jackson and that's only about a hundred miles away, maybe an hour and a half or so, two hours at the most, and I'd probably want to go there to find a car anyway because the selection in Greenwood was pretty limited, that's for sure.

And so on they went, until I begged away from another plateful of cheese and sausage and crackers, explaining that I should probably get some sleep before I just passed out right there at the table.

"Oh, please, you don't even have to ask!" Celia exclaimed. "John, we're all over the poor boy and he's probably been up since God knows when!" And as she showed me to my room, her husband called out after me: "Just get up when you get up. We'll be here."

⧼⧽

Of course, by the time I did wake up, after what seemed like days asleep, I had temporarily forgotten that last remark, and everything that had pre-ceded it; and as all the events of the previous day quickly flooded back into my consciousness, I questioned whether they had all been part of some long, elaborate, bizarre dream. But looking around me—first up at the ceiling fan whirling frantically to ward off the heat, and then out the window, across a wide, sloping lawn, obviously green but somehow rendered almost white in the brilliant sunlight—I realized: This is real.

The clock on the nightstand said it was well past ten. Embarrassed by having slept so late, even with the extra hour I had picked up by wandering into the Central Time Zone, I stumbled into the bathroom, rushed through a shave and a shower, threw on a pressed oxford shirt and my best pair of khakis, and found my way back down to the kitchen, where my host and hostess were already sitting and eating, albeit in bathrobes. It was Friday.

"Good morning!" Celia Emmerich called out, her face formed around a broad, bright smile. "How did you sleep?"

"Very well, thank you," I said. Too well.

"There's someone around here I wanted you to meet." She turned to her husband. "Where'd John go?"

"I think he's out with the horses."

"Oh, that's too bad." She turned back to me. "John is our— John, what would you call John?"

"I don't know," her husband replied. *"Houseboy* doesn't seem quite right. Maybe *valet?* No, I don't think so."

"Whatever," Celia continued. "Anyway, John's probably in his early sixties or so, wouldn't you say, John? And he's black, of course, and he's a little off, you know, in the head. Nice as he can be, of course, but a little slow. You understand. Anyway, John worked for years at Medart, and then they closed down whatever part he was working at and he was let go, and of course he just couldn't get any other kind of work like that, so we hired him on here, and he does work around the house and looks after the horses, and he does some cleaning up down at the paper, too. Just the nicest man. You'll get the biggest kick out of him. Very 'Old South,' if you know what I mean. Always says 'Yassir,' 'Yes, Ma'am,' that kind of thing. Just as nice as he can be. I'll have to introduce you to him when he gets back."

By this time, I had awakened and gotten my bearings to the point where I could, for the first time, take good measure of my hosts. Celia was thin and well made-up, elegant even in her bathrobe; she was a handsome woman in her late fifties, and it was obvious that in her youth she had been strikingly beautiful and, I suspected, had traded on that beauty. Indeed, I would soon learn that in her late teens, while living down on Mississippi's Gulf Coast, she had been to finishing school and had won several beauty contests. Later, in her early twenties, she had worked as an airline stewardess, and had met her husband during a flight to Texas.

John Oliver Emmerich, Jr. was also in his late fifties, although with his white hair and somewhat grizzled face he showed his age to a much greater extent than did his wife. They were, in many ways, distinct opposites, most notably in terms of demeanor. Where she was incessantly gregarious, he was reserved. While she was a fount of enthusiasm, he was laconic. She immersed herself in the Little Theater, surrounded by dozens of friends and fellow thespians, while he flew a tiny two-seater airplane. She, lithe and buoyant, was full of frenetic energy, while he, compact and stolid, moved slowly, deliberately. How ironic, I thought years later, when I heard the news that he had died of a heart attack while running up his own driveway; I never even knew he jogged.

He seemed above that sort of thing, a man supremely confident of who he was and unshakable in the belief that neither he nor his life could be improved upon. He had grown up in McComb, Mississippi, the son of a newspaper publisher—the late John Oliver Emmerich, Sr., known as "Oliver"—who had been a legend in Mississippi, if something of a controversial one. Oliver Emmerich, his son told me, had been publisher of the *McComb Enterprise-Journal* throughout the 1950s and 1960s, a time and place that were quite literally an explosive combination. During a single summer, my new boss told me, the Klan and other such groups firebombed no fewer than twenty-seven black churches in Pike County alone. It was then, according to his son, that Oliver Emmerich took a firm stand against such violence and the cause in which it was used, an act that made his name a household phrase across the state and inspired a seemingly endless string of death threats. His son, John Oliver Emmerich, Junior—known as "John" or "J.O."—was understandably proud of his father's celebrity and reputation, and yet I would come to learn that they must have been something of a burden to him, as well. Scarcely a week passed without someone or other telling me that John Emmerich wasn't half the man his father had been, no matter what they had thought of his father.

If this weighed on him, though, he never showed it, at least not to me or anyone else who worked for him. A graduate of Ole Miss, he was exceedingly proud of the fact that he had gone to Harvard as a Nieman fellow. Over the years, he had cultivated contacts and even friendships with some of the nation's most powerful newspaper editors, people whose pictures festooned the wood-paneled walls of his office at the *Commonwealth*, along with those of several presidents and senators. And in every one of them was John Emmerich himself, grinning broadly as he almost never did in the newsroom of his small-town daily newspaper.

On the morning of September 9, 1988—late in the morning, too, at a time when, as I would soon learn, his employees were rushing to get out the day's paper—he seemed to be completely relaxed and satisfied, an avuncular smile spread out across his face as he patiently introduced me to both Greenwood and the *Commonwealth.*

"We've got three reporters on staff," he explained. "There's Dan Johnson, he's our senior reporter. He's from down in south Mississippi, around Hattiesburg. A strange man, strange. Then there's Margaret Dean. She's black. I don't know that much about her, to tell you the truth. She's been working at the paper now for a few years, but we don't talk all that much. She's not really very friendly, but she does a good job. Her husband's a policeman in town, and she usually handles the police beat, among other things. All of our reporters pretty much cover everything, and you'll be asked to pitch in from time to time, too."

"That's fine with me," I said. "I'd like to have the chance to do other stories—news, I mean."

"Good, good," he said, "but remember that sports is your first responsibility, and I expect that you'll have your hands pretty full with that, at least during football season. Football is very important around here, as I've told you. Very important. But if you want to do other stuff too and you have the time, that's fine with me. As long as you get the sports page put together on time every day."

"I understand."

"All right. So where was I? Ah, yes, our third reporter is a fellow named Tom Hayes, from up in Tennessee. Seems like a nice enough fellow. He just started a couple of weeks ago. In fact, when you called me at first I thought you were calling about that job."

I wish I had been, I thought. I didn't know much about high school football and didn't care to; the thought of spending my entire fall covering that and nothing else left me cold. Somehow, I thought, I would have to find a way to get in some regular reporting, too.

"Our news editor is Karen Freeman. Sweet ol' gal from down in McComb, used to work for me at the *Enterprise-Journal.* She puts the paper together every day and every other Saturday, so you'll be working with her quite a bit. You'll like her just fine. Tim Kalich is our general manager; he handles the business end of things, mostly, but sometimes he'll get involved in editorial stuff. Not usually, though. Who else is there? Ah, yes, Susan Montgomery, our features editor. She works mostly on Sunday stuff, but she'll probably ask you to write a thing or two for her from time to time, which I imagine you'll enjoy. Susan's a bit, uh, flighty, I guess. The joke around the newsroom is: How do you know when Susan's been working at your terminal? There's white-out on the monitor!"

"Oh, John, stop!" Celia interjected, forcing back a laugh. "Susan is just fine. She's been very helpful with the Little Theater, Richard. She always gives us such nice coverage."

"O.K.," John continued, "I guess that leaves Mike McNeill. Now, Mike's only been with us a few months, but I'll tell you the truth—I don't like him very much. Not at all. He's always in some kind of foul mood, always has a nasty look on his face. He's just not somebody I enjoy seeing every day."

"He's not that old, maybe thirty-five, but he's just like an old man," Celia said.

"More like an old woman," John countered, chuckling. "I'd love to fire him, but the truth is I just don't think I could find anybody else who would work as cheap as he does, and he does his job all right. I imagine he won't know what the hell to make of you. But just remember that he can't fire you. He makes up the news budget every day and he'll tell you what to cover, so he is in effect your boss, but he can't fire you. I'm sure he'll try it, at some point, but he can't. Only I can. Just remember that."

I wasn't quite sure whether I found this tip comforting or disturbing.

"Now, there's one more person who doesn't work at the paper but you should get to know him anyway. His name is Jack Henderson, and he's the fellow you're replacing as sports editor. He's got a wife and a baby boy and he just decided he couldn't work for what I was paying him anymore, so he went to work for Teddy Shanks, selling insurance. But he's still going to cover games on Friday night, and he'll probably shoot some pictures for us, too. He grew up here and he played on the team at Greenwood High School, and he knows just about everybody in town, so you really do need to get to know him. He can be of a lot of help to you. I recommend you go visit him right away. Maybe he'll take you around, introduce you to the coaches and all. I'm sure he will if you ask him to. I need you to get out there and start covering football as soon as possible. Mike's doing most of it now, and I don't think he knows a damn thing about it, to tell you the truth."

I squirmed uneasily in my chair.

"Maybe you ought to come on by the paper this afternoon. They'll be having their weekly meeting, and it'd be a good chance for you to meet everyone. First, though, go out and find you a place to live in town," my new boss continued. Just then, someone rapped on the door.

"Oh, good, that's John. Come in!" Celia shouted, musically. "I wanted you to meet him before you go out, in case no one else is here when you get back." The man who stepped inside was thin and stooped and looked much older than his employers; his overalls were faded and dirty, his skin darker than any I could recall ever seeing.

"John, this is Richard Rubin," Celia said. "He'll be staying with us for a few days."

I rose from my chair. "Nice to meet you," I said, extending my hand. He shook it and smiled, nodding enthusiastically.

"Now, John," Celia continued, "I want you to take good care of Richard while he's here, all right?"

"H-h-he my new b-b-boss man, yeah?" John stammered, turning back toward me and bobbing in a series of awkward bows. I flinched in mortification at the sight of a man three times my age abasing himself before me. Was he kidding? Or was this really the way things worked down here, still? And did he—and my hosts—expect me to play along too and assume the role of benevolent but stern and aloof white boss-man to John's darkie footservant? I turned to the Emmerichs and silently implored them to tell me that this was all just a little play intended to mock old Southern stereotypes. But they didn't, and we all just stood there in silence for a few agonizing seconds.

"All right, Richard," my new boss finally offered, mercifully. "I have a few leads for you, but why don't you stop by this one, first." He handed me a list of a half-dozen names, addresses, and phone numbers, and pointed to one Carl Kelly, Junior. "He lives in a big ol' house on River Road, and he's got a few apartments out back. Rents 'em month to month. You probably won't want to live there, but take a look, anyway. You ought to meet Carl Kelly, Junior. He's the kind of fellow who's always writing letters to the paper, two or three a week. Usually they start out *I was lying in bed thinking the other night. . . .* He's a character, all right. You'll get a real kick out of him."

⁓✖⁓

River Road is a narrow brown thoroughfare that snakes alongside the southern bank of the Yazoo in Greenwood. Houses line only the south side of the road; the northern side is all levee, built up in the 1930s to protect the town from flooding when rains swell the river, which they do often. The houses toward the western end of River Road are nice but modest, mostly modern one-story ranches; but as one nears the eastern end of the road—the end, that is, closest to downtown Greenwood and the county courthouse—the houses become much wider and grander, sprouting second and even third stories. These are the houses one expects to see in small Southern towns, especially in the middle of cotton country—imposing, whitewashed Victorian mansions with pillars and capacious front porches and fifteen-foot-high windows. Carl Kelly, Junior lived in one of these mansions, but unlike those on either side of him, his was a study in shabby gentility. The white paint was dirty and peeling, the wood underneath it visibly rotting; the lawn was overgrown with dandelions and less attractive weeds, the stones in the walkway cracked and crumbling. This had once been the house of a well-loved local congressman, John Emmerich had told me. No, his wife Celia countered, he was a senator. Or maybe, John mused aloud, it was the place next door.

Carl Kelly, Junior, and his wife, Dixie Mae—really—were standing outside when I pulled up in Wyatt Emmerich's old Mustang. They were old and tiny, Dixie Mae standing barely five feet tall in a bright floral dress, her hair—just a trace of brown in it still—pulled back in a bun. Carl Kelly, Junior, wasn't much bigger. His hair, a pure white, was parted razor-straight on the side and slicked back from his forehead; his eyes were brilliant emeralds. I had never before seen eyes that color set into a male face.

He didn't even give me a chance to wonder how old he might be. "I'm eighty-seven years old," he said to me, very early in our conversation, so early that he was still shaking my hand when he said it. "Lived in Leflore County my whole life. Born up near Sunnyside, Mississippi. I worked on the railroad for more'n forty years, I sure did. The Columbus and Greenville. When I retired, they gave me a big party."

Eighty-seven years old, I thought, and he still uses the "Junior" at the end of his name. Carl Kelly, Senior, had probably been dead for forty years. I was starting to understand why my boss had said I should meet this man. Or so I thought.

They led me on a quick tour of the apartments out back, three tiny, dim cubbyholes with barely enough room for a cot, a chair and a hotplate, all of them even more run-down than the main house.

"All right," I said, walking back outside with them. "I have a few more places to look at, but if I decide to come back here I'll give you a call."

"That's fine, that's fine," Carl Kelly, Junior said. I started to thank him and turn to leave, but he cut off my retreat with a question. "So you're working for John Emmerich, you say?"

"That's right," I answered.

"Tell me—what do you think of the man?"

I started to wonder if perhaps I were being set up. "He seems very nice to me," I said.

"Mm-hm. And what do you think of his newspaper?"

"I don't know," I said. "I haven't seen it yet."

"Well, let me tell you something about John Emmerich. He's not one-tenth the man his father was, and his father wasn't much, either. And that rag he publishes? I wouldn't let that thing inside my house."

"You wouldn't?"

"No sir! He runs too many pictures of niggers in it, for one thing. Got niggers in there every day, just about." He said the word without any emphasis at all, as if he were saying "coffee tables." "Yes sir, he's a big ol' nigger-lover, no doubt about that."

I had absolutely no idea how to respond. Nature took over. My face flashed hot, and a powerful itch developed in my throat. I wondered if I should just turn and leave. Then I had a thought: Perhaps this was all a show, for my benefit. Maybe Mister Emmerich had called Carl Kelly, Junior on the phone this morning after my awkward encounter with John, and my new boss and prospective landlord had plotted out the whole thing. Maybe that was it—a big practical joke. The two of them were actually good friends. Nobody really spoke that way anymore, did they? After all, this wasn't 1958; it was 1988.

I noticed, then, that this little old man was examining me closely, exactly as I had examined his apartments a few minutes earlier. He looked at my clothes and my shoes, at my cheap watch and cheap haircut, both of which I had acquired back in New York during the frantic few days before my departure. I tried to avoid his gaze, but I quickly realized that it didn't matter; he would talk to me whether I looked at him or not.

"So," he said. "What church will you join?" The question stopped me cold, and I was glad I wasn't looking at him. I strained to get a look at his expression out of the corner of my eye, imagining that he already had a good idea what my answer would be, and that he might very well have some choice words on that subject, too.

"I haven't given it much thought," I said, without turning to face him. There—I figured he wasn't expecting *that*.

But he didn't pause a second. "Well, maybe you better had," he said, and I thought I saw a bit of a smile on his lips, even though it was hard to tell, seeing him, as I was, in the penumbra of my vision. "A young man needs to have hisse'f a church. Specially one like y'se'f, so far from home, you know."

I turned to him and nodded, then tried to ease away again, gently. "Thanks again for showing me the apartments," I said. "I'll let you—"

"Tell me," he said, ignoring the fact that I had half-turned away already. "What are your politics?" His voice wavered but it was, somehow, firm, demanding an answer less evasive than the one I had furnished to his last question.

And I was equally determined to evade him yet again. "Mister Kelly," I said, "I'm just the sports editor. I'm not going to be writing any editorials. Just sports stories. So I doubt my politics will ever come into play."

He shook his head vehemently. "Nope, can't say that these days, no sir. Can't avoid the whole thing now, not when the whole world is goin' straight to you-know-where." He pointed a little white finger at the ground. "Everything's all mixed up nowadays. Used to be, everything was clear-cut. Everybody knew where they belonged, and they stayed there, and they were *happy* that way. You didn't have niggers out looking to mix with white people and have yella babies. Those yellas, now, they aren't any better than the rest of the niggers, 'cept they figure they are, y'see, 'cause they're lighter. And when they grow up, they start a whole mess of trouble. They get it into their heads to go somewhere else and pass themselves off as white, and they might just do it, too, which makes 'em all the more dangerous, y'see? Because everybody thinks they're white, now, especially them. But they're not, of course. They're really just yella niggers, that's all, and a yella nigger is still a nigger and they have no business mixing with white people. You follow?"

I stood there, silent. I wasn't trying to figure out a tactful response, one that would spare his feelings and my conscience at the same time. I wasn't really thinking much of anything other than that I knew now that this wasn't a hoax, because no one would say those kinds of things in jest. That's really all I could think about—that this man was serious. That, and my own startling, fervent desire to remember every word he had just said, and how he had said them all. I wasn't sure why, wasn't sure I'd ever want to tell anyone about it, wasn't sure they'd believe me even if I did tell them. But I knew *I* wanted to remember it, exactly as it had happened.

"You're young yet," he said, in response to my silence. "You'll learn. We've got a lot to protect. Here, you want to see something? Let me show you." He reached into the inside pocket of his old polyester jacket and pulled out a folded piece of stationery. As rumpled as the jacket was, the yellowed paper had not been creased at all, except in the folding. He opened it and handed it to me. It was blank except for the letterhead, which was stamped on in gold leaf and took up the entire top third of the page. It read:

The Carl Kelly, Jr. Corporation

Carl Kelly, Jr., President
Dixie Mae Kelly, Vice President/Secretary/Treasurer
Carl Kelly III, Carl Kelly IV, Trustees
Carl Kelly V, Carl Kelly VI, Future Trustees

"You see?" he said. "That's what it's all about—the future. We've got to do our part for our grandchildren, gotta pass on a legacy they can be proud of. Gotta keep 'em pure. That's what really matters: A white man's a white man, and a nigger's a nigger, and it's gonna stay that way as long as *I* have something to say about it."

I turned to look at Dixie Mae, certain that her face would betray disgust with her husband's rantings or at least embarrassment; but I saw only a smile, the same polite, vacant smile with which she had greeted me a few minutes earlier. *Is it possible she agrees with him?* I wondered. Aren't women supposed to be above this sort of thing?

"All right, Mr. Kelly," I said. "Thanks again for showing me the place. I'll let you know."

"Fine, fine," he said, grasping my hand and pumping. "You take care, now."

"Thank you," I said, and then added, reflexively: "It was nice to meet you." And as those words were leaving my lips, I realized what they were and what they meant, and suddenly I grew very ashamed of what I was saying and what it seemed to imply. But they were out already and I couldn't very well rescind them, and I knew that I would certainly find myself in this same kind of situation again and again as long as I continued to live and work in Greenwood, Mississippi. And I understood, too, that if I hoped to have any success at all as a journalist in a place like Greenwood, I couldn't go around picking fights with people whose views I found odious, and who knew just how many of them might be out there, anyway? On the other hand, I thought, I also can't go around agreeing with this sort of vile racism, either, just for the sake of being liked and welcomed. And so I decided, right then and there, that in order to protect both my conscience and my job, I would compartmentalize my encounters with people in Greenwood, separating them from their ideas, and my feelings about them from my actions toward them. Faced with the repugnant and loathesome, I would entertain my outrage on the inside while remaining, on the outside, inscrutably courteous and genial and above all, silent. It seemed workable, in theory; I could not have known, at that moment, just how difficult it would prove to be in practice, or that, while it would indeed protect my job, it would do something quite different to my conscience.

"Nice to meet you, Mrs. Kelly," I said, trying it out. "Take care."

"Come back and see us," she said, still smiling. "You're such a *nice* young man."

⁂

I spent the rest of the morning looking at apartments, an exercise that afforded me ample opportunity to test my new strategy, as several would-be landlords greeted me warmly and assured me that their properties were well-kept and maintained and safe and that I shouldn't worry because they were very careful about who they rented to and they absolutely *never* rented to niggers. I eventually decided upon a one-room apartment in North Greenwood—actually, it was a poolhouse behind a mansion—because the rent was only two hundred dollars a month and because the landlady, a funeral-home heiress and very recent divorcée named Sandra Knight Austin, had not even raised the subject of race while showing me the place. Later I would come to understand that she had omitted the subject not because of a progressive mindset, but because the entire question would have seemed, to her, absurd. North Greenwood was entirely white in 1988. It still is.

That afternoon, I stopped by the newsroom of the *Commonwealth* for the first time, just as the weekly meeting was getting started and everyone was heading toward the conference room. There was Karen Freeman, short and stout, her head crowned with flaming orange hair, her neck ringed by a rainbow of plastic Mardi Gras beads, greeting me with a "Well, hey!"; Susan Montgomery, tall and Popsicle-stick-thin, sputtering out an enthusiastic welcome between frantic puffs on her cigarette; Margaret Dean, even thinner than Susan, her hair pulled back in a tight bun, a cigarette with a half-inch of ash clinging to its tip stuck between scowling lips, letting a curt "hi" slip from the corner of her mouth as she tenuously stuck out her hand for me to shake; Tom Hayes, the new guy and much older than I had imagined, anomalously neat in an Oxford shirt and creased chinos and wing-tip shoes, his eyes magnified behind enormous glasses, smiling genuinely as he pumped my hand; Dan Johnson, the senior reporter, looking as if he had slept in his clothes, his pants smudged and wrinkled, his shirt stained and improperly buttoned with a necktie folded up and tucked into its pocket, his thinning, straight brown hair topping a face that somehow managed to appear both angry and bemused at the same time. At the head of the table sat Mike McNeill, the managing editor: completely bald on top, thick around the middle and wide below the waist, wearing a plain white shirt and Sansabelt slacks, just as, I soon discovered, he did every day. He shook my hand fervently and introduced everyone to me, then offered me a seat and organized his notes, his face taking on an unpleasant grimace which was, I would quickly come to learn, its default setting.

The meeting got underway: Mike read through the agenda while Susan offered blustering objections. Karen interceded occasionally; Margaret and Tom sat quietly. Dan weighed in on every subject and argument but usually waited until the end of each discussion to do so, content to offer his pronouncement as the last word while he sat regally above the fray (or so he believed; in truth, no one was even listening to him). Until, that is, Mike assigned Margaret to cover a certain story up at Parchman—Mississippi's notorious state penitentiary—at which point Dan bellowed: "That ain't right! I'm the senior reporter here! I should get to do that one! I want it!" Margaret just sat there silent, inscrutable as the sphinx. I had no idea what they were arguing about, having drifted off for a crucial few seconds to study the cheap wood-paneled walls of the conference room.

"I'm the managing editor here," Mike said, sharply. "*I* make the assignments, and *I'm* giving it to Margaret."

"It ain't right!" Dan howled. "I'm the senior reporter here. She don't even want it. I do the crime stuff. That's my beat. And I been waiting years for something like this!"

"I've made my assignment," Mike said. "I don't even see why we're discussing this now. The governor just granted him a stay. They're not gon' do it for a while."

A stay? I looked at Dan; he was pouting. What kind of person, I thought, fights this hard to cover an *execution*?

"Last item," Mike said. "Dan—your story about that little girl's rape? We're gon' have to cut out some of the details."

"What are you talking about? It's all substantiated!"

"I'm sure it is, Dan, but our readers don't need to know all of it."

"Like what?"

"Like, uh, for instance, what he, uh, used for, uh, lubrication."

"What?" Dan said, his voice suddenly dropping a few decibels but assuming a new sense of purpose. "That he used *motor oil* to lubricate her? That's an important detail! She was a little girl! How else could he have raped her? The public has a right to know this!" Susan scrunched her eyes closed and covered her ears with her hands. Karen rolled her eyes toward the ceiling. Tom looked as if he were sitting on a stove that was slowly growing hot. Only Margaret failed to react noticeably. I took all of this in during the second or so before my own embarrassment forced me to look straight down at the table. What a fine introduction to the world of journalism, I thought: a story so vile that I didn't even want to think about it, much less discuss it with the entire news staff. And God forbid I should actually have to write something like that up someday. Could I? Would I? Was this my new job? My stomach started to ache.

"Forget it," Mike said. "Now, if nobody has anything else, I think we're through. Anybody? All right then."

"It ain't right," Dan grumbled as everyone pushed away from the table and stood up to leave. "It ain't right to censor news stories like that. I don't even know why I bother writing them up."

"Come on, Dan," Karen said. "You know you couldn't resist writing a rape story if you tried."

"Richard," Mike said, "if you're free, now, why don't I drive you around town a bit, show you what's what?"

"Sure," I said.

We stepped out of the conference room and headed for the door. While passing the reception desk, though, I bumped into a short, slight, dark-skinned black man. He sported a pencil-thin mustache and more jewelry than I had ever seen a man wear before, both of them incongruous with his brown UPS uniform. "Well, excuse *me!*" he said. "Mike, who's this young stud in such a rush?"

"Richard Rubin, Freddie Williams. Freddie delivers to the paper."

"I also deliver to your house, now, Mike!" Freddie said.

Mike furrowed his brow. "Richard's new in town. I'm fixin' to show him around." He stepped around Freddie and held open the door.

Freddie stuck out his hand; there was a gold ring on every finger but one, and an equal number, I noticed, on the other hand. "Well, welcome to

Greenwood," he said, shaking my hand. "If I can ever be of help, you just holler, now, young stud. And you take it easy on the ladies!"

"Thanks," I said. "I'll try."

"Oh, you're a Yankee! Where you from?"

"New York."

"New *York!* Well, now, how'd you end up all the way down here in Mis'sippi?"

"Not now, Freddie," Mike said. "We're in a hurry. Come on, Richard."

Freddie reached out and shook my hand again. "I'll see you around, now, you young stud-hoss. And don't you worry about Mike, hear?"

"Thanks," I said. "Good to meet you." And I followed Mike out the door and into the parking lot.

"Nice guy," I said.

"He's all right," Mike said. "He poured it on a bit thick with that 'young stud' business. I hope he didn't make you uncomfortable."

"Why?"

"Freddie's a homosexual. Couldn't you tell?"

I was mildly stunned by both Mike's revelation and by his use of a technical and archaic term like "homosexual" instead of just saying "gay." "That's funny," I said. "I thought I saw a wedding ring on his hand."

Mike looked at me for a second; I couldn't tell if he were suspicious of the fact that I would even notice such a thing, or merely marveling at my naiveté. "Oh, sure, he's married and all," he said. "Got two kids. Maybe he's *bi*-sexual. But there's something funny going on there. It's common knowledge. I mean, just look at the man! And the way he talks? Come on now, Richard. We may not have as much of that down here as you do up in New York, but we know it when we see it." Again I was surprised, and a bit relieved: If Greenwood had homosexuals—indeed, if people in Greenwood actually knew the difference between homosexuals and bisexuals—then I supposed the town couldn't be all that backward. They might have Carl Kelly, Junior, I thought, but they also have Freddie Williams. It was something.

THREE

THE ALTERNATE STATE CAPITAL OF MISSISSIPPI

*S*ome people, it is said, grow over time to resemble their pets. Mike McNeill resembled his car, an old, tan Buick Skylark that was just about as plain as he was. The headlights were his eyeglasses, square and dense with refracted light; the grill was his mouth, teeth clenched in a compact, unfailing glower. The roof, dull even when reflecting the hard sunlight, bore a striking resemblance to his naked scalp. The seat covers, like his clothes, were well kept but decidedly outdated. There was no tape deck, just an AM radio. The car started with a groan and lurched ahead slowly, a low rumble of dissatisfaction emanating from somewhere underneath its hood.

"Now, this is Highway 82," Mike said, beginning his tour before we even left the newspaper's parking lot. "Usually we just call it the Bypass. As you can see, it runs right by the newspaper. It's the only four-lane highway that runs through town. It crosses the state, from Columbus to Greenville." And from there we were off, through neighborhoods and subdivisions, past churches and schools and factories and cotton fields. Mike took me by Greenwood High School, a square, modern, orange-brick complex across the Bypass from the newspaper, then drove us out Highway 82, just past the city limits, where he turned off onto a partially hidden driveway and passed underneath a wrought-iron archway. "This is Pillow Academy," Mike said, and indeed it was, molded right into the gate, along with the words: Founded 1966. A suspicious date, I thought. "Greenwood High

School will be your first responsibility for coverage," Mike explained, "but Pillow's a close second." As we puttered up the driveway, I expected to find at the end an ivy-covered brick campus populated entirely by white kids, but as the school came into view, I discovered I was only half-right. Pillow Academy was all white, to be sure, but it was also little more than a series of concrete and corrugated tin huts that appeared to have been thrown up in a hurry.

"How are their teams?" I asked.

Mike chuckled. "Not too good, as you might imagine. But this is where the advertisers send their kids, and they want their kids in the paper. Anyway, they only play other academies, so they do all right." Other academies, I mused, also dating back to the midsixties, no doubt. Pillow wouldn't get much coverage on *my* sports page, I decided.

We drove back into town and by the county courthouse and city hall and the police station and the library and Wal-Mart, past the cotton brokers' offices and old shops downtown, and the newer shops and supermarkets on Park Avenue in North Greenwood.

"This is Grand Boulevard," Mike said, turning off Park and onto a wide, green-shaded street lined by stout old oak trees and even stouter old houses. "This is where the rich folks live." We drove to the far end of the street and pulled up onto a short bridge. A river lazed below.

"Is that the Yazoo?" I asked.

"No, that's the Tallahatchie," Mike replied. "It meets up with the Yalobusha about a mile from here to form the Yazoo."

The Tallahatchie, I thought. Emmett Till's river.

And then we rolled forward again, and suddenly crossed a frontier so sharp and stark that it was the visual equivalent of stepping directly from a meat locker into a sauna. In an instant, the landscape changed from lush and verdant to dusty and brown. "This is where the town ends," Mike informed me.

"So what town is that?" I said, pointing out at what lay ahead, which was nothing but two vast, furrowed fields divided by a slender black road.

"It's not," Mike said.

"What do you mean?"

"It's the county."

"I don't understand," I said. "People live out there, don't they?"

"Of course they do. Someone has to own all that land."

"And where do they live?"

"They live in the county."

"But what's their address?"

"I don't know. It depends on where they live. Whatever the nearest town is, I reckon—Greenwood, Minter City, Schlater, Glendora. I imagine the closest P.O. to them is Money."

I was chilled for a second to hear the name of that town; I hadn't realized it was so close to Greenwood. "Wait a minute," I said, trying to chase the specter of Roy and Carolyn Bryant's store out of my mind. "Let me get this straight: Greenwood ends right here, right?"

"Right."

"And over there is just—nothing?"

"It's not *nothing*," Mike said, his patience starting to give out. "It's just not incorporated. That's what the Delta is, Richard—little towns in the middle of what you call 'nothing.' Fact, that's what the South is. Hell, that's what most of America is."

Sensing Mike's imminent exasperation, I chose not to push the point further, but my mind still couldn't process the notion that one could leave a town without simultaneously entering another one.

Mike turned the car around, and we were back in Greenwood again, back in town. We drove back down Grand Boulevard for a few minutes and then hopped another bridge, this one a longer, iron structure over a river I already recognized as the Yazoo. We meandered through the old downtown again, past a few stores that were open and many more that appeared to be half-open or barely open or shut down completely, casualties of the Wal-Mart and the shopping center out on the Bypass. As we hopped over a set of railroad tracks, I noticed a small white hut with a hand-painted sign leaning against the front wall: WE BUY PECANS. Again, I was confused. Why did they need me? Why didn't they just go to a supermarket and buy the pecans themselves? It did not occur to me that some people in town actually grew pecans in their own backyards. It didn't even occur to me that pecans actually grew on trees in the first place. Like many New Yorkers, I grew up believing that the food chain began at the supermarket.

We drove around a bit more and shortly passed what looked like a modern apartment complex, ten or twelve square, two-story wood and brick buildings, the wood painted a bright periwinkle blue. "That's Snowden Jones," Mike said. "The projects. You don't wanna go in there, believe me."

"But aren't we pretty close to the newspaper?"

"We're far enough," Mike said. I craned my neck to try and get a better look, thinking I must have missed something, some ominous detail that betrayed the danger lurking beneath the place's innocuous-looking surface, but Mike stepped harder on the gas and sped away, or at least pulled away as fast as he could in that car. Soon we were in the middle of a poor, run-down, sun-parched neighborhood.

"This is East Greenwood," Mike said. "Not a good part of town. You don't want to come here alone, especially at night."

I looked at the small white shacks and overgrown empty lots and forlorn little stores and abandoned buildings slowly going by, and at the men sitting around in front of them all in the middle of the day, not doing much of anything in the heat. It looked dirty, to be sure, and destitute, but dangerous? "It doesn't look too bad to me," I said.

"Trust me, it is. You see that park over there?" Mike pointed to what I had taken for just another empty lot, maybe a bit larger than the rest. "That's where Stokely Carmichael first used the phrase '*Black Power.*'" His tone was a strange combination of pride for Greenwood's place in history, and distaste for that particular claim to fame.

"Is that so?" I said.

"Yes. Now, coming up on the left is a restaurant you might want to visit some time . . ." And that was it for Stokely Carmichael, and for East Greenwood, at least as far as Mike McNeill was concerned.

༺༻

For the record: On June 16, 1966, Stokely Carmichael, who had recently been made chairman of the national civil rights organization known as the Student Nonviolent Coordinating Committee (or SNCC), stood before a crowd of some three thousand people in that very park in East Greenwood and implored them to reconsider the principles and tactics that had been SNCC's hallmark for the better part of a decade. The gathering was an outgrowth of the "Walk Against Fear," which had started out as a one-man march from Memphis to Jackson, planned and executed by James Meredith, the man who had single-handedly integrated Ole Miss in 1962. Meredith didn't make it too far. On the very first day of his march, just outside of Hernando, Mississippi, he was shot. He dragged himself off the road and was taken to the hospital; his wounds weren't fatal, but they were enough to knock him out of his own one-man march. Hundreds of volunteers, including Carmichael and Martin Luther King, stepped in to fill the breach.

Upon arriving in Greenwood, though, Carmichael was promptly arrested and tossed in jail. The experience changed him somehow, exhausted whatever patience he still had. After his release, he stood before that crowd in East Greenwood and told them that it was his twenty-seventh arrest, and that he'd had enough. "We been saying 'Freedom' for six years," he asserted. "What we are going to start saying now is 'Black Power'!"

There is no plaque in East Greenwood marking the spot, commemorating the event. There's nothing to note the fact that the SNCC offices in town were burned to the ground, or that several SNCC leaders, including Robert Moses, were shot at and almost killed by night riders in a speeding automobile, or that Bob Dylan performed here in support of local blacks who were being starved by government officials who resented their attempts to register to vote, or that Dick Gregory was arrested here while leading a voter march, or that Sidney Poitier and Harry Belafonte hosted a civil rights rally here, or that local police used fire hoses and attack dogs on would-be black voters several months before Bull Connor did it in Birmingham, or that a local man named Byron De La Beckwith drove down to Jackson one night in June 1963 and murdered Mississippi NAACP head Medgar Evers, or that the most powerful segregationist organization in the nation, the White Citizens' Council, had its national headquarters for thirty-five years in the middle of downtown Greenwood, or that Martin Luther King, Jr., was in town shortly before he was assassinated, or even that legendary bluesman Robert Johnson was poisoned by a jealous husband at a Greenwood house party in 1937 and died nearby three days later. There's nothing about Emmett Till.

There wouldn't be. Even more than the rest of the Delta, and the state, and the South, Greenwood, Mississippi, is a conservative place, and like most conservative places, it has a great deal of pride in its heritage and history, but only insofar as it chooses to recognize that heritage and acknowledge that history. If you were to drive through Greenwood today, you would see no historic markers attesting to the civil rights battles that were fought there, no monuments to the local men and women who sacrificed so much to that cause. If you were to stop your car in town and get out and ask the first man or woman who crossed your path—white or black—what important, historic events had taken place there, chances are they wouldn't tell you about the voting drives and freedom marches and firebombings and shootings that punctuated life in Greenwood throughout the 1950s and 1960s. With the exception of a handful of aging veterans of the civil rights movement, the people of Greenwood do not speak of that traumatic, dynamic chapter in their town's history. For the most part, the whites in town would rather forget it, and the blacks have more immediate and pressing concerns.

What you would hear about is cotton. Huge signs alongside the roads leading into town proclaim Greenwood "The Cotton Capital of the World." All of the town's police officers wear on their arms a patch bearing the slightly more modest legend: THE COTTON CAPITAL OF MISSISSIPPI. An old historic marker that stands next to the Leflore County courthouse asserts that Greenwood is "the world's largest long-staple cotton market," and although no one really believes that is true anymore, no one is rushing to revise the sign, either. There is a museum out on the Bypass called Cottonlandia, and another called Florewood River Plantation; the Bypass itself, like all of the roads leading in and out of town, is usually littered with flotsam from speeding cotton trucks, puffy white clumps that line the side of the road like snow in July. The most prominent object in the town's seal—and in the *Greenwood Commonwealth*'s logo—is a cotton boll.

Front Street, which runs parallel to the Yazoo, is lined with the offices of cotton brokers; along with the courthouse, they are among the few vital operations still remaining in downtown Greenwood. Every year, come August, the neighborhood hosts a festival called CROP Day, CROP being an acronym for Cotton Row On Parade; celebrants eat cotton candy as they stroll past dozens of empty storefronts, the departed merchants' names still legible on the splintering doors and cloudy plate-glass windows but inexorably fading, like inscriptions on ancient tombstones. Only King Cotton, it seems, could survive the advent of Wal-Mart.

Officially, in addition to being the seat of Leflore County, Greenwood is the alternate capital of Mississippi, meaning that, should some disaster or catastrophe render Jackson uninhabitable, all state government operations and related agencies and businesses would relocate to Greenwood, a town that in its current incarnation could not possibly hope to accommodate them. Unofficially, Greenwood is the capital of the Delta, a crescent of land that fans out from the Mississippi River and stretches from Memphis to Vicksburg. In ancient times, the Delta was entirely underwater, part of the Mississippi's riverbed; prior to the Civil War it was all swampland, with few passable roads or even trails, and just a handful of lonely outposts, like Greenwood. The Civil War, for the most part, passed the Delta by. Greenwood sent scores of men off to the fight, but the only action the area saw was in March 1863, when Confederate soldiers at nearby Fort Pemberton scuttled a captured Federal ship, *The Star of the West*, in an attempt to keep Ulysses S. Grant's gunboats from using the Yazoo to get to Vicksburg. It worked, but Grant eventually got there anyway. Two years later, legend holds, the citizens of the nearby town of McNutt gathered up all of their gold and silver and handed them over to a local man, who secretly buried them in the town cemetery to keep them from falling into Yankee hands. When Union troops did, indeed, pass through McNutt, they found the man and demanded that he lead them to the hidden store of valuables.

"Show us where you buried the gold, or we'll kill you!" the Federal troops threatened.

"If you kill me," the man replied coolly, "you'll never find the gold."

They killed him.

Today, all that remains of McNutt is the town cemetery, and in it, somewhere—if the legend is true—a buried fortune. The Union troops never found it. No one ever has.

After the war, when the swamp was drained, it was discovered that the topsoil in the Delta was extremely rich and incredibly deep, running in some places as far down as twenty-four feet—perfect for cotton, and later for soybeans, as well. Quickly, the Delta became what it remains today: a region of huge plantations and little towns set far apart, of long straight roads and vast treeless landscapes, of startling wealth and shocking poverty. Because it was an entirely agricultural region with a voracious appetite for labor, sharecropping came early to the Delta, right on the heels of emancipation, and stayed late, until the 1970s, when the mechanization of farms rendered the institution obsolete. Before then, blacks outnumbered whites in the Delta by a considerable margin, in some counties as much as eight-to-one. Even today, in the age of tractors and combines and airborne crop dusters, and decades after the great migration sent so many of Mississippi's blacks up north in search of better jobs and more equal opportunities, they are still a considerable majority of the Delta's population, to a much greater extent than in any other part of the state, a fact that might in some small measure explain why desegregation attempts met with particularly fierce resistance in the Delta. If what is true for the South is doubly true for Mississippi, then the same could be said of the relationship between Mississippi and the Delta. It has been called "the most Southern place on Earth."

And it is arguable that Greenwood, which lies near the region's geographical midpoint, is nevertheless the most Southern place in the Delta. It is not the oldest town in the Delta, or the largest, or the richest or most cultured or most beautiful. But over time it has come to symbolize everything that the Delta is and isn't, and everything it stands for—first and foremost, a resistance to change.

⥈⥆

Greenwood has always been a port; it sits at the point where the Tallahatchie and Yalobusha rivers flow together to form the Yazoo, and its fortunes have risen and fallen with the river. In 1834, only four years after the Choctaws ceded most of north central Mississippi to the United States in the Treaty of Dancing Rabbit Creek, a man named John Williams staked out a claim and established a settlement, which he named Williams Landing. Soon local planters were storing their cotton bales in Williams' warehouse and shipping them out from his docks. One of the most prosperous of these customers was a Choctaw chief named Greenwood Leflore. At one point, Leflore and Williams had a falling out, and Leflore then set out to establish a new settlement named Point Leflore, about a mile north of Williams Landing, with the intention of driving John Williams and his landing out of business. He came so close to succeeding that in 1844 the residents of Williams Landing, in a panic, approached their rival and offered to change the name of their town to Greenwood in his honor. The chief accepted the offer and closed down Point Leflore; nothing remains of it today. Only Greenwood survives.

Greenwood Leflore was born at LeFleur's Bluff, Mississippi on June 3, 1800. The settlement, overlooking the Pearl River, had been founded by Leflore's father, Louis LeFleur, a French-Canadian fur trader and entrepreneur; today it is known as Jackson, the state capital. Leflore's mother, Rebecca Cravat, was at least part Choctaw.

After being sent to Tennessee for a formal education Greenwood Leflore returned to Mississippi in the early 1820s, changed the spelling of his name, insinuated himself back into the Choctaw nation, and began to rise within its ranks. Within a decade, he had become the Choctaws' principal chief. Indeed, he was one of the negotiators of the Treaty of Dancing Rabbit Creek in 1830, and he appears to have done quite well for himself thereby. While most of his nation were being forced off their land and relocated far west of the Mississippi, Greenwood Leflore not only got to stay in Mississippi but was granted title to some of the most valuable land in the newly acquired territory, in the western part of Carroll County, where the Delta meets the hills—that is, suitable for both farming *and* living.

Greenwood Leflore quickly grew rich, amassing vast holdings of land and acquiring large numbers of slaves to work it. He built himself a legendary mansion, which he named Malmaison—"House of Sorrow"—after the Empress Josephine's famous chateau, and filled it with the finest furnishings from France. In 1841 he was sent to the Mississippi State Senate, where it is said he once delivered a speech entirely in Choctaw in order to lampoon the fact that many other senators were flaunting their high levels of education by delivering their own speeches in Latin. When the Civil War broke out, Leflore, despite being one of the wealthiest planters in the state, eschewed secession and the Confederacy and refused to pay taxes to it; nevertheless, he did not free his slaves in his will, but rather passed them on to his children and grandchildren in perpetuity. He did, however, stipulate: "It is my desire and will that my executors see that there be erected a suitable monument in my memory and I hereby appropriate to that purpose the sum of four thousand dollars." Four thousand dollars would have bought quite a monument in those days, but if such a memorial were ever constructed back then, its location is a mystery today. In fact, no one even knows for sure where Greenwood Leflore is buried. Malmaison burned down in 1942.

Leflore died there on August 21, 1865, just four months after the end of the War Between the States. Six years later, Mississippi chose to honor his memory by naming for him a new county, carved out of pieces of Carroll, Tallahatchie, and Sunflower Counties; and they decided, for the county seat, upon Greenwood, the town that he had won in a trade war twenty-seven years earlier.

On the map, Leflore County resembles nothing at all, except maybe a battered, warped old hacksaw. Its shape was determined by the course of rivers and the caprices of land surveyors. In all, it touches six other counties: Carroll, Grenada, Tallahatchie, Sunflower, Humphreys, and Holmes. To the east are the hills; to the west is more Delta, and more, and more, until you reach the Mississippi, fifty miles away. If you were to stand on a rooftop in Greenwood, you might think you could actually see all the way to the big river—the land is endlessly flat, with few trees or houses to block your line of vision. Were it not for the curvature of the earth, you might just be able to see all the way to Oklahoma, where the Choctaws were forcibly relocated. There is a sense one gets, when standing in the midst of the Delta's overwhelming topographical blandness, that it is all there is. It can make you forget mountains and valleys, lakefronts and seashores—not with its beauty, but with its mind-numbing sameness. And yet, there is beauty in the Delta, too, albeit not of the visual variety. It is there in the smell of the fecund soil on a hot night, or in the sound of utter quiet, or in the joy one feels upon stumbling into a little town after thirty miles of absolutely nothing.

In all, slightly fewer than forty thousand souls live in Leflore County. They live in small towns like Itta Bena (allegedly a Choctaw expression meaning "Home in the Woods") and Schlater (pronounced "Slaughter") and Swiftown; and in smaller towns, like Minter City and Morgan City and Sidon and Money, which started out as single plantations; and in still smaller communities, like Half-Mile and Quito and Shellmound and Berclair and Teoc, which also started out as single plantations but never quite grew enough to become actual towns; and way out in the county, far from any town or any place that's likely ever to become a town. And they live—almost half of them—in Greenwood.

ॐॐ

This is Greenwood: a hundred miles north of Jackson; a hundred and thirty south of Memphis. Fifty miles from Greenville, thirty from Indianola, thirty from Carrollton, thirty from Grenada, five from Itta Bena and the traditionally black Mississippi Valley State University. Skirted by Highway 82 and Highway 49 and Highway 7. Bordered by the Tallahatchie. Bisected by the Yazoo.

The population hovers somewhere just below twenty thousand. Sixty-one percent are black, thirty-nine percent white. Many more whites live in neighborhoods, seemingly seamless from Greenwood proper, that are technically unincorporated—an arrangement that spares them from the obligations of paying city taxes and sending their kids to the mostly black city schools. In the epicenter of town stands the county courthouse, in front of which stands, underneath a massive old magnolia tree, one of the largest Confederate monuments I have ever seen, and I've seen hundreds.

In addition to the courthouse and the cotton brokerages, Market Street has law offices and an appliance store and a bank and an old restaurant and an antiques shop and some empty storefronts and an empty warehouse that still bears an old neon sign advertising it as the home of the New Deal

Tobacco Company. The next block is Washington Street, a pretty, tree-shaded road where you can find the public library and the old Confederate Memorial Hall and the old Piggly Wiggly and the First Baptist Church and a score of old Victorian homes in various states of disrepair or restoration and the old town cemetery. After that, the downtown becomes a hodge-podge of shops—some still open and some closed forever—with the Jefferson Davis Elementary School tossed into the mix, along with the police station and the city jail, the post office and the City Hall, the bus station and the train depot, several houses of worship and several pawnshops, a car dealership and the power company and the phone company and stores and restaurants and an inn or two. For all that, though, downtown Greenwood always seems very quiet. The real action radiates outward.

To the south, for instance, are the railroad tracks, and then a neighborhood that used to be white and is now almost entirely black, and then Greenwood High School and a large park with baseball diamonds and tennis courts that white people don't much care to go to anymore, and then the Bypass, where you can find fast-food shacks and gas stations and convenience stores and a motel or two and an industrial park and the Greenwood Chamber of Commerce and the Greenwood Little Theater and the offices of the *Greenwood Commonwealth*. To the east are a couple of unincorporated neighborhoods and then Highway 7 and the Greenwood–Leflore Civic Center, which hosts shows and concerts and dances but mostly high school basketball games. To the north is North Greenwood, big houses and well-kept lawns and Grand Boulevard and Park Avenue, Greenwood's main commercial venue, with its shopping centers and supermarkets and department stores and drugstores and furniture stores and appliance stores and jewelry stores and banks and fast-food drive-ins and gas stations and a Ramada and the town's only movie theater, which has three screens, and the town's only bookstore, which is a Christian bookstore. And to the west is River Road and the Greenwood Leflore Hospital and some fuel tanks and grain elevators, and then the Bypass and more motels and more fast-food restaurants and more gas stations and a bowling alley and another cast iron bridge over the Yazoo and more car dealerships and a lumber store and a farm implement dealership and the Cottonlandia Museum and, as you're leaving town, a fireworks shack with a giant rocket standing alongside it like a picket, and, farther out still, a newer shopping center with a Wal-Mart, and Pillow Academy, and the remains of Fort Pemberton, where they stopped General Grant.

And that's pretty much it. Not bad, I suppose, for a town of fewer than twenty thousand. There's a local television station, WABG, an ABC affiliate which maintains a studio in Greenwood even though almost all of its newscasts are done out in Greenville. There's a local NPR station, WMAO, but in truth it's just a transmitter, broadcasting programming that actually originates down in Jackson. There's a local newspaper, the *Commonwealth*, but most people in town rarely read it, choosing instead between two other papers: the Jackson *Clarion-Ledger*, the choice of the middle class, or the Memphis *Commercial-Appeal*, favored by the upper class and its aspirants. There are a few local radio stations, featuring talk, country, and Christian music, but much of their programming is beamed in via satellite from parts unknown. There is local programming, too, but you have to know where to look for it and when.

There are a half-dozen or so public elementary schools and one public junior high school and one public high school, and there's one private school, where most of the white people who can afford it—and many who can't—send their children. And should Pillow Academy be too expensive or too crowded or too progressive or too secular for some parents' tastes, there are a half-dozen other private academies within a half-hour's drive, more or less. Some have no endowment; some don't even have accreditation. But all have grown astronomically in recent years, some as much as ten-fold, a tribute to the forces and sentiments and fears that have managed to maintain two separate societies in Greenwood and the Delta, even in the face of nearly a half-century's worth of progress that swirls around it like a hurricane. It's a metaphor they would like, too, appreciating being likened to the eye of the storm, calm amidst the upheaval wrought by progress, maintaining traditions and heritage and old-fashioned values and the peace—if only a separate peace.

But if there is much that divides Greenwood, there is one thing that has long united the town, at least for a few hours on Friday nights in autumn: football. Specifically, Greenwood High School Bulldogs football. Whatever else has happened here, Greenwood—all of Greenwood, from North to East—has always rallied around the Bulldogs. This was true in the 1950s and 60s, when the team was all white and the stadium segregated; it was true in 1988, when the team was a good mix of black and white; and it's true today, when the team is almost entirely black. It is not uncommon for the visiting stands in distant towns like Vicksburg and Clarksdale and Starkville to be filled when the Bulldogs are playing there, and for the parking lots at those faraway little stadiums to be filled with cars and trucks whose rear windows sport the words "GO DAWGS!" written in white shoe polish, and for the Greenwood High School gym to host three or four pep rallies in the week before a big game, and for the *Commonwealth* to run three or four stories about the Bulldogs in that same week.

In Mississippi, the saying goes, it's God, family, and football—and not necessarily in that order. And, as is the case with most everything else, what is true for Mississippi is true for Greenwood, only more so. In Greenwood, football somehow touches everything and everybody, and few people can resist its magnetic pull. It draws working people out of their houses on Friday nights, exhausted as they are at the end of the week. It draws shy people out of their shells, transforming them into rabid, shrieking fans. It draws business people away from business, churchgoers away from church, hunters away from hunting, criminals away from crime. And in the fall of 1988, it managed to draw two people who were by definition marginalized in a place like Greenwood, Mississippi—a poor black kid from Snowden Jones, and a New York Jew fresh out of the Ivy League—into the very fiber of the town.

FOUR

THEY'LL EAT YOU ALIVE

Friday's game was an excellent example of two teams playing
at opposite extremes of their capabilities.

My first story for the *Greenwood Commonwealth* appeared on page 11A of
the paper on Sunday, September 18, 1988—ten days after I arrived in
Mississippi—and featured, in addition to several typos and grammatical
errors, the above-mentioned attempt to lend the piece a touch of erudition. The attempt was a miserable failure, and the sentence itself would
almost certainly not have made it into the paper were it not for the fact
that the article's author was also the paper's new sports editor.

Fortunately, the local team involved was not Greenwood High School,
but an almost entirely black county high school, Amanda Elzy, so that few
of the *Commonwealth*'s readers cared enough about the game to even read the
article, much less take umbrage at my use of terms like "phalanx," "brutal-
ization," "preponderance," and "lest"—words which, I suspected, had
never before appeared on the *Commonwealth*'s editorial page, much less in its
sports section.

An Elzy game rarely merited a story in the paper. Most Fridays, in fact,
the previous sports editors didn't even send stringers to cover them, but
merely relied upon a phone-in from the coach afterward, which might in
turn have generated two or three column inches, presented without a
byline. But Mike McNeill had sent me to Elzy that night, as he put it, to
break me in; he couldn't very well send a neophyte without a single clipping to his name to cover a Greenwood High School game. No, that week,

he would be covering the Bulldogs, while I would be broken in on the Panthers of Amanda Elzy. Looking back on it, I'm surprised he even had me write up the Elzy game at all.

"Amanda Elzy?!" my landlady, the funeral home heiress, had shrieked upon learning where I was heading that Friday night. "My God, Richard, you can't go there!"

"I have to go," I said. "It's my job. Besides, I'm sure it can't be all *that* bad."

"Don't do it!" she wailed. "They'll kill you! They'll eat you alive!" I stared at her for a second, trying to discern some small trace of an ironic smile hidden beneath an almost campy look of horror. There wasn't one. Sandra Knight Austin, whom I had rarely seen not holding a cocktail and a lit cigarette in the same hand, was a simple and blunt woman who did not seem to have a sense of humor. She was indeed certain that a trip to Amanda Elzy High School—just a few miles from where we were standing at that very moment—would be a trip from which I could not possibly return.

"I'm sure I'll be fine," I said. And I was. The people at Elzy, surprised as they were to see a reporter (and a *white* reporter, no less) actually covering one of their football games, were nevertheless exceedingly gracious and hospitable to me.

The insects, though, were another matter entirely. A few seconds after stepping out of my car, I felt a sharp tingling at the bottom of my leg, as if a thousand needles were being jabbed into my ankle. I was wearing topsiders with no socks; but as I looked down to see what was hurting me so, it appeared as if I were, in fact, wearing one sock on my right foot—a crimson, shimmering, teeming sock: fire ants. Hundreds of them. Apparently, I had stepped on one of their beds while climbing out of my car. I hopped up and down, yelped, tore off my shoe and feverishly brushed them off me, a task that took several minutes. My ankle was red and swollen for a week.

And then there were the mosquitoes, thousands of them, each looking (at least to me) to be roughly the size and heft of a fist, hovering just underneath the rusty metal lamps that lined the field, largely obscuring the very light that had attracted them. Or maybe they had been drawn by the field itself, which appeared on that night to be the only part of the Delta that hadn't been drained after the Civil War. It had rained earlier that day, rendering the field the consistency of a thick lentil soup. Worse, it felt as if the last of the morning's raindrops remained hanging still in the air, a wall of humidity rising from the earth, and nearly thick enough to lean against. It was a rain forest without the forest, the giant X-winged mosquitoes outnumbering the people in the stands by a thousand to one and seemingly itching for a fight. Just the day before, I had watched, nauseated, as a City of Greenwood pickup truck trawled through the streets of North Greenwood pulling a trailer that pumped insecticide into the air in fat puffs; now I understood.

It wasn't much of a game. The Cleveland High School Wildcats, a somewhat integrated team from a small city about forty miles northwest of Greenwood, beat Elzy 42–0; the thing I remember most about the match was the sight of Elzy's running backs careening around haplessly in the mud. "There was no dramatic turning point, no climactic buildup in this game," I wrote back at the newsroom later that night. Cleveland's quarterback ran in the first touchdown early in the first quarter; "from there," I wrote, "it was all downhill, and rather steep at that." Comparing game statistics, I noted: "Elzy failed to complete a single pass . . . Elzy punted six times, Cleveland but once." ("*But once*"!)

So much for erudition. Still, if it was a boring game—and I'm certain that most of the Elzy fans in the stands that night would rather have stayed at home and given their dog a flea bath—I managed to enjoy myself thoroughly. This was *real* football, I decided—not that bright, shiny, clean and colorful spectacle I had witnessed a hundred times on television, but this 42–0 blowout, played on a dark, muddy field in the middle of nowhere: the rich, dark brown smell of the earth; the cheers and groans emanating from the sagging, splintered old bleachers; the coaches, not clean-shaven men in coats and ties but scruffy fellows, their shoes and pant cuffs caked with mud; the kids, who, it was obvious, were not playing that night as a step to something greater, but for whom this game was the top of the staircase, as good as it would get for them, as much glory as they would ever taste. They wouldn't be playing in college; most of them wouldn't even be going to college. But they ran and kicked and tossed and slid and stumbled and fell with everything they had to give to the game.

And I, the young reporter covering his first game, strode up and down the sidelines that night like the cock of the walk, talking to players and coaches as the whim struck me, and occasionally even striding onto the field during play to get a better view of the action, as much a part of the game as the coaches and players and referees. As it drew to a close, I climbed up the bleachers to the makeshift "press box" and gave an on-air interview to Lake DeLoach, who was calling the action for WCLD-AM in Cleveland. In the course of one football game, I went from untried novice to seasoned commentator.

The following Monday, Mike McNeill informed me that I would be covering the Greenwood game at the end of that week. But first, he suggested, I should drop in on a practice or two at Greenwood High School. And I should go over to Teddy Shanks State Farm Insurance and introduce myself to the previous sports editor, Jack Henderson.

༄༅

"Glad you're gettin' to meet me," Jack Henderson said, pumping my hand vigorously as he flashed his best insurance-salesman smile. Otherwise, though, he looked and sounded nothing like an insurance salesman. He was six years older than I, with a blond crew cut, bright blue eyes, a mouth full of big white teeth and a cheek full of slimy brown chewing tobacco; he spoke slowly and in an accent that was thicker than any I had heard in the newsroom. He looked and sounded like a football coach. He looked and sounded like a sports editor, at least a lot more than I did. He appeared to want the job a lot more than I did, too, but life had intervened.

"Man, I loved that job," he said, offering me a seat in Teddy Shanks's small, wood-paneled office. "Goin' to games, writin' up games, and that's all you have to do? I cain't think of a better way to make a living, now, can you? I'll tell you the truth, now, Richit, I'd still be there today if John Emmerich woulda paid me just a little bit more. He was payin' me two-sixty-five a week, and all I wanted was three hundred. He offered me two eighty-five, and I said no, I needed three, and now I'm workin' here. Hell, he knows I'll still string games for him anyway, and take pictures. He's not a bad man, but he's cheap. What's he payin' you?"

"Two-forty," I said, wondering, as I was doing so, why I was answering a question I almost certainly wouldn't have answered in any other time or place.

"Figures," Jack said. "I know he woulda hated to pay me even two-eighty-five, if I'da said yes. And I couldn'a stayed on that. I got a wife and child to take care of, and even now it's tough. Shit, I'm so broke I cain't pay attention." He pointed to a framed photograph on his desk of a laughing baby with white-blond hair. "That's my boy, Cal. Not even a year old, look how big he is. Just like his daddy." He jabbed an elbow into my ribs, then raised his arm and hammily flexed a bicep. "So what can I do for you?"

"Mr. Emmerich recommended I meet you," I said, "and so did Mike McNeill. You know, I just started, and I don't have much experience and I guess they figure I could use all the help I can get, especially in the middle of football season."

"You can sho'nuff write, though. I saw your story on Elzy. Man, Cleveland beat them like a redheaded stepchild! All right, so tell me, Richit, how much you know 'bout football?"

"I know a bit," I said. Then, after a second or two, I added: "I guess I don't know that much. I had trouble with the stats and some of the rules."

"Lucky you were at Elzy. That wouldn't fly at Greenwood. You know I used to play for them? Hell, I can take you out right now and introduce you to a hundred people in town who used to play for that team at one time or another, and they and their kids and their parents read every word that's written about the Bulldogs. Every word. So you cain't just go out there and cover a game if you don't know what you're doing. Folks'll be all over your ass like white on rice. But I wouldn't worry about it if I'se you. Y'obviously got a good brain in your head. You'll figure it out. And you got me. I'll go cover any game you want; I'll go cover the Greenwood games with you, even. I'll keep you filled in on what's what."

"Great," I said. "I'm supposed to go down to Vicksburg this Friday to cover the game. I could use the help."

"Well, hell, Richit, I was gon' go to that game anyway. All my friends'll be there already. I'll introduce you around. You want me to take pictures for you?"

"That would be good," I said. "I don't have much experience with that either, especially at night."

"Well, all right, then. Now, in the meantime, y'oughta get you down to the high school and watch a practice or two, see what's going on and get to recognize some of the players. And introduce yourself to Coach Bradberry and Coach Smith. I'm sure they need to meet you, and you sure need to meet them. They'll he'p you out, too. But I wouldn't let on you don't know much about football—not right away, anyway."

The admonition made me nervous, but I was grateful for it nonetheless.

"I'd better get back to the newsroom," I said. "But I'll see you on Friday, right? Where should we meet?"

"I'll just see you down in Vicksburg," he said. "Don't worry—you'll find me."

"Thanks," I said, rising from my chair.

Jack extended a hand and pumped mine again. "Good to meet you," he reiterated. "I'll see you at the game. And say, Richit—you buyin' a place in town, or renting?"

"Renting," I said.

"You need any renter's insurance?" he said. "Fire, flood, theft? We got tornadoes 'round here, you know. You cain't be too careful, now."

↏℞⟦

Like Amanda Elzy, Greenwood High School was a square, brick building, but the similarities ended there. While the two were approximately the same age—the former had been thrown up in a hurry during the 1960s in a last-ditch attempt to head off the desegregation of the latter by building a separate black high school that might really be "equal," or at least closer to such than they had been in the past—Elzy looked tired and worn and, if not quite crumbling, then at least as if it might just start doing so any day. Greenwood High School, on the other hand, was not only a much larger school but also a much cleaner, brighter, better-kept one. I wouldn't call it pristine, or a model facility, but it was clearly the gem of Leflore County.

Its practice field, though, was a mess, with only a few blades of grass managing to persevere amidst the perpetual cloud of dust kicked up by a couple dozen kids decked out in white practice uniforms (Elzy barely had game uniforms, much less a practice set). They were running sprints, tossing and catching and kicking footballs, slamming into one another like a mob of rams vying to court a single ewe, a chorus of grunts emerging every few seconds from the gritty brown mist. Punctuating this strange opera was a series of cacophonous whistle blasts, the whistles hanging around the necks of the three men, two white and one black, who were standing on the sidelines. The first, a young, bearded white man named Mike Martin, was the team's offensive coach; while neither aloof nor unfriendly, he was a quiet man, somewhat reticent and not, I would soon discover, a good source for either information or quotes.

Fortunately, the other two men were temperamentally his opposite.

Melvin Smith, the defensive coach, was a fairly small but deceptively powerful black man who sported a mustache and, at least during practice, a
white porkpie hat with the brim turned up. His voice was a raspy sotto
voce, the type that in a 1930s grade-B motion picture could have belonged
just as easily to a gangster as a football coach; I had already heard that his
defensive line was an impermeable wall that had yet to permit an opposing
touchdown that season. David Bradberry was the head coach, and he
looked the part: Thin and standing ramrod straight, with clear blue eyes,
straight white teeth, a slightly cleft chin and dark blond, brush-cut hair
that was just starting to become infiltrated with gray, he looked like a
younger version of the actor Kevin Tighe (who has, in fact, portrayed football coaches on screen). He struck me as a somewhat private man who, in
any other job, would be much more retiring than his current position
allowed him to be. In addition to dealing with players and other coaches
and parents and fans, Coach Bradberry had to deal with the media, and
even though in Greenwood "the media" was me, it was obvious to me,
from our first meeting, that he understood the rules of such an engagement
far better than I did. He was only the coach of a small-town high school
football team, but he was quite skilled at fielding questions with pat
answers that nevertheless sounded spontaneous and sincere. He also managed to win football games week after week, usually against schools that
were much bigger and richer than Greenwood High School. Still, he and
his team were almost entirely unknown outside the state, and even outside
the Delta.

He and Coach Smith greeted me warmly that day, welcoming me to
town and encouraging me to get to know them and their team a whole
lot better; they knew I had to cover the team anyway, but they wanted me
to take a certain personal pride in my task, just as they obviously had in
theirs. The season before they had played spectacular ball, winning every
game and the north state championship. This year, despite having lost
quite a few gifted seniors, they confided to me that the team was even
better.

"What's new?" I asked.

"Well, Coach Smith's defense is just fantastic," Coach Bradberry said.
"Not only do they keep points off the other side of the board, but they
put a bunch of points on ours."

"Not nearly as many as he does," Coach Smith interjected, pointing at a
tall, lanky, loose-limbed kid who was just rearing back to throw a pass, his

dark brown arm—a striking contrast with the white sleeve of his practice jersey—poised in extension like a slingshot. "You want to know what's new? *That's* what's new."

"Yep," Coach Bradberry said. "That's our secret weapon. You see that arm? That's a cannon. He throws that ball forty-five, fifty yards *in practice.*"

"And this is his first year?"

"That's right. He's never played on any team before. Any team, in any sport. Can you believe that? And he's a *senior.*"

"Wow," I said. "Where'd you find him?"

"He found us," Coach Smith said. "This spring, right when we were starting up practice again. One afternoon I walked outside, and I see this ball just flying down the field forever. I said, 'Who threw the ball?' and someone said 'Handy Campbell.' And I said, 'Who the hell is Handy Campbell?' and they said 'That tall guy right there.' I went and got Coach Bradberry, and he said 'I ain't never seen anything like that before.' And I said, 'I hadn't either, that's why I came and got you.'" The two of them shared a short laugh.

"'Handy Campbell?'" I said. "Is that his real name?"

"Far as I know," Coach Smith said. "That's what his mama says. Anyway, when he first came out, we file-checked on his academics and he was in a terrible situation. So we had to work with him, had to get his teachers to work with him. I thought he was Special Ed, but the kid—we found out that he was smart. The kid was bright. You want to meet him?"

"Sure."

Coach Bradberry blew his whistle. "Handy!" he shouted. "Come over here for a second. The rest of you can get back to it."

The quarterback flipped the ball to a wide receiver and jogged over to the sidelines, stopping in front of Coach Bradberry. "Handy, this is Richard Rubin," the coach said. Handy unsnapped his chinstrap, pulled off his helmet and nodded. Up close he looked even darker than he had on the field; and even though he stood a full six inches taller than me, we appeared to weigh about the same.

"Mister Rubin's the new sports editor at the paper," the coach continued. "He came out to watch us practice today, and he said he'd like to meet you."

Handy looked away from his coach and at me for a second, then dropped his eyes to the ground. "Pleased," he mumbled, extending a hand for me to shake. He looked up at me briefly, then returned his gaze to his shoes.

"Handy works real hard," Coach Bradberry said. "He's going places." Handy just continued to study his cleats. "All right then, Handy, get back out there."

"Thanks for comin' out, sir," Handy mumbled without looking up. "You be there Friday night?"

"Yes," I said. "I will."

He nodded thoughtfully and muttered: "We gon' win again. I'll see you there." And with that he turned and trotted back out onto the field.

"Not much for talkin' to reporters," Coach Smith said with a smile, "but he can throw that ball."

And that was it. That was my first encounter with Handy Campbell. If it seems decidedly inauspicious to me now, it seemed even more so then. If one of the coaches had told me right then that the kid I had just met would, within three months, lead his team to supreme glory and in the process become famous throughout the state, I would have had to stifle a dubious chuckle; and if anyone had told me that this same kid, just six years later, would be accused of murdering a good friend in order to steal his truck, I would have just gone ahead and laughed at them.

⁂

"So, Richard," Mike said the following morning after deadline. "You all ready to go on down to Vicksburg tomorrow?"

"I think so," I said.

"Vicksburg?" Dan interjected, turning around from his desk. "That's where we lost the war."

I stared at him for a second. "*We?*"

⁂

On Friday, September 23, 1988, I drove nearly fifty miles west down Highway 82, then turned south on Highway 61 and followed it for another hundred, a trip that took more than three hours. Throughout the journey, I was passed by cars with Greenwood banners flapping furiously from their antennas and "Dawgs Eat Gators," or some variation on that theme, scripted upon their rear windows in white shoe polish. Even so, when I finally arrived in Vicksburg, I was startled to see that the entire visitors' grandstand was already full. Hundreds of people had made the drive ahead of me.

I had not come down alone, but had brought a date, my first in Mississippi. Sharon was a petite blonde, a college student who also worked as a cashier at the Wal-Mart in town. I had spoken to her briefly a few times before, and finally, on the previous Wednesday, had mustered up the nerve to ask her out right there in the checkout line, while the two middle-aged ladies behind me inadvertently humiliated me by loudly cooing and whispering "In't that sweet!" to each other. To my surprise, Sharon, who knew even less about football than I did, agreed to accompany me to the game. Later that night, she would bestow upon me my first Mississippi kiss as we sat atop a cannon at the Vicksburg battlefield park. As a former student of history, I thought it entirely appropriate.

"Hey, Richit!" someone called at me from the sidelines. Baffled to think that one of the fans actually knew me—I had only been in town for a couple of weeks at that point—I spun around and saw Jack Henderson, wearing a maroon Greenwood cap and clutching a huge camera. "You get here all right? Got y'a date, huh? You Yankees move fast, I reckon. Come on, lemme introduce you around." He led me up into the stands. "This here's Kirk, we played football together in high school and now we play baseball in summertime. I run a semi-pro league. And this is Snuffy Everett, he played with us too in high school. He's so damn big I bet you thought he's a linebacker, right?"

"No, I was a kicker," Snuffy said.

"Snuffy got a scholarship up in your neck of the woods."

"I was at Pitt. I went for a tryout with the Steelers. They almost picked me up."

"But they didn't," Jack said, "and you didn't even graduate, you dumb-ass, and now y'ain't got no job and no diploma and you're stuck right back here with the rest of us. And this here's Bubba Ruscoe. He lives up in Carrollton. We go huntin' sometimes. Bubba damn near killed hisse'f one time drivin' into a bridge up by Coila, didn't you, Bubba? Got a metal plate in his head."

"Right here," Bubba said, rapping his knuckles against his forehead. "See? Y'wonna knock on it?"

"That's O.K.," I said.

"No, go on," he insisted. "Try it!" I held out my arm, crooked a finger and tapped it against his plate. It felt just like bone to me.

"Richit took over for me at the *Commonwealth*," Jack said. "They payin' him even less than me, and he's Ivy League. Richit's from *New York*." They nodded appreciatively, or so I presumed. "We gon' teach him all about Mis'sippi football. Come on now, Richit, you can talk to these boys later. Let's go down and get us a good spot on the sidelines."

And with that we pushed our way back down through the grandstand, which was even more crowded than it had been when I'd arrived. I looked around me at the people, hundreds and hundreds of them, all of whom had driven a hundred and fifty miles on a hot night at the end of a long week just to watch a high school football game; they were laughing and clowning, waving maroon-and-white pom-poms and seat cushions in the air, passing beers and Cokes back and forth, joking and chatting as if they were at a class reunion or a wedding. They were white and black, young and old, male and female, well-dressed and in glorified rags, but every last one of them was smiling and alive, and I just knew that there was nowhere else any one of them would rather be, and that every one of them would have driven twice as far just to be there. It was Mississippi and it was high school and it was only a few weeks into the season, but for them it might as well have been an NFL playoff game, and when the announcer introduced the visiting Greenwood Bulldogs, the stands behind me let out a roar that shook my very bones, and I roared, too.

> *The bad news is that Vicksburg scored more points against Greenwood than the Bulldogs had given up during the entire season previous.*
>
> *The good news is that it doesn't really matter.*
>
> —"Bulldogs pin Gators, win 20–7"
> *Greenwood Commonwealth*, Sunday, September 25, 1988

And so I, too, became a fan.

☙❧

There was another team I came to follow that week, and to write about, and root for. Leflore County High School, a small, almost entirely black school in Itta Bena that made Elzy's campus look splendid by comparison, didn't have much of a football team. But one afternoon, during the same week that I met Jack and Coach Smith and Coach Bradberry and Handy Campbell, I got a call at the paper from a man out at LCHS named Lester Smith. Two years earlier, Lester Smith (no relation to Melvin), who taught math at the school, had put together a cross-country track team which had since won every single meet in which they'd competed; nevertheless, his team had never gotten any coverage in the *Commonwealth*, and, in the hope of changing that, he invited me out to meet with him and his boys. Mike told me I was free to fill my sports page as I wished, but warned me also that most *Commonwealth* readers didn't give a damn about cross-country track—or, for that matter, any fall sport other than football—and didn't even give half a damn about Leflore County High School, even though Itta Bena was well within our circulation area. I decided to go anyway, in part because I, too, had run track in high school, and in part out of curiosity: I had always thought of the sport as a middle-class northeastern white kid's pursuit, and I was intrigued, to say the least, at the notion of finding such a team at a poor black high school in the middle of the Delta.

Short and round and dressed not for the practice field but for the classroom, Lester Smith was self-effacing and humble, with crooked teeth and a slight stammer. But he was also ambitious and determined to win. Somehow, without any money or support to speak of, he had managed to scrape together a squad of fourteen runners, each of them better than anyone I had ever run with or against. On the hot September afternoon when I first visited the school, every last one of them was out there, running laps around a track that was only partially visible through a veil of grass and weeds. The heat was such that the air was shimmering; but the runners did not slow down or slack off, and as they passed the part of the track nearest to me, I was surprised to hear some of them shouting and laughing with each other. Coach Smith called a few of them over to meet me; like Handy Campbell, they were all shy and humble and polite to a fault, calling me "sir" even though it was obvious to all of us that I was only a few years older than they. But they were also confident that they would win the state championship, undeterred despite the fact that no one came to watch their practices or even their meets. Still, as I shook their hands, I detected in their eyes a silent plea to give their team some publicity on my sports page, something that might lure to this year's meets some spectators and even fans, an enthusiastic presence which the runners obviously didn't need in order to win—they'd been winning for two years without it, after all—but clearly wanted very badly, nonetheless.

And by the time I left him and his team that afternoon, I wanted it, too, and was determined to do my part to make it happen. My story, which started in heavy from the very first paragraph, ran that Sunday:

> *Thankfully, the unsung hero is a dying breed. The omnipresence of the media in our lives demands that we pay proper heed to most human accomplishments, no matter how small or obscure. Certainly, in an area such as this one, that places such high emphasis upon athletic achievement an individual or team which excels is rightfully showered with attention and adulation.*
>
> *Strangely, such recognition has escaped the Leflore County High School cross country team . . .*

I wince today when I read those words and recall the blind and indignant idealism that wrought them. I didn't listen to Mike McNeill; I was certain that I could, somehow, make the *Commonwealth*'s readers care about Lester Smith's team.

But I was wrong. Instead, on Monday, I received nearly a dozen calls from readers, not thanking me for enlightening them, but criticizing me—politely, for the most part, though a few were rather sharp about it—for using up so much of the sports section to write about such a team (one of the callers referred to them as "a bunch of running niggers," and the rest were scarcely less blunt) when there were football games in other parts of the state that had gone uncovered.

The following Saturday, I attended LCHS's first meet of the season, at nearby Mississippi Valley State University. They won handily.

I didn't write it up.

FIVE

THE LAST OF THEIR
KIND

*O*n the afternoon my byline first appeared in the *Greenwood Commonwealth*, I received a strange phone call at the newsroom.

"Hello, *landsman!*" bellowed a stout voice just dripping with Delta. I had never heard Yiddish spoken with a Southern accent before; I had not even imagined such a combination possible. Yet here it was, booming through my telephone's earpiece.

"Hello?" I offered.

"This is Richard Rubin, right?"

"It is," I said.

"Well," the voice continued, as firm and warm as a handshake, "this is Joe Martin Erber, and on behalf of the Jewish community I wonna welcome you to Greenwood."

The Jewish *community*? It had never occurred to me that I might not be the only Jew in Greenwood. To learn that there were other Jews here—enough of them to form a community—well, it was almost too much to believe.

In fact, by the time I came to Greenwood, in the summer of 1988, the town's once sizeable Jewish community had been whittled down to maybe two dozen souls. But by the end of that day, I had received calls from just about every one of them.

⚬

For starters, there were the Kornfelds: Leslie and Gert and their son, whose given name was Murray but whom everyone called "Bubba." (Bubba Kornfeld!) They owned a store in town, on Johnson Street—"Kornfeld's," what else?—that had been founded early in the century by Leslie's father, Wolfe. Leslie, tall and lean with a sharp chin and heroic nose, was in his seventies when I first met him; he'd been born to both Greenwood and Kornfeld's, and had grown up nearby on George Street, in a house with chickens and a cow in the backyard. When America entered World War II, Leslie enlisted in the army and was sent first to Philadelphia, where he met Gert. To this day, I cannot imagine exactly how Leslie managed to convince Gert to return to Greenwood, Mississippi with him after the war, but he did, and she did, and more than forty years later, I could still detect traces of her native Philly accent mixed in with her acquired Delta drawl; they intensified whenever she discussed how much she missed cheese steaks.

Kornfeld's (which was typically mispronounced by its customers as "Cornfields") was an old-fashioned general clothing store, the kind which, in the days before the proliferation of massive retail chains, could be found in most Southern small towns, and which was often owned by Jews, even in the Delta. Born in England to Russian parents, Wolfe Kornfeld had immigrated from Europe as a child through the port of Galveston, Texas, and had set about making his living as an itinerant peddler. Eventually he saved up enough money to open a store in Greenwood, which still stands, mocking the passage of time and the shifting of demographics and the encroachment of Wal-Mart. The floors' wide wooden planks resonated gratifyingly when trod upon, and its ceilings were high, both to dissipate the heat and to provide extra storage and display space for the clothes they sold—hats and boots and work shirts and dress shirts and work pants and dress pants and kerchiefs and neckties and sneakers and shoes and jackets and suits and bathing suits and underwear and lingerie and children's clothes and always, hanging over the whole thing like a talisman, a pair of blue jeans with a seventy-five-inch waist. "We sell five or six of those every year," Bubba told me once. He wasn't joking.

Usually, though, Bubba was joking about something or other; in the store, he never failed to combine a Southern-accented sales pitch with some Yiddish-tinged shtick, a combination of Lyndon Johnson and Henny Youngman. He looked that combination, too, his face dominated by eyeglasses and a trim beard, his body clothed in western shirts, pressed blue jeans, and ostrich-skin cowboy boots. Bubba had served in the Mississippi

National Guard during the sixties, and he once told me that the most useful thing he had learned during his service was how to immolate fire-ant beds with kerosene. He also acquired a deep respect for firearms, and implored me, almost every time we spoke, to get myself a gun, lest my car break down on some dark and deserted highway late one night. I once asked him what good it would do me, in such an instance, to shoot my own car; he laughed, then repeated his admonition as if I had said nothing at all.

At their store, the Kornfelds still used an old brass cash register, behind which was posted a large sign: "Let's stay friends—don't ask for credit." "I keep that up there for the *veissers* as much as the *shvartzers*," Leslie explained to me one afternoon.

"The what?" I asked.

"You never heard the word *shvartzer* before?" Leslie exclaimed, incredulous that the Yiddish term for a black man might have eluded the ears of a native New Yorker.

"I have," I said, not mentioning that I would never actually use such a term. "But what was the other one?"

"Oh, you mean *veisser*? That's the opposite of *shvartzer*."

It made sense—I had studied some German in school, and I knew that *weiss* meant "white"—but I had never heard such a term before, and hearing it that afternoon in Kornfeld's, I began to understand that the binary world of race pervaded everything in Greenwood, even Yiddish. It was a world that would not recognize nonpartisans: You were either on one side or the other, and if you failed to choose sides for yourself, someone else would do it for you. I don't know how it had happened with the Jews of Greenwood—whether they had chosen it for themselves or not—but in the eyes of the town, and the Delta, and the state, they were, most definitely, *veissers*. If that designation spared them the harsh oppression that their ancestors had faced in Europe and the blanket discrimination that their own cousins were still facing elsewhere in America—and make no mistake, it did—then I suspect it must have also engendered in them a certain ambivalence, as it did in me. And yet, for the most part, they seemed completely comfortable with the high station they held in Greenwood—with it, and in it.

Few people exemplified this phenomenon for me more clearly than Ilse Goldberg, the proprietress of Goldberg's shoe store on Howard Street. Short and stout, her head crowned by a beautiful thick black mane that looked even more striking next to her pale white skin, she was the consummate Southern lady, right down to her genteel accent and mannerisms;

anyone you asked would have confirmed what was obvious: that she was one of the most prominent and respected people in town. I was astonished, then, to learn that she had not been born in the South—nor, for that matter, in the United States. She was, in fact, a native of Germany who had fled that country just months before World War II began. Unable to gain entry into the United States, the family sat out the war with other Jewish refugees in, of all places, Shanghai. After the war, they were allowed to emigrate to America and ended up settling in, of all places, Greenwood, Mississippi, where Ilse married Irving Goldberg, whose family had been there for a couple of generations already. The experience of flight and displacement did nothing to shake Ilse Goldberg's sense of her identity, nor her pride in that identity; she was the only person I knew in Greenwood who actually kept kosher, going so far as to have her meat shipped in from Chicago, and when, months later, she had me to her house for a Passover *seder*, we all dined on dishes that the family had somehow managed to carry with them when they had left Germany in 1939.

Nevertheless, in most other ways she had assimilated to life as a Delta *veisser* extremely well. She had sent her sons, Mike and Jerome, to Pillow Academy, and had encouraged them to play for the school's football team, where they shone. Mike later married Gail Moyer, whose father had owned the general store in the tiny Delta town of Glendora, where they were the only Jews. Mike and Gail worked in the Greenwood store; they had two boys, who were enrolled in Pillow and preparing for their bar mitzvahs. Jerome ran another Goldberg's shoe store in Indianola, thirty miles to the west.

Ilse's husband, Irving, had been incapacitated by a stroke, and so Ilse, in addition to being the family matriarch and taking care of her own octogenarian mother, also ran the family business. She was, above all, an unfailingly strong woman. And she was Greenwood—white Greenwood—through and through: She lived in North Greenwood, was a booster for Pillow Academy, and supported those politicians and public servants who represented the town's white old guard. Her store was the antithesis of Kornfeld's, being modern and neat and brightly lit, with extremely courteous help and without even the slightest hint of Yiddish or anything else that might suggest Jewishness, save for the name. She once told me that when he still lived in town, Byron De La Beckwith, the man who assassinated Medgar Evers and who was also known to be a rabid anti-Semite, would nevertheless cross the street just to tip his hat to her. She related this fact without a sense of disgust or embarrassment, only amusement and a small measure of delight for being able to tell me something I didn't know and couldn't have imagined.

I respected her immensely and liked her a lot, besides, liked visiting her store and talking in her office. And every time I did, I wanted so much to ask her one question: How could someone who had fled murderous racism as a child, and whose own mother still bore a thick German accent that must have served as a daily reminder of that childhood persecution, have assimilated herself so well into the upper ranks of a society dominated by a notion of white supremacy—not the virulent and violent brand, perhaps, but no less determined to keep *us* separate from *them*, and to ensure that *us* remained on top. Had she forgotten what it was like to have been one of *them?*

I never asked. Mrs. Goldberg's presence and bearing were such that I could never bring myself to do so.

I did, however, get the chance to pose that same question to another member of the community. Marshall Levitt was already in his sixties when I first met him, but was still living with his ninety-five-year-old mother, Nancy, in the same house on Washington Street in which they'd both been born. Nancy Levitt was, by birth, a Davidson, a member of a large extended family with branches in both Greenwood and Meridian, Mississippi, some three hours to the south and east. Joe Martin Erber, whose mother had also been a Davidson, once described one member of the Meridian branch of the family as "the orneriest Jew I ever met"; another member, Meyer Davidson, was so outspoken that he had come within seconds of having his house blown up by the Ku Klux Klan on the night of June 29, 1968, before FBI agents, who had been tipped off, intercepted the would-be bombers. At ninety-five, Nancy Levitt seemed every bit as feisty as her cousins; she could scarcely hear or see, and her memory was pretty well shot, yet she was anything but mute, frequently issuing assertions and declarations in a loud voice that smacked of defiance and even contempt for her age and infirmity.

Marshall, though, was made of different stuff. He had served with a bomber crew during World War II and had flown quite a few dangerous missions over Europe, but after the war he had simply returned to Greenwood and the house on Washington Street, taking over his father's scrap metal business and never marrying. He was embraced by the rest of the Jewish community and was related, it seemed, to at least half of them, but was always regarded as something of an eccentric, a bit off. One afternoon, I asked Marshall if I could record his reminiscences on audio tape, something I enjoyed doing from time to time with people whom I believed had lived particularly interesting or unusual lives or who merely had great stories to tell—war veterans, immigrants, former civil rights activists, the very elderly, and most of the members of Greenwood's Jewish community. Marshall, ever polite, readily obliged, and we sat down in his mother's living room, my tape recorder set in front of him, discussing the life he had lived thus far. We spoke of his parents and grandparents, his schooling and service in the war, and life in Greenwood during the 1950s and 1960s. When the topic turned to the civil rights movement, Marshall promptly told me that he had served as an officer on the board of the local chapter of the White Citizens' Council, and that his appointment to said board had been one of the proudest moments of his life.

I stared at him, astonished. "Marshall," I sputtered, "don't you think it's strange that a Jew would be an officer in such an organization?"

"No," he said with a shrug.

"But don't you think that you, as a Jew, have a responsibility to fight that kind of bigotry, or at least not to perpetuate it?"

"No."

"But don't you think it's wrong that you would be involved in perpetuating the same kind of prejudice that your own grandparents faced in Russia?"

"No."

"But—"

"Look, Richard," he said, obviously growing annoyed but still smiling, nonetheless. "We can go around and around like this all day. My answer's not going to change."

Instinctively, my lips pursed to form the word "but" yet again. Years of collegiate debate had instilled in me a devout faith in the power of logic, and a firm belief that all intelligent people will succumb to reason if pressed hard enough; surely, I thought, there must be some way I can put this that will reach Marshall Levitt. But as I began to speak, I saw his eyes harden and set; and it occurred to me, for what was quite possibly the first time in my life, that no one can be made to hear something that they just do not want to hear. It was a lesson I would have to learn again and again in Greenwood.

❧❧

There were other Jews in Greenwood, too, like Harry Diamond, a first cousin of Leslie Kornfeld's, who had played football at Greenwood High School (class of 1930) and then had gone on to play for the Alabama Crimson Tide; later he opened a general store in tiny Moorhead,

Mississippi, about twenty-five miles west of Greenwood, and during the 1950s served as commissioner of public schools in Sunflower County, where he quietly advocated gradual desegregation. Harry was already a widower when I met him, living in a modern ranch house in North Greenwood and driving into town every afternoon to have lunch with his cousin at the Crystal Club. They often took me along with them; Harry had a grandson at Penn, and I think he believed he was adopting me as a surrogate.

And there were Sam and Eva Kaplan, an elderly couple who lived in a condo on River Road, and their son David, who had married a girl from Arkansas and had moved back to Greenwood with his wife and children but who was not happy there and would soon be leaving again; and Joe Orlansky and Meyer Gelman, whom I had trouble distinguishing even though they looked nothing alike—Joe lived in a big old brick house on Market Street, and Meyer and his wife and daughter nearby, on a dirt road next to the Yazoo levee, in a white house with a large blue Star of David painted over the garage—and Jerry Wexler, a smooth-talking businessman in his forties who had just bought the L&L Catfish restaurant down on Highway 49 and who once told me that he had frequently played chess with James Meredith at Ole Miss. And then there were the ghosts of people, Jewish people, who should have been there but weren't, children and grandchildren and neighbors and friends who had moved away to enter college or the army or to get married or take a better job and had never returned, but who were always spoken of as if they were still in Greenwood, really, as if they were just traveling for a bit in Memphis or Birmingham or New Orleans or Atlanta or Miami or Chicago or New York and would soon be returning, even though everyone knew that in fact they would not be returning, not even for a visit, that there was nothing for them in Greenwood and that they had done the only thing they really could have done, which was to get out. This was why my arrival in town had caused such a sensation among the town's *landsmen*; no one could remember the last time a young Jew had moved *to* Greenwood.

All of this was explained to me by Joe Martin Erber, who was the community's unofficial historian and rabbi and cantor and caretaker and cemetery keeper. Joe was a big man and in his late forties when I met him; he sported a waxed handlebar mustache, drove an ancient Volkswagen Beetle covered with bumper stickers of every ilk, and lived in a neighborhood near the high school where he and his wife were the only remaining white residents. His speech was slow and thick, his accent as deep and authentic as any I would hear in Greenwood; he was a postman and part-time police officer in town. On the day I met him he reached into his mail sack and pulled out a copy of a Memphis news monthly called *The Hebrew Watchman.*

"I've never heard of it," I said.

"What?" he bellowed. "Never heard of *The Hebrew Watchman?* What kind of Jew are you? Oh, that's right—you're a *New York* Jew." He laughed heartily, his belly shaking underneath his regulation United States Postal Service work shirt. He was also the union local's shop steward.

It was Joe who filled me in on the town's Jewish history, informing me that, up until recently, Greenwood had had not one but two synagogues— an Orthodox and a Reform.

"What happened to the Orthodox one?" I asked.

"That's the one that's still open!" Joe announced with a chuckle. "You see, the old Reform Temple was started by the German Jews, who were here first, and then later, when the Russians came, they joined it, too. Built a big ol' Temple right over on Washington Street, across the street from Marshall's house, you know, where the First Baptist Church is now. And that was O.K. for a few years, but you know what they say—'Where you have two Jews, you have three opinions'—right? So after a while some of the Jews got fed up with the Reform temple, said it was getting too reform. Story was that one time an old Jewish woman died and when they unveiled her tombstone in the Jewish cemetery it actually had a cross on it! So a bunch of them left and started up their own *shul*—my grandfather, and Les Kornfeld's father and Harry Diamond's father and Marshall Levitt's—and they collected money for a new synagogue. And they didn't like the fact that the old Greenwood Jewish cemetery was right next to the Christian cemetery out on Carrollton Avenue— it's really the same cemetery; go out there and you'll see what I mean—so they bought some land on Bowie Lane and started another Jewish ceme-tery, too, to go along with the new congregation and the new synagogue."

The "new" synagogue—Congregation Ahavath Rayyim, erected in 1923—still stood on Market Street, next to the New Deal Tobacco Company and across from Joe Orlansky's house, and it was still in use, but just barely: Joe Erber confessed to me that they hadn't had a *minyan* —a ten-man prayer quorum, according to Jewish law—in years. But the building itself was beautiful and well-kept, a classical Georgian structure with immaculate pews and a pristine ark and sterling Torah scrolls and a pol-ished memorial board with more names on it than the entire remaining Jewish population of Greenwood and all of their friends and neighbors combined. Still, the truest and most profound sense of loss that pervaded every gathering of Greenwood's Jews was not for those who had died—like Jerry Wexler's father, a colorful figure who had played Tevye in the Little Theater's production of *Fiddler on the Roof* and had passed away shortly before my arrival in town—but for those who had left. "You see those rooms in the back of the *shul?*" Joe said, pointing. "That's the Hebrew School. We used to have dozens of kids in there at one time—so many we had to have several classes going at once. Nowadays, we've only got Mike Goldberg's two boys and David Kaplan's two boys, and his are only half-Jewish. And that's it. And when they're done, I reckon we'll have none." He worried about what might happen to the synagogue after the congregation had dwindled down to nothing. "There's a lot of history in this place," he said, a hint of emotion creeping into his otherwise stolid drawl. "A lot of memories. A lot of people worked awful hard to build it, and to keep it going."

"What about the cemetery?" I asked.

"Oh, that'll be all right," he answered. "We have a trust set up for perpetual care. So at least we know that'll always be there. And we have a saying about it, too: 'Last one in, close the gate behind you.'"

Later that afternoon, I drove out to the other Jewish cemetery, the old one out on Carrollton Avenue, the one that had helped inspire the rift in Greenwood's Jewish community. It was just as Joe had described it: a part of the Christian cemetery, the westernmost part, to be exact, indistinguishable from the main, but with its own wrought-iron gate bearing the legend "Greenwood Jewish Cemetery." It sat in a part of town that was now an industrial slum and almost entirely devoid of visible pedestrian traffic. Still, the cemetery itself was verdant and fairly well kept, and most of the several dozen stones in the Jewish section were still legible. One of the graves appeared to be freshly dug; reading the temporary marker, I discovered that it belonged to a man in his late seventies who had died just weeks before I'd first arrived in Greenwood. Later I would learn that he had moved away from town decades before, and had only returned to be buried with his *mishpocha*, his relatives.

I walked through the rows of stones, reading their inscriptions, looking for the woman whose marker had been inscribed with a cross. I couldn't find her; perhaps, I thought, someone had since corrected the mistake. I did find Berthas and Maxes and Juliuses and Gertrudes and Ferdinands and Annas and men who had had "Junior" affixed to their surname, contrary to European Jewish tradition. I found people who had been born in Germany before the American Civil War and who had, at some point, crossed an ocean and traveled overland by horse-wagon in order to settle in

Greenwood, Mississippi in the nineteenth century. *And for what?* I asked myself—is this what they had hoped for in America? To be a minority in another small town, only this time an even smaller minority, and in a town plagued by heat and violence and xenophobia and yellow fever?

But I hadn't known these people then, and I didn't know them now. Perhaps they had found in Greenwood some kind of pastoral paradise, free from centuries of old-fashioned blood-lust Jew-hating. Perhaps they had been welcomed here, and had prospered, and had assimilated and intermarried, and perhaps the cross on that old woman's tombstone hadn't been a mistake, after all. Perhaps they had believed that they couldn't have done any better than they did here then, and perhaps they were correct in that belief. From everything I could see and could glean from that seeing, it appeared to have happened exactly that way, and they did just fine by it all, and the only loss sustained in the whole affair was that sustained by the few Jews who still remained in Greenwood, clinging fast to their heritage and identity in the face of their own dwindling numbers and advancing age and without a next generation there to survive them—and by me, who never got to meet them, or to know what they lived or how, or to understand.

I drove over to where Joe Erber had said the Reform temple's last home had been, on West President Street in North Greenwood, not far from where I lived. I had expected an elegant edifice, worthy of the old cemetery and the names and stones in it, but what I found was a small, bland modern building, its name affixed to its outer wall in plain, austere letters, dull even against the dull red bricks. There was a realtor's sign stuck in the lawn; a few weeks later, someone bought the place and turned it into a day care center.

𝔰◦𝔔

When I first arrived in Mississippi, I had anticipated passing the High Holidays in private, or perhaps just ignoring them altogether and working. By the time Yom Kippur had arrived, though, I had learned of the existence of Congregation Ahavath Rayyim, and it was assumed, by Kornfelds and Goldbergs and Erbers and Levitts and Kaplans and Gelmans and the rest of Greenwood's Jews, that I would be spending the Day of Atonement at the synagogue on Market Street. I had never attended a service there, and, in truth, I did not want to go then, either, finding the prospect of observing such an event in an all-but-empty house of worship to be somewhat depressing. Nevertheless, nearly four thousand years of residual ancestral guilt prevailed, and on the night in question I donned my only suit and drove down to Market Street.

I could scarcely find a parking space.

Inside the synagogue, to my surprise, were scores of people, most of them in their sixties and older, but dressed smartly and as surprised to meet me as I was to meet them. They had driven in from a handful of small towns scattered in orbit around Greenwood—Belzoni and Sunflower, Moorhead and Schlater, Ruleville and Inverness, towns where they were the only Jews—just to attend services on the holiest day of the year. As they introduced themselves to me one by one, I felt as if I were witnessing a bizarre ceremony, an annual revival of a defunct Jewish community, people who had risen from the dead just to recite *Kol Nidre* and say *Yizkor.* But no, I thought, these people are really survivors, coming together for one day a year in the kind of place, and with the kind of numbers, that can make them feel as if they are not merely walking anachronisms, vestiges of a community and a way of life that no longer exists. I don't know who was more grateful, them or me—for the opportunity, and for the display.

Then Joe Martin Erber came charging in, apologizing for his tardiness and still dressed in his Greenwood policeman's uniform. He greeted the congregation quickly and hurried up to the *bimah,* donning a *yarmulke* and cracking open a prayer book. He turned to face the ark and the eternal light, and began to lead the crowd in prayer in Southern-glazed Hebrew. As he rocked back and forth, *davening* as Jews have done across centuries and around the world, I noticed the .38 caliber pistol bobbing in a holster on his hip.

⊰°⊱

Late one night, a couple of weeks later, I was driving back from Jackson when I passed through the small town of Lexington, Mississippi. Lexington was about thirty-five miles southeast of Greenwood and was the seat of Holmes County; the whole place seemed to be arranged in a square around a beautiful old courthouse. On the road into town, a black wrought-iron sign asked travelers: *Is Jesus Christ Lord of Lexington?* I did not know the answer, and wasn't sure I wanted to know.

A few minutes later, though, as I drove by the courthouse, my headlights fell upon the sign over the largest store in the town square: COHEN'S. I was stunned, and, I confess, a bit relieved.

Not long thereafter, I had occasion to drive through Lexington during daylight, and I stopped into Cohen's. Phil Cohen, the proprietor, was a thin, slight and balding man in his 40s who smiled warmly and frequently. As I introduced myself, he seized my hand and shook it vigorously; despite the fact that Lexington fell outside the *Commonwealth*'s circulation area, he had heard tell that there was a young new reporter in Greenwood who was Jewish.

"Really?" I said. "How?"

"Oh, I don't recall, exactly," he replied. "Probably from one of my cousins. I've got *mishpocha* all over the Delta, especially in Indianola. There's a Jewish network all across Mis'sippi, you know. They get word around faster than Western Union."

Phil Cohen's store was a somewhat smaller and dimmer version of Kornfeld's—not surprising considering that Lexington was little more than one-tenth the size of Greenwood. I asked Phil how his family had come to live in Lexington, and to open such a store.

"My grandfather was taking a train down from Memphis to some town with hot springs in it," he replied. "Something to do with his health, he must have had a cough or something. His family were all up in Memphis. And on the train he fell into a pinochle game with some Jews from Tchula, Mississippi, just down a few miles from here. Anyway, these Jews owned some stores in Tchula, and a farm or two, too, and they somehow convinced my grandfather to get off the train with them there, and the next thing he knew he was working for one of them, and then he saved up enough to open his own store up here. This was around the turn of the century. His parents stayed up in Memphis, though. His father had been a tailor in Memphis, and when the Civil War came along the Confederate army drafted him to make uniforms for them. He made all the uniforms for Nathan Bedford Forrest's cavalry. Did you know that one of Forrest's top lieutenants was a Jew named Moe Sternberger?"

"Is that right!" I said. In my mind, I conjured a scene of some Union scouts crouching on a bluff, peering through a spyglass and catching a glimpse of the dreaded Rebel horseman. "Run, boys!" one of them shouts, his voice afire with terror. "It's Forrest, and he's got *Sternberger* with him!"

I caught myself smirking, and quickly chased the image out of my head. "So your grandfather started the store, and then he passed it on to your father?"

"That's right," Phil Cohen answered. "And I left town for college, and then the army, and then I went down to San Antonio for a while and worked as a stockbroker. But then my dad got sick and he couldn't run the store any-more, and my mother couldn't run it by herself, so I came back to town with my wife and kids. I never thought I'd be back here, but here I am. We take the kids to Hebrew School down in Jackson a couple of times a month."

"Was your family the only Jewish presence in town?"

"Heavens, no!" He laughed. "Used to be the whole town square was Jewish, or almost all, anyway. There are still a couple of the old Jewish stores left, too—there's Herrman's insurance, and Flower's store, right around the corner. The Flowers were originally called 'Blum,' but then they took it upon themselves to anglicize the name. There used to be some Jews over in Meridian, I think it was, and their name was 'Threefoot.' They anglicized it from 'Dreyfus.' Anyway, Flower's and Herrman's still have the names, but they're not run by Jews anymore. I'm the last one left." He smiled as he said it, but he still looked sad.

I felt bad, wanted to change the subject. "Was your grandfather the first Jew in town?" I asked.

"Oh, no, there were plenty of Jews here even before he came—they owned stores and farms, some of the nicest houses in town. Very well-liked, too. When they decided to build a temple in 1905, the whole town got together and put on a benefit opera to raise money for the cause. Somewhere around here I have a special newspaper from the event."

He dug out the ancient, yellowed clipping and showed it to me, and we talked for a few minutes more. Phil Cohen spoke vividly of Greenwood, how he and his friends would pile in the car and drive down there for Jewish dances, how Jews from every little town in the Delta would show up at these mixers, how they all knew each other and each others' parents and siblings and aunts and uncles and cousins and second cousins. And, as I had done with Sternberger's charge earlier in our conversation, I began to drift off into another fantasy, this one about a vast network of Jewish families spread out across the Delta, more intricate and interconnected and involved than any I would ever find even in New York: Mississippi as the Promised Land. And yet, this time I believed I was not all that far off from the truth, or at least from what had once been the truth.

Some minutes after that Phil Cohen and I shook hands and parted company. On my way out of town, I stopped by the old synagogue, sitting just yards off the square on a side street. It was a small, whitewashed building, plain but dignified, indistinguishable from a church but for the lack of a cross atop its peaked roof. I tried the door, but it was locked. Of course—Phil Cohen had said it hadn't been used for years; there was no congregation left. I peered through the dark leaded glass, hoping to catch a glimpse of the eternal flame that sits over the ark holding the Torah scrolls, but I couldn't spot it. Phil Cohen had told me that Lexington had sent forty-seven Jewish young men off to World War II, but only two had returned. The rest, having seen the world beyond a small town in Mississippi, chose to remain in it. Phil Cohen and his family were the last of their kind in town, and he was certain that his kids would move away after college, leaving him alone with the store. Unlike him, they would not return, and one day, perhaps not too distant, he would close up shop for good, leaving nothing behind but the sign and a few tombstones and an old whitewashed sanctuary to show that he and his family and an entire Jewish community had ever been there.

⚓

Not long thereafter, I was driving east on Highway 82 one afternoon when I came upon the little village of Eupora, Mississippi, about fifty miles from Greenwood. Houses lined the road on both sides, their driveways snaking down to meet the blacktop. At the bottom of one of them, on the right side of the road, stood a bright wooden sign, staked into the dirt: "Randall W. Kohen, Eupora, Miss."

I slammed on the brakes, drove up the driveway and knocked on the door. A thin man in his late twenties, sporting a brush mustache and a baseball cap advertising a dealer of farm implements, answered the door. "Are you Randall W. Kohen?" I asked.

"I am," he answered in a friendly tone. "What can I do for you?"

"Nothing," I said. I explained that I was surprised to find a Jew living in Eupora, Mississippi, and that I just had to stop in and introduce myself.

The smile did not leave his face, though it muted some in bemusement. "But I'm not Jewish," he said.

"Oh," I offered; then, overwhelmed by the pounding surf of embarrassment, I attempted to reason my way out of it: "W-well," I stammered, "you know that 'Kohen' is a Jewish name, of course."

"No, I never heard that," he replied. "I was always told it was German."

I thought about correcting him, considered informing him that the origin of his surname was, in fact, Hebrew, that it denoted that he was a descendant of the priestly caste that had presided over the Great Temple in Jerusalem in the time of Herod. But I didn't. Instead, I muttered an apology and slunk away. If Randall W. Kohen of Eupora, Mississippi had been raised to believe that he was not Jewish but German, it was not for me to tell him otherwise.

Six

THERE IS NO NEWS

*F*rom the newsroom of the *Greenwood Commonwealth:*

A daily deadline of ten-thirty a.m. When first informed of this, I somehow took it to mean that ten-thirty a.m. was the deadline for actually arriving at work. I was very much mistaken. In fact, ten-thirty a.m. was the deadline to have the day's sports page ready to be sent to press, and later, when I left sports and moved over to straight news reporting, the deadline for handing in all of that day's assigned articles and wire editing. The *Commonwealth*, you see, was an afternoon newspaper. On a typical weekday, it was printed and stacked and ready for delivery by one-thirty or two p.m., although it sometimes appeared a little bit earlier and frequently a good bit later, depending upon how rigidly we adhered to the morning deadline, which was in turn dependent upon whether or not J. O. Emmerich was in town. When J. O. was out of town, which was often, the deadline was viewed more as a guideline; nevertheless, we tried to respect it anyway, if only in an attempt to get the day's real responsibilities behind us and bring on the much more relaxed atmosphere that filled the newsroom once the deadline had passed. The hours before deadline—three hours, to be precise, since most of us arrived in the newsroom between seven and seven-thirty a.m. (the notable exception being Mike McNeill, who never seemed to go home)—were frenzied, awash in the work of writing articles and taglines and cutlines and headlines, and editing articles and wire copy, and shooting pictures and developing film and printing photographs, and laying out your section and proofreading other peoples' articles and fielding phone calls from people who had questions or comments or who believed they had some little piece of news that just had to get into the paper that very day. Almost always, these were cut off politely after no more than a few syllables; when you were on deadline, there was no time for telephones, or conversation, or anything other than what was incontrovertibly necessary to getting your articles and pictures and pages in on time. And if that included driving somewhere to cover breaking news or shoot the local photograph (there had to be one on every front page, and the responsibility rotated among the reporters), it didn't include braking for Stop signs. There would be plenty of time to work it out with the police after ten-thirty a.m.

A typical workday at the *Commonwealth* followed an asymmetrical arc, beginning with the morning scramble, which ended promptly at 10:30 or thereabout (how well you could afford to slip something through at 10:47 or 11:03 was dependent entirely upon the mood and graces of Karen Freeman, the paper's news editor and unsung workhorse, who coordinated all of the articles and photographs and cutlines and wire copy and somehow managed to alchemize it all into a daily newspaper), whereupon the newsroom would plunge into a state of decompression, in which it might very well languish for the rest of the day. Somewhere in the remaining five hours or so you might take a long lunch with some coworkers, think about stories you'd like to do, process and print more film, take more phone calls, return the calls of people who had phoned while you were on deadline, call friends and relatives back home, run errands, and, if absolutely necessary and if you were so inclined, go out and cover a story or two. I quickly discovered that one could do many other things during the time one was supposed to be out covering stories; my favorite was going home for a nap, which I managed to do two or three times a week. When the next deadline was still twenty-one hours away, anything seemed entirely possible, and nothing terribly urgent.

☙❧

Smoke: It filled the newsroom day and night, like a fog bank, like mosquito netting, like the angel of death in Cecil B. DeMille's *The Ten Commandments.* Everyone at the *Commonwealth*—from the reporters and editors to the advertising salesmen and the press operators—smoked. Correction: chain-smoked. Some intermittently smoked and chewed tobacco. A few did both at the same time. I was the lone exception. I was asthmatic.

People talked on the phone and to each other without removing the cigarettes from their lips; they rained ash constantly, charring their desk-tops, the fabric on their chairs, their own shirts and pants. The smell was inescapable: It infiltrated your hair and your clothes and the lunch you had brown-bagged that day; it coated your notepad and your camera and your computer terminal. People smoked incessantly while on deadline, then cel-ebrated making deadline by lighting up. The only time they didn't smoke was during the paper's weekly news meetings, because J. O. had designated the conference room a smoke-free zone. As a result, weekly news meetings were brief and brusque and riddled with virulent arguments about matters of little or no importance.

∿∿

Responsibilities: You were responsible for doing all of the articles Mike assigned you in that day's news budget.

You were responsible for shooting pictures to go with those articles, and for developing those pictures and printing them and making sure you knew who all the people in the pictures were and how old they were and where they lived and how all their names were spelled.

You were responsible for profiling businesses when the advertising sales-men, via J. O., asked you to.

You were responsible for covering all of the stories that fell within the purview of your beats, and all of the stories generating from tips you had gotten over the telephone, and if you did not care to do so you were responsible for passing them off onto someone else.

You were responsible for keeping your desk and your person neat in case a visitor should stop by the newsroom.

You were responsible, when leaving the newsroom, for looking neat and being courteous and for telling Edna the receptionist where, roughly, you were going and when, roughly, you would return.

You were responsible, once or twice a week, for shooting some kind of local photograph for the front page of that day's newspaper, even though there was almost always no news of any kind (much less photogenic news) happening in town that day and you were more likely than not to return with a picture of crossing guards helping children walk to school, or garbagemen emptying cans into the back of their truck, or someone from the Army Corps of Engineers taking inscrutable measurements at the Yazoo.

You were responsible for writing up cutlines to accompany photographs people sent in to the paper for publication, the most common type of which featured a seven- or eight-year-old boy holding aloft the severed head of a deer he had just shot while hunting with Daddy, his cheeks smeared with the deer's blood in the traditional commemoration of a young man's first kill, "First Kill" being the most common title for the cutline that would accompany such a photograph, although one Saturday night, feeling tired and punchy, I opted for "Sick Little Bastard" instead, and was caught by Karen only at the last minute before we went to press.

You were responsible for proofreading other *Commonwealth* reporters' articles before they went to press, because it was rightfully believed that no one could catch all of his or her own typos.

You were responsible, once or twice a week, for editing the "people" column that came in over the AP wire, and for putting into boldface every single name that appeared in the column, even if neither you nor anyone else in the newsroom actually knew who they were.

You were responsible for editing articles and developing film that was dropped off in the newsroom by stringers, usually high school or college kids working for no pay but possibly a course credit or two.

You were responsible for scanning the wire for other Mississippi stories that might be used to flesh out a particularly thin or dull or non-local-news-heavy edition.

You were responsible for covering Rotary Club luncheons, because J. O. was a Rotarian, and for making it sound as if the guest speakers, who usually had very little of import to say, had had a great deal of import to say.

You were responsible, at those rare times when Mike wasn't around, for keeping an ear tuned to the police scanner he kept on his desk, a battered old contraption with a ripped paper speaker that spewed high-pitched gibberish only he could understand.

You were responsible for maintaining good relations with the police department and the fire department and the sheriff's department and the city council and the county board of supervisors and the farm bureau and the chamber of commerce and the board of education and the public library and the town's planters and businessmen and attorneys and merchants and restaurateurs and hoteliers and teachers and ministers and funeral directors, with whom maintaining good relations meant writing up and running in full every obituary that you took over the telephone, even those where the deceased was an obscure person who hadn't lived in

Greenwood for forty years and left behind twenty-four grandchildren and was being attended by six pallbearers and a dozen honorary pallbearers, all of whom had to be listed by name and town of residence. (Black funeral homes, I soon learned, were much greater sticklers for this kind of detail; white funeral homes would usually let you go with only the names of the deceased's immediate family and actual pallbearers.)

You were responsible for fielding your share of open news and obituary calls, the kind that were heralded only by Edna's voice over the intercom announcing "news, line two" or "obituary, line four," and not always running into the darkroom or out back or sitting at your desk pretending to be engrossed in some wire copy until someone else fielded the call.

Most important, you were responsible for scooping the competition, which in Greenwood consisted of two understaffed, underfunded, remote network affiliate outposts, WABG Channel 6, an ABC station, and WXVT Channel 15, which carried CBS. They both listed their domain as "Greenville–Greenwood," but both did their nightly newscasts entirely out of Greenville, and only WABG even kept a studio in Greenwood, a tiny room that was filled with antiquated equipment and that was never, as far as I saw, actually used for anything other than storage. Nevertheless, WABG made some measure of noise about competing with the *Commonwealth,* and occasionally sent one of their reporter–anchors— Richard Dean or Kendra Farn, who were rumored to be secretly engaged to each other—to cover some event or other, although most often they merely edited down the paper's articles and read them over the air.

Scooping WABG and WXVT were tricky propositions. While the notion of competition between the *Commonwealth* and these television stations struck me as absurd—the paper's circulation hovered somewhere underneath 9,000 (the cutoff for competition in the smallest category of competition for statewide awards), and viewership of the stations' local news programming couldn't have been much higher—most people in Greenwood, from the mayor and police chief down to the guys who pumped gas at the Double-Quick, seemed more taken with the notion of having their face appear on-screen than having their words appear in print, and were more likely to call a TV studio when they spotted breaking news than they were to call our newsroom. Sometimes it came down to timing: If it happened between ten P.M. and ten A.M., it was ours; ten A.M. to ten P.M., it was theirs. Once in a while, it was a matter of good old-fashioned journalistic ingenuity, elbow grease, and legwork. And occasionally, when a reporter didn't care for an assignment or was feeling angry at Mike or just plain lazy, he or she would leak a scoop to someone at one of the stations in time for that night's newscast, thus nullifying the need to write up the same story for the newspaper the next day. I did this so often with WXVT that the station manager took to sending me gifts.

⁓⁓⁓

The *Commonwealth* did not put out a paper on Saturdays—no Saturday morning deadline, no Saturday morning deadline rush. This was a pure blessing in the fall, when the sports editor—that is, me—spent Friday nights covering at least one football game, and then repairing to the news-room and jotting down notes about the action in between fielding calls from stringers covering other area games and jotting down notes about them, too, a somewhat chaotic exercise that usually stretched until one or two in the morning.

On Saturdays, I would saunter into the newsroom around three in the afternoon—later, if I were covering a game at Valley—and confront the unpleasant task of turning a small mountain of hastily scribbled and often illegible notes, along with a half-dozen unlabeled canisters of film, into a sports section, a goal that was always somehow realized, although rarely before the midnight deadline, and never without the help of Karen or Mike, who alternated Saturdays as well. There was a reporter on duty every Saturday, too—like the editors, they rotated through that particular shift to handle any kind of news that might break between noon, when they arrived, and seven, when they completed writing up the day's police log and headed home. Their early departure never failed to spark in me some virulent strain of envy; months later, when I switched over to report-ing myself, I would come to regard the short working Saturday as the greatest of the job's perks, which were admittedly few to begin with.

A vague but potent stupor would overtake me on those Saturday nights, when I would stumble out of the newsroom at one in the morning and head off into the moist night, most often toward Park Avenue for some fast food and then the shopping center closest to Grand Boulevard, which had a video store called Fun Flicks and a cavernous warehouse grocery named Country Market. After picking up a video or two, I would grab an enormous cart and cruise the aisles, looking for items that might spark enthusiasm in my tired mind. There were always a few young families, white and black, in the Country Market after midnight Saturdays, tired-looking men and women with toddlers in tow, dressed in torn and soiled sneakers and shorts, pushing carts filled to the brim with food and beverages in colorful boxes and bags and bottles, smiling and laughing and touching and kissing and rarely looking as if this were not the high point of their week. These people were not my readers; they did not take the *Commonwealth*, or any newspaper at all. We didn't see each other at work, or eat at the same restaurants, or go home to the same neighborhoods. But because we were all out there together at the Country Market late on a Saturday night—me celebrating the end of the work week and the imminent advent of a day of rest, them celebrating the same thing or perhaps just the rare opportunity for all of them to be together in one place at one time, if only to shop for the week's groceries—we became members of the same community, even if none of us could have possibly hoped to define that community. Somehow, it made me feel satisfied about the work I had spent the previous week doing; I was in Greenwood now. I was in it, and of it, a part of it. It was enough.

And then I would go home and microwave some more food and watch a movie or two and somewhere in there fall asleep, usually without giving much thought at all to Sunday. That was what I did after work on Saturdays.

❧❧

The rest of the week, though, was different. If the most potent urge I felt upon leaving work on Saturday was to settle into the bosom of Greenwood and there drift off to sleep, the urge that overcame me most weeknights was to get out of town and look around, wide-eyed and wide awake. The destination didn't matter nearly as much as the trip itself.

Sometimes, my coworker Karen and I would get into her Chevy and head down to Jackson, usually with no more ambitious a goal in mind than to explore a mall or a neighborhood and hit the Krystal hamburger stand, returning just in time to get enough sleep to allow us to manage the next morning's deadline rush. More often, though, I set out alone, drawn only by some point on the map, an unfamiliar road or a town with an alluring name: Shaw or Leland or Drew or Ruleville or Kosciusko or Duck Hill or Rosedale or French Camp. Like my Saturday night trips to Country Market, the ostensible objective was not really the point of these weeknight jaunts. There was rarely much to see in any of these towns but some houses and churches and a small store or two and a small bar or two and a cotton

gin and perhaps a school and a host of other buildings long since abandoned and boarded up. It was the roads that were the true attraction—not
that they were much to look at, either, but merely being on them, straight
and narrow and flat and paved in a such a rough way that driving over them
at a certain speed made your tires hum like a monk reciting a Gregorian
chant, was the perfect antidote to a day spent in the newsroom, loud and
crowded and agitated and tense. On a Delta road out in the middle of
nowhere it was easy for me to believe that the road itself came from
nowhere and went nowhere, and that I didn't have any particular need to go
anywhere, either. Driving down Highway 49 or Highway 8 or Highway 7
or Highway 61, the rows of cotton and soybeans stretching out forever on
either side become almost hypnotic in their perpetual sameness. They are,
it appears, as they ever were, and will always be so, and I would think:
There is no news. Yesterday is today is tomorrow. And sometimes, when
the sun set and the moon was new and the road appeared to stretch out
straight ahead without end, I would turn my headlights off and slip into a
darkness so profound that I couldn't even see the steering wheel in front of
me, and the road and fields and sky would all disappear, and it was just me
there, just me and silent black space and nothing else in the world.

Of course, I couldn't do that for more than a second or two before
beginning to feel weird and frightened and scrambling to turn the lights
back on, and truth be told you can't even drive down a road to nowhere
through fields of forever for very long at all before it stops being soothing
and starts feeling eerily lonely. Occasionally I would see some bright lights
glowing in the distance and my spirits would lift for a bit, and then I
would discover that the lights in question lined a grain elevator or cotton
gin or catfish processing plant or some other industrial outpost that was at
that hour as devoid of humanity as was the black emptiness that surrounded it, and then I would feel even more lonely. Fortunately, though,
there was also always some slightly inhabited point on the map out there
somewhere, no more than twenty or thirty miles from the last point on the
map, to break the silence and the monotony, at least for a minute or two.
And there was the radio.

I was quickly becoming a fervent devotee of the medium of radio, even
though I had taken it for granted almost since birth. Now, the truth is that
Mississippi radio is nothing special, especially up in the Delta. There are
few local stations, for one thing, and most of them actually pipe in their
programming from satellites linked to enormous sterile studios in

Colorado and other points unknown; the rest seem to favor formats of country or Christian or both, two musical genres for which I did not much care. But at least they were local; they were company, reminders that there was still life out there, somewhere, that I could not drive so far as to be out of their reach, out of the range of their voices and music, cacophonous to my ear as they were and yet soothing as well. Out there, where people lived so far apart from one another that you could not see the light from your nearest neighbor's house in the middle of the night, the radio was sometimes the only thing that kept me from believing that I had dropped off the planet altogether.

I had a friend who moonlighted at a small mom-and-pop—owned Delta AM radio station that carried some local programming during the day but switched over, at night, to a satellite feed from somewhere out west. The programming on this feed was particularly odious—fifteen-year-old bubblegum music punctuated by an announcer who never identified himself or his satellite service or even the names of the songs but merely recited, in a voice reeking of broadcasting-school smarminess, quasireligious homilies like "Do *you* know where *you're* headed?" and "What is expected of *you?*" and "Have you done your part today?" and "A man with faith and family is a rich man, indeed." My friend's job consisted of making sure the station didn't lose the feed (not that he could have done much if it had) and announcing, every half hour, the time, the temperature and the station's call letters. Sometimes, if he were reading something interesting, he might skip the half-hour break; he told me once that on any given night he had between three and eight listeners, and that the station's owners were never among them, being inclined to retire early in the evening.

When I would visit, my friend would cut off the feed—usually in the middle of a song—toss me a set of headphones, and begin chatting with me on the air. We would talk for a few minutes about anything and nothing and then someone—one of the three to eight—would call in and we'd put him or her on the air, too. Often they would talk mostly to me, asking what on Earth had brought me down to the Mississippi Delta from New York and what was New York like for real and now that I was here how did I like it and did I think I might stay a while and even settle down here and they certainly hoped I would. Every one of them knew the station's owners, I am sure, but no one would tell; and the next day, when the owners invariably asked my friend if anything unusual had transpired during the previous night's shift, he invariably answered, "Not a thing."

As soon as I left the station, in fact, my friend would switch back to the satellite feed as if not a thing really had happened; and then, driving back to Greenwood, usually past midnight, I would spin my car radio's analog AM dial to see which distant cities I could pick up: St. Louis and Denver and Houston and Baton Rouge and Chicago and Omaha and Boston and Indianapolis and Baltimore and Cleveland and Pittsburgh and Dallas and Atlanta and Des Moines and Minneapolis and Buffalo and Detroit and Philadelphia and, if conditions were right and I was vigilant in my search and if I were really lucky besides, New York.

I'll tell you the truth: The first time I drove in total darkness across that flat alluvial plane far from anywhere and even farther from anywhere that meant anything to me and picked up a New York radio station—WABC, AM 770, with Dr. Bernard Meltzer dispensing advice on health and finances and human relations—I cried.

The second time, I laughed. I laughed because I was somehow even more amazed by such a find than I had been the first time, and because I was no longer far from anywhere that meant anything to me, and because spattered out in front of me on a black canvas were more stars than ten mathematicians could count, and because it was only eight hours until deadline and I had three stories to write that morning and three pictures to develop and print and two pages to lay out and I hadn't slept more than four hours a night all week and here I was driving around in the middle of nowhere, even though it was no longer nowhere to me.

SEVEN

HOW PEOPLE REALLY LIVED

*E*rik Werner was himself no product of the Delta. He had grown up in Memphis, the son of a television weatherman, and had graduated from the University of Tennessee. In 1988 he was a television reporter at WXVT-TV; we were often sent to cover the same stories at the same time, and gradually we became friends. Erik was, in some small way, famous in the area: Every night his face appeared on thousands of television screens from Greenwood to Greenville. But none of that seemed to matter in the Delta. One Friday, I invited him to visit me at home; when my landlady saw Erik, a black man, walking across her property and heading for my door, she became hysterical and had to be convinced not to call the police.

A few weeks later, he invited me over to his place in Greenville. When I arrived, I was stunned to discover that he actually lived in a dilapidated housing project. Seeing me pull into the place's pitted and littered parking lot, he rushed out to meet me and immediately advised me that we shouldn't waste our time hanging out there, but rather head right off to some party across town. Then he quickly changed the subject; it was clear that he was embarrassed and wondering why he had asked me to meet him at his home rather than the studio, which was clean and bright and which I had seen many times.

Now, I was young and naive and perhaps not all that astute, but I knew this: Erik Werner had a more glamorous job than I did, and made more money than I did. He lived in a town that was twice as large and prosperous as the one in which I lived, and which had a reputation for being much more open and progressive than mine. But I lived in a neat, well-maintained apartment in a safe, clean neighborhood; he lived in a fetid, isolated ghetto.

From that night on, I began to see Greenwood, and the Delta, as a series of ghettoes—black and white, rich and poor. They are jagged and jumbled but always clearly demarcated and always pure; they may shift from time to time, but they do not crumble, nor diminish, nor give, not even slightly. There are white restaurants and black restaurants, white bars and black bars, white parks and black parks, white baseball diamonds and black baseball diamonds, white swimming pools and black swimming pools, white clothing stores and black clothing stores, white barbershops and black barbershops, white gas stations and black gas stations, white mechanics and black mechanics, white attorneys and black attorneys, white doctors and black doctors, white clinics and black clinics, white funeral homes and black funeral homes. Most important, there are black and white neighborhoods, black and white schools, and black and white churches. Legal segregation may be dead, but its ghost still stands guard at doors all over town.

The best and most popular restaurant in Greenwood was located in the heart of the old downtown, right across Johnson Street from Kornfeld's. The sign said it was the Crystal Grill, but when I lived in town it was still commonly known as the Crystal *Club*. To gain admittance, it was said, one had to hand one's membership card through the door. Lifetime membership cost a dollar; a typical entrée cost three or four. I ate there frequently with coworkers and friends; a week never passed that I didn't lunch there with Leslie Kornfeld and Harry Diamond. In all, I probably had hundreds of meals at the Crystal Club. I never once was asked to produce a membership card. And I never once saw a black customer there.

Today, I am told, the membership requirement has been officially abolished. But the clientele, as far as I can tell, is still all white.

⚜

When I lived and worked there, Greenwood, Mississippi was more than half black. The Greenwood *Commonwealth*, however, was almost entirely white, from the editors and reporters to the men who ran the presses and delivered the paper to subscribers (most of whom were white, too).

Margaret Dean, one of the paper's three reporters, was the only black presence on the entire editorial staff.

I could tell from the beginning that I would have a hard time getting to know Margaret. For one thing, she didn't seem to want to have much to do with me. Everyone else at the paper had welcomed me warmly, eagerly sought to engage me in conversation, invited me out for lunch or over for dinner. Not Margaret. My early attempts to engage her in conversation were futile; during my first month or two at the paper, she seemed to regard me with suspicion and wariness. Later she would confess that she had not initially thought it worth her while to befriend me, imagining that I would not last in Greenwood more than a few weeks, and that, my unusual origins aside, she had viewed me as nothing more than the latest in a parade of white men to march through the newsroom, earning as much as or more than she despite their relative inexperience, and making her feel ever more the token.

Eventually, though, Margaret and I did become friendly. She still remained somewhat aloof, and could be intensely private, but sometimes, without warning, she opened up in strange and stunning ways. Once, when we were down at the police station and she was teaching me how to do the police beat—that is, how to read the police log and copy down its entries (the most common being "public inebriation") for reprint in next day's paper—she stopped and told me a story.

"One time, Richard," she began, "I was down here on a Saturday, doing this, and a voice comes over the scanner sayin' there's a house fire goin' on, and announcing the address over and over. And they must have said it four or five times, and all of a sudden I thought: Wait a minute—that's *my* house! So I ran out to my car and raced on down there, but it was just about gone already. Ain't that something, now?"

Margaret said this with a wry smile; I didn't know how to react.

It was Margaret, more than anyone else, who introduced me to black Greenwood and taught me to see, at least to some extent, what things looked like from the other side of the color line. She herself had a fairly unusual perspective: She had grown up in Yazoo City, some fifty miles down Highway 49, close enough to know how things were in the Delta but far enough from Greenwood to be able to contrast the two towns. And in her mind, Yazoo City always compared favorably. This never failed to confound me; Yazoo City struck me as smaller and uglier than Greenwood, dominated by sulphur plants that rendered the sky a perpetual yellow. But

Margaret told me that as a child, she had once seen Dr. Martin Luther King lead a march there, and hearing that, I figured that if he had gone to Yazoo City then there must be something more to the place than I could perceive through the jaundiced haze that hung over it.

What truly made Margaret's perspective unusual, though, was that she was part of an exceedingly small Greenwood demographic: the black middle-class. Margaret's husband, Reginald (she always called him "Dean," leading me to think, early on, that his name was actually "Dean Dean"), was a police officer in Greenwood, and they lived with their two sons in a house that they owned. Their house was very nice; the surrounding houses were not. Greenwood's black middle class was so small that they did not even have their own neighborhood. Instead, they lived among the rest of the town's blacks, who were, for the most part, truly poor.

In that regard, Greenwood is no different from the Delta as a whole. Vast swaths of it are consumed by devastating poverty just as Margaret's old house had been consumed by fire. The unnatural landscape in these places—houses and sheds and stores—looks to the initiated eye to be ravaged, not by conquering armies or the wrath of nature, but by neglect and deprivation. There is habitation aplenty but not much life. There is languor, hopelessness, purposelessness. There is devastation, the human kind. The Delta is a third-world country in the middle of America. The Delta is poverty, and poverty is the Delta. The two are inseparable, and have been, I suspect, since Emancipation. And, like everything else in the Delta, poverty exists and persists and flourishes in two varieties: black and white.

ॐ∾

In the late 1980s, several of the very poorest counties in the United States were in the Mississippi Delta; the poorest of all, Tunica County, has since been swept up by an economic boom in the form of riverboat casinos. But the next poorest, Holmes, is inland—no river, no casinos, no economic revitalization; the biggest thing to hit Holmes County in the past few years is a new state prison (prisons and casinos were, in fact, two of the biggest growth industries of the 1990s; throughout Mississippi, and the rest of the South, and much of the nation, for that matter, small towns and communities competed vigorously to land one or the other). Holmes borders Leflore County a few miles south of Greenwood; a few miles south of that border, one comes across Tchula, Mississippi, the poorest town I have ever seen.

Tchula sits on Highway 49, a two-lane blacktop that is the shortest route from Greenwood to Jackson. Along the way, it runs through towns like Cruger and Edwards and Sidon and Thornton and Bentonia and Pocahontas and Flora and Eden, past catfish farms where the ponds are as perfectly square as if they had been drawn on a piece of paper with a pencil and ruler, around stagnant bayous spiked with the hollowed trunks of dead trees and covered with green slime so thick it appears you could just stroll across it like a moldy old carpet. Mostly, though, it cuts across flat, dusty farmland, vast brown expanses interrupted only by the occasional irrigation rig and, out near the horizon, an old brown house or a white-washed church or a line of trees, planted out there to prevent the Delta from turning into a dust bowl. That's what you're looking at when you're driving down Highway 49, stuck, perhaps, behind some hopelessly slow combine or log-truck or jalopy. And then you pass a small, rectangular green sign: Tchula. That's it. That's all you need to know.

Except that, a few yards later, there is another sign, warning of a drastic drop in the speed limit: Tchula is known as a speed trap, and although I never once saw a police car there, my radar detector rarely failed to register a long, shrill tone as I drove slowly through the town. It would be easy to presume that Tchula's low speed limit serves no purpose other than being a lucrative source of income for the place. But the word "lucrative" implies that there is money somewhere in Tchula, and if this is true then it is the most ingeniously hidden money in America. Besides, the speed limit's true purpose quickly becomes apparent: In Tchula, people are constantly crossing back and forth over the highway, slowly and without even looking for cars.

The first few times I observed this phenomenon, it baffled me. Just what were these people doing in the middle of the road while cars and trucks whizzed by? Were they trying to get struck by a passing motorist, perhaps, hoping for some kind of insurance payday? Were they seeking to alleviate the monotony of life in Tchula by playing some sort of automotive Russian roulette? Why were they there?

It took several more such encounters, several more trips down that slender blacktop alley lined with sheds made of plywood and cardboard and tarpaper and looking as if they had survived several fires ("survived," perhaps, being too optimistic a term; rather, *endured*) before I realized that "why?" was only part of the proper question—the other part being "why not?" There was nothing for them on either side of the road: No jobs, no hope for employment or much of anything else, and no homes—just the crudest form of shelter from the elements, which were, most often, no more threatening than merely oppressive heat. Why be on one side of the road or the other? Why not be right there in the middle? Any spot in Tchula— whether off in a field or a parking lot or on some dirt shoulder or on the blacktop or right on top of the double-yellow line—was just as good as any other spot, no better or worse. Tchula was beyond hope, beyond even despair. Anyone could see that.

Or so I thought. One day, in the break room at the *Commonwealth*, Vic Laurent sat down next to me and said: "Hey, Richard, y'wonna get rich quick?"

"Sure," I said.

"Well, then, all you gotta do is open you a fried chicken shack down in Tchula," he asserted, laughing. "You'll be a millionaire in no time a'tall, I tell you what!"

A moon-faced man in his midforties, Vic Laurent was the paper's book-keeper. He wore loud madras plaid shirts, smiled constantly, and seemed to have a decided fondness for beer, which he frequently drank in his office or the break room. In other words, he was the epitome of what is known down South as a "good ol' boy"—relaxed, quick with a joke or a bit of advice, and always up for some kind of good time. I liked him a lot, despite the fact that we disagreed on almost every matter of any real importance.

Vic had enrolled as a freshman at Ole Miss in the fall of 1962, just as the National Guard and angry white mobs were convening upon the cam-pus for one last showdown over desegregation; "yes, me and Mister Meredith were in the same class," he often said to me with a grin. But he had also been born and raised in Leflore County, and was Greenwood through and through. He had strong opinions on all the most controver-sial subjects, and he was not shy about sharing them. One day, while we sat in his office and chatted amiably, I made the mistake of commenting, in passing, that the staff of the *Commonwealth* seemed to me to be dispropor-tionately white.

"I tell you what!" he said. "And you know why that is?"

"No," I said. "Do you?"

"Hell, yes," he replied. "Blacks don't wonna work here."

"Why's that?"

"It's not just here. They don't wonna work anywhere. And why the hell should they? They got their welfare and their food stamps, and then you drive by their houses, these little ol' shotgun shacks, and they all got brand-new Cadillacs settin' in their driveways! And if they need some more money, they just go out and have them a few more kids. They got it made, I tell you what!"

"What the hell are you talking about?" I spat, horrified.

"Listen, Richard, I'm not bein' prejudiced here. I'm not a racist. I don't have anything against the blacks. But that's just the way it is. They don't work like white people do. They don't have to work like white people do. All they do is get that check from the gov'ment and cash it and then drive around in their Cadillacs and go out and have them a good ol' time. You know what they say? *If you could be a nigger on Saturday night, you'd never wonna be a white man again!"*

I opened my mouth to speak, but nothing came out. Unquantifiable notions flailed around in my mind, careening off the walls of my consciousness, slamming into one another and creating a logjam in my throat. Vic had grown up in Greenwood and had driven through Tchula hundreds of times, and he was certainly not blind or stupid. He could see that there were no Cadillacs in a place like Tchula, that people there didn't work not because they were lazy but because there was simply no work to be had there now that the mechanization of farms had rendered sharecropping obsolete, and that no fried chicken stand, or any other kind of restaurant, would last a week there unless they did all of their business in food stamps. I couldn't understand how he could make such an absurd statement, one so riddled with falsehoods that I could not even grasp where I might begin picking it apart; and yet I knew, at the same moment, that I understood perfectly.

"Jesus," I mumbled. "White people."

Vic's eyes opened wide; his jaw fell open. "What do you mean, 'white people'? For God's sake, Richard," he said, leaning in close to me, his face awash in sad concern. "Look in the mirror. *You're* white!"

I didn't know what to say. What could I say? There was no denying it: I *was* white. No matter how I saw or thought of myself, as far as Greenwood was concerned, I was white, as white as any other white person in town, so obviously white that it was presumed, by most other whites I met, that I saw the world exactly as they did, that terms like *nigger* and *bluegum* and *porch monkey* and *moon cricket* didn't offend me, that I probably used them myself and certainly wouldn't mind hearing someone else use them in conversation with me, that I too said things like *If you could be a nigger on Saturday night*

you'd never wonna be a white man again and that even if I didn't say them I
believed them, believed that blacks didn't want to work and were scamming
the government out of welfare millions which they then used to buy steaks
and gold chains and Cadillacs. And if I should choose to protest these pre-
sumptions about how a white man like me thinks, and should think, would
anyone listen and take heed? And why should they? After all, I lived in a
white neighborhood. I ate in white restaurants. I worked in a white office,
had a white job, and availed myself, consciously or not, of the uncountable
advantages and privileges and opportunities and freedoms afforded me
solely because, yes, I was white. But the truth was that, as obvious as it was
to Vic and everyone else in town, up until that moment I had never really
thought of myself that way; I'd always enjoyed the luxury of not having to
think about it at all.

No more.

I never did come up with anything to say back to Vic; instead, after an
uncomfortable moment or two I just turned away, frustrated and embarrassed, and went back to the newsroom. I made a point of walking by
Margaret's desk, hoping, perhaps, that she could absolve me of something—I didn't really know what—but she wasn't there.

ॐ

Like me, Carroll Academy was white. All white. As were Pillow Academy,
and Star Academy, and Cruger-Tchula Academy, and Central Holmes
Academy, and East Holmes Academy, and Strider Academy, and Sunflower
Academy, and dozens of other small private schools throughout the Delta,
all of which had been founded in the mid-to-late 1960s, when it had
become apparent that the federal government wasn't just going to forget
about the *Brown* decision. Most of them were housed in corrugated metal
sheds; most of them weren't accredited. Most of them hardly had classrooms and libraries and playing fields. Some of them barely had enough
students to field football teams. All of them played football, but only
against one another.

One Friday night, I was up in Carrollton, covering a football game at
Carroll Academy (team name: Rebels), when a man walked up and started
making conversation with me. Soon his wife joined in, and his two sons
and three daughters, all asking me what New York was like and how did I
like Mississippi and was I enjoying the game. Their kids were not enrolled
at Carroll Academy; they attended J. Z. George, the local public high

school, where they were among the few white students. But the Wildcats, as J. Z. George's team was known, were playing out of town that night, and so here they were. Their clothes were not torn or dirty but were well-worn and obviously old; it appeared to me that none of them had bathed in a few days. But the conversation was friendly and engaging, and by the time the game ended, they had invited me to their house for dinner later that week.

They lived not in town but out in the county, near the small community of Coila (pronounced "Coe-AHL-lah"). The road upon which their house stood was not marked or named or paved. I drove around for a half hour trying to find the place; when I finally did, I was stunned and a bit frightened. The house was a small, crude wooden shack, riddled with holes and looking as if a lazy breeze might turn it into a pile of firewood. I wanted nothing so much as to turn around and drive off, to scurry back to my cozy and solid apartment and call them and tell them I couldn't find the place and it was just as well anyway because I had a bad stomachache and we'd just have to try again at some unspecified point in the future. But I couldn't call. I didn't have their phone number.

They didn't have a phone.

Nor did they have electricity. Nor running water.

They had had these things at one time, they explained, but then the man of the house had hurt himself somehow and hadn't worked in quite some time, and the medical bills had eaten up what savings they'd had. Now they got by on welfare and food stamps, which wasn't nearly enough, so they did without things like electricity and running water and insurance for the man's old pickup truck, and patched up their clothes as best they could, and hunted for food as best they could with a slingshot, as the man had pawned his old rifle some time back to pay a gas bill. On that night, what had been hunted down and killed and cooked over a can of sterno was squirrel. And I ate it. It tasted—well, it didn't taste like chicken.

❧

A week later, while I was covering a Greenwood Bulldogs game, Handy Campbell's mother, Hattie, walked up to me and invited me over to their place for dinner with the family. At that very moment, her son threw a missile that soared over half the field and hit squarely a wide receiver in the end zone. The crowd erupted in cheers; the Bulldogs had already held a commanding lead that night—thanks in large part to Campbell's efforts—

and the game was almost over, but this pass was so beautiful that it seemed to transcend something as petty as the score. It was artistry, a moment of physical brilliance that brought the people in the stands, even those rooting for the other team, to their feet. They had just seen something rare and special, and they knew it. And minutes later, after the game had ended and I was interviewing him—he spoke softly, his eyes pointed at the ground, of the contributions of his wide receivers and running backs and defensive line—those same fans strode onto the field and surrounded Handy Campbell, some shouting plaudits, others merely looking, staring, basking in his presence. Just a few months earlier, none of these people had even known he'd existed. He didn't seem to notice the difference.

The following Tuesday evening, I drove over to Snowden Jones, the blue-and-white housing project about a half-mile from the *Commonwealth*'s offices. Although it looked from the road like an ordinary apartment complex, Mike McNeill had warned me on my first day in town to stay away from the place, especially after dark. Jack Henderson had told me: "I wouldn't go there, except with my .44, maybe, in broad daylight." As I pulled into the parking lot and locked my car, I could see through the twilight that the asphalt was littered with broken glass, and that there were men sitting on the buildings' steps and talking who grew silent and stared as they saw me approach, but I tried hard to forget all of the warnings and walk as if I were not at all apprehensive about being there.

I hurriedly found apartment 3-G and knocked on the door. After a few seconds—no doubt it seemed longer than that to me at the time—the door opened and I was greeted by Handy. As his mother set the table, he gave me a tour of the apartment: a small living room and three small bedrooms in which Hattie and Handy and Anthony and April and Tracy and Zondra lived. Handy was the oldest.

Dinner was served: ground beef in tomato sauce on macaroni. It was delicious, and I raced through a large plate of it and heaped on another helping. Looking around, though, I began to notice that everyone's plate but mine appeared old and chipped, and that no one else was taking seconds, and that the chairs upon which we were sitting were cheap and worn and splintering. What decorations there were on the wall were not framed and hung but merely tacked up; the walls themselves were dark and mottled and in need of repair. In my first few moments in the apartment, I had seen everything in the glare of being a new visitor receiving gracious hospitality, but now I could see the place for what it really was—a dingy apartment in a housing project, poorly furnished and poorly maintained and far too small for its six occupants. And these people were poor. They didn't wear it like the family up in Coila or the road-wanderers down in Tchula, maybe, didn't appear quite as exposed and bereft, but they were truly indigent.

That in itself didn't surprise or shock me, I suppose; I'd been in the Delta for some time by then, and I knew how things were there, how people really lived. But I couldn't quite reconcile the image of Handy Campbell as a triumphant football hero, standing on the field of play and being mobbed by adoring fans, with the image of Handy Campbell as a skinny, underfed, ill-clothed kid who lived in the projects. And if I couldn't reconcile the two images, how could all those fans? And how could Handy Campbell himself?

Here's how: They didn't even try. The fans never thought about it, I am sure, never considered where Handy Campbell went and what he did when he was off the gridiron. As for Handy Campbell himself, I suspect he just took those Friday nights as a gift, and spent the rest of the week clutching close the hope that someday, the rest of his life might rise to their level.

EIGHT

THE BRIEFEST EXPERIENCE OF PERFECTION

Handy Campbell, at least, had those Friday nights.

> *It's been a long, hard road for Leflore County High School's cross-country team. And it's about to get much steeper. Literally.*
>
> *This Saturday, Coach Lester Smith will take his team down to Mississippi College in Clinton. There they will be setting their sights on the only meet and title they have failed to win: the state championships.*
>
> —*Greenwood Commonwealth*, Friday, November 11, 1988

For most of that fall, I had refrained from devoting space in my sports section to the weekly exploits of Lester Smith's running Tigers, remembering with some pain the rather graphic calls I had taken from readers following my original article on the team, not to mention the grumbling disapprobation that had been broadcast in my direction by John Emmerich and Mike McNeill. Even Jack Henderson, the former *Commonwealth* sports editor who had since become my friend, and who professed respect for both Lester Smith's team and my interest in it, confessed that he wouldn't have run anything on the team in *his* sports pages. "Hell, no!" he said. "This time a year, folks 'round here 'spect to read about football, football, and football, and that's it. Y'already piss people off by runnin' the hockey scores. You know you're the only sumbitch in Greenwood,

100

Mississippi who gives a shit about hockey, you Ivy League Yankee Jew."

"I know," I laughed. "That's why I run them."

"Well, that's one thing," Jack said. "They don't take up that much space, and most folks probably just figure you're a crazy sumbitch, which of course you are. But you go take up serious football space runnin' stories on a *cross-country team* from a school like Leflore, and people ain't likely to consider whether or not y'in your right mind before they go on and shoot your Yankee ass."

And so I refrained from writing about L.C.H.S.'s cross-country team that fall. But I followed their progress anyway, calling Lester Smith every Monday morning, without fail, to see how they had fared in the previous Saturday's meet. Every Monday morning, without fail, Coach Smith had the same news. His team had won. And no one had been there to see it happen.

But by the beginning of November, football fever had hit such a pitch in Greenwood that I began to believe there might just be a surplus of fan enthusiasm in town, and that some of it could, with a certain measure of interference, be channeled toward cross-country. Naturally, I would provide that certain level of interference.

On Friday, November 11, when I should have been devoting all of my energy to previewing that night's Bulldogs playoff game, I wrote and printed an article on the Tigers, "Leflore Cross-Country Hopes Third Try for State Championship Works." I summarized the team's undefeated season, in part to generate reader enthusiasm and in part to assuage my guilt for having ignored them all fall.

> *First there was their own meet, where they ungraciously made off with the top honors; then there was the Mississippi College Invitational, the Coahoma County Invitational, the Leland Invitational, the Delta Valley Conference Meet in Rosedale, and most recently, the Class 3A District Championships in Greenville. All throughout, Leflore has never broken stride. And every week, the victory margins get bigger.*
>
> *But all that means nothing to the Tigers now. What lies ahead is the only hurdle that has ever tripped them up.*

I extensively quoted Coach Lester Smith and team captain Tyrone Davis, a slight kid with close-cropped hair and a quiet, polite demeanor. And I closed the piece by reiterating the time and place of the state championships—11 o'clock the following morning at Mississippi College in Clinton. I was certain that fans would make the trip down to the meet the next day; and later that night, as I marveled at the sight and sound of the thousands who had come out to see Greenwood High School beat Jackson Provine, 28–0, in the first round of the state football playoffs, I felt even more certain.

The next morning, I drove down to Clinton to see the cross-country state championship. In the movies, an underdog team like Leflore pulls through and wins in the end. As for real life:

> CLINTON—*Leflore County High School's cross-country team, barely two years old, succeeded in winning the Class 3A state championship by a slim margin here Saturday.*
>
> *The last state title LCHS won was in 1973, in basketball. At that time, Leflore was a 1A school.*
>
> *Seven schools competed in the 3A finals, including old rival Port Gibson, and heavily favored Pontotoc. The 3A is traditionally the most competitive conference for Mississippi cross-country . . .*
>
> *"I owe all the credit for this to the team* [Coach Smith said]*, and to our administration, which gave us great support. This will be good for the county, and great for the school . . .*
>
> *"It's very satisfying," he said. "I really enjoyed helping these guys grow, and guiding them as they reached to be their best."*
>
> *And it is official: Leflore County High School's cross-country team is the best.*
>
> —"Leflore cross-country squad wins 3A crown"
> *Greenwood Commonwealth*, Sunday, November 13, 1988

But even though they occasionally collide, the movies and real life are, of course, almost entirely divergent. In the movies, for example, Leflore's seven runners—Tyrone Davis, Richard Holston, Walter Magee, Juan Jones, James Ramsay, Dexter Saffold, and Reggie King—would have been terribly jittery before the race, while their coach would have stood steady as an oak, cool as an iceberg. In real life, the opposite was true. While his team calmly went through their stretching regimen, with Holston telling me "this is going to be our day," Coach Smith confessed to me: "I have butterflies; it's as if I were going to run the race myself. I'm a nervous wreck." And in the movies, the runners would have been swallowed up by a jubilant mob after crossing the finish line. In real life, they were greeted only by Coach Smith. No one else had made the trip.

Still, they left with a medal. I left with a story that would later win an award from the Mississippi Press Association. In the movies, that Saturday in November would have been a turning point in all of our lives. But this wasn't the movies; this was Mississippi. In America, life doesn't get any more real.

⁂

Mere 70-millimeter film, though, could scarcely have done justice to a Greenwood Bulldogs football game. In the fall of 1988, I spent every Friday night experiencing that particular slice of Mississippi real life.

Perhaps more than anything else, it was a religious experience, and I mean that literally. The band closed every game by playing "Amazing Grace," while most everyone in the crowd loudly sang along. One night, I had the temerity to ask Jack what exactly that old hymn had to do with football. He thought about it for a few seconds, then explained: "Shut the hell up."

Every game began with a preacher giving a benediction, an act that I soon came to regard as my own personal auto-da-fé. "Heavenly Father," the minister would intone into a microphone, his voice booming from enormous amplifiers and ricocheting off the grandstands, the scoreboard, eyeglasses, and teeth. At that point, everyone present—fans, players, and coaches, all of whom were already standing—would bow their heads. Everyone, that is, except me. I would stand there for a few seconds, feeling naked and marked and alone, until I couldn't take it anymore and bowed my own head, too. Maybe, I consoled myself, he won't say it this time.

"We ask Your blessing for these boys tonight," the minister would continue. "Keep them safe on the field of play, and later, when the contest has ended, guide them safely back home. Bless the parents and siblings and friends and neighbors who have come out here tonight, and keep them safe from harm. Bless the teachers who have taught these boys, and the coaches who have coached them."

So far, I would think, so good.

"We ask that the game which is about to be played here be fun and fair, and that all who participate, whether they win or not, might take away valuable lessons which they will carry with them as they travel through life, and that those lives will also be fun and fair and fulfilling. We ask that the spectators here tonight might also carry away valuable lessons, and lead fulfilling lives, and that they will continue to bind together as a community in faith and love. And that, on the field or in the stands, at work or at play, at school or at home, they do right by each other, and follow the teachings and commandments laid out in Your Holy Bible."

Inevitably, at this point, I would think: All right. He's not going to say it.

And then, just as inevitably, he would, indeed, say it: "We ask these blessings in the name of our Lord, Jesus Christ."

And every time, I would flinch and then deflate as if punctured. I don't know why I was always so surprised: Even though it was a public school, Greenwood High never once failed to start their games with a prayer, and to direct the crowd in the grandstands to rise and bow their heads for that prayer, and to address that prayer specifically to Jesus Christ, and to utterly ignore the fact that not all of their boosters were Christians. And so, every Friday night, in an effort to not stand out, I bowed my head, too, and hoped with tightly closed eyes that this week's prayer might be a bit more inclusive. But it never once was, not even a bit; and always, afterward, realizing that once again I had inadvertently prayed to Jesus, I would think: God forgive me, whatever Your name really is.

Most of the time, though, a little unwitting apostasy seemed an acceptable price to pay for the privilege of watching a Greenwood Bulldogs game, not merely for what went on on the field, which was usually pretty exciting, but for the way those Friday nights vivified the town itself. For most of Greenwood, Saturday and Sunday were for sleeping, shopping, visiting, running errands, going to church. Monday through Thursday were for work. But Friday was for football, for joy, for life.

There were pep rallies in the gym. Tailgate picnics in the parking lot. Sing-alongs in the stands. There was a good bit of something approximating brotherhood. I never saw blacks and whites get along as well anywhere else in Greenwood. The team was split nearly fifty-fifty, black and white. So was the school. For most of its history, Greenwood High School football, like Greenwood High School itself, had been a segregated affair. There was no sign of it in 1988.

They were kids, the Bulldogs, but suited up and charging onto the field, they were more than men. They looked huge, towering; they looked like they had been born to play football, and had been playing it since birth. As they trotted purposefully onto the gridiron, buffeted by a loud pulse of cheering, the announcer called out their names: Kenny Smith. Bennie Jackson. Trey Bullock. Trennis Livingston. Scott Atkinson. Marvin McDowell. Frederick Ervin. Edward Jordan. Cedric Spivey. Dexter Williams. Odis Dean. Mark Jones. Bobby Goss. Corder Ward. Wallace Melvin. Torrance Johnson. The

Bonner brothers, Carlos and Antonious. Vasheen "Tony" Noland. Frederick "Blue" Steele. Handy Campbell. When the game had ended and the stadium emptied out and the cars left the parking lot and the lights were shut off, many if not most of them returned to poor homes and resumed the life of poor kids, anonymous and hungry and without much hope. But for a few hours on fall Friday nights, they were titans in maroon-and-white uniforms. The people in the stands idolized them, wanted to be them, to adopt them, to date them, to raise kids who would take after them.

They were individuals. The Bonner brothers—Carlos was a wide receiver, Antonious a defensive back—were outstanding and versatile players, but shy. Kenny Smith, a huge linebacker, was amiable, kind. Cedric Spivey, a defensive lineman, was eager to please. Trey Bullock, a kicker, was earnest, serious, focused. "Blue" Steele, a compact running back, was cocky and a cut-up. I once asked him how he'd earned his nickname; "I'm so black I'm blue," he explained with a sly smirk.

Handy Campbell was all of them in one: shy as the Bonner brothers, amiable as Kenny Smith, eager to please as Cedric Spivey, focused as Trey Bullock, and, on the playing field, cocky as "Blue" Steele. But off the field, he always kept about him a quiet confidence and dignity, always gave due credit to his teammates. He had joined the team later than most of them; he hadn't come up through the freshman team (the "Bullpups," as they were known) and the junior varsity. He didn't swagger, at least not off the field. On the field—well, I guess the act of throwing a fifty-yard pass is a kind of swagger, but if you can do it, you're probably entitled.

The fans in Greenwood tended to swagger, too, but they were also entitled. Throughout the season, their team had managed to find increasingly breathtaking ways to win, usually by lopsided scores and often against teams that were ranked much higher than they were. In eleven weeks, they compiled a record of 10–1, their only loss, a 10–0 shutout, coming at the hands of Clarksdale, an old Delta rival. With that record, Greenwood sailed into the playoffs and trounced Jackson Provine—they even managed to score on a 99-yard touchdown drive—in the first round. As the team celebrated on the field, word came down: For the next round, they would face Clarksdale again.

ॐ≪

My friend Jack Henderson was a true redneck, and he was proud of it— "damn proud!" he would tell you. He drove a pickup truck fitted with a toolbox and Confederate flag bumper sticker. He chewed tobacco whenever he wasn't eating or sleeping. He owned eight guns, none of them less powerful than a .44. And every Friday night, when he and I would go stand on the sidelines at Greenwood Bulldogs football games, Jack would wear a pair of cowboy boots that cost more than a trip for two to Gulf Shores (pronounced "Guff Shows"), Alabama (pronounced "Alla-BAMMAH!"). These boots were calf-high and made of ostrich skin, dyed gray, with lac-quered cherrywood soles, and steel bands stretched across the sharply pointed toes, polished so thoroughly that they shone even in the dark. Jack and I went to quite a few Bulldogs games that fall, many of them played out on fields laden with deep, dark mud, but mysteriously, I never saw a speck of it get anywhere near those shiny steel bands.

Jack and I ribbed each other a good bit during those games, and his boots were a favorite target of mine (after all, I knew better than to make fun of the man's guns). Usually, I tried to be somewhat subtle; but when the home team charged onto the field at Bulldog Stadium to face the Clarksdale Wildcats in the North Mississippi 5A semifinals, and a wild, shrieking rebel yell assaulted the air, I was suddenly emboldened to launch a more direct attack. Looking down at the ground, I whistled long and low and said, with a sneer: "Nice boots! Where can I get me a pair?"

Jack squirted a stream of chaw in the direction of my sneakers. "Richit," he said, "ain't nothin' stupider lookin' than a New York motherfucker in Mis'sippi boots."

The strange thing was that as the season had worn on, I had started to feel more and more comfortable in Mississippi boots (figuratively speaking, of course). A day before the game, I had written an article that reeked of boosterism—"Bulldogs determined to make good on second shot at Clarksdale." J. O. was pleased; even Mike McNeill, who had never quite adjusted to having an alleged Yankee intellectual cover Mississippi high school football, seemed impressed. The coaches, ever more confident of my loyalty, began giving me a bit more than just the standard boilerplate when it came time for quotes. Instead of merely praising his boys' dedication and promising that everyone would go out there and give 110 percent, Coach Bradberry issued an earthier prediction: "If we don't make any boneheaded mistakes and give up the big play," he speculated, "we'll be O.K."

Those words came back to me on the first drive of the game, when the Wildcats picked up the opening kickoff on their own 20-yard line and managed to move it to Greenwood's 8-yard line in a matter of minutes, poised to score at least a field goal or, more likely, a touchdown. This is it,

I thought. The only game I could remember in which Greenwood had not put the first score on the board had been the previous loss to Clarksdale.

But then Melvin Smith's defense woke up and, on two consecutive downs, sacked Clarksdale's quarterback, Joe Golden, for lost yards. On the fourth down, Clarksdale tried to fake a field goal attempt and run for the end zone, but Greenwood's defense shut them down again. In all, Clarksdale had lost twenty-one yards on the play.

Greenwood was unable to convert a first down on their first possession of the game, but Bobby Goss was able to punt the ball an impressive sixty-nine yards. On the next play, Golden, visibly flustered by the reversal of momentum, bobbled the snap. Kenny Smith rushed in and hit Golden hard, forcing him to drop the ball. ("I saw him, I hit him, and that was that," he told me after the game. "Coach always taught us to make big plays when we can.") Corder Ward rushed in and recovered the ball, giving the Bulldogs possession on Clarksdale's 12-yard line.

Handy Campbell trotted out, but now it was his turn to be sacked, for a nine-yard loss. On the next play, he threw for an interception, which was run up to Clarksdale's 21-yard line just as the first quarter ended. I couldn't recall having seen Campbell ever turn the ball over before; but as I looked at him, standing on the sidelines, I saw no trace of worry or disappointment. Indeed, his face was inscrutably calm, betraying nothing inside. Then I looked down at his hands hanging at his sides, clenching and unclenching slowly, and I saw in that scarcely visible gesture an anxious, searing desire to get back into the game, to make things right.

He would soon enough. Greenwood's defense quickly shut down Clarksdale's brief drive, forcing them to punt to Greenwood's 37-yard line. On the next play, running back Mark Jones picked up the ball and ran it twenty-one yards. Then Handy Campbell hit Carlos Bonner with an eighteen-yard pass; then, taking the snap and biding his time, he reared back and threw the ball another twenty-four yards and again hit Carlos Bonner—in the end zone.

The crowd screamed in delight and jumped to its feet. Greenwood had drawn first blood from the team that had shut them out seven weeks earlier.

From there it was easy, or at least looked that way. On the very next play, Clarksdale fumbled the ball on their own 34-yard line; one run, two passes and a kick later, the score was 14–0. After the half, Campbell threw the ball forty-five yards to hit Torrance Johnson in the end zone. Antonious Bonner intercepted a Clarksdale pass in his own end zone and ran it back forty-one yards. Campbell got the ball down to Clarksdale's 3-yard line, then handed it off to "Blue" Steele, who ran it in for the final score of the game. This time, it was Greenwood who shut out Clarksdale, 28–0.

Bulldog Stadium was jubilation. Fans streamed onto the field, picking up the players, embracing the coaches. Jack tried to shoot some pictures of the celebration but quickly gave up and joined in instead. Coach Bradberry, who typically shunned hyperbole and tended toward understatement, beamed and told me, "This is undoubtedly our biggest win." Melvin Smith and Mike Martin agreed. So did the players. *Sweet Revenge!* read the headline of my article about the game; and then, just to make certain my choice of clichés was fully appreciated, I added: "If revenge is sweet, then you can bet that Greenwood will be developing cavities after this game." Bleh.

Handy Campbell alone seemed at that moment more given to contemplation than elation. In all, he had thrown the ball 114 yards that night, including three touchdowns, but he was far from satisfied. "I still think I need to get a lot better," he told me. "I'm going to work hard on that this week."

Σ∂∞Θ

That same night, several hours northeast of Greenwood, Tupelo High School's star quarterback, Todd Jordan, had thrown for 284 yards, a season high, and led his team, the Golden Wave, to a 17–7 victory over Jackson Calloway High School. In doing so, Tupelo progressed to the North Mississippi finals, just as Greenwood had done in beating Clarksdale, meaning the two would face each other the very next week. This time, though, when the news of their upcoming opponents' identity was handed down, it was greeted with anything but trepidation. "I don't worry about our kids facing Todd Jordan," Coach Bradberry told me while still on the field celebrating the win over Clarksdale. "They face Handy Campbell in practice every day, and I can't think of anyone in the state of Mississippi who throws the ball better than he does." Coach Smith crowed: "Tupelo will be a challenge, but we're red-blooded all-Americans, and we love challenges."

By Saturday morning, though, the intoxication of the previous night's triumph had started to fade, exposing the sober reality of the situation. In beating Clarksdale, Greenwood, now 11–1, had advanced to the rank of number seven in the state. Tupelo, though, was ranked number one. One nationwide poll ranked them twenty-second in the nation. Another ranked them sixteenth; yet another, twelfth. No one had beaten them all season; no one, it was widely believed in Mississippi, could.

Few even bothered to speculate on the source of Tupelo's immense prowess. The answer was obvious: Todd Jordan. A golden-haired, all-American boy, Jordan had recently been named one of *Parade* magazine's top American high school athletes. College scouts, it was said, had been courting him since the eighth grade. A revolving gaggle of them had attended every Golden Wave game that season. Jordan was the face of Mississippi high school football.

Handy Campbell, on the other hand, was faceless, at least beyond the city limits of Greenwood. Despite David Bradberry's assertion that he was the best quarterback in the state, Campbell hadn't made anyone's list of anything. Not a single college scout—from anywhere—had come out to see him all season. Other than Bradberry and Smith and his teammates, the only people in Mississippi who knew what Handy Campbell could do were those he had beaten on the field of play. Otherwise, he was utterly unknown, a nobody who had come from nowhere and, it was assumed, was heading there, too.

In fact, Handy Tyrone Campbell was entirely a product of Greenwood, born there on October 15, 1971. He was named for his father, Sam Handy, a native of Minter City, Mississippi, a little community some twenty miles north of town. At the time his son was born, Sam worked for the Dixie Amusement Company, fixing and delivering jukeboxes. Sam Handy later moved to Chicago; he was visiting relatives in Minter City when he died of a heart attack on December 20, 1993, at the age of forty-four. He never married Handy's mother, Hattie, who gave her son—and all the children she had borne, five of them from four different fathers, none of whom she'd married—her last name.

His siblings were all talented athletes, but Handy exhibited the greatest physical gift. By the time he was a junior in high school, he stood 6' 4" and weighed 190 lbs., and believed, as everyone around him did, that he could do well at any sport he chose. "He had what you call that *thang*," his friend Lanardo Myrick told me years later. "That *thang*, man—talkin' 'bout football, basketball, baseball, soccer, track. We had a little thing called 'The Fastest Man at Snowden Jones.' And I was the man. So one time we raced. And in the 40, I'm running a 4.4 or a 4.41—and he *beat* me."

But football was always Campbell's favorite. "We used to play a lot on Taft Street," Handy told me, referring to the neighborhood he'd lived in as a small boy, before the family moved into Snowden Jones. "We had sandlot teams and we used to play games like that a lot. Out of school all I did was play sports at the sandlot." He had not thought of trying out for the team at Greenwood High School until his junior year, and even then, he said, it wasn't his idea. "A lot of people just saw me throwing the ball, and they liked the way I threw it. They said, 'Maybe you should go out for football,' and after hearing a lot of people say that I finally decided to do it." Not that he had many misgivings. "I was kind of anxious and nervous at the same time," he remembered, "but I was waiting. I wanted to show everybody I could do it."

And now, in Tupelo, he would finally get his chance.

❦

The week that followed the Clarksdale game was enveloped in a mixture of anxiety and excitement that grew ever more intense as Friday approached. In practice that week, everyone seemed tense, nervous; even Handy Campbell, normally as slack as an unused rubber band, now appeared to be stretched taut. Again, it was mostly visible in his hands: Even when standing on the sidelines of the practice field, he gripped the ball so tightly I thought it would burst.

The coaches betrayed their own inner tension that week by reverting to awful sports clichés when interviewed. "We're just going to go out there and play 48 consistent minutes of good football," David Bradberry told me.

"I don't see how being an underdog is bad," Melvin Smith said. "Rooting for the underdog is the American way. Anyway, our kids don't see themselves as underdogs no matter whom they're playing."

As story quotes go, this was dreadful stuff. But in the charged atmosphere that possessed Greenwood that week, I hardly even noticed. Besides, I needed all the quotes I could get: Mike had ordered me to devote an entire page of that Thursday's sports section to the upcoming game. My article, *Greenwood, Tupelo Prep for Final North 5A War*, was subtitled "For Greenwood's Coaches, Players, It All Comes To This." This had been true of last week's game, and the game before that, too, but the fact had gone unmentioned; now, it hovered so obviously and oppressively over everyone and everything in town that to leave it yet unmentioned would somehow, I imagined, make things even worse. In a desperate attempt to inject some levity into the situation, I titled the accompanying column—comprising mostly an interview with Golden Wave head coach Ricky Black—*Just What Does Tupelo Want With Us, Anyway?* No one laughed.

At one point during practice that week, though, Coach Bradberry's vaguely cool facade cracked just a little bit, when he spoke about his quarterback's strengths. "Handy has a lot of courage," he asserted. "He'll hang onto the ball and take his licks. I'm not taking anything away from Todd Jordan, but going into the playoffs, if I had to pick a quarterback for us to have, I'd pick Handy Campbell."

It was a bold statement, the kind Bradberry had refrained from making throughout the season and that he was under no obligation to make now; I certainly hadn't asked him which quarterback he'd prefer to have on his team. But I took it as a declaration of confidence aimed not so much at me and the *Commonwealth* readers as at Handy Campbell himself, who had told me, that same afternoon, "I'm going to continue to work hard and try and get it together," as if throwing three touchdown passes the week before had signified some kind of falling apart.

I don't remember putting the sports page together that Friday morning; I'm not even sure if I did. I do know that around noon, Jack, Snuffy Everett, Bubba Ruscoe and I piled into Jack's wife's Mercury and headed off down Highway 7 toward Tupelo. That was the plan, anyway; I had no idea how to get to Tupelo, and I wasn't sure Jack did, either.

In fact, there was no simple, direct route between the two towns, which lay about 150 miles apart. Greenwood was thirty miles from the nearest interstate; Tupelo was nowhere near one at all. Jack showed me a map, and with his finger traced a bizarre, serpentine route that meandered through more than a half-dozen small highways, including the Natchez Trace. It seemed farther to go than Chicago. Luckily, we had seven-and-a-half hours until kickoff.

Snuffy had brought along a cassette which he insisted on playing at full volume as soon as we got out of town and onto an open road. I grimaced and braced for Hank Williams, Jr.'s "If the South Woulda Won," but what blasted out of the car's speakers was Tone-Lōc's "Wild Thing." To my astonishment, these three Mississippi-born white men—one who had played football at Pitt, one who was never without a plug of Beech Nut chewing tobacco in his cheek, and one who had a metal plate in his head—sang along with the song and danced as best they could while sitting down. When the number ended, they rewound the tape and played it again—seventeen times.

We stopped at least twice every hour, as Snuffy, who incessantly chugged Mountain Dew, always seemed to be in need of a rest room. We drove with the windows down in brisk autumn weather, ate Slim Jims by the dozen, ranked on each other mercilessly, and flirted ineptly with every female who crossed our path. In Houston, Mississippi, we circled the town square a dozen times fruitlessly; in Calhoun City, we actually convinced a coquettish pair of girls to make the trip with us (Snuffy's pick up line: "Hey! Come here!") before realizing that we had nowhere to put them.

In Vardaman, Jack ran into a store and returned with a small bottle of white shoe polish, the kind that comes with its own brush applicator. Tearing off the cap, he scribbled "GO DAWGS!" on his rear window; then, just in case any passersby might not know which dawgs he meant and where exactly they should be going, he added, underneath: Go Greenwood! Beat Tupelo!

"Is that O.K.?" I asked, never having seen someone deface his own car before.

"Damn, Richit!" Jack replied. "What you think they sell this stuff for? Ain't nobody wearin' white shoes in November!"

Later, standing in a convenience store parking lot in Okolona, I pointed to Jack's pouch of Beech Nut and asked for a pinch.

"You sure you can handle it now?" Jack asked. "This ain't Big League Chew."

"Come on," I said. "How bad could it be? They make *baby food*." I plucked out a generous wad with my fingers and deposited it between my cheek and gum, exactly as they said to do in the Skoal commercial. A few seconds passed, and then my cheek and tongue and the roof of my mouth began to burn as hot and painfully as my bare ankle had while under siege by an army of fire ants.

"Jesus!" I shouted, then promptly set about spitting out every last bit (a process that took several minutes) and rinsing out my mouth with two cans of Coke. "I can't believe you actually put that shit in your mouth! It's like acid!"

Snuffy and Bubba Ruscoe doubled over with laughter; Jack grinned broadly, spat at the ground, and patted me on the back. "Richit," he said, warmly, "I do believe you're on your way to becoming the world's first Jewish redneck!"

"I reckon," I shrugged.

※

By the time we got to Tupelo the sun had just about set for the evening. We tagged on to the end of a seemingly endless line of cars, headlights lit, slowly slithering like an incandescent python through a labyrinth of streets leading up to the stadium; another line passed us going in the opposite direction, and every twenty seconds or so Jack or Snuffy or Bubba would recognize one of the cars—their windows covered with white shoe polish, too—and would honk the horn hysterically, hooting and shouting and waving their arms, their heads fully out the windows as the cars slowly crept toward each other. Soon, they began doing that at every car, even those obviously from Tupelo; and soon, I began doing it, too.

Once we'd parked, I bounded toward the school, feeling as if I were on my way to an NFL game. No, not just a game: the Superbowl. All around me, people walked in the same direction quickly and with purpose, even skipped, while keeping up a steady stream of increasingly excited chatter. At the entrance gate—the entrance gate!—I flashed my Mississippi Press Association badge, the first time I had ever done so, then tipped my head toward Jack and said, cavalier as Bogart: "He's with *me*." The man nodded, obvious respect in his eyes, and promptly ushered us through. We were from *Greenwood*, dammit.

The bleachers were already filled to capacity, and now people began packing into the spaces in between the grandstands. Some carried signs ("Go 'Air' Jordan!", "Bite 'em Bulldogs!"); some had painted their faces (maroon and white for Greenwood; blue and gold for Tupelo), and no one, it appeared, had come without something—pom-pom or pennant, flag or foam finger, seat cushion or streamer—to wave wildly in the air. The bands stood on opposite sides of the field, playing fight songs that crashed and clashed cacophonously in the middle. The lights, scores of gleaming silver beacons poised high atop gleaming silver poles, shot brilliance over every blade of grass. I remembered the lights at Amanda Elzy High School: rusty and dented and barely capable of casting illumination beyond the overlapped wings of massive mosquitoes. Elzy seemed the other side of the world from here.

The teams charged onto the field, slapping and patting each other, as an announcer stirred the crowd to a frenzy. A minister stepped up to a microphone and delivered the benediction. This time I barely even noticed the incantation to Jesus. A coin toss, a lineup, a kickoff—it was as if I'd never seen any of it before, as if this were a brand new game that was being created and refined right here, right now, before my eyes.

And here came Handy Campbell, a giant, a gazelle, loping onto the gridiron, getting into position, catching the snap, darting to and fro, looking around, his arm rearing back and then snapping forward like a slingshot, like a mousetrap. Thirteen yards to Carlos Bonner, square in the sternum, the Greenwood grandstand going wild, anticipating the beginning of an unstoppable drive to Tupelo's end zone. But Tupelo stopped them on the next set of downs. Then Greenwood stopped Tupelo. Then Tupelo recovered a Greenwood fumble. Then Greenwood stopped Tupelo again. Then Tupelo lined up for a punt, Coach Bradberry on the sidelines shouting "Watch for the fake! Watch for the fake!" and Tupelo did fake and went for the pass and Greenwood blocked that, too. Then Greenwood took possession and Tupelo stopped them yet again, and back and forth and back and forth, a groaning, crunching pas de deux that ran out the first quarter and bled over into the second.

And then Greenwood's Cedric Spivey found his way around some Tupelo defensive lineman and slammed into Todd Jordan, who had only been sacked twice all year. Jordan fumbled; Bennie Jackson recovered the ball for Greenwood on Tupelo's 27, getting them closer to the opponent's end zone than they had been all game. "Blue" Steele, who had been penned in all game, broke out at last and ran the ball to Tupelo's 12, then the 9. Handy threw the ball toward Edward Jordan, waiting in Tupelo's end zone, but Jordan missed the pass, and on the next play Greenwood fumbled. They managed to recover the ball themselves, but not without losing twenty yards in the process. A ten-yard face-mask penalty against Tupelo took the ball back to their 19, and then, on third down, "Blue" Steele ran it to the 7, well within Trey Bullock's field goal range. Bullock trotted out and did his thing, and just like that, Greenwood made it to the scoreboard first with a 3–0 lead. Greenwood's fans shrieked with glee, and their band raced into a march, double-time.

Tupelo took possession again and the teams resumed their dance, back and forth, back and forth, until, late in the quarter, Handy Campbell completed a fifteen-yard pass, and then another for nineteen yards, and then hauled back and threw a third for fifty-five yards. The ball came to rest on Tupelo's 3-yard line; a defensive penalty pushed it up to within three feet of the end zone, with only ten seconds left on the clock. Campbell tried to hit Carlos Bonner in the end zone, but a Tupelo defenseman intercepted and slapped the ball to the ground. There was time for only one final play: Handy Campbell ducked around and, clasping the ball in his enormous hand, leapt over a writhing pile of maroon and white and blue and gold and touched the ball down just over the line.

Greenwood's side of the field erupted ecstatically, the band playing even faster than before. But then there was a whistle, a conference of the referees; and, emerging, one of them reported that the play had been called dead before Campbell had made his leap. Catcalls and cheers spiked the air; the 9 was yanked off the scoreboard, restored to a 3.

I'll probably never know what happened in the two locker rooms during that halftime, but I do know that out on the field there was a certain silence that defied even the marching bands stomping around, a tension I had never felt at any of the games I had covered that fall—indeed, at any sporting event I had ever attended, anywhere. The muted laughter and chatter and cheer that buzzed about the Greenwood crowd then was uneasy, without any of the confidence that had been there before the opening whistle, as if tethered on a rod and reel, ready to be yanked back and hidden at any time. Jack did not circulate about the crowd as he always did, but stood still on the sidelines, checking his film, his stats. I reviewed my notes again and again, as if I had missed a Greenwood touchdown in there somewhere. After twenty-four minutes of championship football, only three points had been scored. True, it was Greenwood who could claim those three points, but three points wasn't much of a lead against the top-ranked team in the state, not much of a bulwark against a Golden Wave that had seemed, throughout the rest of the season, more like a tidal wave. They had the statewide reputation. They had the national ranking. They had Todd Jordan. We had obscurity. We had a bunch of dirt-poor kids. We had three little points. It didn't seem like much at all.

All too soon they were jogging back onto the field, a little more tired than the first time, a little more scuffed and scraped, a little more trepidatious.

Tupelo kicked off, and Greenwood got the ball on its own 20-yard line. Immediately, Handy Campbell called a play, took the snap, danced back a few yards, and hit Carlos Bonner on the 32. The Greenwood stands issued a soft cheer, hesitant; but Handy Campbell didn't hesitate. Clapping his hands, he trotted back into the huddle, called a play, trotted out again, shouted out a few numbers, and took the snap.

And then, in a handful of seconds, everything changed forever.

I saw it all, every millisecond of it, watching from just over the sideline in midfield, knowing even as it began how it was going to end, and I can see it yet, as if viewing a slow-motion replay on television: Handy Campbell gliding back, pedaling back, hopscotch, triple-jump; his offensive line lunging forward, crashing into Tupelo's defensive line, buying him a precious second or two; a blurry white streak, Greenwood wide receiver Edward Jordan, dashing for the end zone as if he were being chased by the Angel of Death with the Devil in tow; Handy poised, turned sideways, his left foot rising up off the grass an inch or two, his arm, long and skinny and dark and looking as if it were elastic, stretching back, back, back, spidery fingers clenched over the laces, and then shooting up and out all at once like a javelin; the ball, in a flawless spiral, arcing up over the field, up, up, now blocking out the lights, up, and now hanging still for just an instant before beginning a slow descent, down, down, now just over the upstretched fingers of Tupelo's backfield, now behind them, down, down, now framed against a white jersey with maroon numbers, Edward Jordan, standing in the end zone, arms out, pulling it from the sky like a pie from an oven, and into his chest like his own newborn baby—seventy yards away from where Handy Campbell stood, motionless, watching.

Sure, there were cheers, a few—but not many. Mostly there was a stunned silence, gaping mouths. Mostly there was astonishment, awe. We had just witnessed a graceful and graced seventy-yard pass in a high-pressure high school championship football game. We had, all of us, just witnessed history, and we knew it, and we were somehow different because of it. There was now in our consciousness the briefest experience of perfection, and it would forever taint, if only unconsciously, everything else we would ever see or do. That moment changed everyone who was there that night. Especially Handy Campbell.

"What happened after the half," Coach Bradberry told me after the game, "is something you don't go over on the chalkboard. That's Handy's talent, and that's what he's capable of doing."

It was all over then, really. Antonious Bonner intercepted a pass from Todd Jordan, "Blue" Steele ran the ball twenty-six yards, and Handy Campbell threw another touchdown pass, this one for a mere twenty-three yards, to Torrance Johnson. Tupelo managed to kick a field goal and score two touchdowns, narrowing Greenwood's lead to a single point ("a thread of a lead," I later wrote in the paper), but no one on Greenwood's side of the field seemed at all worried. We had seen what Handy Campbell could do, and we knew, somehow, that he would find some way to do it again. And we were correct. Quickly, he took the ball on Tupelo's 43, threw it forty-one yards—again to Edward Jordan—and then ran it in himself. They missed the extra point, then recovered a Todd Jordan fumble and turned it into a field goal. With five minutes left on the clock, the score stood at 26–16, where it would remain for the rest of the game. With two minutes left, a steady, unabated roar began to rise from the Greenwood stands, ever louder, louder. With ten seconds left, fans began pouring onto the gridiron, embracing players, coaches, even members of the opposing team. It didn't matter who; there was no sign that someone had just lost a football game.

Jack let his camera fall to his side and rushed into the mob, but I stayed on the sidelines, scribbling notes, and thinking. Ever since Handy Campbell had thrown that seventy-yard pass, fragments of notions had been swirling around in my head, colliding with other fragments and struggling to fuse into some coherent whole; now I believed I had it. Watching that football sail through the air in a sublime arc, it occurred to me that what I was really witnessing was the rise of Handy Campbell's fortunes, and with them, in a parallel arc, my own. They were, I believed, tied together, and not only because I needed him for copy as much as he needed me for coverage. We had come up together at the same time, inexperienced and yet confident, not knowing exactly what we should be doing but knowing, nonetheless, that whatever it was we could do it. We had been given a great and largely unearned opportunity—him on the gridiron, me in the newsroom—and were now paying back those who had gambled on us with fat and glorious dividends. Up until that moment, I had wondered, every day, whether I had made a mistake in coming to Mississippi, whether I should have just stayed at home and taken some low-level job at some small suburban newspaper; now, I had seen a sign. I was on the right path—we both were, Handy Campbell and I—and from here it was only going to arc up and up and up, like that football. And in that moment, I was able to believe that, unlike that football, our arcs were never going to come down.

And Handy Campbell, at that moment, believed the same thing, at least of himself. Seven years later, recalling that night, he would smile and shake his head and muse: "It was the best feeling in the world. It was just—mmm!"

"The Tupelo game was the killer," Lanardo Myrick recalled the same seven years later. "After that game, he was in a daze. Everybody was pullin' him, wanting to interview him. He was like a god."

"Handy's story is a Cinderella story," David Bradberry told me. "He went from anonymity to being in the spotlight. His life was like a fishbowl. People all over the state wanted to know who Handy Campbell was."

That conversation, too, took place seven years after that legendary night in Tupelo. By then, David Bradberry and Melvin Smith and Mike Martin and I had all left Greenwood. Only Handy Campbell remained, and he only against his will, quite literally a prisoner of the town, languishing in a small jail cell on the second floor of the Leflore County Courthouse. If any of his five cellmates had seen the famous Tupelo game, they never mentioned it.

NINE

MY JOB

On the drive back from Tupelo, with Snuffy and Bubba Ruscoe asleep in the back seat, Jack and I reviewed the game in barely hushed tones. We ran through every play, it seemed, trying to work out just how I was going to capture and render some small fragment of the night's electricity for the benefit of Sunday morning's readers—those who had missed the game and wanted to experience it secondhand; those who had been there and wished to relive it, as Jack and I were doing now; and those who lived far away, in Jackson or Meridian or Biloxi or Batesville or Hattiesburg or Natchez, where the hometown papers would pick up my article off the wire and run it that same Sunday morning, giving readers who had never heard of the Greenwood Bulldogs or Handy Campbell a first impressive glimpse of both.

"When Tupelo tried to fake that punt," I recalled, "and our line just shut them down? I think that was a turning point."

"No, no, Richit, the real turning point was when Spivey sacked Todd Jordan."

"Maybe. But of course the real watershed was that seventy-yard pass."

Jack laughed. "Ain't that an understatement. I been watchin' high school football my whole life—hell, I prolly been to thousands of games by now—and I ain't never seen anything like that. Never. When he sorta hopped back and—" Jack abruptly stopped speaking.

"What?" I asked, after a few seconds of silence. "What is it?"

"I tell you, Richit," he said, his voice muted but determined. "You don't know how jealous I am of you."

"What are you talking about?"

"Damn! I cain't tell you how much I miss that job. I swear, I don't think I was ever happier in my life than when I was doin' what you're doin' right now. Don't get me wrong, Richit, you do a fine job and you can sho'nuff write better than I'll ever be able to, but I think that was just what I was born to do. Ain't no sport I ain't played at some time or other, and ain't no one in town I don't know. John Emmerich couldn't find someone could do it better'n me at twice the price."

I nodded, thought for a few moments. "You know Tom Hayes?" I said.

"Sure. Third reporter."

"Well, he just gave notice yesterday. He got a job at a paper in Little Rock. He's leaving in a couple of weeks."

"So?"

"So, I've been wanting to write straight news ever since I got here, but I haven't had the time, with football season being what it was. But now, with him leaving, maybe I'll be able to switch over to his job, and then you can come back to the sports desk."

"That's mighty white of you, Richit, but you're forgettin' why I left. I just cain't afford to keep workin' for what he was payin' me."

"Yes," I said, "but maybe he'd rather give you the raise then run another search for a new reporter or sports editor. I think it's worth a try, anyway. I'll tell him I want to replace Tom, and then you go in and see him and tell him everything you just told me—about how nobody could do the job better than you at twice the price. In fact, I'd say it just like that. Make him feel like he'll be saving money, somehow, instead of spending it."

"All right," Jack said, smiling hopefully. "Let's do it first thing Monday, right after deadline."

❧❧

On Monday morning, right after deadline, I walked into J.O. Emmerich's office and informed him that I would like to leave the sports desk to take over Tom's reporting slot. He nodded, adding that I could switch over just as soon as he found a replacement for me. I thanked him and left.

Then Jack walked in and shut the door behind him. I returned to my desk and waited; a few minutes later, the door opened again and Jack walked out. His face betrayed nothing as he made his way over to my desk.

"Did he give you what you wanted?" I asked.

"Nope," he said.

"I'm sorry," I offered.

"Don't be," he replied with an uneasy half-smile. "I took the job anyway."
He would figure out some way, he explained, to make up the difference—
maybe umpiring baseball games in the summer, or running a baseball clinic,
or doing some other kind of writing for local schools in his spare time, or
selling Amway if he had to. He'd work it out, somehow. For now, though,
all he knew was that he was coming back, and that just the thought of it
made him as happy, he said, as a pig in shit.

And that was it: Jack was taking over the sports desk, and I was moving
over to news. He was returning to the only job he'd ever loved, and I was
getting a chance to see Greenwood, Mississippi as it really was, and not
merely through the lens of sports. Only after I'd worked in news for a few
months would I come to understand just how similar, in the peripheral
scenes and subtle details that never made it into any section of the newspaper, those two views were.

⳾⳾⳾

That fall, I had written quite a lot about football and a bit about cross-
country track. I had also written about baseball, and softball, and basketball, and soccer, and swimming, and tennis, and golf, and track and field,
and hiking, and fishing. The variety of subjects didn't surprise me; what
did surprise me was how much I'd enjoyed writing about sports—with one
notable exception: hunting. I had no use for any of it: the guns, the goofy
camouflaged uniforms and orange vests, the little pouches full of deer
urine hunters squirted on themselves to attract their prey, the lame ratio-
nalizations they offered about thinning out the deer population to protect
the environment and ecosystem, the pictures that came in the mail every
week of eight- and nine-year-old boys, their cheeks smeared with deer
blood, grinning satanically as they held aloft the severed head of their first
kill. Before I'd come to Mississippi I'd known of hunting strictly in the
abstract and had found it only vaguely distasteful. Now, having seen its
tools and fruits up close, and having had to cover it as if it were as noble a
pursuit as any other athletic contest—as if both sides were equally
equipped and armed and victory was achieved without death—the mere
thought of it sickened and angered me, and I asserted, loudly and in the

middle of the newsroom, that the thing that made me most glad about my impending switch to news was the fact that I would never again have to write a single word on the subject.

The next morning, on the news budget, Mike had typed under my name: "Go on a real Mississippi Delta duck hunt and write about it."

I appealed the assignment to J. O. He supported Mike. People came from all over the country to hunt ducks in the Delta, he said, and the season was about to begin. Jack wouldn't settle in to the sports desk in time to catch any of it, and besides, they wanted the perspective of someone who had never been on a hunt before. I would do as Mike said, at least in this case.

Mike had already taken the liberty of contacting two of Greenwood's most inveterate duck hunters, Mike Rozier and Roger Easley. Rozier owned a construction company; Easley, an insurance agency. They were an unlikely pair, Rozier brawny and bearded and gruff and laconic, Easley slim and clean-shaven and refined and gregarious. Mike told me he wasn't sure if I'd come back alive, but that either way he'd have a pretty good story to run.

They picked me up a few minutes before four on a frigid morning in December. It was the first time I had ever felt cold in Mississippi, and I couldn't recall ever having felt quite so cold anywhere else. Just a few months before, the notion of being able to sit in a car without the air conditioning on seemed impossible. Now, as I climbed into Mike Rozier's immense Ford Bronco, already swaddled in several layers of clothing— thermal underwear and wool socks (borrowed from Jack), sweaters and hat and gloves and boots (purchased from L.L. Bean with other applications in mind) and, yes, camouflage fatigues (also borrowed from Jack)—I was relieved to find the heat on full blast.

Seven hours later, shivering and exhausted, I stumbled into the newsroom, found my way to a terminal, sat down and began to type:

> The hunter is up at an ungodly hour. He leaves his comfortable bed, his warm electric blanket and his loving wife to don long johns, army camouflage, three pairs of socks and twenty-pound boots, and venture out into the pre-dawn chill of a December morning.
>
> As he drives through the deserted town, he envies the lucky souls who have never hunted and remain snuggled

inside their warm houses, oblivious to the compulsive and frigid way of life that has seized control of his free will.

The hunter will meet up with his hunting buddy, another poor soul like himself who has also lost control of his destiny. The two will get in whosoever's truck is pulling the boat trailer, and speed off to a destination both dread reaching.

Eventually, they turn off the road and follow a path that winds its way through the darkness, down to the landing. The hunters congratulate themselves on once again being the first to arrive at the site. Hunters are able to choose their specific hunting spots, or holes, on a first-come, first-served basis. They convince themselves that this option was worth getting up at 3:30 in the morning for. These are the same two people who, just a week before, arrived at the landing at 9:30 P.M.—on the night before duck season opened.

Other trucks arrive, other boats slide in. The men all congregate in the center and talk. A group that could easily pass for the cast of the latest Rambo movie discusses manly things like hunting, working, and how badly each got shafted by his wife's divorce attorney.

I set out to write a satire.

The hunters pull the top over the blind and sit as still as is possible in a tiny boat atop a frigid lake in pitch-darkness.

Then begins the wait.

They talk about how cold it is. They berate themselves for not bringing the heater. They set a time limit for their expedition, the shorter the better. No doubt they will get their limit within minutes. They exchange hunting stories that seem to substantiate this point. They check their watches and drink more coffee. Once in a while, they have to lower the blinds to go to the bathroom. Drinking an entire thermos of coffee in short order will do that to you.

They shake their legs to keep their feet from freezing. They rub gravel "heat bags" between their palms. They tell more hunting stories. This time there is less conviction in their voices. They talk of unfortunate people they know, suckers who went hours, days without seeing a duck. They disparage shooters who go to Cadillac clubs in heated boats with venetian blinds. They postulate on just how lousy the morning will be. They curse the jerk who told them the ducks would be out in force. They swear this is the last time they will ever do something as insane as going duck hunting.

They have been at their hole exactly fifteen minutes.

My objective was to make hunters, and hunting itself, look ridiculous.

Nine o'clock. The pre-established time for the waiting game to come to an end. The hunters have decided to write the day off as a bizarre fluke. None of their friends know they have gone hunting today, anyway. No one will be the wiser.

The blinds are dropped. The hunters unlash their boat and head for the decoys. A few are scooped up into the boat.

And then, they appear. First, there are two of them. Then a flock of five flies overhead. And another.

The hunters beat a hasty retreat to their tree clump and once again lash up their boat. They blow the calls. Within minutes, a group of three ducks flies overhead. The hunters throw back the cover and fire several shots in rapid succession. None seem to hit.

At 9:45, a green-head circles around the area and drops gracefully to the water amidst the decoys.

The hunters flip their top. The duck is startled and flips its wings furiously. It is too late.

What came out, though—fifty-four column inches later—was more like a paean.

As they wind their way back to the landing, they discuss the clouds on the horizon, the jobs that they must now go to, the way the lake level is steadily dropping. But mostly, they talk about the next time they will return to this spot, probably tomorrow.

After all, the duck season in Mississippi is only 31 days long this year. And there's a lot of hunting to do in one short month.

And somehow, despite the lack of sleep, the cramped quarters, and the barely bearable temperatures, this dedication makes sense. Even beyond the fact that the hunters spend thousands of dollars each year on this stuff; even notwithstanding the camaraderie of the event and the gratifying achievement of a kill; there is something more to hunting that keeps people like this going.

One of the hunters explained it to a novice this way: "I could never shoot another duck as long as I live, and I'd still hunt," he said. "The sight of that duck swooping down onto the water besides those decoys—that right there is what it's all about."

I couldn't figure it out. I sat in front of the monitor and scrolled through the article, wondering what had become of all my smug and self-righteous contempt for hunting and hunters. I couldn't find a trace of it. Somehow, it had evaporated on the path between my brain and my fingers; somehow, it had been neutralized, catalyzed into admiration, or at least appreciation. How could such a thing have happened to me? What, I wondered, could have alchemized my disdain into—well, into something that was clearly not disdain?

I sat there and pondered it. Maybe, I thought, it was their graciousness as hosts and guides, the way they generously shared their coffee and hot sausage rolls with me, their avuncular manner in patiently explaining to me the folkways of the sport; maybe it was the fact that they actually let me handle a shotgun myself, sliding the bolt back and forth and hearing the delicious, unmistakable snare-drum-like sound of a live shell being loaded. Maybe it was the fact that at one point Roger Easley, sensing that I felt as if the frigid wind were slicing the skin off my cheekbones, pulled the warm wool facemask off his own head and handed it to me, magnanimously insisting that I wear it. Or maybe it wasn't the result of any particular incident at all, but rather the residue of a testosterone high, the natural product of a morning spent huddling in a small boat laden with weapons and live ammunition and buoyed by an incessant stream of guy-talk.

Later, though, I would pin it on a conversation the three of us had had about halfway through our two-hour wait between duck sightings. It started, strangely enough, when Mike Rozier asked me if I were divorced.

I laughed. "No," I said. "Why would you think that?"

"I don't see no wedding ring on your hand," he said.

"I'm only twenty-one!"

"Oh, that's right, I almost forgot. You're a Yankee."

"Down here, Richard, people get married pretty young," Roger Easley added. "Mike and I were both married by the time we were twenty-one."

"The first round, anyway," Mike interjected. "You got to be careful with these girls down here, Richard. They know how to lure a man in, a lot better than we seem to be doing with these ducks. But they can be just as deadly, now."

"Really?" I said.

"Mike may be exaggerating a little bit," Roger said. "But don't you think we've got some beautiful girls down here?"

"Sure," I said. "Plenty."

"That's right. And they can be as charming as all get-out, too, I'm sure you've seen that already. They know how to appeal to a man, and you've got to mind what you're doing. It can be very dangerous for the unsuspecting. If you're not paying attention, they're liable to—"

"Sink their claws into you and not let go," Mike chuckled. "'Course, there are worse fates to suffer. Just make sure that you don't go get you a divorce. They can be *very* expensive."

"Now, why would Richard go and get a divorce?" Roger asked. "Young fella like him could have him the pick of the crop down here."

"You think?" I asked.

"Absolutely. Someone like you could go pretty far in a place like Greenwood. You could write y'own ticket here, yes you could. I can guarantee you'd be a big success down here."

I was about to ask him why, exactly, someone like me (whatever that meant) would do so well in a place like Greenwood—a town so different from the one in which I had grown up that I had difficulty imagining that they existed within the same country—when Mike Rozier jumped in with an answer. "What do you got down here, Richard?" he asked. "White trash and rednecks, mostly. Hell, we *need* more people like you, we really do. A place like Greenwood, you could do anything you want here. You could live anywhere you want, have any girl you want. I tell you what, I think you might oughta think about settling down here for good."

"Absolutely," Roger Easley concurred.

"Well," I said, "maybe I will." And they said good and then we moved on to some other topic which I've long since forgotten. But from time to time that morning, and in the days that followed it, I would return to that conversation, and to the last thing I said on the subject, and in doing so I would never fail to be genuinely and gravely surprised, not only at what I had said—"well, maybe I will"—but also at the fact that I had really meant it as I said it. I had set out on an assignment I had considered distasteful, profiling a "sport" I had believed to be abominable and men I had speculated would be ignoble, but determined, as I had been ever since the day I had met Carl and Dixie Mae Kelly, to act amiable and accepting and keep my revulsion to myself. But this time, while acting as if I liked these men, I actually began to like them; and in liking them, I actually began to like hunting, and to show a genuine interest in it. And they, sensing this, made me feel not only accepted in Greenwood, but valued, as well, and that was something I found just plain intoxicating. And writing while intoxicated is always dangerous.

And so I had signed my name to an article that seemed to condone and even glorify a pursuit I found repugnant. It was the first hint I'd had that the deal I had made with myself that morning in Carl Kelly's front yard might, in the end, prove untenable. As time went on, that realization would increasingly gnaw on me until I could scarcely take it anymore.

ॐ

Mike and Karen and Margaret and Dan quickly initiated me into the world of the *Commonwealth* staff writer, a world composed largely of beats and local photographs, wire-copyediting and telephone-obituary taking. I was assigned the Greenwood City Council beat, the Leflore County Board of Supervisors beat, the Chamber of Commerce beat, the business and industry beat, the bank beat, the hospitality and tourism beat, the parks and recreation beat, the Board of Education beat, the Army Corps of Engineers beat, the Fire Department beat, the Sanitation Department beat, the Greenwood Housing Authority beat, the Greenwood-Leflore Hospital beat, the weather bureau beat, the museum beat, the waterworks beat, the power company beat, the telephone company beat, the post office beat. I asked for (at Karen's suggestion) and was granted (by a bemused Mike) the Greenwood Voters League beat, meaning that I would attend the semiregular meetings of an old civil rights organization that hadn't been covered by the paper in years; this, in turn, meant that I was also assigned the unofficial "black beat." I was also, at Mike's whim and almost certainly because of his strange sense of humor, assigned both the farm beat and the church beat, at least until Dan nagged and tormented Mike into giving them back to him (but not before I shot and published a photo of Mike Goldberg's seven-year-old son, Scott, lighting a Hanukkah menorah—ah, yes, Jewish control of the media!). Finally, I was assigned to cover the Exchange Club, the Lions Club, the two Elks Clubs (white and black) and the Rotary Club, the last of which was deemed the most important because John Emmerich was a member and attended every monthly luncheon.

And so I attended every monthly luncheon at the Rotary Club, too. I also attended Exchange and Lions and Elks club luncheons (typical entrée: ham) and every meeting of the City Council and the Board of Supervisors and the Greenwood Voters League. I attended power company meetings and housing authority meetings and Chamber of Commerce meetings and Board of Education meetings. I attended innumerable church revivals: Methodist, Episcopal, African Methodist Episcopal, Presbyterian, Pentecostal, Evangelical, Charismatic, Baptist, Missionary Baptist, Primitive Baptist, Church of God, Church of Christ, Church of God in Christ, and one sect up in the hills who called themselves the Dirt Eaters. I wrote stories about crop yields and crop dusters and insects and insecticides and cotton brokers and cotton gins and once, I actually spent an entire day picking cotton by hand. I didn't much care for it.

I followed the travails of the Greenwood Tourism Board, which struggled to pass a one percent tourism tax and find new and enticing ways to lure tourists to Greenwood, despite the fact that there wasn't much to see in Greenwood and no one who wasn't from the Delta seemed to know quite where it was, anyway. I followed a three-way battle between the City of Greenwood, Leflore County and Carroll County over who was supposed to pay how much in taxes on the Greenwood-Leflore Airport, which despite its name was actually in Carroll County and was besides not much more than a single runway that always appeared to be overgrown with weeds. I followed the plight of Greenwood's savings and loan institutions, which were ranked among the least safe in a generally unsafe state, and the agonizing decision of one of those S&Ls, First Federal, to close its North Greenwood branch, which was shaped like an old railroad station, complete with a little red caboose. I followed the mayor's crusade against the local cable company, which he felt had added too many home shopping channels to its lineup, and the city's war against blackbirds, a half million of which invaded Whittington Park, across the bypass from the newspaper, and threatened to take over the town itself before being chased out by screaming flares and ultrasonic cannons.

Oh, the riveting headlines that graced my stories in those days! There was "Use caution while making deposits, bankers say" and "Board promotes tourism" and "Industrial prospects eyed" and "Weather watchers keep eyes on nearby rivers" and "Energy agency's manager assists development" and "Council, housing office at odds" and "Council OKs paper ballots" and "Medart officers proud of firm" and "Counterfeit $100 bill passed to business" and "Flu vaccines available now" and " 'Friends' gather together" and "Restaurant group calls off petition" and "Valley radio station closer to being on air" and the series inspired by the blackbird saga: "City to lower ultrasonic boom on unwelcome roosting birds" ("The city of Greenwood will be taking new measures to reclaim an area which has, as of late, gone to the birds. Literally."), which begat "A-hunting we will go" (accompanied by a picture of police officer Reginald Dean, Margaret's husband, pointing a screaming flare gun at a flock of birds), which begat "Sounds chase birds from park," which begat "Greenwood says 'Bye-bye' to blackbirds." That was a particularly eventful week.

Sometimes, though, stories that had portended boredom actually turned out to be interesting, even frightening. One day Mike assigned me to write a piece on the increasingly severe penalties that local judges were handing down to people convicted of drug offenses, like one Greenwood man who got thirty years in prison for selling sixty-five dollars worth of cocaine to an undercover police officer. The story consisted largely of an interview with Circuit Judge Gray Evans, considered by many to be the toughest judge in the Delta, if not the state; that same week, Judge Evans had presided over the sentencing of three Greenwood men tried for drug offenses. One was convicted of selling twenty dollars worth of marijuana to an undercover agent, another of possession of one ounce of cocaine and three grams of marijuana laced with cocaine, and the third of possession of thirty-six marijuana cigarettes and a bag containing five dollars' worth of the drug. All three were black, and all three—even the last, who was a first-time offender—were given the maximum sentence of three years in prison and a $3,000 fine. Remarking on the week's events, Judge Evans, a large, square-jawed and jowly man who was imposing, intimidating, and seemingly humorless, told me earnestly: "I sometimes wish I had more time and fine to give some of these people. I have made the statement in sentencing people, 'I regret that I can't give you more, but the state has tied my hands.'" Seeing the look of astonishment on my face, he added: "People ask me, 'Doesn't it bother you to hand out these kinds of sentences?' And I tell them, 'Hell, no!'" Now, I had no intention of violating any laws—drug-related or otherwise—while in Greenwood, but I nevertheless left Judge Evans's chambers that afternoon with a newly spawned yet profound fear of the man, and from that day on, whenever I saw him at the courthouse or anywhere else in town, I experienced something akin to a mild panic attack.

⁂

One morning, seeing that Margaret had been assigned to cover a murder trial, I asked her and Mike if I could take the story instead. They both just shrugged—Margaret apathetic, Mike vaguely incredulous—and said fine. I drove excitedly down to the courthouse, determined not to miss a minute of the drama. After all, it was my first trial, and my first murder.

As I stormed into the courtroom, Circuit Judge Howard Q. Davis was just beginning to preside over the selection of a jury. Settling into a seat, I thought about how much work I was going to get to miss while covering this trial: Based on what I had seen in the movies and on television, I figured the jury selection was bound to last a couple of days, the trial itself a couple of weeks, followed by a few more days of jury deliberations, and then the story's climax—the dramatic presentation of the verdict. This was going to be quite a saga, I thought while straining to get a look at the back of the defendant's head. If I'm lucky, I might be here, filing dramatic dispatches, for a month.

Jury selection took only a few minutes, however, and as soon as it was completed the judge banged his gavel and called the trial to order. The case was *The State of Mississippi vs. Ronnie Ray Strong.* The defendant was black, as was his lawyer. The prosecutor was white, as was most of the jury. In his opening remarks, the prosecutor, Charlie Swayze, fervently told the jury that on the night of September 10, 1988, the thirty-year-old Strong had shot his wife four times in the neck with a .22-caliber pistol at their house in Itta Bena, and that he had done so with premeditation and malice aforethought. Then Strong's court-appointed attorney, Willie Perkins—a fairly colorful figure who was known as something of an orator and dabbled in local politics—rose and asserted, without much enthusiasm, that his client had been under the influence of alcohol and marijuana at the time of the shooting, that he had believed his wife was fooling around behind his back and was planning to do him physical harm, and that the shooting had been an accident, besides. The jury seemed unmoved.

Swayze and his assistant, Merle Bouchard, put up their witnesses. A coworker who spent the evening of September 10 with Strong testified that they had *not* imbibed alcohol and smoked marijuana that day, but that after he had dropped Strong off at his house that night, he noticed that the .22 pistol he kept under the front seat of his car was missing, and that when he returned to the house he saw Mrs. Strong lying on the floor, her children crying and screaming, "Our mama's dead!" A thirteen-year-old niece, who was in the house when the shooting occurred, testified that she had seen Strong go out to the coworker's car while he was in the house and "get something and put it in his pants," and that later, when Strong and his wife were arguing, she heard a shot, ran to the kitchen and saw Strong straddling the body of her "auntie," choking her and pressing the gun against her neck, at which point she ran away and heard three more shots, as did a fourteen-year-old neighbor, who was also in the house at the time of the argument and fled after hearing the first shot. Itta Bena's police chief and his deputy testified about hunting down Strong after the shooting, capturing him, and tracking down the murder weapon, which Strong had hidden atop a water tower at nearby Mississippi Valley State University. A forensic scientist testified that the four bullets found in Mrs. Strong had come from that same gun. A pathologist testified that at least one shot had been fired at close range, and that the state of the body, particularly the hands, indicated that there had been no violent struggle before the shooting. All of this took about an hour and a quarter, more or less.

For his part, Willie Perkins called only one witness—Ronnie Ray Strong himself. The defendant began by recalling how he and his late wife had met, at Parchman Penitentiary in July 1986, when the future Mrs. Strong was a guard and Ronnie Ray was serving a term for armed robbery. They moved in together upon his release, and married in April 1988, but soon there was trouble: Mrs. Strong, he said, began an affair with another man. When asked, during cross-examination, the name of his late wife's alleged paramour, Strong stammered that he couldn't remember it just then but that he saw the man around Itta Bena often and that he would recognize him on sight. Willie Perkins softly groaned.

On the night of September 10, Strong testified, he and his coworker drank "three or four quarts of beer, and smoked two joints." Then, he said, he told his coworker "that something wasn't right, and asked if I could borrow his gun." His coworker, he claimed, had responded: "You know where it is, go get it." He walked out to the car, Strong recalled, and took the gun, which had two bullets in it already; he then loaded two more bullets, which he claimed he had found underneath his dresser at some previous but unspecified date and had been carrying around ever since for no apparent reason. "I wasn't going to hurt anyone," he said from the witness stand, explaining that he had merely intended to confront his wife's unnamed but nevertheless recognizable lover.

Then, he said, things got ugly. He walked into the house and found his wife, who had been gone for much of that day, sitting in the kitchen and doing her hair. He requested an explanation of her absence. "When I asked her where she had been," he recalled, "she told me it was none of my damn business." They began to argue, he said, and then Mrs. Strong reached into her purse and "put on a pair of brass knuckles." When informed, upon cross-examination, that a thorough search of the residence had failed to turn up any brass knuckles, Strong just shrugged.

Feeling threatened and seeking only to defend himself, Strong pulled out his coworker's gun, hastening to add: "I never intended to use it." A scuffle ensued, and then, as Ronnie Ray Strong testified: "The gun went off."

"And what about the other three shots?" Willie Perkins asked his client.

Strong shook his head. "I can't explain that," he said. "I don't know what happened, or why I did it." From the corner of my eye, I thought I saw a juror snicker, but when I turned to look at him, he stopped.

"Here's a person who was caught in the heat of passion," Perkins told the jury in his closing, which he delivered with even less vigor than his opening. "This is not a murder case. It doesn't take a genius from Ole Miss Law or a scholar from Harvard to find that there was no premeditation in this case."

Charlie Swayze, on the other hand, rendered his closing with relish. He pointed at the defendant and called him "mean as a snake and dangerous," then urged the jury to find him guilty of murder instead of the lesser charge of manslaughter. "Where in the world is the evidence of passion?" he shouted. "So what if he's mad at his wife? That doesn't give him the right to pull a pistol and unload it on her. If it did, we'd all better start wearing flak jackets."

He took a moment, drew a few deep breaths, clasped his hands, and smiled patronizingly at the jury. "Ladies and gentlemen, let's be reasonable about this. If you don't think this is a murder case, then let him go, because it's not manslaughter."

The jury deliberated for less than a half hour, then filed back into the box and handed a slip to the bailiff, who passed it to Judge Davis. Ronnie Ray Strong had barely stood up before the foreman announced the verdict: Guilty of murder. Strong did not appear to react; Willie Perkins gazed vaguely into space without turning to his client. Immediately, Judge Davis banged his gavel and sentenced Ronnie Ray Strong to life in prison.

I looked at my watch: It was a few minutes past noon. The whole thing had taken a little more than three hours. I would be back in the newsroom in time to write the story up and do a few more assignments that same day.

That afternoon, I sat in the break room with Jack and Karen and Margaret and recounted the morning's events, sparing no detail. Everyone laughed a lot, including me. But that night I sat in my apartment and wondered about Ronnie Ray Strong, whose defense came down to a few quarts of beer, two joints, a nameless rival, a pair of disappearing brass knuckles, and three unexplained shots. Why had he even bothered with a trial? No one else there—not the prosecutor or the jury, not even his own defense attorney—seemed to take the whole thing very seriously. No one had thought it worth much of their time. Why hadn't he plea-bargained? Why did he go through with a trial?

He did it, I figured, because he'd had nothing to lose; he probably hadn't been offered a plea bargain, and the only thing he had left at that point was his constitutional right to a trial. He was entitled to have his day in court, and now he'd had it, even if that day had really lasted only about three hours. But a woman had been murdered less than six months after her wedding day, and a man was going to Parchman for the rest of his life, and the only emotion I had felt throughout the whole ordeal was amusement. Two lives were gone, and I had found it funny.

꧁꧂

Not long thereafter, I came into the newsroom one morning and was told by Mike to drive down to an East Greenwood bar, Orlando's, where a man had been murdered the night before. The man, Mike told me, had become embroiled in an altercation, possibly over a woman, which had spilled out into the parking lot, where the assailant had pulled out a shotgun and blew off the leg of the victim, who then bled to death.

I grabbed a notepad and my camera and drove down to Orlando's, got out of my car, ducked under the yellow police tape, and stepped into the parking lot. A police officer I knew fairly well was standing there, guarding the crime scene. I asked him where the shooting had occurred, and he led me over to a section of the lot near the street. He pointed down at the ground: there, on the asphalt, was a brown spot, roughly the size and shape of a large manhole cover, with a small tail trailing off at the bottom. I stared at this spot for a few seconds. I knew right away that it was blood, a lot of blood. I knew that a man had bled to death right here, on this spot, not eight hours before, and that this large brown spot was his blood. But I felt nothing. I tried to make myself feel something, anything other than the shame I felt for my impassivity. But I couldn't. Instead, I picked up my camera, trained it on the spot, and took a picture. That was my job.

TEN

SOME KIND OF CLUB

When Europeans first landed on American shores, the most powerful weapons they carried to subdue the indigenous population were not rifles, but microbes. Native Americans had never before been exposed to old European illnesses like smallpox and typhus and cholera, and while the British and French and Spanish had had centuries to develop immunities to these killers, the Iroquois and Cherokee and Seminole had not. The Indians had no natural resistance to these old but new diseases and, helpless in the face of them, they succumbed time and again.

So it was, five centuries later, with me and Southern women.

I had grown up on tough New York women, and then graduated to tough Ivy League women. The females I had known and befriended and dated during the first twenty-one years of my life had been taught from birth that they were the equal of men in most ways and their superior in many, and they took the lesson to heart. They walked like men, talked like men, dressed like men, and acted like men. You did not hold doors open for them, or rise from your chair when they entered the room, or pull out their chair when they endeavored to sit down. Nor did you offer them your arm to hold when strolling side by side. And you did not look to them for adulation or admiration or, certainly, a home-cooked meal. This was neither bad nor good; it was simply the way it was, and I knew no different—until, that is, I arrived in Mississippi.

By the end of my first week in Greenwood, I could tell I was in completely unfamiliar territory. By the end of my first month, I had determined that I was utterly lost. But then again, I wasn't in much of a hurry to find my way out, either. After all, I was surrounded by women who made me feel omnipotent, charming and irresistible simply because I was male. They flirted with me, fawned over me, flattered me to excess. They clung to me, cooed at me, coddled and cared for me. They dressed for dates as carefully as if they were going to a cotillion, and invariably acted as if they had never had a better time in their life, even if we were doing nothing more than taking a drive down some lonely back road surrounded by stagnant bayous. If bonding with Southern men could be as intoxicating an experience as drinking whiskey, dating Southern women was as addictive as cocaine. I made less than a thousand dollars a month, but I spent almost every penny of it—after rent, food, gasoline and utilities—on dates. I would have spent more, too, if I'd had it.

It started with Sharon, the Wal-Mart cashier who had come with me to my first Greenwood Bulldogs game, in Vicksburg. For our second date, Sharon and I drove up to Memphis to have dinner and see *The Last Temptation of Christ*, which had recently opened nationwide but which was not playing in a single theater in the entire state of Mississippi. Arriving at the theater, I noticed that it was being picketed by several dozen people, most of whom were carrying signs condemning the film as blasphemy, and a few of whom were toting very large plywood crosses. I fell into a discussion with one of them while attempting to cross the picket line, asking him how he could condemn as heresy a film neither he nor anyone he knew had actually seen. He predicted that I would someday wind up in hell. I replied that I looked forward to seeing him there, whereupon he struck me on the head with his cross. As it happened, Sharon and I enjoyed the movie thoroughly; when we emerged, the man was gone. I never saw him again—in Memphis, hell, or anywhere else.

A few days later, Sharon left Greenwood and returned to college. I wasted no time in mourning, embarking, instead, on a great dating spree.

I dated a twenty-year-old Kappa Delta from Ole Miss and a twenty-year-old high school dropout who lived with her parents and six younger siblings in a tiny shack up in the hills. I dated a librarian and the head of the Greenville Chamber of Commerce, a social worker and a policewoman, an artist and an accountant, a letter carrier and an opera singer, a doctor and a nurse. I dated secretaries and teachers and lawyers and students and chefs and store clerks and musicians and women who seemed to do nothing at all. I took them to restaurants and movies and nightclubs; they took me to picnics and family reunions and little towns that didn't even appear on the map. I told them about my job and my coworkers and my friends back home, taught them Yiddish expressions and New York slang and the meaning of certain Jewish holidays; they cooked for me and made me clothes and cleaned my apartment and did my laundry, and one very nearly killed me in a car accident, which I took as divine retribution for allowing her to clean my apartment and do my laundry. Being with them was like gorging on cheesecake: I felt guilty and decadent, but I assuaged my conscience with the understanding that when this particular chapter of my life was finished, I would have an opportunity to eat cheesecake only infrequently, and an appetite for it even less frequently. So for the time being, I was content to overindulge in this particular delicacy. I liked Southern women, respected them, appreciated them.

Even so, I was far from being able to understand them, as I found out one night when I took out a woman named Denise. Denise was a pretty little blonde girl, maybe nineteen or twenty, a student at Mississippi Delta Junior College who always wore a ponytail and bright pink lipstick and had one of the thickest Southern accents I had ever heard. We met late one night in the Jitney Jungle—specifically, as she tallied up my groceries. We chatted for a few seconds about nothing at all; then, stepping back, she fluttered her eyelashes, gazed deep into my eyes, and said, soft and slow: "Payaper or playastic?"

"Pardon me?" I said.

She motioned to the bags at the end of the conveyer belt. "Payaper or playastic, sir?"

"Oh," I said. "I'm sorry. Plastic, please."

Her smile expanded. "Say . . ." she said, coyly. "Where you from?"

"Uh, I live here," I offered.

"No, silly," she laughed, and reached out to pat my hand with hers. "Before here. I can tell you're not from Mis'sippi!"

"That's right," I said, and patted her hand back. "But I can't tell you where I'm from unless you promise not to tell anyone."

"Oh, I promise," she said. "Cross mah heart." And she did just that.

I leaned in close, and she followed suit. "New York," I whispered.

"NEW YORK!" she said, somehow clasping my hand and rearing back at the same time.

"Shhhhhh," I said, brushing a finger across my lips and winking. "You promised."

"Oh, shoot," she said. "Ain't no one 'round to hear us!" As I said, it was late. "You're a long way from home! What brings you down to Mis'sippi, anyway?"

I thought about making up some elaborate yarn, but I worried that she might just believe it. "I'm a reporter," I said. "For the *Greenwood Commonwealth*."

"Is that right!" she said. "Why, we take the *Commonwealth*!" she said. "Mama and Daddy, I mean. I read it, too. What's your name?"

"Richard Rubin," I said.

"I've seen your name!" she said, excited. "I know I have!"

By the time my ice cream started to melt, we had made a date for the following evening. It didn't matter to me that she was undoubtedly of a stock that the "nice people" of Leflore County—a class to which I was clearly expected to belong—would have called "white trash." Denise was Southern and female and thus possessed of that potent charm to which I had as yet developed no immunity.

The following night, after dinner, we took a drive to Carroll County, up into the hills, miles away from the lights of Greenwood and the Delta. It was a very dark and clear night, and after driving around for a few minutes, I suggested to Denise that we pull off the road into a rest area and, uh, "search for constellations."

"Whatever you wonna do, Richard, that's fine with me," she said, grinning. Back home, I'd never known a woman who seemed capable of uttering such a sentence. It was, I repeat, a potent charm.

I pulled my car off the road and we got out and leaned against it, staring up at the sky. For a few minutes we just stood there like that; then, without a word, Denise moved closer to me. Our arms touched, just barely.

Still looking up, I instinctively lifted my arm and draped it over her shoulders, pulling her in closer to me. There was another moment of silence; then she leaned in, very close, her strawberry-scented breath and hair giving me flashbacks to high school, and whispered, so softly that I could hardly hear it: "Baby, did you bring me *all the way up here* just to lay me?"

∛ℤ

The next morning, after deadline, Jack swaggered up to me in the break room, his face creased behind a leering grin.

"What is it?" I asked.

"Heard you had a date with that little blonde girl works at the Jitney. *Denise.*"

"Yeah, and . . . ?"

"Heard you went to a lot of trouble to git you somethin' you coulda got just by askin' for it."

I felt my face heat up. "First of all," I huffed, "I didn't go up there for that. I really did just want to see some stars. And second——"

"Damn, Richit, don't bust your britches! I don't care what you did. You're free, white and twenty-one—you can do whatever you want. Hell, I know when I'se your age, I'd stick my dick in a bush if I thought there's a snake in there'd suck it for me. I just thought we'd have us a little talk."

"What about, the birds and the bees?"

"Didn't they give you that back at home? Do we have to teach you every-thing down here, Mister Ivy League New York Jew? I just wanted to tell you a few things about the kind a women we got in Mis'sippi."

"I've already met a lot of them."

"I know, but I don't think you really know what's goin' on, and you're liable to get yourse'f in some trouble if'n you don't figure it out right quick."

"What are you talking about?"

"What I'm talkin' about, Richit, is this: Girls down here got one thing in mind, and only one thing, and that's gettin' married. Now, they know all about how to snag a man—they know how to get dressed up and put on makeup and perfume, and how to cook and sew and clean, and they sho'nuff know how to stroke your ego, and I can tell you from personal experience that quite a few of them know how to fuck y'brains out, too, but the point is that they learn all these things for one reason, now, and that's to he'p them land them a husband, you see? That's what they want, now, and that's what they gon' get, and if you're not careful one of them's sho'nuff gon' end up married to you, and I pity that poor girl, I surely do."

"Married? Are you insane? I just got out of college!"

"I know that, Richit," Jack laughed, "but don't worry—it ain't too late!"

Just then Vic Laurent, the paper's accountant, strode into the break room. "Jack, just what are you teaching our fine Yankee friend today?" he said, his lips pressed tightly in the smirk I'd seen him wear more often than not.

"It seems Richit's a bit in the dark when it comes to Southern girls," Jack replied.

"That ain't how I heard it," Vic said. "I hear he's been out with half the white girls in Leflore County, and he's just waitin' for the other half to come of age."

"S'about what I heard, too," Jack said. "But now I'm tellin' Richit what they really after."

"Oh, I reckon he'll find out for himself soon enough," Vic said. "I tell you what."

"Excuse me," I said. "I *am* in the room, here."

"Well, I'm sorry about that, Richard," Vic said, turning to me. "Is this about that girl Denise?"

"No," I said. "Just Southern women in general."

Vic smiled paternalistically, threw an arm across my shoulders. "Well," he said, "that just happens to be my field of expertise, I tell you what. So, what do you need to know? You just ask Dr. Vic, now."

"Jack says they're all just looking to get married ASAP."

"Did he, now. Well, it seems our ol' friend Jack is smarter than I thought." Vic winked at Jack, who laughed. "Are girls around here just lookin' to get married? Abso-damn-lutely. Are they lookin' to marry a Yankee like you in p'tic'lar? That I cain't say, but it's a safe bet that if they goin' out with you, now, they got that on their minds, I tell you what. Lemme ask you this: Do they cook for you?"

"Usually."

"And do they sew stuff for you?"

"Sure."

"All right. And do they tell you how big and strong and handsome y'are, even though we all know y'ain't, really?"

"What's your point?"

"Now, hold on, there, Richard, I'm gettin' there. They ever let you see 'em without their makeup on?"

"I don't think so."

"Do they make any kind of demands on you?"

"Not really."

"Do they let you get away with saying and doing all kinds of stupid stuff without calling you on it?"

I started to shake my head, then stopped and thought for a second. "I guess," I muttered.

"Oh, my," Vic said, grinning and shaking his head. "It's worse than I thought. Richard, you better be *real* careful, now, I tell you what, or you gon' find yourself down at First Baptist one a these days, saying 'I do.' Although I figure you to be more of an Episcopal type, actually."

"What do you mean? These are the most easygoing women I've ever dated!"

"Exactly," Vic said, nodding. "That's just how it works. It's like one of those plants—you know, the ones that eat the flies and all?"

"The Venus Flytrap?"

"Exactly. Draws you in, looking real nice, smelling real nice, and before you know it you're stuck in there and the jaws are closing. Or look at it this way: It's like a mousetrap. Mouse comes along, sees a tasty piece of cheese, goes over to have hisself a snack and then BAM! No more eating cheese, no more scurrying around. No more nothin'. You see, Richard, your problem is you think you can get that cheese without springing the trap. You think you know what you're doin', but in reality you ain't got a clue. You keep eatin' that cheese, now, and one of these days that trap's gon' come right down on your head, and then you're stuck and the game's over. It happened to me. It happened to Jack. And it's sure as hell gon' happen to you, I tell you what."

I thought about that conversation quite a bit afterward, about what Vic and Jack seemed to be saying about the shifting roles of predator and prey and the strange rules of the hunt, about my own cockiness and naiveté and egotistical stupidity, and about how little control any of us had over events and relationships despite what we believed, but in the end my mind kept returning to one question: How did Jack and Vic know about Denise?

ॐ

They knew because we all lived in a small town in a small part of a small state. Mississippi may have had two million people in it, but everyone—or at least everyone white and middle-class—seemed to know each other. And if you didn't actually know a particular person, you were bound to know someone else who did.

One day, for example, I happened to mention to a woman I was dating that I was a fan of the Mississippi writer Eudora Welty. The very next day, I received an invitation to Ms. Welty's eightieth birthday celebration, which was to be held at the governor's mansion in Jackson. Weeks later, while I was passing through the receiving line at the Welty celebration, I introduced myself to the governor, Ray Mabus. "Oh, I know who you are," he said warmly, then complimented me on a couple of articles I'd written recently. I would soon have precisely the same experience with two different Mississippi congressmen, Mike Espy and Trent Lott. Espy, the Delta Democrat, and Lott, the Gulf Coast Republican (who had just recently left the House, after eight terms there, for a seat in the Senate), did not agree on much, but they both knew who I was well before I met them, and they both quoted my own work to me. No more than nine thousand people read the *Greenwood Commonwealth*, but apparently they were the right nine thousand people.

But it went well beyond that. If I had to write an article on a large Mississippi company, for instance, I could just call up the company's president. If I was a bit confused about some arcane state law, I could just call up the state legislator who had authored the bill twenty-five years earlier. Never once was I handed over to someone's assistant—absolutely no one was inaccessible. It was as if merely by being who I was and moving to Mississippi, I had joined some kind of club where the members all knew and liked one another and could deny each other nothing. It was an extended family without the genes, one that took in new members all the time, whether or not they wanted it or even realized it. It could be comforting and flattering to be drawn in to such a fold, but it could also be claustrophobic and stifling, and after I discovered that Jack and Vic had heard all about my date with Denise—whom neither of them actually knew—less than twelve hours after it happened, I began to feel as if everything I did and said was being done and said on a stage before an audience comprised of the entire town of Greenwood, and possibly the entire state of Mississippi. There was no cover and no anonymity, and for a while I found it increasingly difficult to write about people knowing that I would almost certainly run into them at the Piggly Wiggly or the Crystal Club or the Wal-Mart or the Double-Quick, especially considering that they already knew as much about me as I did them—and often, more.

On Friday night in December, I drove down to Jackson to visit the synagogue there—it was Hanukkah, and though I did not feel a need to celebrate the holiday in temple, I took it nevertheless as an opportunity to see and meet the state's largest Jewish community for the first time. Now, despite the fact that I was not religious, I had grown up in a Conservative Jewish congregation, meaning that the kosher laws and Sabbath were strictly observed at the synagogue, the service was conducted mostly in Hebrew, the men and boys all wore *yarmulkes* (and, if they had been bar mitzvahed, *tallises*, or prayer shawls, as well), and there was no music at all except for that provided by the cantor's tenor voice; the rabbi, while vibrant, always seemed a bit fatigued from his two-mile walk to the place. As soon as I walked into the temple in Jackson, though, I could tell I was in a different kind of synagogue.

For one thing, no one wore a *yarmulke*. For another, the service was conducted entirely in English—and not just English, but in a style and tone of prose nearly identical to that which I had heard and read in dozens of white Protestant churches throughout the Delta. The synagogue itself, which had been partially destroyed by a Ku Klux Klan bomb in the 1960s and immediately rebuilt, looked more like a church than any of the Jewish houses of worship I had known back in New York. The rabbi, Eric Gurvis—a youngish man who sported a trim brown beard and a slight New Jersey accent—spoke in a folksy, informal tone, more chatting with his congregation than preaching to them, skipping some of what I had believed to be the most basic prayers and hymns in favor of others I had never heard before (and which sounded suspiciously like "Amazing Grace"). Finally, though, he came to a point in the service I did recognize—the *Amidah*, the silent prayer and meditation. I was relieved to see the congregation rise to their feet rather than remain sitting, and recite the prayer in silence rather than aloud. As I stood, head bowed, I comforted myself that at least some traditions remained intact, even here.

A few seconds later, though, I thought I heard a faint hint of music—not much, just a few notes, but loud enough to make me wonder. I shrugged it off, told myself I was imagining it; but instead of vanishing it grew louder and louder, until I looked up at the *bimah*, or pulpit. There stood Rabbi Gurvis in his white clergy gown, picking and strumming a guitar like Roy Clark, a wide and colorful leather strap draped over his shoulder. I choked back a laugh; if he does "Kumbaya," I thought, I'm going to lose it.

Fortunately, he didn't, and I managed to hold my peace until the end of the service. As the congregation shook hands with one another and wished each other a good Sabbath and a happy Hanukkah, I walked up to the *bimah* and introduced myself to Rabbi Gurvis. "Ah, yes," he said, eagerly shaking my hand. "I've heard all about you."

ॐ∾ॐ

Hanukkah came and went, but by mid-December, Christmas had infiltrated and occupied Greenwood so thoroughly that I could easily imagine Noel lasting until Memorial Day.

I first noticed it the Monday morning after Thanksgiving. On the short drive to work, I passed no fewer than two dozen houses already decked out in colorful lights—red, green, blue, bright white—and a few with light-up reindeer and sleigh parked on the barren brown grass. The front door of the *Commonwealth* was covered by an immense wreath, a red ribbon drooping underneath. Inside, a fat fir tree sat decked out right in the middle of the newsroom, blocking my view of just about everything. In twelve hours, Christmas had invaded and conquered the Delta. I had been taken prisoner in my sleep.

I almost liked it, though something about the whole thing seemed very wrong to me. While I'd observed only Hanukkah, I had fond memories of Christmas from my childhood in New York—the cheer, the spirit of brotherhood, the music, the decorations. But for me, this bounty had always existed in a certain atmosphere, and that atmosphere was cold. Christmas just wasn't Christmas without snow, or at least without iced puddles on the ground and frosted air in front of your face. And though Mississippi wasn't really warm anymore, it wasn't—with the exception of a freak frosty morning every couple of weeks, like the one I'd chosen to go duck hunting—very cold yet, either. It was just gray.

Still, this was a place that assumed the posture of taking Christmas seriously. The Rotary Club always held a three-day Christmas Carnival at the Civic Center. Every school, no matter how small or poor, staged an elaborate Christmas pageant. And Greenwood hosted an annual Christmas parade down Market Street, culminating in a fireworks show over the Yazoo.

It was the parade and fireworks show that captured my imagination—not for what they might be, but for what they once had been. These were the two things that everyone at the paper could agree upon: that the parade had sure been something special once, and that it wasn't much these days. But no one would dream of skipping it, not even Vic, who seemed to miss the old parade more than anyone. "I tell you what, Richard," he would drawl, "that was one hell of a show. Hundreds of marching bands, from across the state. Even other states—Alabama, Tennessee, Arkansas, Louisiana, Missouri, Texas—all over the South. Each band was better than the last, too. They'd just march right on through town, one after the next. I tell you what, that parade ran all day, twelve hours or more. Sometimes they'd split it up to two days. Man, it was something to see, I tell you what. Hell, now it's pitiful. Just pitiful. They'll let any old band with two horns and a drum march now. Parade's over in an hour. Fireworks last about five minutes. Used to be the fireworks would go all night. Boy, that was some kind of show. You should have seen it back then. That was something, not like now." Still, Vic would be there; he said he wouldn't miss it, and I couldn't imagine that he ever had.

Across town and out in the country, in Schlater and Sidon and Glendora and Cruger, in North Greenwood and East Greenwood and everything in between, strange things were happening, a few more each day. Satiny red wrapping paper and green ribbons appeared on the doors of the rich and the poor. Rusted-out cars squatting on untended lawns became crèches. A raggedy scarecrow metamorphosed into a regal Christ on the cross, "INRI" spelled out in corncobs over its head.

People were not immune, either. By the second week in December, everyone in the newsroom seemed to be infected with the spirit of the times. Even the dourest of my colleagues, like Mike and Margaret, were wearing bright colors and broad smiles. But though I fought the feeling, I couldn't help but sense something sinister about all this good cheer. Maybe that was because it seemed that everyone grew giddier as the month progressed—it was as if spirits rose higher and higher in the office exactly as the sun's arc sank lower and lower in the sky outside it. And then one night after work, Karen Freeman, our news editor, invited me to visit a cemetery with her.

"This isn't just any cemetery," she explained. "No, indeed! You need to see it. Trust me."

"Why? What is it?" I asked. I'm sure I looked at Karen as if she'd suggested we drive over to the hospital and break into the morgue.

"Well, now, baby, that'd spoil the surprise, wouldn't it? You just come on. I'm drivin'."

"O.K., so . . . uh . . . where is this place?"

"Well, now, that's an interesting question. I know it's about ten miles outside of Carrollton, but that's about all I know. I've got directions from Jack. He's been there a bunch."

"You haven't been?"

"Yeah, I went last year, but I didn't drive, so I wasn't really payin' attention. And there aren't street signs. Besides—" she winked—"it gets pretty dark out there, you know."

That was enough for me. I begged off, telling Karen that I had some laundry to do, and I didn't know when I would be able to make it there, so if she really wanted to see this place she should just go without me.

"Go out there *by myself?*" she said, laughing. "No, indeed!"

☙❧

The biggest Christmas party in Greenwood every year took place at Morris Office Machines on Howard Street. It was a store that was less than a half-mile from where I lived, yet I'd never even noticed it before. Its broad plate-glass facade looked like it hadn't been dusted since before the *Brown* decision; behind it, displayed on a Formica platform, were desks and chairs and a couple of adding machines from the same era. They hadn't been dusted, either. From the sidewalk, it was hard to see anything behind them.

But the window displays weren't the anachronisms. I was. When I went to the party, I pushed open the front door of Morris Office Machines and stepped back forty years. Hundreds of people, some in black tie, some in jeans, crammed into a couple thousand square feet. Against the left wall, between some wooden file cabinets and an assortment of water coolers, a five-man combo swayed in white dinner jackets and skinny black bowties, graying crew cuts and big smiles. One of them plucked at a bass taller than he while singing into a microphone: *Tall and tan and young and lovely, the girl from Ipanema goes walking . . .* Their audience was a large chunk of Leflore County, white against white broken only occasionally by a black waiter with a tray of hors d'oeuvres or empty glasses.

I believe I talked to just about everyone there that night, including the mayor, the chief of police, the fire chief, several judges, several members of the city council, the heads of the Rotary Club and the Lions club and the Exchange club and the Elks club and the Garden club and the local chapters of the Daughters of the American Revolution and the United Daughters of the Confederacy and the Ole Miss alumni organization and the Mississippi State alumni organization and the Delta State alumni organization and the Mississippi University for Women alumni organization and the Pillow Academy alumni organization and the Republican Party and the Greenwood Little Theater and Mothers Against Drunk Driving and every white church congregation in Leflore County. I talked to morticians and schoolteachers and planters and insurance agents and lawyers and ministers and salesmen and builders and shopkeepers and restaurateurs, hundreds of people in all. I'd never met most of them formally, but they all addressed me by name, as if they'd known me all my life. Not one of them made any mention of the fact that I was from New York, or anywhere else. For a moment, I imagined that this was the essence of Christmas in the Delta—a brief time when everyone broke themselves down to the lowest common denominator and related to everyone else as if there were no differences between people, as if everyone in the world had grown up right next door to everyone else. Then a waiter walked by and I handed him my empty glass.

❦

I admit that I didn't get much work done on the day of the Christmas Parade, but then again, none of us did. The work ethic was on vacation. Everybody seemed excited, even Vic. I couldn't wait to see this grand old spectacle, whatever was left of it. At 3:30 we closed the newsroom down and drove to Market Street; Jack and Karen and Vic and I and about fifteen other people parked ourselves in front of the New Deal Tobacco Company and waited for the festivities to begin.

I can't say if nostalgia had blurred Vic's hindsight, but it didn't seem to hamper his view of the present. The parade—what there was of it—didn't start until around six. It straggled on until about eight, drawn out so long only by several gaping holes in the procession, most notably one high school band who all lost their music and couldn't themselves be found until someone thought to look in their bus. Still, their performance towered over some of the better-prepared bands, like the one who somehow managed to have only one of eighty-four feet hit the ground at any given moment. I almost laughed when one of the girls from one school's color guard speared another in the back with her flagpole; but as the sentiment was making its way to my mouth, I turned and looked at Vic and saw that perpetual grin of his twisted downward in agony, and I realized that this entire affair was farcical only to me and maybe Karen, and only to her because she'd grown up two hundred miles away in McComb. To Vic and Jack and just about everyone else packing the sidewalk of Market Street that night, the pathetic procession through the heart of town was a reminder that the Greenwood, Mississippi of their past was really dead, as dead as the Confederacy; and though most of them hid it behind cordial smiles of feigned appreciation, the people standing all around me were themselves dying, and dying painfully. Yet they did not leave, did not even turn away, and I knew as sure as I knew anything that every last one of them would be standing here again this time next year, and the year after that, and as long as Greenwood could still muster up some form of a parade for Christmas. They could not help themselves.

As for me: It seems that the sad spectacle of the parade, followed by the scraggliest display of fireworks I had ever seen, softened me so much that toward the end of it all, when I saw Karen walking over to me, I did not turn and flee, even though I knew she was going to ask me, again, to go see this old cemetery with her. And when she did, I did not say no.

❦

"Now, this is the story," she said after we'd driven out past the Leflore County limits. "Back in 1966, there was this girl named Sandra Faye Haley who lived with her mama and daddy up in the hills. She was fifteen or sixteen and I guess she was a student at J. Z. George, you know, and she was an only child, right? I think her parents were a lot older than normal and for sure they were out there, even for hill people. Well, you'll see.

"So Sandra Faye's mama didn't like this boy she was seein'. Don't ask me why, sometimes it just happens that way. And she didn't want her daughter datin' this boy any more, or maybe she just didn't want her to go to the prom with him. But a girl in love, you know, so Sandra Faye goes to the prom with this boy anyway, and afterward she makes the mistake of lettin' him bring her home and they start neckin' right there on her front porch. I mean, who hasn't? But her mama's waitin' up and she sees 'em and runs out and chases this boy away and drags Sandra Faye in by her hair and sends her to her room and tells her she ain't never gonna see that boy again because she's just been grounded for the rest of her natural life. You follow?"

I nodded. We had already turned off 82 into Carrollton, and now the county courthouse loomed up on the right. I looked up through Karen's moonroof: cloudy, but no sign of rain. Legend held that when it rained here at night, the courthouse walls ran with blood, a reminder that twenty freed blacks were slaughtered on this spot one night in 1886. I'd never learned what had precipitated this massacre, and I had never seen the courthouse in the rain. I wanted to, though I wasn't sure what I would do if the walls really did run with blood. I had once walked through the old cemetery on the wooded slope behind the courthouse and accidentally set my foot down on a shallow depression near a grave, my leg plunging down into the soft ground, almost to the knee. Worse still, this had happened at dusk, and I was so spooked by it that I'd avoided even looking at the cemetery since. This was Carrollton, the ancient county seat where white-frame houses from the 1830s and 1840s lined skinny, twisty streets, where a new building hadn't been raised downtown since P. G. T. Beauregard fired on Fort Sumter, where the courthouse walls turned rain into blood and the dead pulled you down into the grave with them. I couldn't believe I had actually agreed to go along with Karen, without a word of protest. I suddenly wanted to ask her to turn back, but she was talking at a pace that made interrupting her impossible.

"So there's Sandra Faye," she went on, "sent to her room for good, and the boyfriend chased away, probably with a bloody nose, I wouldn't be surprised, and Sandra Faye's mama—Mayzell's her name—sitting in the

living room, readin' or knittin' or what have you, and she thinks everything's under control. But you know a girl in love, or maybe you don't, but
a girl in love or thinks she's in love will do the damnedest things. She's
what you might call an unstable atom, if you remember your chemistry. So
what does Sandra Faye do but run into the bathroom and lock herself in
there. And then, she finds some arsenic somewhere in there, and she eats it.
Now, she doesn't eat that much—the police said they thought she was just
tryin' to put a scare into her mama—but here's where it gets really weird.
You know Rhonda Smith, works paste-up at the paper? You know her.
Well, back in 1966, her mama, or maybe it was her mother-in-law, I cain't
remember exactly, but anyway she was a nurse in the emergency room at
Greenwood-Leflore, and she was there the night they brought Sandra Faye
Haley in. She says they tried and tried to pump that girl's stomach, but it
wouldn't do any good. You see, because she only took a little arsenic, it
didn't stay in her stomach long. It went right into her bloodstream. If she'd
taken more, it wouldn't have dissolved so quickly, and they could have
pumped it out. But because she only took a little, just to scare her mama,
they couldn't save her, and she died. Right there, in the E.R."

Suddenly, Karen was quiet. I waited for her to resume her tale, but she
didn't. Finally, I prodded her. "So, that's it? She just died?"

"Yep."

"That's the story? What about her mother?"

Karen smiled, briefly. "You'll see," she said.

"What, she killed herself too?"

"You'll see."

"What, are we going to see a mother-daughter ghost team?" I wished I
really believed it was as ridiculous as I tried to make it sound.

"Just have patience, baby. We'll be there in a few minutes."

"Come on," I said. "*Tell me.*" But Karen would only smile as the dim
glow of Carrollton sank into the darkness behind us. She turned onto a
road without a visible name, then another, and stepped on the gas, sending
us speeding over the soft curves and hills of a road without houses or
lamps. A few more minutes and the road itself seemed to vanish from
under us; we were just hurling onward through dense black space. Then we
tipped over one last hill, and I saw it all.

Lights. Thousands of them, and more, unthinkable numbers of blue
and green and red and yellow and bright white lights, hovering in the darkness. They pulled us in, soaring forward to meet them. I looked at the

speedometer, but it said we were actually slowing down. I didn't believe it.

The lights grew larger and multiplied, splitting apart into dozens of smaller lights, which also grew larger and multiplied. A fireball hovering a hundred feet off the ground became a gold star, sitting atop a massive evergreen. There were cardboard figures, Santa and elves and reindeer and angels and Joseph and Mary and the Magi and the infant in the manger. And there was music, electronic notes that sauntered shyly out of the inanimate crowd and into the night, beeping "Hark the Herald Angels Sing" and "Oh, Come All Ye Faithful" for no one at all. And there was a little whitewashed church just across the road. And I looked closer, narrowed my eyes, and yes: Amid the lights and the reindeer and the Magi and the tree there were *gravestones.*

And then we were there, Karen slowing to a stop right next to it all. For a couple of minutes, we just sat there. Then we got out of the car.

The graveyard was closed off by a chain-link fence. Just behind it, facing the road and the church, was a large gray stone with the name HALEY engraved near the top. Underneath, "Sandra Faye, August 1, 1950–June 24, 1966," and in the top center, just above her name, was an oval photograph of the girl, wearing her prom gown, her dark hair piled high atop her fair face, a corsage strapped to her wrist. A tiny doll with rouged cheeks sat on top, her legs dangling just above the picture. Spread out in front was a dirt mound, covered with plastic to keep it from washing away. To the left was a smaller HALEY stone with two humps, one marked for Earl, 1908–1985, the other for Mayzell, 1912–. I looked back at the silent white church, up at the silent black sky. There were no stars, only the vague gray mist that slipped out of my own mouth. I stared into the cemetery; I thought I could see a music box, tucked behind the tree. It chimed out "Oh Holy Night." I listened to the whole thing; I didn't want to miss a note. I stood there for a long time, so long that I forgot where I was. I forgot that I was miles out in the country, in a place so remote it would never even make the pages of our small-town newspaper. I forgot that I'd ever been in a newsroom. I forgot that I'd ever been anywhere else. I forgot that there *was* anyplace else, really—anyplace other than this Mississippi, the only place in the world, I imagined, where such a bizarre tragedy could have produced such startling, stunning, shocking, sad beauty.

"Now, you tell me," Karen said. "Have you ever in your life seen anything like that in New York?"

And I told her: No, indeed.

ELEVEN

THE HIGH-WATER MARK OF MY CONFEDERACY

Winter fell on the Delta like slate. The sky was perpetually gray, the cold air sharp and dry. It seemed absurd that this same place had stunned me with its oppressive wet heat when I'd first arrived only a few months before. I soon forgot what the summer had felt like, and I decided, at that point, that as unbearable as September might have seemed at the time, January was worse. The flat, frigid land stretched out endlessly ahead. I couldn't conceive that it would ever be warm again.

I almost looked forward to work, needing to see the color in another person's face, to feel the glow of fluorescent lights and the warm air that filled the newsroom when everyone was racing to make deadline. I found myself craving the company of other people, or at least their presence. The frozen stillness of what lay outside made it difficult to believe that this was indeed the beginning of a new year, and not merely the death of the old one.

Just a few weeks before, I had sought any excuse to get out of the newsroom. Now I wanted to stay there as much as possible. I think we all felt that way; no one rushed to answer their phone anymore. Even when paged, we would let the phone sit there for a minute or two, unanswered, hoping the caller would grow impatient and just hang up. Usually, they did.

Then Karen, who had good-heartedly assumed as a personal mission the responsibility of making my Mississippi sojourn as pleasant as possible, came up with the idea of having me take over the Carroll County beat, which no reporter had covered for years—anything, she figured, to get me out of the newsroom and back into the world. "Come on," she implored when I hesitated. "It'll be interesting. It'll be *fun*."

It was neither. Not much seemed to happen up in Carroll County, which lay directly east of Leflore and marked the end of the Delta. It was the hills, an old, mostly white and mostly poor region; hill people weren't as friendly as Delta people, and they carried about them a somewhat less subtle air of menace. If people in Greenwood were often too polite to say "no comment" to an inquiring reporter, people in Carrollton often had no compunction about saying "none of your damn business!"

Only a few thousand people lived up in Carroll County, and for better or worse the only news worth covering up there was the semiregular meeting of the Carroll County Board of Supervisors. It was a matter of government, democracy in action and thus open to the general public and the press; but on the day I first attended, there was no general public there at all—only the five county supervisors, who regarded the reporter suddenly appearing in their midst with surprise, and not the pleasant variety.

No one bothered to introduce himself to me. Instead, a squat, powerful man, who appeared to me to weigh at least four hundred pounds and who wore a belt buckle the size of my face, simply called the meeting to order and passed out carbon copies of agendas. He was, as I would soon learn, the board's chairman, Lloyd "Honey" Ashmore, and despite both his nickname and the stereotype that men of such size are supposed to be jolly, I would never see him smile or say a kind word, although Jack told me he once saw him snap a monkey wrench in two with his bare hands. How he got tagged with "Honey" remains a mystery.

The meeting lasted only about a half hour and was as boring and inconsequential as the Kiwanis' Lunch I had covered the previous day. I left wondering how I was going to get six inches out of it.

Then Karen told me that the Board preferred to conduct its "important" business unobserved. They handed out incomplete agendas, went through them, and then sat around, eating and grunting, as if they were done. A reporter, bored and assuming the meeting was over, would just get up and leave. Then they'd resume. "You have to wait them out," Karen said.

The next month, I did. I sat through more than an hour of chomping and snorting, and I didn't leave until all five had frustratedly climbed into their trucks and driven away.

Later that afternoon, back at the newsroom, Jack ambled over to my desk, his cheek, as always, full of chew. "Richit," he said with a nod, eyebrows raised, "I just got me a call from Honey Ashmore."

"Really?" I offered, my voice cracking nervously. "What did he say?"

"He said," Jack replied, "and I quote: 'Can you tell me why I *shouldn't* kill that boy?'"

I laughed, nervously; and then, desperate to camouflage my fear, added: "Yeah, right."

Jack just shook his head, raised a Styrofoam cup to his lips, and spat into it. "Richit," he said, visibly suppressing a grin, "they got places in Carroll County to bury a body, ain't *never* gon' find it."

⁕⁗

One morning, Mike told me to drive up to Vaiden, a small Carroll County town about forty miles northeast of Greenwood, and the furthest point in our circulation area. "They're finishing up work on the new county courthouse up there," Mike said. "Go visit it, and the old one, too."

"But the Carroll County courthouse is in Carrollton," I said, thinking of the old gray cube where the walls ran red every time it rained, and where the Confederate monument bore the unregenerate motto: THEY FOUGHT AND DIED TO DEFEND THEIR CONSTITUTIONAL RIGHTS.

"Well, they've got one in Vaiden, too."

"But I thought Carrollton was the county seat."

"Well, apparently Vaiden is, too. Now just go on up there, all right? I don't have time to argue with you, Richard." And with that Mike turned and walked off, as patient and indulgent as ever.

In fact, Carroll County has *two* seats, a vestige of a time when roads were poor and folks in the eastern half of the county would have to sacrifice several days' worth of work if they needed to travel to Carrollton to pay their taxes. And so a second seat of local government was established in Vaiden, a town that, as far as I knew, bore no distinction whatsoever, except as the site of a truckstop along Interstate 55 and a nightclub, the Country Music Palace, which was actually a large wood-beam and corrugated metal shed; on Valentine's Day, 1989, I saw one-time Motown star Percy Sledge perform there for a crowd of several dozen. Tickets cost five dollars.

There was no direct route from Greenwood to Vaiden. The quickest way to get there was to take Highway 82 up past Carrollton, then turn onto Highway 35, a hilly, twisting two-lane road lined with piney woods and littered with dead armadillos, their tiny legs reaching stiffly toward heaven. Despite the ubiquity of these shelled omens, there was something about Highway 35 that made me want to drive fast, and I rarely took it at less than eighty miles per hour, even at night. And so it was that I roared into Vaiden that winter morning.

The road into town was lined by a slight ridge, making it possible to imagine the experience of riding in on a covered wagon a hundred and fifty years earlier. The approach was marked on the left by a small yellow high school building, a product of the WPA; on the right, by a rolling cemetery that seemed to stretch back forever. Only about nine hundred people lived in Vaiden, but many times that number appeared to have died there.

Near the center of town stood the old courthouse, a striking and imposing edifice built of red brick and marked by stout Doric columns, a peaked roof and a broad, square clock tower. It seemed like a proud old building, at least until you looked closely—then you saw that the brick was faded and crumbling, the pillars peeling and splintering, the clock faces marred by large holes and streaked with ancient dirt. Only the monument standing outside—"Sacred to the memory of the Confederate Soldier who fought for principles that can never die, as long as a sense of right and patriotism dwell in the human breast"—appeared to have been spared the relentless assault of time and the elements.

Perhaps that was because it was relatively new, having been commissioned by the United Daughters of the Confederacy in 1912. The courthouse dated back to 1905, and its courtroom, on the second floor of the building, had recently been used as the site of a scene in the movie *Mississippi Burning*, which was already the cause of much controversy throughout Mississippi, even though it had yet to play in a single theater in the entire state. The rest of Mississippi was concerned with how the film negatively portrayed their home state (or so they had heard, anyway). But in Vaiden, the object of controversy was not the film itself but rather the filmmakers, and how they had treated the townspeople and their old courthouse.

"This was just last year," Vernon Welch, the county supervisor from Vaiden, recalled as he walked me through the courtroom, an old, dark chamber lined with old, dark wood and featuring a balcony and a large ceiling fan. "They said they wanted to film a trial scene in here, but we told them the floor wouldn't be able to support the weight of all the equipment and the actors and all, so they said fine, we'll build supports underneath so it can, and they did. And then they said they wanted to use the balcony—that's where the blacks used to sit, back in the old days, you know. Well, we haven't used the balcony for years and years, because it's not safe, and we told them so, but they said no problem, we'll just build supports under it, too. And they did. And they put on these fancy new doors downstairs for another scene, and they used a bunch of people here as extras, and they used the courtroom for about a week, and then when they finished they just packed everything up, took their doors and their supports, and left, and now the courtroom is even weaker than it was before."

"How much did they pay you to use the courthouse?" I asked.

"Three thousand dollars," he spat.

"And how much did they pay the extras?"

"Not one dime."

Clearly, Hollywood had not made any friends in Vaiden. I asked Vernon Welch about the courthouse itself.

"We've got to get out of here before it falls down on us," he said without a smile as he walked me through the offices downstairs. The building, he explained, had been condemned back in 1973 by a grand jury, which had ruled it "not structurally sound." The county, though, did not have the money to build a new courthouse, so they were forced to continue using the old one, which grew ever more hazardous. "Some people say it will fall tomorrow," said Charles Ellis, the Circuit and Chancery clerk, who overheard my conversation with Vernon. "It seems like the walls are pulling apart. But I have to work here; I can't think about it, because if I did, I probably wouldn't be able to come in every morning."

Margie Laugherty, a deputy justice court clerk, chimed in: "It will be much easier to work when I don't have to worry about mortar falling on my head."

"You'd be safer in a tent than you are in here," Vernon sighed.

"We've got one judge who's granted all his cases a continuance until the new courthouse is done," Charles Ellis said. "He says he doesn't think the courtroom can take another trial. Every time it rains, water pours into the courtroom and the records get all wet. Every time it rains the whole courthouse is flooded. The state Supreme Court just overturned a murder conviction down in Greene County because it said their court-room was unfit for trial, and ours is even worse."

As Vernon led me out of the old courthouse, a look of relief crossed his face; I imagined he experienced such a feeling every time he left the build-ing alive. "Now there," he said, pointing at the construction site across the street, "is our salvation. The lowest estimate we got for renovating the old courthouse was $1.5 million. We're building that one for $438,000."

"When will it be finished?"

"Couple of months, hopefully."

"And when will you move over?"

He laughed. "The day it's ready."

I shook my head in wonder. How was it possible that such a place still existed in America, a place where people risked their lives every day in order to keep the county operating and dole out some semblance of jus-tice, where people had no choice but to endure such dangerous working conditions *for fifteen years* simply because there was no money to do things another way?

Is this America?

⋙⋘

By this time I had started to develop a real curiosity about Vaiden, Mississippi—and, since I had already missed the paper's morning dead-line, I was left with no reason to refrain from indulging it. I asked Vernon Welch where I might learn more about the town; Vernon referred me not to a book or a library but to his sister-in-law, Frances Jordan Welch, who was known as "Bud." Bud, in turn, took me to meet her mother, Frances Wright Shivel, who was known as "Red Mama"—not because of latent Communist sympathies but rather her hair, which was still a muted crim-son even though she was now in her seventies. The three of us sat in Red Mama's living room, surrounded by one-hundred-and-forty-year-old ancestral portraits and a one-hundred-and-forty-year-old Kimball square grand piano, drinking tea and talking Vaiden.

"The first thing you need to know," Red Mama said, "is that Vaiden wasn't originally called 'Vaiden.' The original name was 'Shongalo.'"

"Shongalo?"

"That's right, Shongalo. That's what the Indians called it—the Choctaw, you know—and that's what the first white settlers called it, too, back in the 1830s."

"What does the word mean?"

"No one really knows," Bud admitted, smiling. "When I was coming up, I heard some people say it meant 'sturdy oak,' and other people said it meant 'lark,' and other people said it meant 'laughing maiden.' I always liked that one the best."

"The story is," Red Mama interjected, "that one day a beautiful Indian maiden went down to the crick to do some wash, or maybe to bathe, I don't know. I think it was to bathe. And this young brave was hiding in the thicket, you know, watching her, and then she just sprouted wings and flew away. Up and flew away. And this brave, he was there watching this, and when he saw her fly away he just stared and said 'Shon-ga-lo!' And that's the story."

"So why was it changed to 'Vaiden'?"

"Back in the 1850s, the railroad wanted to come through town," Bud said. "Wanted to put a depot here. By then Shongalo was a thriving place—we were already a major stop on the stagecoach that ran from Black Hawk to Kosciusko, you see—and the railroad wanted to come through and stop here, on the way down to Jackson and then New Orleans. And they wanted to put their depot on a piece of land that was back then right in the middle of town, not far from where we're sittin' right now. And this land belonged to a man named Louis Whitfield Herring, who was one of the founders of Shongalo, owned a lot of land. Mama and me are kin to the Herrings—we're kin to most of the important early families in town, actually, like the Cains, and the Kennedys, and the Whiteheads, and the Pleasants, and the Wrights, and the Durhams, and the Jordans."

"My mama was a Wright," Red Mama interjected. "And her mama was a Vaiden."

"So the railroad wanted this land that belonged to Louis Whitfield Herring, or I should say to his estate. And they went to the executor of his estate, Dr. C. M. Vaiden, who was Mr. Herring's brother-in-law. Doctor Cowles Meade Vaiden. We're kin to him, too. He was from Virginia, originally; he came down to Shongalo in the 1830s, when he was a young man, and he married Mr. Herring's sister, and a little later his own sister came to visit and she ended up married to Mr. Herring. That kind of thing happened a lot in those days. So then years later Dr. Vaiden is the executor of Mr. Herring's estate and the railroad comes to Dr. Vaiden and wants to buy this piece of land that had belonged to Mr. Herring to build their depot on, and Dr. Vaiden says O.K., and he arranges it. He arranges for the railroad to buy the right of way, and some land to build a depot on, all for fifty dollars. And in gratitude the railroad people renamed their depot 'Vaiden,' and the town, too."

"And do you know," Red Mama added, "that this is the only town on Earth named 'Vaiden'?"

"Is that right?" I said, trying to think of another. I couldn't.

"It is," Red Mama said, "and this was quite a place, now, back when. At one time Vaiden was the wealthiest town of its size in all of Mississippi. That's right. A lot of very important people lived here or came through or started out here. You wouldn't know any of them, because you're too young and you're not from around here, but we had quite a few, yes we did. You've heard of J. Z. George, have you? He was a United States senator, a very rich man, one of the richest in Mississippi. He grew up around here. This was fertile ground, I tell you, very valuable."

"There was money to be made here," Bud said. "And some of the earliest settlers in Shongalo were Jews, you know."

My face began to grow warm and I stared at Bud, trying to discern the significance of what she was saying, and to determine why she had said it. Was she tossing out the old stereotype that Jews gravitate toward money? Or was she trying to suss out whether I was Jewish? Or both? My mind gyrated with a half-dozen different snide remarks, but I was far too interested in hearing more of what she had to say on the subject to release any of them—Vaiden, after all, was the last place I had expected to find Jews, or their ghosts, anyway—so instead I simply said: "Really?"

"Absolutely. There was a big family in Shongalo named Hirsh, the father and mother came from Germany, and their oldest son, Joe Hirsh, he went off to fight on the war with the 1st Regiment, Mississippi Light Artillery, they fought at Shiloh and Vicksburg both. Did you know that we had some local boys who fought at Gettysburg? That's right, 'The High-Water Mark of the Confederacy,' as they say, and we were there. So anyway, after the war Joe Hirsh came back to Vaiden and went into business and got rich and at one point he owned the deeds for just about every piece of land in town. He sat on the board of the Vaiden Male and Female Institute, which was founded by Dr. Vaiden. In fact, there were several Jews on that board at one time."

"There were a lot of Jews who owned stores in town," Red Mama said. "Shongalo and Vaiden both. There was Simon Lichtenstein and Solomon Saber and a fellow named Stein who owned a big store with Charlie Eskridge, who might of been Jewish, too, for all I know. They were all here very early. And there was Mister Rosenthal, Benjamin Rosenthal. I didn't know him, but I knew his wife, his second wife, Elizabeth. She was a McCaskill. She lived to be a hundred years old. And I knew his son, Leo, and his wife, Bettie. Bettie came in to town shopping one day in an old housecoat and when she got home he yelled at her so bad about it that she never came in to town again. She's the one gave me that piano, she sure did. They were lovely people, the Rosenthals."

"And there was Charles Kopperl," Bud added. "He was one of the first postmasters of Shongalo, back in the early 1840s. He converted and he was made a deacon at the Shongalo Presbyterian Church. That's the pretty little red brick church you see, right next to the old courthouse, the original one."

"There used to be a plaque on the wall in the church," Red Mama recalled, "saying he was 'a cultured man, of exquisite taste, wonderful energy, and of unstinted hospitality.' I don't know if it's still there."

"I don't think it is, Mama," Bud said. "But he's mentioned in Carl Sandburg's *Abraham Lincoln: The War Years.* I have a copy of it around here somewhere." She rustled through some papers and pulled out a yellowed photocopy of page 331 of the first volume of Sandburg's four-volume history of the war. The passage dealt with the arrests of hundreds of Confederate sympathizers following the Union's defeat at the first battle of Bull Run in September 1861. Amidst a list of those interned at Fort Lafayette in New York Harbor I spotted: "Another prisoner, Major Charles Kopperl of Carroll County, Mississippi, had made the rounds of hotels and saloons along Broadway, New York, wearing a revolver and a bowie knife, telling of how at the battle of Bull Run he had made mincemeat of Union soldiers." I smiled: At the connection between Vaiden and New York, sure, but more at the image of a middle-aged Mississippi-accented Jew in a Confederate uniform drunkenly raising hell on the streets of old Gotham. It was almost too beautiful a vision to accept as historical fact.

"Major Kopperl was killed in the war," Red Mama lamented. "And did you know that there was fighting right here in Vaiden? Yes, yes there was. There were skirmishes outside of town, and then Grierson's Raiders came through and made all kinds of trouble, they sure did. You've heard of Grierson's Raiders, haven't you? They rode all through here on New Year's Day, 1865, they sure did. They were on a mission to tear up the railroad, the Mississippi Central, and their leader was from Illinois, Colonel Benjamin Grierson, he was a music teacher, and around here he's still known as 'The Gray Ghost.' And when they came through Vaiden a bunch of ours met them outside of town and they mixed it up; some were killed on both sides. But that didn't stop them, now, and they rode into town and did all kind of awful things—burned houses and stores and the train depot, tore up the train tracks, said ugly things to the people, things like that. They stopped at the Kennedy house, that's still there. I'm kin to them; I remember my uncle used to own that house and he would sit out on the porch with his feet up on the railing and look out over all his land. And Grierson and his men took over that house and they kept their horses *inside the parlor* and let them eat hay off the keyboard of the family's grand piano. And then when they left they were going to burn the house to the ground and the little girl took them to the woods and showed them where the family had buried its wine, so they just took the wine and didn't burn the house down, and I'm kin to her, too. I *knew* her."

"And there was another big house, outside of town," Bud said, "named Briarwood, it belonged to the Canon family, and it was right near where the soldiers fought their skirmish, and afterward Grierson billeted some of his wounded men there and the Canons treated them so well that when it came time for them to leave Colonel Grierson ordered his men not to destroy Briarwood, and it's still there, too, although no one's lived in it for as long as I can remember."

"Can I see it?" I asked.

"Sure!" Bud said. "Tell you what. I'll give you a tour of the whole town. It'll be good to get out and get some fresh air, what do you say, Mama?"

Red Mama just nodded her head, and in a couple of minutes we were all in Bud's car and driving through town, past the old Kennedy house and the old Watkins house (which was located, I noted with a smile, on Hirsh Street), the current courthouse (which was still known as "the new courthouse," even though it was eighty-four years old) and the old courthouse (built in 1874) and the Shongalo Presbyterian Church, the site where the *new* new courthouse would soon be and the site where the train depot used to be. Then we turned off onto a dusty dirt road and drove a couple of miles east of town, until we spotted an enormous Georgian plantation manor, brown and rotten and splintering, sitting about two hundred yards off the road. "There she is!" Bud pronounced. "That's Briarwood."

Bud and I climbed out of the car—Red Mama stayed in the backseat, not caring to make such a hike on a cold winter afternoon—scaled a slight rise and started to bushwhack our way through waist-high weeds toward the abandoned old mansion. From the road, it resembled nothing more than a sagging beige mass, but as we slowly made our way closer to it, the house began to take form, gradually revealing both its former splendor and the depth of its decay. There were the floor-to-ceiling windows, blackened and broken; the roof, slanted steep and pocked with gaping holes; the chimneys, fat and thick and crumbling; the doorway, wide and empty and surrounded by a portico, atop which sat a triangular pediment, atop which sat an enormous scowling bird, vigilant and majestic but faded to the same old brown.

"What a place!" I said to Bud as we drew within twenty yards. "It must have been gorgeous. Look at all the detail—look at that eagle carved over the door! It's huge! I've never seen anything like it!"

Bud froze, turned to me. "That's not an eagle," she said softly. "And it's *not* part of the house."

I looked at her, bemused. "What do you mean?"

"It's a buzzard. They must have nested in there."

"A buzzard!" I froze too.

"Shh!" Bud said, but it was too late. Already, that which I had taken for a wooden representation of our national bird was rising off its haunches. It spread its wings out horizontally—at full span they were even wider than the pediment—and issued a series of shrill shrieks. As it flapped its wings and took off, five or six other buzzards shot out of the windows and roof and joined it above our heads, circling in a spiral that grew ever smaller as their cacophonous calls grew louder.

"Come on!" Bud said, turning around. "They're mad! We gotta get back to the car before they attack."

"Attack?" I yelped. "But we're not even dead!"

"Doesn't matter!" Bud called back as she pushed aside a dense clump of something that wasn't quite green. "They think we're going to harm their nest."

"O.K.," I said, already puffing. "But, uh, what exactly do you mean by 'attack'? Do they bite?"

"Worse."

"What?"

"They vomit on you."

"They *what?!*"

"They vomit on you!" Bud repeated. "And let me tell you something. There's nothing on this earth that smells worse than buzzard vomit. Hurry now! I hope Mama didn't lock the doors! She does that sometimes, I don't know why, but she does."

Somehow, we managed to make it back to Bud's car—which was, blessedly, unlocked—without being hit by any buzzard vomit, although a few minutes later, after we had driven back to town and managed to ditch the squadron of enraged flying scavengers, I did spot a splatter of the stuff on the roof of the vehicle as I reemerged. I took it as an omen against getting too close to the past. Or something.

And Bud was right: I never have smelled anything worse.

ॐ

The following week, an interstate truck driver whose name I would never learn pulled his rig onto the shoulder of I-55, just a few miles north of Vaiden, and stepped into the woods to relieve himself. Looking down at the ground, he noticed what at first seemed to be a strange pattern of sticks; he soon decided, though, that what he had stumbled across was a human skeleton, partially covered by leaves and weeds but not buried, and spread out over a distance of eight feet or so. The truck driver called the authorities, who arrived on the scene but were immediately faced with a problem—in which county, exactly, did the remains lie? It seems that the spot the truck driver had chosen for a rest stop sat at the conjunction of three counties—Montgomery, Grenada and Carroll. A surveyor was called in to determine jurisdiction, and after some measuring and map-reading, the decision was handed down: Carroll County. A radio call went out to the Carroll County Sheriff. Mike picked it up on his battered old police scanner, somehow managed to interpret it, jotted down a few details, and walked over to my desk.

Minutes later I was on my way up to Carrollton to see Sheriff C. D. Whitfield and his deputy, Don Gray. Sheriff Whitfield resembled Oliver Hardy squeezed into a ten-gallon hat, holster and cowboy boots, while Deputy Gray was known among *Commonwealth* staffers as "The Hair," due to the extravagant amount of time he apparently spent on his elegant coiffure—with his sweeping sandy-blond locks and his mirrored aviator sunglasses, he resembled a small-town Mississippi sheriff's deputy far less than he did an extra on *Miami Vice.* And, like an extra, he never seemed to utter a word.

Sheriff Whitfield, on the other hand, was quite gregarious, if largely humorless, and rarely hesitated to share every bit of information he had. The first thing he told me, when I arrived at his office in the Carrollton Courthouse, was that he had quickly discovered "a small, round hole in the skull," and had deduced that death had resulted from causes other than natural—namely, a bullet to the head. "If it looks like we've got a homicide, we'll proceed with a full investigation," he told me. "I wouldn't be surprised if we'll have to do just that."

"How long has the skeleton been there?" I asked.

"It could be a matter of months," he said, "but I think it's been there for years."

The bones were gathered and shipped down to the state examiner's crime lab in Jackson, where, with the help of dental records, the remains were identified as those of a thirty-year-old college professor named John Paul Scott, who had disappeared in June 1973, while driving from Trent University in Ontario to Franklin, Louisiana to visit his fiancée. Two weeks after Scott's disappearance, a twenty-one-year-old man named Donnie Gene Silcox was arrested on a controlled substance charge and promptly confessed to killing Scott, who had picked up Silcox in Bowling Green, Kentucky, as Silcox was attempting to hitchhike from his hometown of Toledo, Ohio to Houston, Texas. Mississippi authorities took Silcox with them and combed the area where Silcox told them he had disposed of Scott's body after the shooting, but they were unable to find it, and thus unable to charge Silcox with murder. After a brief stint in jail for possession of a controlled substance, Silcox was released.

Now, fifteen years later, Carroll County Sheriff C. D. Whitfield issued a warrant to have Silcox extradited from Ohio to Mississippi, then personally drove up to Toledo to get the man and bring him back. The morning after he returned, Sheriff Whitfield called me at the newsroom to let me know that he would be escorting Silcox to his first court hearing later that day, and invited me to come witness what I would come to know, years later and back in New York, as a "perp walk." Unlike New York perp walks, though, which were always attended by anything from a cadre to a throng of reporters, photographers, and cameramen, this Carroll County version of the old police tradition would be attended by only one journalist.

At the appointed time, I perched myself on the Carrollton courthouse's front steps—there were only a few of them—and waited. Slowly, three men ambled up the sidewalk, then turned at the old black wrought-iron gate and headed right for me. On the left was Don Gray, hair perfect as always, mirrored sunglasses dangling from his left breast pocket. On the right was Sheriff C. D. Whitfield, a faint smile on his lips, a noticeable bounce in his step. And in the center was Donnie Gene Silcox: pale skin, thick dark hair and mustache, light blue shirt open at the neck, black trousers, scuffed black loafers, his wrists pinched together in handcuffs, his ankles linked by a foot of chain. I raised my camera and pointed it at them. Gray glanced off to the side; Whitfield raised his jowly chin and stared right into the lens. And Donnie Gene Silcox, without lowering his head a bit, turned his eyes to the ground. Within minutes, Judge Cooper "Pete" Misskelley had set Silcox's bond at $100,000 and had assigned Greenwood attorney Leland H. Jones III to Silcox's case. Lee Jones was perhaps Greenwood's best-known criminal defense attorney. He was a short, colorful man, always impeccably dressed; with his thick brown beard and perpetual grin, he struck me as a cross between Ulysses S. Grant and a leprechaun. Lee Jones was atypical of Greenwood's lawyers in that he rarely failed to give a reporter a usable quote devoid of legalese, and never said "no comment." Despite the fact that he blatantly affected a folksy Southern charm whenever he spoke to me, I'd always found him somewhat endearing. Most of polite Greenwood considered him a shyster.

When the hearing was over and Silcox had been escorted back to his cell—which was also in the Carrollton courthouse, a fact that had somehow eluded me during the perp walk—I asked Whitfield if I could go see the prisoner. He led me to the jail and left me standing outside the bars of Silcox's cell; inside, the man I had photographed earlier turned away from me and cowered in the corner, like a dog fearing a beating.

"Why are you doing that?" I asked.

"I'm not very proud of being in here," he replied, softly.

As I drove back to the newsroom, I thought about the man and what it must have been like for him, and somehow, despite the fact that I knew he had murdered someone while hitchhiking, I began to pity him. After all, he had been snatched out of his home, whisked down to the middle of nowhere, Mississippi, and tossed in a dark, musty jail cell, where he would wait until he was tried for murder and then, like Ronnie Ray Strong, sent to Parchman for the rest of his life. Later that afternoon I shared this with Mike, who, seemingly possessed of some information I did not have, simply sneered and said: "Yes, the dangers of being a *homosexual* hitchhiker."

As it happened, we were both wrong. Donnie Gene Silcox soon made bail, and at his trial, which I did not attend, he was actually acquitted. Later, I asked Lee Jones how that could have happened. "He confessed, didn't he?" I said.

"Well, now, Richard," he replied, "he made a statement that said he *killed* the guy. But every killing is not a crime. Whereas every breaking and entering is a crime—if you go on and break into someone's house, that's always a crime. But not every killing is a crime."

I tried to sift through any number of interpretations of Lee Jones's statement, but quickly gave up. Frequently, when talking to him, I found I had no idea what he was saying. But he was a fairly successful criminal defense attorney, and he had managed to get Donnie Gene Silcox acquitted despite a confession. "Who did you put up in your defense?"

"Just him, but he made an excellent witness. They ate it up."

"What did he say?"

"That the guy tried to queer off on him, and it scared him, and he pulled out his gun and shot him. Then he got scared, pulled out the body and got the hell out of there."

"He tried to do *what* on him?"

"Queer off. Those were *his* words—'queer off.'"

"And that was his entire defense?"

"Listen, Richard, when they found this guy's bones, they called his father, asked if he wanted the skull, and he said, 'As far as I'm concerned we buried him already, and I don't care what you do with that skull.' Don't you find that a little strange? His own father? And down here, with the time lapse, people in Carroll County didn't care. And the victim wasn't from here. Hell," Lee Jones chuckled, "he was a *Canadian*."

❧❧

By the time C. D. Whitfield had driven up to Ohio and returned with Donnie Gene Silcox, spring had just started to dawn over Mississippi. While we in the newsroom quietly celebrated the winter's thaw, it brought serious flooding up in parts of Carroll County, trapping many people in their homes, some for weeks. One day I drove up to interview one of them, an elderly woman who lived up in the woods, far off any paved road. Her tiny house was essentially a single room, furnished only with a chair, a cot, and a small table, atop which sat an enormous Bible. As I entered, she was already sitting in the lone chair; behind her stood her son, who appeared to weigh even more than Honey Ashmore and sported a beard that ran halfway down his overalls. He eyed me suspiciously as I squatted down in front of his mother and began asking her questions, careful to remain faultlessly polite.

About fifteen minutes into the interview, though, she suddenly stopped me in the middle of a question. "Say!" she said, seeming a bit agitated. "Wha'd you say your name was, again?"

"Richard Rubin."

"Rubin!" she exclaimed, slapping a hand on her knee. "Rubin!" She leaned over to scrutinize me, her eyes—nearly blind though they were—working up and down furiously. Her son mimicked her, and somehow looked much more dangerous in doing so. The two of them silently inspected me for a few very awkward, if not extremely uncomfortable, seconds. "Are you," she said, "a *Jew?*"

Now, at this point in time I'd been in Mississippi for about six months, and had often worked out just such a scenario in my mind; still, somehow, when it finally materialized, it took me entirely by surprise. And so I did what I usually do when taken entirely by surprise: I told the truth.

"Yes, I am," I said.

"Well!" she declared, leaning forward even further, tipping her chair onto two legs and pointing a crooked finger at my face. "Let me tell you something about Jews. *Jews,*" she said, drawing out the word to several syllables as her son grew ever more massive overhead and I attempted to calculate whether or not I could actually make it out to my car and start it up and peel away quickly enough, figuring that it would all come down to whether or not I had left my car door unlocked, and what kind of New York idiot was I, anyway, to lock his car all the way out here in the middle of absolute nowhere—"*Jews,*" she repeated a bit louder, then paused a tormenting extra second to draw in more breath, "are the *finest* people on this earth!"

And with that she pushed herself up out of her chair and ambled over to the table for her Bible, her son's face erupting into an immense grin, my own going completely slack with shock. The old woman leaned far over the book and flipped through it, pressing her face up almost to the page and pointing her finger to specific passages that declared the Jews to be God's Chosen People and the bearers of His Word. She hadn't seen one in many years, she explained, and had never had one in her house; it was, she crowed, a great honor. I don't recall how I managed to return to the interview, but as I wrapped it up and rose to leave, her son clasped my hand firmly, and she herself stepped forward and gave me a brittle hug.

I staggered out of the small house, dazed. One moment I had felt acutely anxious and threatened, and the next I was, quite literally, embraced. Six months after it had begun, my transformation in Mississippi was now complete: From being designated, solely due to the circumstances of my birth, an ambiguously defined and somewhat suspect alien; to being designated a white man; to being designated one of the nice people and a valued member of the local society; to being designated, solely due to the circumstances of my birth, one of the finest people on earth. I was flattered, of course, and gratified. But from that moment on, the capriciousness of it all would nestle in my mind like a burr, and gradually I would begin to comprehend, if never fully understand, the frustration and sadness and rage that must have been daily companions to the million or so Mississippians who, with equal capriciousness, had been designated undesirable and inferior and beneath contempt, solely due to the circumstances of *their* birth—namely, that they had been born black.

That kind of insight would come slowly. What would come slower still—and mercifully so—was the inkling that, in Mississippi, at least, someone like me could have been effortlessly raised up so high only because so many others had, with great effort, been kept down so low.

ॐ๛

But all of that would only come much later. At the time, all I really felt was a strange mixture of disorientation from the morning's bizarre encounter, and relief from having stayed up in the hills past the daily deadline. In all likelihood, I was also a bit giddy from being overtired (a function of my job), not to mention cocky (a function of my personality) and hyperactive (a function of all the coffee I had consumed in the newsroom that morning). The floodwaters were receding, revealing supple brown earth, its rich scent beckoning spring like a lover; the next deadline was still twenty-three hours away. So I started up my car, found my way to Highway 35, and was soon taking its rises and dips and curves at eighty miles per hour. And then, without planning or even realizing it, I was back in Vaiden. There was the little school, the vast cemetery, the Baptist church, the Methodist church, the Episcopal church, the Shongalo Presbyterian church, the three courthouses—the oldest pristine, the largest collapsing under its own tired heft, the newest still unfinished and unoccupied. Then I spotted Bud and Red Mama crossing Hirsh Street, heading toward the library. I rolled down my window and called out: "Hey!"

Bud started at the sound, but Red Mama didn't flinch at all, just turned toward me. "Hey!" they replied in unison, and walked over to the car.

"Stayin' away from them buzzards?" Bud asked.

"So far, so good," I said. "What are you doing now?"

"Just walkin'. What'd you have in mind?"

"What do you know about the cemetery?"

Red Mama laughed. "I know a little bit," she said. "I'm a founder of the Vaiden Cemetery Association."

"They're the ones take care of the place," Bud said. "They keep it up, and they're trying to raise enough to establish a trust-fund for perpetual care. As it is they keep it pretty nice, especially considering how big it is, and how old."

"It's just about the nicest cemetery in Mis'sippi," Red Mama said. "My husband just died a few months ago, and he's in there. And I'm gon' be in there someday, and Bud, too."

"Hush, Mama, let's don't talk about that now!"

"Will you show me around?" I asked.

"I don't see why not," Red Mama said. "We're just walkin' anyway. Come on, park that thing and we'll all walk up there."

I pulled over and got out and the three of us hiked up Hirsh Street, past the old Watkins house up on the hill, then cut through to Highway 35, dashed across and made our way up a short rise and onto a dirt path. Immediately, we were surrounded by gravestones—headstones and foot-stones and obelisks, limestone and sandstone and granite, solid and cracked and crumbling, tall and lean and short and squat and some just tiny, their inscriptions ranging from sharp and clear to fading and barely legible to vanished entirely. And directly in front of us, surrounded by an ornate black wrought-iron fence, was a massive marble seraph standing atop a pedestal, maybe fifteen feet tall, its eyes lowered toward the ground in mourning, its arm raised high, finger pointed toward heaven. Engraved in the pedestal was a likeness of the deceased, a somber-faced man in jacket and vest and cravat and surrounded by two draped urns, and beneath them was a long epitaph, carved in letters too small to read at such a distance. The word "gaudy" did not do it justice.

"That's Dr. Vaiden," Red Mama said. "His monument came all the way from Italy, it did. Cost ten thousand dollars, and that was more than a hundred years ago. It was so heavy that when they were transporting it a bridge collapsed under its weight. They almost lost it."

A bridge collapsed under its weight? What could have been worth all that? "Can I read the inscription?" I asked.

"Sure," Bud said. "Just open the gate and go in."

I did.

SACRED TO THE MEMORY OF
DR. COWLES MEADE VAIDEN

Born in Charles City County, Virginia, April 21, 1812
Removed to Mississippi in 1837
Died in Carroll County February 6, 1880

*In early life an instructor of the young, he afterwards became succes-
sively a Physician, an Agriculturalist, and a Merchant in all of which
vocations his integrity and industry were crowned with merited success
as well as with the esteem of all who knew him.*

*As a Husband he was gentle and loving, as a Friend sincere and
unchanging, as a Citizen, generous, public spirited and devoted to the
interest of his adopted State. In an ardent zeal for the more general
education of our youths, he showed the true spirit of the Philanthropist.*

*The wealth which rewarded his labors dispensed both public and private
with no sparing hand. Through the many ordeals of long and varied
life he held himself bravely, came out, at the last that
Noblest work of God is honest man.*

I let out a long breath.

"In't that something?" Bud offered.

"During his funeral," Red Mama said, "someone ran up shouting
'Horse thief! Horse thief!' And a bunch of the men ran off after the cul-
prit, and they caught him and then they came back and resumed. And do
you know that Dr. Vaiden never allowed any of his slaves to take his
name? We're descended from his nephew, Henry Merritt Vaiden. Dr.
Vaiden didn't have any children of his own." Except, I mused silently, for
this monument.

"Now over here is the oldest part of the cemetery. We call this the
Shongalo Cemetery. And here's the oldest gravestone in the cemetery: Eliza
Pleasants Wells. Died in 1837." Red Mama leaned over the small rectangular slab, comprised of an ornate inscription beneath a carving of a
sprawling weeping willow. "See here, she was just eighteen years, five
months and three days old. Her mama and daddy gave the land for this

cemetery. We're kin to them. And there's another one from 1837, James H. Cain. We're kin to him, too."

They certainly have, I thought, a very large extended dead family.

"Come on," Red Mama said, leading me to a small stone obelisk no taller than I was. There was a DAR badge stuck into the ground at its base, and a tiny, faded American flag. The wording on the stone was barely readable.

"That's old John Cain," she said. "Came to Shongalo from North Carolina. He was a drummer boy in the Revolution." She paused for a moment in reverence for that other war, the one that was won. "Used to be a whole mess of Cains in town. Old John migrated with a couple of his brothers, and they all had big families. We're kin to them."

"Mama," Bud sighed, "you done said that already."

Red Mama did not respond, but simply turned back to me and continued her tour. "Now over here is Captain John Hugh Wilson. He died . . . let me see here . . . he died in 1849. He was the first sheriff of Copiah County, down in south Mississippi." I glanced at the stone for a second, but my eyes drifted to a small white marker standing humbly next to the sheriff's. It read, simply: UNKNOWN MEMBERS OF THE FAMILY OF CAPT. JOHN WILSON.

"That's sad," I said. "How did that happen? Didn't they keep records?"

"Oh, you'd be surprised," Bud said. "It happened all the time. We don't know how many people are buried in here without markers, but there are plenty of them, I tell you what. Come, look over here." She led me across a broad open lawn to a new stone, low and wide, with a sharply etched, elaborate inscription:

CIVIL WAR 1861–1865
32 SOLDIERS KNOWN ONLY TO GOD

UNDER THE LEADERSHIP OF COL. BENJAMIN H. GRIERSON, A MUSIC TEACHER AND BAND DIRECTOR FROM JACKSONVILLE, ILLINOIS AND COL. PHILLIP H. SHERIDAN OF THE 2ND MICHIGAN CAVALRY.

"WITH MALICE TOWARD NONE, WITH CHARITY FOR ALL, WITH FIRMNESS IN THE RIGHT AS GOD GIVES US TO SEE THE RIGHT, LET US STRIVE ON TO FINISH THE WORK WE ARE IN, TO BIND UP THE NATION'S WOUNDS, TO DO ALL WHICH MAY ACHIEVE AND

CHERISH A JUST AND LASTING PEACE AMONG OUR-
SELVES AND WITH ALL NATIONS."

> *ABRAHAM LINCOLN'S*
> *SECOND INAUGURAL ADDRESS*

"Hmm!" I said, nodding my head. I certainly hadn't expected to find something so magnanimous here.

"Isn't that nice?" Bud said. "A local woman raised some money and had that made, Mrs. Mable Bruce. You know, let bygones be bygones."

Red Mama, however, did not look convinced. "I don't know," she said. "Tell you the truth, no one's even sure if those boys are theirs or ours. Now over here is one we know for sure." She walked me over toward the fence and knelt down beside a solitary arched sandstone marker, no more than eighteen inches high. She brushed aside some weeds so I could read it:

LUCAS.
C.S.A.
-ALABAMA-
DIED
1862.

———

"This boy was a soldier from Alabama," she said, "and he took sick around here and Mrs. Mary Pleasants—I'm kin to her—she took him in, nursed him in her own house, but he died anyway, and she buried him here."

"Was Lucas his last name or his first?" I asked.

"No one knows," she replied. "That's all we have on him, that one name: Lucas."

I shook my head and wondered if, in the subterranean community of Vaiden, the unknown dead were still alone and anonymous, or if everyone at that point knew everyone else's name in full, or if, perhaps, appellations were merely a vanity of the living and unnecessary beyond. Red Mama rose and slowly walked off, back toward the more crowded parts of the cemetery. I pulled a few more weeds away from Lucas's lone name, and followed her.

"Now here are the Kennedys," she said. "We took you by their house last time you were here. We're kin to them, you know. And here are the Kaiglers. They came to Shongalo very early, too."

I read their names—Augustus, Sarah, Julius, Henry—and thought of other names I had seen in the cemetery, too: Kalberg. Weis. Shamburger. Seelbinder. Gross. "Were they Jews?" I asked, timidly.

"Now, I don't rightly know," Red Mama said. "I always thought they might be, but I cain't say for sure."

"Where were the Jews buried?"

"Again, I cain't say for sure, but I imagine most of them chose to be buried up in Memphis, in one of the Jewish cemeteries they have up there, or maybe down in Vicksburg. But come on, let me show you something." And she took my hand and led me to a small plot of stones, the oldest tall and arched in alabaster. "This is Benjamin L. Rosenthal, born January 15, 1827, died November 7, 1889. He was a Jew, I know that for sure, and I think I remember knowing that he was called 'Mister Bennie' around town. And see that symbol etched up there, over his name? He was a Mason, too. And over here is his first wife, Nannie—she died young, you see, in her thirties—and here's his second wife, Elizabeth McCaskill, she's the one lived to be a hundred years old. And here's Bettie Rosenthal, the daughter-in-law, she gave me that beautiful piano we have, and here's the son, Leo. They were lovely people, just lovely. I remember one time, they came over to see Mama and Daddy . . ."

Red Mama's voice faded in my consciousness as I became distracted by one of the headstones in front of me, a broad, modern granite slab, plain but for a single flower carved in each of the upper corners. It was the epitaph, in particular, that distracted me:

LEO J. ROSENTHAL

FEB. 28 1873

MAR. 30 1944

ASLEEP IN JESUS

Red Mama must have noticed me looking; "Well," she sighed, "I don't reckon that's very Jewish now, is it."

I looked at her, tried on a small smile, shook my head.

"But I suppose that happens," she added. "You get away from the rest of your people and you get swallowed up. I imagine that's how it happened. The Jews who wanted to stay Jews moved to Memphis or Vicksburg or Natchez, or else their children did. The ones who didn't really care one way or another, they stayed here."

"What about that other fellow?" I asked. "The one who became a deacon at the Presbyterian Church?"

"Oh, he's over here," she said, and led me to an alabaster obelisk that was about as tall as I was. It bore a masonic symbol, a ladder ascending skyward surrounded by the letters "K. S. H. T. W. S. S. T.", underneath which was carved:

IN MEMORY OF

CHARLES KOPPERL
DIED
JAN. 1, 1865
AGED
51 YEARS

"New Year's Day, 1865," I said. "How did he die? In jail, up in New York?"

"No, no," Red Mama said. "They let him go, eventually, and he was mustered out, came back home. He was nearly fifty by that time, I suppose, and maybe he'd been wounded or something, or maybe they just wouldn't let him fight anymore, I don't know. But he came back here and settled in, and he was a big man in town, now, one of the best, and he lived in a very nice house right here in town, and he was here when Grierson came through. Now this was New Years' Day, 1865, like you said, and the Yankees, they had a group of cullud soldiers with them. Well, these cullud soldiers, now, they were here to loot, you know. And they marched on up to Major Kopperl's house to do just that, but he came out and met them on the porch. He had a watch, and they wanted it from him, but he wouldn't give it up. So they shot him, right there on his own front porch. And that's how it happened."

She spoke of it as if she'd witnessed the whole thing, even though it had happened a half-century before she was born. It seemed to me that she was still traumatized by this act, and it was suddenly obvious to me that the death of Major Charles Kopperl had crippled Vaiden, and that Vaiden had never really recovered. It had once been a bold place, confident in its ability to carve itself out of the wilderness, to live amongst the Choctaws and the copperheads, to thrive in its own remoteness, to become the wealthiest town of its size in the state, to survive a raid from the dreaded Gray Ghost. But there was blood over the town now. There was fear—not much, but enough to blunt their pioneer steel. There was defeat in their past, and the memory of it would always be there with them, holding them back in some small way.

Something seized me right then, and I cursed myself for not having been born a hundred and fifty years earlier, for not having been one of that generation that got word of the Treaty of Dancing Rabbit Creek in 1830 and set out for the unsettled parts of north central Mississippi. I cursed myself for being born too late to be the postmaster of Shongalo, or to open a store or a tavern off Hirsh Street, or to swap stories with Mister Bennie Rosenthal and Doctor Cowles Meade Vaiden and old John Cain, or to set up a synagogue and a Jewish cemetery to keep Simon Lichtenstein and Joe Hirsh and Solomon Saber in town, or to tell Major Charles Kopperl to just hand over his damned watch. And then I cursed myself for not being able to meet Eliza Love Wells and the rest of Red Mama's dead kin and Captain John Wilson and the unknown members of his family and Lucas C.S.A. Alabama, and for the knowledge that whatever I might do in the future, I could no more be a part of Vaiden than I could go back and see and do all those things.

I turned away, not wanting Bud and Red Mama to see the pain I imagined was conquering my face; and as I did I spotted, a few yards off, something I had not noticed before: a fence, an ordinary steel chain-link fence, plain and low and modern, as out of place there as I was, behind which lay what appeared to be an entirely separate burying ground, its stones stubby and spread sparse and mostly overgrown, sitting side by side with the Vaiden Cemetery but quite obviously of a different piece entirely. "What's that?" I asked.

"Oh," Red Mama said. "That's the cullud cemetery."

The colored cemetery—kept apart from the white cemetery by an ugly little fence, a fence not high enough to keep out even a child, a fence constructed obviously not for security purposes but solely as a symbolic gesture. In the community of Vaiden's dead, I thought, names might no longer hold any significance, but skin color apparently still does.

And that right there, that frontier between the white and black Vaiden cemeteries—that was the high-water mark of my confederacy. A minute before, I had wanted, more than anything else, to shed what little remained of my sense of Yankee alienation and be wholly of the place, of Mississippi. Now, I began to feel grateful for that same sense of strangeness, to cling to the remnants of it, to understand that in the end, it might just be my saving grace.

TWELVE

BYE, BABY

*T*here was a place on Claiborne Road in North Greenwood called Webster's, a good-times-bar-and-grill type establishment that Jack and Vic and Karen and many of the other men and women who worked at the *Commonwealth* often visited after work to have a drink or two and perhaps some dinner. It was casual and loud, the kind of place where nothing seemed to matter very much, least of all who you were or where you came from or what you had done that day to earn your keep. I liked it, liked the shelter it seemed to provide from the newsroom and the rest of Greenwood, and at one point I was dropping in several times a week.

One night during this period I drove over in a rainstorm and, in the slick darkness, found myself not in the parking lot but stuck in some deep mud across the street. I stepped harder on the gas pedal but only managed to mire myself deeper; realizing the futility of the situation, I climbed out of the car and just stared at it sadly, shaking my head at the other cars speeding by.

Then a large black sedan pulled up alongside me and stopped. The driver, a middle-aged black man in a three-piece suit, stepped out and asked me what was wrong. I told him I was stuck.

He smiled sympathetically. "All right," he said. "Don't worry, we'll get you out. You start her up, and when I tell you to, hit the gas." And with that he stepped behind my car, the mud immediately swallowing up his shoes.

"But your suit!" I said. "I really should push."

"Don't worry about it," he said. "I'll have you out right quick."

"But—"

"Really," he said, still smiling, "I done this more times'n I can count. Go on."

I climbed back in the car and cranked up the ignition. "All right," he said, "hit the gas!"

I did, though not very hard, and the wheels just spun around in the mud as they had before. "Hold it a minute!" he called, then shifted around behind the car. "All right," he said, "now hit it hard this time!"

I did as he said, and after a second or two the car broke free and climbed back onto the road. I stepped out to thank the man and immediately noticed that his pants were now thoroughly covered with mud.

"I'm sorry," I said, rushing up to him. "Let me pay for the dry cleaning."

"That's O.K.," he said, still smiling. "You don't have to do that."

"I want to."

"No, no, it's all right," he said. "My dry cleaner owes me a favor."

I chuckled, then turned toward Webster's. "Well, at least," I said, "let me buy you a drink."

Again, he shook his head. "I appreciate it," he said, "but I couldn't."

"Come on," I said. "I insist."

"No, really," he replied. *"I couldn't."* And in that instant his smile changed just a little bit, enough for me to notice but not enough for me to discern how or why.

I thanked him and we shook hands and then he drove off, and I managed to get my car into Webster's' parking lot and went in and quickly found the *Commonwealth* table and greeted everyone and sat down. I told them what had happened and everyone laughed, and then the waitress arrived with menus and took our orders, and the evening began to seem like any other. But as we were waiting for our food, I started looking around—something I had never really done there before, since I had always regarded Webster's as one of the few spots in Greenwood where I didn't have to be a reporter. I looked at my tablemates and the people sitting at the other tables, at the men and women sitting on barstools and standing behind the bar and talking on the pay phones and running around with trays in their hands, and for the first time since I had started going to Webster's, it occurred to me that every last person in the place was white. And I understood, then, that the Good Samaritan hadn't been coy or excessively gracious in declining my offer. He was speaking the plain truth. He *couldn't* go in there.

Now, this wasn't anything new, certainly not in Greenwood. Many of the town's sit-down restaurants, including my favorite, the Crystal Club, were segregated. But they were old establishments, places that had been around since the days when segregation was a matter of law, and most of their patrons had been steady customers since those days. These places upheld a morally corrupt tradition, but they were open about it, and assumed no pretensions of transcendence. They were racist establishments, but at least they were openly racist.

Webster's, however, was new and young and assumed the pretense of abandoning pretension. Their atmosphere had been carefully crafted to exude the impression that everyone was welcome there, which made the realization that some people remained yet unwelcome all the worse, at least in my mind. I had taken them at their word; now I knew better, thanks to the man who had helped me emerge from the mud.

I never saw him again.

৵৹ঌ

Whatever Webster's was, good and bad, there was one thing it wasn't: significant. True, Webster's was a de facto segregated restaurant in the age of integration; but it was a small place, situated neither downtown nor out on Park Avenue, and it maintained a fairly low profile. It stood not as a defiant symbol of segregation, but as a little establishment overlooked by the forces of integration, like one of those little white puffs that fall ubiquitous to the sides of Delta highways in the wake of speeding cotton trucks. Besides, calling the late 1980s the age of integration in Mississippi would be a statement of extremely dubious accuracy, not because of how many institutions in town were still segregated, but because there didn't seem much hope that any of them would be desegregating anytime soon—anytime at all, really. The people who had marched and fought in the 1950s and 1960s for school desegregation and black voter registration were old and tired. The next generation, the ostensible heirs to their movement and beneficiaries of the progress they had won, didn't know much about the previous generation's struggle, and didn't seem to care. In fairness, they had other things to worry about—drugs and crime and severe poverty and poor educational facilities and rapidly dwindling employment opportunities. But they didn't appear to stand for anything, really, except maybe a determination to survive somehow.

This decided lack of idealism was particularly striking in a place like

Greenwood, a town that was shot through with reminders, living and dead and inanimate, of the civil rights movement. In the years following the Civil War, a large proportion of Mississippi's state budget was dedicated to the care of Confederate veterans who had been crippled and maimed during the War Between the States; this image, of a state overrun with hobbling amputees, was one that often entered my mind as I made my way around Greenwood and the rest of the Delta. The civil rights movement had hit the region like a cold civil war, and its veterans, while not usually physically handicapped, still bore deep psychic wounds, no matter which side they had been on.

They bore a certain degree of celebrity, too. One afternoon, I was walking down Howard Street with Joe Martin Erber when he gestured, subtly, at a skinny old man in a straw porkpie hat strolling on the opposite sidewalk. "You know who that is?" he quietly asked me.

"No, who?"

"That, Richard, is Byron De La Beckwith."

I froze for a second, stared tactlessly at the man who had shot Medgar Evers in the back. "You *know* him?" I asked, stunned.

"Sure," Joe said. "Everybody in town knows Dee Lay. His wife and my mama were den mothers of the same Boy Scout troop. He used to say my mother was one of the finest ladies he knew." He laughed. "Even if she *was* a Jew lady."

I looked at Joe for a second, then shrugged and continued walking. By then I knew better than to be surprised that a man who was known by almost everyone in Mississippi—even by me—to have assassinated an icon of the civil rights movement could just saunter blithely through town unmolested and unconcerned. After all, a former member of the local chapter of the Ku Klux Klan worked in the newsroom at the *Commonwealth*, just a few yards from my desk, and never failed to treat me as if I were his own nephew. One leader of the old KKK organization lived just a few blocks from me; another was a founder of Carroll Academy and still sat on its board. The founder of the national White Citizens' Council, the most powerful segregationist organization in the country during the 1950s and 1960s, lived nearby in Itta Bena and was one of the most respected men in Leflore County; he had been a founder of Pillow Academy, and still gave the school generous financial support. And it seemed that most of the white people I knew—those of a certain age, that is—had belonged to the Council's local chapter at one time or another. It was rumored to still meet once a month on the second floor of a bank downtown, just as the Klan was rumored to still meet at the Delta Burger.

They were the extreme, to be sure, but Greenwood was full of other people, more moderate in appearance and reputation, who were at heart unreconstructed rebels still lamenting the second Lost Cause—white men and women, middle-class and professional, who yearned for the Greenwood of their youths, who spoke mournfully of what had happened to the public schools and Whittington Park and downtown, who refused to acknowledge Martin Luther King's birthday as a holiday and instead referred to it as "Robert E. Lee's Birthday," who groused about the abuse of power by the federal government and the usurpation of states' rights. Not a day passed—in truth, scarcely an hour passed—without someone casually tossing the word "nigger" about in conversation with me, not in anger or fear or disgust or contempt or even in an attempt to gauge my reaction, but simply because they had always used it and saw no reason not to now.

I said nothing, of course; I had long since learned to do so, an effort that went back to my encounter with Carl Kelly, Junior on my first day in Greenwood. I gradually trained myself to avoid wincing visibly, as well. But I also sought out the company and conversation of veterans of the other side of that cold civil war, people in whose presence I could sit without feeling like a spy, whose stories I could nod to without feeling like a liar and a fraud. It made me feel better to do so, better about Greenwood and humanity, though mostly just better about myself.

Unfortunately, such company was hard to find, such conversation harder still. With few exceptions, the men and women who had been the foot soldiers in the war against segregation in Greenwood, people who had fought terrible battles outside the Leflore County Courthouse and the Jefferson Davis Elementary School and had in the process made unthinkable personal sacrifices, did not carry themselves about as heroes, and did not speak of their heroism. Whether it was due to humility or some vestigial survival instinct or a combination of the two, they looked and acted like everyone else and, when asked about the 1950s and 1960s, simply shrugged and muttered that those were some bad times. I did not press them on the matter; as much as I wanted to hear their stories, I wasn't willing to force them to revisit memories they obviously would have preferred, for the most part, to let alone.

There was one story, however, that I wanted to hear more than any

other, and as my months in Greenwood passed, I only became more determined to do so, no matter what I would have to do to get the one person
who still could to tell it to me.

⁂

During my first six months at the *Commonwealth,* I confided in several of my
colleagues that I was fascinated with the murder of Emmett Till, if not
obsessed, and that I had a keen interest in meeting and talking to anyone
who had been personally involved in any facet of it. Almost everyone
reacted to this by laughing and dismissively wishing me luck, and for a
while I satisfied myself by driving out to Money and sniffing around the
building that had once been Bryant's Grocery and Meat Market, the building where Emmett Till had had what would prove to be a fatal encounter
with Carolyn Bryant. I would pull up and park across the road and just
stare at it for a few minutes—the loose screen pocked with holes, the sagging second-story enclosed porch, the rusty sign that had become partially
detached and limped out from the wall like a flag on a still summer afternoon. The Bryants were long gone, or so I was told, and the place was now
another small grocery, this one called Young's. Invariably, after a few minutes, I would get out of my car and stroll across the road, slowly enough
that I could examine the little building more closely while pretending to be
on my way inside to buy something or other. I would search the dirt on
either side of the front steps, trying to discern where the tables had been,
tables upon which someone had once set out checkerboards and around
which Emmett Till and his cousins and their friends had gathered that
afternoon, talking and joking and clowning until the fourteen-year-old
from Chicago passed around a picture of a white classmate and told the
stunned and disbelieving others that she was his girlfriend. And after a
short while I would slowly and with a false and shallow calm saunter on
into the store itself and greet the clerk behind the counter and engage in
meaningless conversation for no other purpose than to allow me to study
the counter itself and silently postulate: she stood there, a little to the left,
probably, and he stood here, right on this spot where I am right now, right
here. And after another short while I would step back and glance briefly at
the shelves and then turn back and say good-bye and leave, never buying
anything because I had no use for Vienna sausage and sardines and deviled
ham and because, more important, I did not wish to patronize the place,
no matter what it was called these days. Still, I went back there often for

the first six months or so of my time in Greenwood; by *often* I mean once every few weeks—frequently enough to sate my curiosity without arousing suspicions, or so I hoped.

Then one night, I was sitting in the gym at Pillow Academy with Jack, watching a bad basketball game and feeling profoundly bored; Jack perceived this and took pity on me. "Hey, Richit," he whispered loudly. "Y'see that guy settin' across the way there in the plaid shirt?"

"Which one?"

"The one that's kinda orange and yellow?" He started to raise a finger to point, then caught himself and tried to gesture with his eyes instead. "Stocky guy with the black hair slicked back? Three rows up from the floor, settin' next to the blonde lady?"

"O.K.," I said.

"That's Ray Tribble. Lives on a big farm outside Money, one of the biggest cotton growers in the area. Gave a ton of money to this place."

"All right . . ."

Jack paused, looked around, dropped his whisper a level or two. "He was on the jury."

"What jury?"

"Shh!" Jack spat. "Sound carries in here." He looked around again. "The jury that let those two guys go that killed your friend."

"What—"

"Up in Money."

I straightened up suddenly and jerked to look at him, then at the man, then him, then the man. "You mean—"

"Damn, Richit!" Jack said, jabbing an elbow into my side. "Keep it down! Everyone in the fuckin' place can hear you!"

"Sorry," I muttered. I stared at the man for a few seconds more. "Are you sure?" I whispered.

"You damn near made the ref call a time out!"

"No, I mean about—"

"Would I have told your Yankee ass if I wasn't?" He raised a cup to his mouth and spit into it. "Listen, Richit," he said, offering a faint conciliatory smile, "let's just keep it between us, all right?"

I nodded my head, but as I did so it occurred to me that everybody in that gym—players and coaches and cheerleaders and parents, and every last one of them white—knew exactly who that man was, knew what Jack had just told me, and that none of them cared one bit. I looked at the players. They're too young, I thought. They might not. But their parents do.

Not long after that, I was sitting in the newsroom, languishing after deadline, when I saw another man, reed thin and in his seventies but with still sandy brown hair, walk into the newsroom, shake J. O.'s hand as if he'd known him for years, and step into the publisher's office, shutting the door behind him. Karen spun around in her chair to face me and leaned in close. "You see that?" she said, winking at me. "That guy was one of the lawyers who defended those men." By then I didn't have to ask just who "those men" were.

"What's his name?"

"John Whitten," she said, speaking out of the side of her mouth like a gangster in an old movie.

"Like the congressman? The guy who's been there forever?"

"That's *Jamie* Whitten. His cousin. Big family in Tallahatchie County. This guy, John Whitten, he still practices law out of the same office as he did then, up in Sumner."

"I'd love to talk to him about it," I said, but Karen just laughed and told me that would be an excellent way to start collecting unemployment.

Even Dan Johnson, the senior reporter with whom I rarely spoke at all, somehow had learned of my apparently peculiar interest and had decided to foster it. One afternoon, as we sat next to each other at a county board of supervisors meeting—I was there to cover it, he for reasons known only to himself—he leaned over and said, too loud for my comfort: "You see that guy over there? The old guy?" He twitched his elbow in the direction of another man sitting in the gallery, maybe eight or ten seats away from us.

"Uh-huh."

"Well," Dan said, grinning and bobbing his head, "that was his gin fan they used on that boy up in Money. To pull his body down when they threw him in the Talla—"

"I know what they did with it," I said, trying hard not to look over at the man. "Did he give them the fan or did they steal it from him?"

"I don't know. I know they was never tried for stealin', I can tell you that."

"Maybe he gave it to them without knowing what they wanted it for."

"I don't know."

"I mean, why would he do it otherwise?" I said. "It doesn't make sense. I can't believe he knew what they were going to do with it." Then I remembered that I was speaking to Dan, the man whose greatest pleasure as a reporter came from covering stories involving some kind of rape, and I shut up.

Back at the newsroom, I related the story to Karen, who merely shrugged and said: "Yeah, I knew that."

"You did?" I said. "Why didn't you tell me?"

"You dit'n ask. And what are you going to do with that little tidbit anyway? Go interview the guy?"

"I might."

She laughed. "Right," she said. "And while you're at it, why don't you interview the killers, too?"

"I didn't know they were still alive."

"One of them in't," she said. "But the other one's got himse'f a store up in Ruleville. That lady's husband. Ex-husband, I hear it. I can tell you exactly how to get there."

"Good!" I said, stiffening with bravado. "Maybe I'll just go on up there and do that!"

"Go on," she smirked. "You're free, white and twenty-one."

"O.K.," I replied, and then added, with a glaze of self-righteousness: "And for your information, I don't care for that expression."

Karen stopped smiling, lowered her eyes, nodded her head. She was, in my limited experience, a rare creature—a white Mississippian who was deeply and personally wounded by the ubiquitous racism endemic to her state.

"Me neither," she said.

♣♣

I knew better than to run such a story idea by Mike first, and decided to go over his head and ask J. O., despite the fact that we'd had words that very morning, when I returned from a break to find him sitting at my computer terminal. "Uh, *excuse* me," I'd said. "I was using that." He'd stared at me incredulous for a second or two, and then exclaimed, his voice loud and high: "Tell me, Richard, who's the publisher of this newspaper, and who's the cub reporter?"

But now he was out of his office, and Edna, the receptionist, had no idea when he might return. Desperate to discuss the matter with someone, anyone, I ran into Vic's office, figuring he'd have some insights on the story.

I was right.

"S'a damn shame," he said, then took another gulp of his beer.

I nodded, but quickly looked away, unsure of what he'd meant.

"Hell," he sputtered, "this thing happens, and it's ugly and all, but it happened and the kid's dead and he's not comin' back. But then these reporters and TV crews come in from all over the world, Richard, and they just set out to make us look bad. All they wanted to do was make us look like a bunch of savages, to make Mis'sippi look like the most backward place in the country. Hell, in the world. Worse than the jungles of Africa, with the cannibals."

"Well," I said, "it was a pretty brutal thing, and those guys just got away with it, scot free."

"See, Richard, this is your problem," Vic answered, shaking his head to express his disappointment in me. "You've only heard one side of the story. Who wrote those books? I bet they've never even set foot in this state."

"The story's pretty well known."

"You see? There you go. You're an expert on the whole thing already. Tell me, how long you been here?"

"I don't know. Almost a year."

"Almost a year! Well, forgive me, sir! I've only been here goin' on forty-five years. But then, I reckon you know better."

"So tell me, then."

"Gladly." Vic polished off his beer and tossed the bottle into the garbage can. Then he pulled another bottle out of the cooler he kept under his desk and cracked it, unleashing a sound like a tiny snare drum being punctured. "Let's talk about what you 'know,' first. Now, what did that kid do in that store?"

"*Do?*"

"Did I stutter? What did he *do?*"

"He didn't *do* anything," I said.

"Not a thing, huh? They just came and took him away for nothing?"

"They said he 'acted fresh.' He mumbled 'Bye, Baby' on his way out the door."

"That's it?"

"That's it."

"Nothing else?"

"Nope."

Vic put his beer down on the desk and leaned over, putting his round, cherry face within a few inches of mine. The smell of a waning fraternity party drifted out of his mouth, but Vic's eyes were as sharp and focused as I'd ever seen them. "Now, I want you to do this, Richard," he said. "You call up that fancy Ivy League college of yours, and you tell them to give back your mama and daddy all their hard-earned money, because they didn't teach you a *Goddamn thing*. That boy didn't walk in there and just mumble 'Bye Baby' or nothing like that. He grabbed that woman and he pinned her hands down and then he put his hands all over her and he rubbed his body all up against hers and pushed his pecker up against her through his pants. *That's* what that boy did. And I'll tell you something right now: If he'd a did that to *my* wife, or *my* little girl, I'd a shot him just as dead, and so would you."

"Well," I said, startled at Vic's vehemence but determined not to back down. "I've never heard *that* story before. What makes you think *that's* the truth?"

"Hell, everybody knows that's the way it happened! You just ask around. Go on!"

"Funny you should say that," I offered. "I was thinking about going up to Ruleville to talk to Roy Bryant. Maybe I'll interview him for the paper."

Vic laughed, so hard he had to put his beer down on a spreadsheet. "Whoa, there, pardner. Let's not get carried away, now. You're not going to do any 'interview' for this newspaper, not with that man. J. O. wouldn't touch that one in a million years."

"Why not?"

"'Why not?' Son, are you tetched? Can you just imagine the fire that would rain down on J. O.'s head if he ran that story? Hell, he's lost half his advertisers already because they think he runs too many pictures of niggers in the paper. He's not gonna go piss off the other half just for your sake."

"But it would make a hell of a story. Isn't that what's really important here?"

Vic sighed, picked up the bottle, and took another drink. "Richard, you know I like you," he said, reaching out with his free hand and patting my shoulder. "Hell, I might even let you date my daughter, if you weren't a damn Yankee and a pinko, to boot. But there's something you just don't realize, when you come down here and start yellin' about the blacks and racism and stirring up all kinds of old stuff that should just be left dead and buried. You don't see any problem with that, because someday, when you're through here, you're just gonna pick up and move on back to New

York or to Los Angeles or someplace else. But when you're long gone, I still have to live here, and so does J. O., and so does everybody else in this place but you. This is our home; we got *no place else* to go."

Vic tipped back his head then and polished off the bottle. He turned and tossed it toward the garbage; it hit the rim and fell down onto the first bottle, the clink muffled by wadded-up paper towels and Styrofoam cups and the rest of the trash. "Damn," he said. "Richard, I gotta get back to work."

🐾🐾

Vic was right: J. O. informed me coolly, when he returned a few minutes later, that I would not be interviewing Roy Bryant for his newspaper or any other, at least as long as I worked for him.

I decided to drive up to Ruleville anyway that afternoon. I didn't know what I would do when I got there, whether I would actually have the nerve to go into Roy Bryant's store, what I would say or not say to Roy Bryant if I did find the nerve. I drove slowly, and used the extra time to search for a compelling reason to go complete the trip or abandon it. I found neither, and when I arrived at the store, nearly an hour later, my impetus was nothing more than inertia.

The store itself was a small shack, a former gas station that bore no sign, at least none that I could see. It sat a few blocks off Highway 8, which was itself nothing more than two paved lanes that ran for fifty miles between the Mississippi river and I-55. The little store sat in the middle of what appeared to be a black neighborhood; I wondered why the man had chosen to open his store here, or if any of his customers knew who he was and what he'd done thirty years earlier, just a few miles away. Maybe they did know but went there anyway; maybe they coexisted under some kind of uneasy truce that both parties recognized as distasteful but necessary. After all, he needed to make a living, somehow, and they needed to eat. Piggly Wiggly wasn't about to open a store here.

I pulled into the parking lot and cut the motor. I sat there, hands on the steering wheel, wondering what I was going to say to this man, how I was going to ask for an interview, how I was going to respond to the excuses and recriminations and outright lies I was sure he'd offer—that is, if he didn't just pull out a gun and shoot me, too. I didn't really expect him to do that, but on some level, I think, I wanted him to. Not to shoot me, of course, but to threaten me, maybe, to do something that would allow me to empathize with this fourteen-year-old kid, thirty-three years dead, to feel the kind of rage I wanted to feel but couldn't, not for something that had happened more than a decade before I was born. I imagined I was about to get close to some sort of pure historical evil, the kind that people read about for many centuries afterward but can never really hope to understand, or even envision, separated from it as they are by so many years and sensibilities. I wanted to get as close to it as I could; I worried—stupidly—that I might never have the chance again. I had a microcassette recorder and a reporter's notepad in my jacket pocket.

Pulling the flap over the obvious bulge in that pocket, I opened the car door and climbed out onto the burnt cinders that covered the tiny parking lot. There were flowers planted out in front of the store. Flowers!

I walked up to the door and stopped. It was warped and splintering, badly in need of a couple of coats of paint; the screen, having peeled away from the upper right corner, lilted down, its wire ends frayed and splayed. The ancient wooden boards underneath my feet creaked ominously. I looked down: The cinders had left black streaks all over the cuffs of my chinos. I hoped they weren't stained.

I pushed the door open and stepped inside. There was nobody behind the counter, nobody in any of the aisles. The place was dark, lit only by two or three yellow bulbs.

There wasn't much to see: Mostly rickety shelves, stocked with the very same kind of provisions I had found in his old store over in Money, and a lone cooler. There was a cat sleeping in a back corner, curled up on some newspaper; I almost laughed at the sight of it, a pet I associated with sweet old ladies, not killers. Where was the German Shepherd, the Doberman, the Rotweiler? A cat? A cat that looked like it had been sleeping for years?

I walked toward the counter and peered through the door that led to the back room; there was a light on in there, but no shadow. Where was this guy? Would he just walk away, leaving the cash register wide open? That wasn't really so uncommon here; actually, people did it all the time, retiring to some back room to watch TV or play cards or smoke, trusting that their customers would alert them when the time came to pay for something. Still, it seemed strange, knowing this man's history and who his clientele were. Maybe someone had warned him I would be coming. But that was impossible. No one knew. Well, no one except Karen and Vic. And J. O. But they didn't know for sure; I hadn't told them I was going that very afternoon. And they wouldn't have called, would they? They didn't know the guy; and this place didn't even appear to have a phone, anyway.

I walked back down the center aisle toward the snacks, picking up a package of cheese-and-peanut-butter crackers. I tapped them against my wrist and stared lazily at the shelf, looking for a better option. There they were: Moon Pies. The old Southern staple, two cookies sandwiching molten marshmallow, covered by chocolate. They were a bad habit I'd picked up during my time in Mississippi, sweet and messy and possessed of absolutely no nutritional value and I knew it, but I couldn't help myself; they tasted too good. I grabbed a second one and pulled a Coke out of the cooler, too. I didn't intend to buy any of it—if I couldn't bring myself to spend money at Young's, how could I possibly do it here?

Just then, he appeared behind the cash register and smiled. Smiled. My God, he looked exactly the same as he had in that picture taken after the trial, except that his hair was much thinner and his waist much thicker and his lips seemed shrunken and there was no cigar in sight. But those eyebrows were as wide and black as they'd been in those old news photographs. And he was younger than I imagined he'd be, not yet sixty. And he was *smiling* at me.

"He'p you, sir?" he asked. He called me *sir.*

"Uh . . ." I said, a bit dazed, then slowly approached the counter and laid down the Moon Pies and the Coke. "Uh, just this," I mumbled, assuming what I hoped was a reasonable impersonation of a Southern accent. It seemed to work.

As he rang it up, I saw his wrists shake. The register was as old as everything else in the place, one of those mechanical behemoths with punch keys and numbers that popped up on cards behind a window. It was a struggle for him to push those keys; his hands, pale and bony and covered with dark spots, moved between them with trepidation.

I dug a five out of my wallet and tried to hand it to him before he'd finished ringing it up, but he doggedly continued hunting for the right numbers. At one point, he picked up a Moon Pie and, squinting, held it up not three inches from his nose. "Don't mind me," he said, smiling. "I'm just legally blind."

Divine retribution, I thought. A lightning bolt to the eyes. Years later, after he was dead, I would learn that it had been much slower, much more pedestrian—he'd actually destroyed his own vision by working as a boilermaker, a profession he'd taken up after local blacks had boycotted his store out of business, and local whites had refused to stake him the money he needed to start farming. His training as a welder had been paid for by the G.I. Bill.

He took my five-dollar bill and pressed the 'sale' key on the register, throwing the drawer open. He fumbled around in the change. "Napkins?" he asked.

"Yes, please," I said, accidentally dropping my fake accent for just a moment. It was enough.

"Say," he said, squinting now at me as he pulled a few napkins from the top of a stack and mixing them in with my change. "You're not from around here."

My face suddenly felt hot; a faint tingle raced across my scalp. "Pardon me?"

"Y'accent. Where you from?"

"Greenwood."

He smiled, snorted; I could not have imagined a sight so strange as this man smiling at me. "No, really," he said.

"Really, I live in Greenwood."

"But you weren't born there, now, were you."

I tried to laugh myself, but it came out as a squawk. "Is it that obvious?" I asked.

"Well, I'll tell you," he drawled. "Not many folks around here speak the way you do, sir." *Sir.*

"I guess not." I'm not sure how I arrived at the lie I spoke next, whether I consciously decided to do so or just did it reflexively, guided by some survival instinct. Whatever the case, what I said was: "I'm from St. Louis, originally."

It was a good choice. "St. Louis?" he said. "Really! I've heard a lot of nice things from there. Friend of mine went up there a few years back. Said he liked it a whole lot. Said everybody up there was nice as could be. For a bunch a Yankees, that is." He winked at me.

He *winked* at me.

I nodded. He still had my change in his hand; I thought he might never hand it to me.

Then he did, but he held back the Moon Pies as he fumbled around for a paper bag. "Well, then," he said, grabbing one by the edge and snapping his wrist, flipping it open. "What brings you to Mis'sippi?"

For some strange reason, then—maybe just because I wasn't thinking clearly—I told him the truth: "I'm a reporter for the *Greenwood Commonwealth.*"

He froze for a second with his hand, still clutching the Moon Pies, halfway immersed in the bag. I froze; my bones froze.

But then the color flooded back into his face, and he dropped the Moon Pies onto the bag's flat bottom, pulled his hand back out, and went for the Coke. He nodded, murmured something like "mm-hm." We stood there for a few seconds, nodding at each other, saying not a thing. I flicked my eyes down at my wrist, the one with the watch, but I couldn't quite see it without moving my head. It didn't matter; I could feel the time passing with every weak pulsing of the vein that was squeezed between my arm and the watch's band. I could feel it slipping by, but I couldn't do anything about it; and I believed, at that moment, that there wasn't much in this world that I could do anything about.

"Thanks for stoppin' in," he said without much conviction, and laid the bag down on the counter, still clutching one edge with his trembling hand. I stared at that hand: tan and spotted, callused and twisted, knuckles so sharp they looked like they would tear through his skin at any moment. That hand, I thought, that frail, brittle old pitiful hand had once pressed the barrel of a .45 up against the temple of a fourteen-year-old boy and pulled the trigger and got spattered with the kid's blood and brains. I could feel them now, running off onto my own hand as I reached out for the bag. I quickly scooped it up off the counter and turned to leave.

"Come on back now," he said, weakly.

I nodded without turning around and pushed through the old door. I stepped out into the parking lot and started walking toward my car, but then I stopped and slid my hand into my jacket pocket. I ran my finger over the tape recorder's buttons: I hadn't turned it on, hadn't even considered it. I had forgotten it was even there. I pulled my hand back out and continued on to my car. It wouldn't have made any difference. I didn't want to interview him for the *Commonwealth,* or anywhere else; I didn't want to hear what he had to say. What I did want was to not have driven up to Ruleville and gone into that store in the first place. I never told anyone at the paper that I did.

⊰⊱

As I was climbing back into my car, but before I turned the key and started it up and drove away as fast as I could, I tossed that bag, with the bottle of Coke and the two Moon Pies, onto the floor behind the front passenger's seat. It lay there, just like that, not moved or even touched, until I left Mississippi for good a few months later.

When I first started working at the *Commonwealth,* Mike McNeill would frequently tell me that while I might write well enough, I didn't have what it took to be a reporter; gradually, his opinion began to change and he said it less and less, until finally, after a few months, he stopped saying it altogether. And it was around that time that I started to suspect that he may have been right in the first place.

One morning, when it was my turn to shoot the local photograph, Mike picked up off his police scanner a bulletin about a house fire in East Greenwood and gave me the address. By the time I got there the blaze had been extinguished, but there were still plenty of firemen milling about the scene, including the chief. I asked him who had lived there, and he pointed at a man in a light-colored windbreaker bobbing in and out of the darkened shell of what had been, until that morning, someone's home. The fire had burned for only about fifteen minutes, but in that time it had completely consumed the interior of the little shotgun house. The chief said it had been an electrical fire. When I asked him if I could go into the house and take a few pictures, he nodded.

I wasn't even inside the door when the burnt air attacked my nostrils. It seemed sharper than usual, with more of a poisonous edge, as if it were plastic that had burned and not a man's house. There were no walls left, only charred wooden beams which had so many minute cracks in them they looked like the skin that covers a man's knuckles. I touched one and felt a chunk of it dissolve into soot in my fingers. The roof didn't look much sturdier; a hole about a yard wide had opened up toward the back, and sunlight charged through it, leaving a bright oval on the blackened floorboards. In one of the side rooms, I could see the remains of a couch—a wooden frame with a few springs curling up through the base like they were gasping for air. A mirror had fallen on the floor and broken apart when the wall it was hanging on had dissolved. It was hard to see how the shell of this shack was still standing. I felt adventurous just being in there.

I shot a few good pictures, and figured that between those and the ones I'd taken of the firemen, I was covered. Now all I needed was some information. But the guy in the windbreaker was nowhere to be seen.

"Sir?" I called. There was no answer. "Sir? *Sir?*"

Something stirred in the dark rear of the house, and the man suddenly moved into the bright oval on the floor, like an actor stepping into the spotlight.

"Sir," I said, "Richard Rubin, from the *Commonwealth*. Is this your house?"

The man nodded.

"Mind if I ask you a few quick questions?"

A shrug.

"Good. It'll only take a minute. Could I have your name?"

He looked confused, even offended. But finally, after a few seconds, he spoke. "John Austin," he mumbled.

"Could you spell that for me, please?"

"A–u–s–t–i–n."

"Were you here when the fire broke out?"

"Uh-huh."

"What were you doing?"

"Eating my breakfast."

"And what alerted you to the fact that your house was on fire?"

"Smelled smoke."

"So the fire didn't begin in the kitchen?" I glanced over his shoulder at an ancient, blackened refrigerator.

"No. There." He pointed at the room with the couch and the mirror.

"Are you sure?"

Again he looked confused. "I ran out. This is where the fire was."

He wasn't very talkative, but I got enough out of him for a solid photo cutline. I turned to leave, then stopped for one last look. John Austin was standing in his former living room, staring at the skeleton of his couch. It looked to me like one hell of a picture, just waiting to be taken. I got one off quickly; the flash alerted Austin, and he turned to me and stared mutely. I excused myself and left.

Now, getting good pictures for the paper was always tricky, even under the best of circumstances. For one thing, John Emmerich was too cheap to buy cameras for all of his reporters, so we had to supply our own. In my case, that meant an ancient Nikon that my father had given me, a camera so old and ungainly that in order to focus the lens on an object one had to look through the viewfinder and slide a lever back and forth until a yellow ghost image aligned itself with the image you hoped to shoot. J. O. was also too cheap to hire someone to work in the darkroom, so we were all responsible for processing our own film (which we spooled out of cartridges in short strips onto reusable canisters—another money-saving trick of J. O.'s) and printing our own pictures, both of which we did with the benefit of perhaps fifteen minutes of training. As a result, only a fraction of the pictures I shot came out well, and of those only a fraction survived the darkroom.

As it happened, though, on that morning that last picture I had shot of John Austin looking at his scorched couch came out very well indeed—the look on the man's face, as if he wanted to cry but were determined not to do so in front of the camera; the charred beam, with a small piece of singed posterboard still clinging to it, level with the man's head; the skeletal couch; the man's arms, hanging limp at his sides, like a boxer saying, "Enough!" It was a great picture, yes, and I was so proud of it that I went back into the darkroom after deadline and made myself a few more prints of it, glossy 8 x 10s.

A few days later, I pulled those pictures out of my drawer and looked them over again. But something strange happened: Instead of feeling proud I was overcome with shame, not for the pictures but for what I had done to get them. I winced as I remembered barging into John Austin's gutted house, brusquely asking him some questions and then just as brusquely turning to leave before picking up my camera to eavesdrop further on his grief and shock and capture it on film—not for his benefit but for mine, and for the benefit of nine thousand readers who didn't know him and didn't care about him. I remembered what Margaret had told me about the time her house had burned down, how she and Dean had lost so many things that money could never replace, how they had worried about where they would live afterward and that even when they found a place it was in a different school district and how she still had trouble sleeping at night sometimes because she thought she smelled smoke. Mike had congratulated me on the photograph, even mentioned entering it in a contest, and I could tell he was thinking that at last I was becoming a real reporter. And I believed that he was right. But I was also starting to believe that that might not be such a good thing, after all.

✧

One Saturday night in the late spring, I went on a date with a woman I had seen a couple of times already. Diana was twenty-one, had just graduated from Ole Miss, and would be entering law school there in the fall. Like most of the other women I had dated in Greenwood, she was perfectly pleasant, charming and intelligent and unfailingly gracious. That night we went to Lusco's, an old steak restaurant situated in the no-man's-land between downtown and East Greenwood. We were joined by her best friend, Jeannie, and Jeannie's boyfriend, Denton. Like Diana, they had just graduated from Ole Miss, and Denton would also be enrolling at Ole Miss Law that fall.

Much of Lusco's comprised several small private rooms—no more than booths surrounded by curtains, really—the kind of atmosphere that lends itself to frank conversation. Denton, possibly being protective of his girl-friend's best friend, tried at first to draw out my political beliefs and atti-tudes, but after a while, faced with my usual initial guardedness on such subjects, he gave up, decided I was O.K., and started talking about how "the niggers" were ruining Greenwood and the Delta and hell, all of Mississippi, and the only reason they hadn't ruined Ole Miss yet was because they were only about ten percent of the student body but that was gon' go up soon and you just wait, the niggers are sho'nuff gon' ruin Ole Miss, too, and then where would a white man be able to get a decent pub-lic education in Mis'sippi? And on and on he went, and at one point Diana turned toward me ever so slightly and flashed me a subtle look that said: Please don't hold this against me. I just smiled back at her reassuringly, but in fact I did hold it against her, as unfair as I knew that was.

And I soon realized it was even worse than unfair. It was completely hypocritical. The truth was that the only close white friend I had in Greenwood who *wasn't* racist was Karen. Most of my closest friends in Greenwood said things to me every day that were just as bad as Denton's little harangue, if not worse; and yet, these same people, people whose minds were shot through with ideas and prejudices I found utterly odious, were also some of the best friends I had ever had in my life, people who would have done anything for this New York Jew, even at great cost and perhaps danger to themselves. They were truly some of the finest people I had ever met; at the same time, though, there ran through them a repug-nant vein of bigotry that I could not seem to separate from all of the good in them. How could I? I asked myself if I could have understood and for-given my friend Erik Werner for befriending someone who was virulently anti-Semitic; in the end, I decided, I could not. How, then, could I expect Erik Werner to understand and forgive me for befriending so many racists? And how could I forgive myself? Still, how could I just dismiss them as friends after everything they had done for me, after they had gone to great lengths to make me feel welcomed and valued by Greenwood, after they had personally interceded with others on my behalf more times than I would ever know? How could I reconcile the fact that some of the very best people I had ever known were also, in that one sense, some of the very worst?

I couldn't. I refrained from thinking about it as much as I could, but as the months passed, those thoughtless intervals became shorter and less frequent, and in the end, it started to make me crazy. And that's when I knew I had to leave Greenwood.

Before I did, though, I came to understand just how good things had been for me in Mississippi by catching a glimpse of just how bad they could have been. One afternoon, as soon as I walked in the paper's front door, Karen rushed up and handed me a copy of the latest edition of *The Winona Times*, fresh off the press. "What's this?" I asked.

"Page two," she said, grimacing. "You'll see."

Winona was a small town about twenty-five miles east of Greenwood; the *Times*, its paper, was a weekly. Like most of the weekly papers in the area, the *Times* was too small and poor to have its own printing presses, so it had contracted with John Emmerich to use his. Once a week, Waid Prather, the *Times'* editor, would bring his page paste-ups down to the *Commonwealth's* newsroom and sit and wait while the presses churned out his newspaper. Frankly, I don't remember very much about Waid Prather, except that he was gangly and innocuous-looking and always wore suspenders, often with a belt; I doubt I ever had a real conversation with him. Apparently, though, I managed to make an impression on him, because his editorial in that week's paper was all about me:

> There's a Jewish fellow I've been running into on a regular basis of late who's found what he wanted.
>
> He hasn't necessarily gotten everything his life has to offer or even everything he's dreamed up, but when he came to Mississippi he found what he wanted.
>
> Or at least what he wanted to find.
>
> He had hardly been in the state any time at all before he began to downplay and bad mouth the state, the entire South for that matter, for its rinky-dink religion, its prosaic outlook, its pedestrian lifestyle, its prejudice and its pride.

In only a matter of weeks he had learned everything he'd been told about the South was just as it was. He was not disappointed.

But he no more understands what it is to be Southern, than I understand what it is to be Jewish.

Should an anthropologist go to some remote island and spend a few weeks, months, even a year, no more, then propose to explain what it meant to be a member of that island's society, his colleagues would laugh him to scorn.

No one even in a year's time could understand a people, even if they were met without preconceived notions.

I wouldn't even dream of going to New York, my friend's home turf, spend a few weeks or months working or living there and then announce how things were.

I don't pretend to know how it is to be Jewish, even though I've seen this ole boy almost weekly for several months, any more than I would explain the Catholic religion based on rooming most of two years in college with a Catholic . . .

"Isn't that just the ugliest thing you ever saw?" Karen said, looking as pained as if Prather had been writing about her instead of me. "And he has the nerve to say *you're* prejudiced! I'll never talk to him again!"

"Lemme see that," Jack said, trotting over and snatching the paper out of my hands. He read it quickly, then tossed it down on the floor. "That just ain't right," he said. "Richit, I'll be the first one to admit that you're a loudmouth and a Yankee bastid, but why'd he have to go on and make a big point outta you bein' a Jew? What the hell's that got to do with anything?"

"I don't know," I said. "But he seems to think it's important."

Jack was right: I was a loudmouth, and I had said more than a few disparaging things about the South right there in the newsroom; it was, after all, one of the only places I could really speak my mind without worrying about it affecting my ability to do my job. But I had never had such a conversation with Waid Prather, and I was surprised that he would attack me in print over things he had merely overheard me saying to other people, or perhaps had even just imagined I would say if given the opportunity. I wondered if the old axiom was, after all, true—that Southerners are unfailingly polite to your face and relentlessly vicious behind your back.

But ultimately, what I saw in that surreptitious attack was not the petty, spiteful prejudice and resentment of one man, but the absence of it in everyone else. If Waid Prather, with whom I'd never actually discussed the South, could nevertheless be so malevolent toward me, then how accepting and forgiving must have been my friends and coworkers in the newsroom, people who had heard me critique their native town and state and region more times than even I cared to count? And how many times had they defended me behind my back, to people like Waid Prather, without ever telling me so?

Inadvertently, they had flashed me the hands they'd been holding for most of a year, revealing to me all that had been and all that could have been; and while the memory of this encounter and of my colleagues' deep decency would, in the months and years to come, sometimes make me a little more crazy, I was very grateful for it. I could not have asked for a better going-away present.

⤳❦⤶

A few days later, I heard the news that Handy Campbell would also soon be leaving Greenwood—headed off to Starkville for what was certain to be a glorious role as quarterback for a different pack of Bulldogs. After a heady spring, during which he had received solicitous visits from dozens of college recruiters and coaches, Handy had signed with Rocky Felker and Mississippi State, as good a springboard to the NFL as any in the South. I was exceedingly proud; I suppose I had developed a somewhat proprietary sense about Handy Campbell's talent and his future, and I strutted around the newsroom as if *I* had been drafted by Rocky Felker.

After deadline I left the newsroom and drove over to Snowden Jones to congratulate Handy. I found him in the parking lot, tossing a football around with his brother and one of his sisters and grinning just as broadly as I had imagined he would be.

"Congratulations!" I called out.

He pivoted, tossed the ball to me. "Thanks," he said. He was quiet and subdued as always, but there was an electric quality to his movements and gestures that betrayed his combustible excitement. And that grin.

"When are you leaving?" I asked.

"A few weeks, I guess," he said. "I'ma be there on the first day they let me in."

"Am I going to see you on the Giants someday?"

"I don't know," he said, earnestly. "Maybe the Bears."

"So that's it, huh? Bye-bye Greenwood?"

He laughed. "That's right," he said. "I'm outta here for good."

ॐ

I left for good one morning an hour or so before dawn, easing out of my landlady's driveway in neutral to avoid waking her or any of the neighbors. It was a long drive back to New York, more than a thousand miles, and I wanted to get a good jump on the day. But I also left early just because I could; after nearly a year in Mississippi, a place few people ever visited or even passed through and fewer still ever seemed to leave, I could leave.

For most of that drive, and for much of the months and years that followed it, I tried to make sense of that fundamental contradiction I'd found at the center of Mississippi, of how I could scarcely find very good there without very bad, and very bad without very good, and how I couldn't figure out how to embrace one without appearing to accept the other, to reconcile the conundrum that had tugged and torn at the fiber of my sanity until I'd had to flee Greenwood in order to save what remained. Like Handy Campbell, I believed I would never return.

We were wrong, of course, both of us. He would return, utterly humiliated and defeated, only four years later. I would return, a year and a half after that, to witness the waking nightmare that his humiliation and defeat had wrought. I came back to see him literally fight for his life, tried for a crime I was certain he couldn't have committed; I came back because I believed that I had, at last, found a small arena in Greenwood where right and wrong were both pure, and separate, and about to square off against one another in battle. Handy Campbell came back to Greenwood in 1993 because he had nowhere else to go; I came back to Greenwood in 1995 because I believed that I had finally found there something that was not some or other extreme of gray, but a clean and clear-cut matter of black and white.

I could not have known then how gravely mistaken I was. Nothing in this world is a matter of black and white—not even in Mississippi, where everything is a matter of black and white.

PART TWO

A BAD PLACE TO BE

THIRTEEN

THE NEW OLD SOUTH

Leflore County Courthouse
Greenwood, Mississippi
Monday, May 22, 1995

I slipped into town late at night, just as I had the first time, even though now I was arriving by car rather than by bus. But despite the fact that this time I was not just coming but coming *back,* having once lived in the place for nearly a year, I felt exactly as I had that first time, seven years earlier, when I'd walked down three narrow steps and stepped onto the parking lot of the Greenwood Greyhound station: anxious; terrified; powerless. I drove through the town well under the speed limit, steered my rental car into the parking lot of the Greenwood Ramada Inn, cut the motor, and just sat there, unsure of what to do next, whether I should get out of the car and check into the motel, or start it up again and drive right back to the Memphis airport.

But when, just before midnight on Friday, May 19, 1995, I finally did open the car door and the hot, moist night air hit me in the face, my fear melted into memory—not of the *Commonwealth,* or of the Greenwood Bulldogs, or of Handy Campbell, or of my home in New York and the quest that had drawn me away from it and back to a place I'd believed I would never see again. It was a memory of Amanda Elzy High School, and of another hot, moist Friday night, this one back in September 1988, when I had covered my first football game, when I had emerged from another car and had been immediately overwhelmed by the voluptuous smell of the earth, a scent that I had never since encountered—not in

201

Alabama, where I'd spent a year in graduate school; nor in Memphis, where I'd lived and worked as a freelance writer for more than two years after that; nor anywhere else, north or south—nowhere else but here, where it again embraced me instantly and this time touched off in my mind a wild cyclone of memories so vivid and random and irrepressible that I actually looked around for fire-ant beds. There weren't any. Unlike Elzy's, this parking lot was paved.

The following Monday morning, as I stood outside the Leflore County Courthouse, where Handy Campbell was about to go on trial for capital murder, I was confronted with another assault of memories—of trials I had covered, interviews I had conducted, off-color sotto voce conversations I had been invited to join, all of them within these white walls. Mostly, though, I thought about the murder trial of Ronnie Ray Strong: how the whole thing, from the jury selection to the sentencing, had been disposed of in the course of a single morning, how the defendant's conviction had seemed assured from the moment the judge banged his gavel to start the proceedings, and how no one there seemed to care at all about any of it, not even the defendant. Was this what Handy Campbell could expect? Would his life be thrown away that quickly, with so little care and effort?

No. This is a capital trial. Ronnie Ray Strong had never faced anything more than life in prison. Besides, I thought, Strong was guilty. Handy Campbell is innocent. That takes longer.

I looked around at the courthouse, at the lush green lawn, at Market Street, bleached in the morning sun. There was that massive magnolia tree, that elaborate Confederate monument; there were those brick law offices, those wooden cotton brokerages, those concrete appliance shops and clothing shops and antique shops, those empty glass storefronts, that wrought iron and steel bridge tripping over the Yazoo into North Greenwood, the white neighborhood where the lawyers and cotton brokers and merchants all lived. None of it seemed to have changed a bit.

I walked up the steps and pushed open the door. Like the hot Friday night wind, the courthouse had a distinct and evocative smell—a combination of old documents and floor polish, air conditioning and hair tonic. It brought to mind that afternoon in Judge Gray Evans's chambers, when he had gloated about the draconian sentences he handed down every week, sparking in me a terror that in turn evoked a mild form of posttraumatic stress disorder whenever I found myself in his presence thereafter. It was that sensation, specifically, that this courthouse scent evoked in me that day; but when I walked into the courtroom and saw Judge Evans himself sitting on the bench and presiding over the selection of the jury that would try Handy Campbell, I felt not fear but merely surprise, and a vaguely warm sense of recognition.

And I thought: Greenwood may not have changed, but I have.

⁓

In fact, the Greenwood I had known had changed quite a bit, though not in ways that I could tell just by looking at buildings and trees and streets. There was, for instance, no one left in the *Commonwealth* newsroom that I knew, save for Tim Kalich, who was now the editor-in-chief. Dan was said to be working at a newspaper in Tennessee. Mike had returned to Arkansas. Karen had returned to McComb. Vic had left for an accounting job at a local furniture manufacturer. Margaret had left for an administrative job at Greenwood High School. Jack had left for a teaching and coaching job at Pillow Academy. John Emmerich, the man who had hired me and brought me down to Greenwood in the first place, had dropped dead while jogging up his driveway. When I had stopped by the newsroom that Saturday, on my first morning back in town, I felt as if I had returned to the house in which I had grown up to find another family living there.

I experienced the same sensation when I walked over to the practice field at Greenwood High School early Monday morning. The players I had known were all gone, of course, but so were the coaches. Mike Martin was said to be at a high school in Tennessee or Arkansas. Melvin Smith had left for a job coaching at Delta State, from which he was later lured away by Mississippi State. And David Bradberry had left to become head coach at the public high school in Clinton, Mississippi, an affluent, mostly white community near Jackson. The Greenwood High School varsity football team, which had in the fall of 1988 been split nearly even between black and white players, was now almost entirely black. So was Greenwood High School itself, which in less than seven years had gone from being just about fifty-fifty to being 92 percent black. The vanished whites had fled to Pillow Academy, which was now significantly larger than it had been back when I'd lived in town, and to Carroll Academy, which was more than twice as large as it had been, and to Cruger-Tchula Academy, which was ten times as large. I didn't know this Greenwood High School, didn't know these coaches and these kids. They seemed strange to me. They seemed less.

But then, almost everything in town did. I had gone by the synagogue, Ahavath Rayyim, that Saturday morning; it was closed, as it usually was Saturday mornings—the few congregants who still made an effort to hold services preferred to do so on Friday nights instead—but this time that fact struck me hard, as if the old temple would never be open again. I stopped by Goldberg's shoestore and Kornfeld's, went across the street to the Crystal for lunch with Leslie Kornfeld and Harry Diamond, visited Jack and Margaret and Vic and Celia Emmerich and Joe Martin Erber, drove over to Itta Bena and up to Carrollton and even out to Money, but I couldn't seem to connect to anything quite as acutely as I had before. There was a buffer there now, something that had sprung up between me and Greenwood at some point during the six years I had been gone. Everything was just as familiar as it had ever been, but for some reason I had trouble imagining that I had once lived and worked in this place for nearly a year, and not even that long ago. I felt like a visitor—not to anything in particular, just passing through.

The worst for wear was Vaiden, the town I had liked most of all outside of Greenwood itself. The 1905 courthouse, the thing that had first brought me to Vaiden, was completely gone. The little green hill upon which it had perched was now naked but for the Confederate monument, which looked much smaller than I'd remembered. Gone, too, was the old original courthouse—a boiler had exploded and demolished it. The worst shock of all, though, lay in the cemetery, where Dr. Vaiden's massive seraph no longer stood atop its marble pedestal, but alongside it, leaning against it, snapped from its base and cast down into the dirt, losing its confidently upraised arm in the process.

"Tornado did that," Bud Welch said as we gazed at the fallen angel; her mother, who had so energetically led me through this same cemetery the first time, was now ensconced in a nursing home over in Winona. "A few years back. Tore the place up pretty good, but this was the worst. And you wonna see somethin' else that's changed in here?"

"I don't know," I said.

"Come on, now," she beckoned and led me to a remote corner of the burial ground, which had once been the sole province of Colonel Grierson's men and the mysterious, mononymic Lucas. Now, the open green lawn was covered with identical arched white military tombstones, six rows of seven. I walked up and down, perusing the inscriptions: There were Mississippians and Alabamians, Tennesseans and Arkansans, even a Virginian. But not a Yankee in the lot.

"In't that something?" Bud exclaimed. "A few years back a historian came through town and told us there never was any Union soldiers buried here, not according to the records. Just our boys. Turned out we had it all wrong. Some time later he came back with the records, had the names of all the soldiers who really were buried here, so we sent out for these stones. Did a really nice job with 'em, don't you think?"

"Yes," I said, then turned and pointed at the back of the large memorial stone. "But what about Grierson's men?"

"We sent that back to where we got it, had 'em smooth it down and inscribe it again. Cost us a lot, too, tell you what. But they did some job, you cain't even tell there was ever another inscription on it. Come and see."

She led me around to the front of the little monument. She was right— it looked brand new, the letters sharp and bold, perfect:

DEDICATED TO THE MEMORY
OF THE CONFEDERATE SOLDIERS
KNOWN AND UNKNOWN
WHO GAVE THEIR LIVES DURING THE
WAR FOR SOUTHERN INDEPENDENCE
1861–1865
AND ARE BURIED IN THIS CEMETERY

I did my best to keep a straight face for Bud, to hide my distaste and disillusionment, but I was mortified. The Civil War, an honest disagreement, had reverted to the War For Southern Independence, a struggle against despotic oppression. Gone were thirty-two Union soldiers, known only to God. Gone was a music teacher and band director from Jacksonville, Illinois. Gone was President Lincoln's plea for a merciful reconciliation, his call to bind up the nation's wounds, his appeal to the better angels of our nature. Gone was a just and lasting peace among ourselves; gone were malice toward none, and charity for all. Left in their place was only defiance, as cold as the stone into which it was chiseled.

Perhaps, I thought, I should not be so surprised. Of late, I had come to understand that the Mississippi I had experienced in 1988 and 1989, as troubled and divided and segregated as it had been, was in fact a state at its progressive apex, a Mississippi better integrated and more harmonious than it had ever been before and, it now seemed, would ever be again. I knew very well that in 1991, two years after I had left Mississippi, the electorate had cast out Ray Mabus, the state's first and only New South governor, replacing him with Kirk Fordice, a businessman from Vicksburg whose attitudes and rhetoric reminded me of no one so much as Ross Barnett, the governor who had vowed to defend segregation to the death and had done everything he could conceive to keep James Meredith out of Ole Miss. Fordice represented what I was coming to regard as the New Old South, an unofficial but popular movement dedicated to stanching integration and federalism and progressiveness in general and returning to such old-fashioned values as de facto segregation, economic feudalism, laissez-faire government, and a defiant Southern pride tinged with a sense of extraregional persecution. The New Old South had transformed Mississippi into a Republican stronghold for the first time since Reconstruction; it had kept labor unions out, wages and public benefits and literacy rates low, and the clientele of the Crystal Club white. It had diminished the power of old civil rights organizations, held the line on the proportion of black students attending formerly all-white state colleges, and swelled enrollments at unaccredited private academies that were still all-white.

I knew all this. I knew that this movement, this state of mind, was powerful and diffuse, that it had reach. But I hadn't imagined that reach could extend all the way into a small-town cemetery and change the inscription on a tombstone. If this is what Handy Campbell is up against, I thought, he's as good as dead.

❧

On Monday, May 22, 1995, at 9:30 A.M., I walked into the courtroom on the second floor of the Leflore County Courthouse and claimed a seat in the back row, the only one that still had any available. Almost every other row, I would soon discover, was packed end to end with prospective jurors, seventy of them in all.

I dropped a notebook on the seat to hold it open for me and walked slowly around the edge of the courtroom to see what was going on up front. The judge was not yet present; nor were the defendants and their lawyers. But as I approached the prosecutor's table, I noticed that the door behind the judge's bench was open, and through it I could see there, standing in the stark white hallway that led to the judge's chambers and lawyers' conference rooms, Handy Campbell. He did not notice me, nor, it seemed, anyone other than the short, burly, bearded white man who stood directly in front of him. Rather, he stood hunched over, leaning in toward the man, his attorney—Lee Jones, who had been appointed by the court to defend him—who in turn leaned in very close to him in what I assumed to be an important last-minute pretrial strategy session. It was only a second or two later, after my eyes adjusted to the light, that I realized my mistake: The lawyer was merely cutting the tags off his client's new suit.

It was a dark suit, and it made Handy Campbell look at once more imposing and more respectable, although no doubt only the latter was intended. Lee Jones's suit was lighter and pinstriped and much more expensive, which only made him look to me like a nattily attired sprite. He seemed to have avoided aging since I had seen him last, and indeed, when I had talked to him on the phone a couple of weeks earlier, he spoke and sounded exactly the same as he had during the Donnie Gene Silcox affair, as if nothing that occurred in the past six years had touched him in any way. Handy Campbell, on the other hand, appeared to have lived not only his six years but Lee Jones's, as well, and perhaps a few more on top of those. Yet as he stepped into the courtroom, he merely looked down at the floor and betrayed no more emotion than he had while trotting onto the gridiron at Tupelo for the first time, which is to say: none at all.

Right behind him, though, strode in two decidedly more animated figures. Willie Perkins was calm, but buried in that calm, and none too deep, was the laconic yet brazen confidence he carried with him everywhere, even into this same courtroom on that morning he had walked in with Ronnie Ray Strong, a man whose defense boiled down to a vanishing set of brass knuckles and a shrug. Now he walked in with someone I had never seen before, the only person in this entire ordeal whom I did not already know: Lanardo Myrick, Handy Campbell's codefendant, the man who, I had already decided, had to have been responsible for whatever unfortunate misunderstandings and mistakes generated this whole ugly mess—who had even, perhaps, set Handy Campbell up for such a fall.

Yet Myrick thoroughly defied every vision of him I had formulated since I had first heard his name, during that Thanksgiving conversation with Jack. He did not look like a dangerous thug, a bad seed who had no use for the law except to violate it and cajole his friends into doing the same. He looked, quite simply, like a geek: Tall but absurdly skinny, with close-cropped hair, glasses that bore a striking resemblance to the safety goggles I had been issued in my tenth grade chemistry class, and an enormous exuberant grin, which he flashed liberally throughout the gallery until Perkins grabbed him by the jacket and gracefully shoved him into a chair. Even then, he turned around every few moments, smiling at whoever met his eye, as if he were encountering them at a party. All the while he clutched in his bony hands a large and thick volume bound by a red leather cover. I couldn't quite make out its title.

Soon the bailiff appeared and commanded all present to rise for the Honorable Gray Evans, and the judge himself walked in, his broad six-foot-three-inch frame cloaked by an enormous black robe with a swatch of blue velvet in the center and red piping on the sleeves, his face looking as if he were tasting something bad that he had tasted a great many times before and so could not be too offended, still a bit annoyed but resigned to it. (I jotted a brief description down on my pad, then added: "A stern Dave Thomas?") He wordlessly sat down and shuffled a few papers, and that was when I noticed that I was no longer terrified of the man, a revelation that made me a bit sad for the detachment it implied, but for which, nevertheless, I was quite grateful.

Judge Evans looked up and out over the jury pool of seventy local souls—split nearly evenly between black and white—and delivered a speech that sounded very familiar to me, a short lecture about how essential jury trials were to the American system of justice, and how exactly they fit into the picture. "Your duty is one of great importance," he intoned. "Even though you do not get paid very much, it is something we have to ask you to do in order for the jury system to work." He promised to move things along as quickly as possible. "I will assure you," he said, "that I will do my best to make sure that you do not have to wait any longer than absolutely necessary. Just remember that I have to wait with you, and I do not like to wait." A few people in the jury pool chuckled; the judge just glared at them.

"Keep in mind the importance of what you have to do," he continued. "Please don't request for me to excuse you unless it is very, very important." Then he ran through a list of qualifications for serving on a jury: "You must be neither an habitual drunk nor a common gambler," he said. "You must be at least twenty-one years old, a resident of Leflore County, able to read and write, and not been convicted of any crimes of infamy. If you are over sixty-five years of age you may be exempted, if you wish. Is there anyone here who would like to claim such an exemption?"

A hand shot up immediately; an elderly black man, Mister Campbell, told the judge he was eighty-two years old and was promptly excused. "Anyone else?" the judge asked.

For a moment, no one stirred; then another elderly black man, nudged by the woman sitting next to him, raised his hand.

"Yes?" Judge Evans said, pointing his gavel at the man.

"I'm eighty-three!" the man declared. The gallery broke into applause for the man, and the judge quickly dismissed him, too.

The judge asked the jury pool if anyone else had a good reason to be excused. One woman stood up and said her mother had just had a stroke and was in the hospital; another rose and announced that she was six weeks pregnant and suffering terrible morning sickness. Yet another woman said she lived in Itta Bena and had no ride to court, and a man slowly rose to his feet and said the same thing, then added: "I have arthur-itis."

"I do, too," Judge Evans said, then dismissed all four of them.

When they had cleared out, the judge pulled out the indictment and read it to the court. "The State of Mississippi versus Handy T. Campbell and Lanardo Myrick," he declared, in which the state alleged that on October 25, 1994, the defendants did "kill and murder Freddie Williams, a human being, against the laws of the state of Mississippi, and did also commit armed robbery." That was harsh, I mused, and blunt, and yet none of the charges struck me nearly as hard as the phrase "Freddie Williams, a human being." Gone was Freddie Williams the UPS driver who seemed to know everyone in town, Freddie Williams the flamboyant bon vivant who wore a shiny ring on every finger, Freddie Williams the gregarious stranger who had greeted me on my very first day in town and led me to suspect that Greenwood might not be such a scary place after all. None of that mattered here; only the fact that he had once been a living human being was relevant now. I wasn't sure whether I found that comforting or not.

Judge Evans looked out over the jury pool and asked: "Do any of you think you know anything about this case that you think might affect your judgment in deciding the guilt or innocence of these two defendants?" A half-dozen hands shot up. The judge asked them, one by one: What opinion have you formed? One by one, they answered: They did it. One by one, the judge thanked them, then dismissed them.

Next: "Have you seen anything, read anything, heard anything about

this case?" Nearly every remaining potential juror raised a hand. The judge
let out a groan, then continued. Anyone related by blood or marriage to
either one of the two defendants? Anyone know either of these two defendants? Could you lay that aside and act as if you don't know them, or do
you think this might affect your judgment? Anyone know Freddie
Williams?

This last question effectively killed the jury pool. Nine or ten people
rose and stated that they did know the victim—he delivered to their house
or their store, they grew up with him or had been friends with him as
adults. One woman stood up and told the judge that something very similar had happened to someone in her family. She, like almost everyone else
who had answered any of Judge Evans's questions, was dismissed.

And just like that, the jury pool had been reduced from seventy souls to
thirty-seven. Lee Jones slowly rose and, declaring that since both the prosecution and the defense could dismiss a dozen potential jurors for any reason they saw fit, the remaining pool of thirteen people—just enough for a
jury and only one alternate—was too small to offer his client a fair trial,
and so he was compelled to move for a change of venue. The judge asked
the prosecutors and defense attorneys to approach the bench. A moment
later, he announced to the gallery that he was granting Jones's motion. The
trial would be relocated to Batesville, Mississippi, sixty miles north, and
rescheduled for the end of July. The jury pool—still numbering thirty-
seven—just sat there, not sure what to do next. Judge Evans told them to
go home.

And then he himself stood up and walked out the door behind his
bench, followed by the prosecutors, and the defense attorneys, and finally
the defendants, each reshackled and then escorted out by a sheriff's deputy
and led back to their jail cells, where they would sit for another two
months. And when all of them were gone, the people sitting in the gallery,
spectators and former prospective jurors, slowly rose and filed out the
door, chatting and laughing, no doubt a bit more appreciative of their freedom for the experience.

And then there was no one left but me and the bailiff, who studied me
for a minute or two until, apparently satisfied I wasn't a vandal, he turned
and walked out the back door. And I just sat there some more, not because
I was stunned or tired or uncertain what to do next, although I was in fact
all of those things. I sat there because, unlike everyone else who had been
there, I had no place else to go. I had traveled more than a thousand miles

to witness a trial that wasn't going to happen, at least not now and not here.

Eventually I rose and left the courtroom, walked down the stairs and out through the courthouse's front doors. Out on the front steps I found Lee Jones, who was himself just leaving the courthouse and heading back to his office across the street. We shook hands, and I asked him if he had been surprised at how quickly the jury pool had been annihilated.

"Surprised?" he laughed. "Hell, I was shocked. I had no idea the queer was that well-liked!" I did not immediately comprehend that he was referring to Freddie Williams; and even after I did, I considered the remark nothing more than a casual quip tossed off by a man who saw no reason to give much thought to what he said before he went ahead and said it. Only much later would I come to understand that it was anything but.

Lee Jones grabbed my hand once more and shook it vigorously, then charged off toward the plain two-story townhouse that housed his office. And then I was alone again, standing out on the courthouse lawn, staring off at nothing in particular and trying to determine what I would do next. I had spent most of my time in Mississippi so far thinking about how Handy Campbell could have landed in such a mess; but there was another question that had vexed me for the past six months: What had happened to his football career? It seemed like a straightforward enough question, one for which a simple answer would not be too hard to find, and yet critical to the story; after all, had Handy Campbell followed the trajectory everyone had assumed he would—from stardom at Greenwood High School to stardom at Mississippi State University to stardom in the National Football League—he almost certainly would never again have passed within a thousand miles of Greenwood, and not within a million of the Leflore County jail. Yet a clear-cut answer to that question was already proving to be elusive, and I would pass most of the next two weeks in a deeply ambivalent hunt for one, wanting more and more to learn the truth, but coming to understand, as I got closer and closer to it, that it would be the kind of truth that few people really do want to know, much less speak.

A tall, slender black woman, seventeen or eighteen years old, walked across the courthouse lawn and approached me. "Did they start the trial yet?" she asked me.

"No," I said. "They couldn't get an impartial jury, so they're putting it off for a couple of months and moving it somewhere else."

She looked disappointed, but did not turn and walk away. After a moment or two of silence, I asked what her name was. "Corvette Walker," she said.

"Did you know Freddie Williams?"

"Yeah," she said. "I don't know why anybody—why they'd do him like that." She let out a sigh. "Some people think they can just do whatever they want."

"Do you know Handy Campbell or Lanardo Myrick?"

"I don't know that other guy," she said, "but I grew up down the block from Tyrone."

And I knew she was telling the truth, because only the people who had grown up with Handy Campbell still referred to him by his middle name.

"Do you think he did it?" I asked, hoping that maybe she, who seemed to know him better than anyone else I had posed that question to, might have a different answer.

But she just tipped her head to the side and rolled her eyes. "Tyrone was a wild child," she said. "You never could tell *what* he was going to do."

It was not the answer I had hoped for, to be sure, and the Handy Campbell I had known had been anything but a wild child. But I could not easily dismiss the judgment of Corvette Walker, not just because she had grown up with Handy Campbell but because, unlike everyone else I had posed the question to over the past three days, she confessed that she really *did not know.* Unlike most everyone else in town, it seemed, she would reserve judgment until she got Handy Campbell's side of the story, until she heard his testimony.

And now it became clear that she and everyone else was going to have to wait another two months to hear that testimony. Everyone, that is, but me. I had already heard it, two days before.

FOURTEEN

THE BENEFITS OF BEING
A WHITE MAN

Leflore County Jail
Greenwood, Mississippi
May 20, 1995

The Leflore County courthouse is an impressive building, three Federalist storeys of limestone and marble topped by a triple-tiered, golden-domed clock tower. It was built in the first decade of the twentieth century, a time when Mississippi and the rest of the South were just beginning to emerge from the disgrace of Appomattox, reassuming a fierce and assertive pride about their region. Southern county courthouses from that era were designed to stand as symbols of such disinterred chauvinism; they are often the most impressive structure in the county, sitting on the choicest real estate. The archetypal Southern county courthouse stands in the middle of a town square, but because the welfare and destiny of Greenwood have always been closely tied to the Yazoo River, where cotton is loaded onto barges and shipped to markets all over the world, the town's epicenter is not a square but rather a line, spread out along the riverbank. The Leflore County courthouse marks the center of that line—the corner of Market Street, where the cotton brokers have their offices, and Fulton Street, where that wrought-iron and steel bridge spans the Yazoo, connecting the mostly black downtown with the all-white neighborhood of North Greenwood.

The halls inside the Leflore County courthouse are lined with granite, bathing the space in a mysterious gray light. Just inside the front entrance, on either side of the hallway, there are doors marked "Records"; behind

213

them lie large, bright rooms where the whitewashed walls, a dozen feet high, are scaled by shelves built specially to hold massive ledgers, some more than a century old. Back out in the hallway, just under the main staircase, sits a concession stand: an ancient, dusty glass case containing shoe laces and shoe polish, hair combs and hair tonic, chewing tobacco and chewing gum. Sales are slow; even on weekdays, the building almost always seems empty. Walking through the Leflore County courthouse, it is easy to imagine that you have somehow stumbled through a chronological loophole and reemerged somewhere in the last few months before the Supreme Court agreed to hear arguments in the case of *Brown v. The Board of Education of Topeka, Kansas.*

But all of this is true only if you enter through the front door.

The side door, which can be found around the corner and facing west, opens into an entirely different world, one devoid of lazy courtliness or any other hint of the past. These are the offices of the Leflore County Sheriff.

Unlike the rest of the courthouse, the sheriff's office is not a quiet, sedate realm. It is constantly filled with dissonant noise, voices shouting into telephone mouthpieces or out of police scanner speakers or at each other, face to face. In here, everyone—deputies and probation officers, lawyers and social workers—seems to be in constant, frantic motion, even the people handcuffed to chairs.

Years before, as a reporter, I had spent quite a few hours in this office, trying to scrounge a quote or some small grain of information out of someone. Usually I left frustrated, having failed to secure a moment of someone's time or even discern whom I should be asking for such a favor. The place was—is—a perpetual blizzard of activity, even on Saturday mornings.

Such was the case when I found myself back in that office on the morning of Saturday, May 20, 1995. The fact that six years had passed since my last visit—that I was a freelance writer now, and no longer a reporter at the *Commonwealth*—changed nothing; as always, no one seemed to notice me. I found an empty chair, sat down, and waited.

The man I was waiting for was Lee Jones, with whom I'd spoken on the telephone a few weeks before. After renewing our acquaintance, I asked him about Handy Campbell's case. He chuckled and said that the state's case against his client was so flimsy—based entirely on rumors and circumstantial evidence—that he couldn't believe they'd had the nerve to arrest him in the first place.

"Mm-hm," I said, not at all comforted; I had expected Lee Jones to say exactly that sort of thing. That was his job. Besides, everyone else I had spoken to in Greenwood believed that the police had so much evidence against Handy Campbell that they could have just sent him on to prison—the Mississippi State Penitentiary at Parchman—without a trial.

"Uh, Lee," I asked, after some more small talk, "do you think I could interview Handy?"

I had no reason to expect that even Lee Jones would grant such a request; his client was awaiting trial on a capital charge, and there was no way talking to me could help him. Indeed, even the small risk that their client might say something damaging before such a trial would, I imagined, have prompted most lawyers to dismiss my request with a laugh, if they didn't hang up on me first. But Lee Jones didn't even seem to think about it before saying: "Hell, yeah! Why not?" I was so astonished that I stumbled over a few simple words of gratitude, set up a date and time, and hung up before he could change his mind.

Perhaps I should not have been so surprised. As far as I could tell, Jones's defense of Handy Campbell had, thus far, been little more than perfunctory. He had only met with his client once or twice, and hadn't met at all with Willie Perkins, who had been appointed to represent Campbell's codefendant, Lanardo Myrick. From our conversation, I had come away with the distinct impression that Lee Jones didn't even know very much about the case. His casual attitude left me gravely concerned about his client's prospects; but it was that same casual attitude, I knew, that was granting me such free access to Handy Campbell, and I did not hesitate to take advantage of it.

⁂

Lee Jones had advised me to be at the sheriff's office at ten that Saturday morning. By ten-thirty, he still hadn't shown up, and I was becoming impatient. At a quarter to eleven, I spotted Sheriff Ricky Banks coming out of his office. I asked him if he'd seen Lee Jones that morning.

"No," he said. "But he already told me you were coming by to see Handy Campbell today."

"He's not coming in?"

Sheriff Banks shrugged. "I reckon not."

The sheriff had a deputy escort me up to the jail, through two iron doors, and into a whitewashed hallway pocked with solid iron doors, each having only one little square opening, near the top, ruled with thick black bars. I was only there for a minute or two, but I took the opportunity to peer through one of these openings and into what I would later learn was Handy Campbell's cell: ten feet square of concrete, with three bunkbeds, a payphone, a television, five cellmates—all of them black, all of them charged with robbery, theft, aggravated assault, or some combination of the three—and another barred window, somewhat larger, through which I could see Lee Jones's law office, and, behind it, a small swatch of the Yazoo.

The deputy quickly steered me away from the cells and toward what I initially mistook for a storage closet. It was a tiny triangular room, its windowless walls covered with cheap wood paneling. Stacked up from the floor were some thirty-odd boxes of coffee; there were two ladders, a couple of chairs, a broken television set, and a gray metal desk, old and dented, on top of which sat a large piece of scientific equipment that looked like it came from the set of *Lost in Space.* It was labeled: THE INTOXILIZER.

This, my escort informed me, was the jail's "Lawyer Room." He excused himself and closed the door.

He knocked a few minutes later and pushed the door open again. Handy Campbell shuffled inside. He was wearing his "street clothes": a black visor emblazoned with a red Nike swoosh, a red t-shirt with a crest on the pocket, blue-and-white-striped shorts, white socks, black and white Nike hightops with velcro ties. I had plenty of time to write all of this down: Handy moved very slowly. His ankles were linked together by a shiny metal chain perhaps six inches long.

He looked, at once, larger and smaller than I had remembered him. I'd forgotten just how big Handy Campbell was; my memories were mostly of his speed and grace and humility, and, in fusing those with my knowledge of his squalid childhood and adolescence, I had retained a somewhat distorted image of a lanky kid about my height. In truth, Handy Campbell had stood six foot four inches tall in high school (six inches taller than me), and weighed 190 pounds. If anything, the passing years had only served to fill him out a little more. And in this room, with its cramped walls and low ceiling, he appeared even larger.

Even so, he struck me as being, somehow, diminutive. Perhaps it was the leg-irons and handcuffs, or his stooped posture, or the mixture of surprise and embarrassment on his face, or his initial inability to sustain eye contact for longer than a fraction of a second—whatever it was, at that moment Handy Campbell appeared to me little more than a child. I reminded myself that I was only four years older than he. Six-and-a-half years earlier, when he'd been a seventeen-year-old star quarterback and I a twenty-one-year-old cub reporter (my boss's term), I had drawn quite a few parallels between the two of us: We were both just starting out, both trying hard to impress people around us and people we had never met, both a little cocky about our abilities and our prospects (although his cockiness had manifested itself much less frequently than mine), both, to no small extent, dependent upon the other. Now the dynamic between us was hopelessly lopsided. I was still moving forward, but Handy Campbell had reached the end of the line. Nothing appeared to lie ahead for him but life in prison, and quite possibly an untimely death. At the end of our interview, I would walk out of this jail, and this courthouse, a free man; he would return to his cell to await the inevitable.

The deputy guided Handy toward a chair and told him to sit. That accomplished, he told me I could have as much time as I wanted, and advised me to let him know if I needed anything. I asked him if he could remove the prisoner's handcuffs; he did so without hesitating. Then he stepped through the door and, to my surprise, closed it behind him. Only at that moment did I fully realize that I was being allowed to interview Handy Campbell alone, without his lawyer or even a guard present. I could scarcely believe it; I certainly couldn't imagine such a thing happening anywhere but Greenwood, Mississippi.

I opened my briefcase and pulled out a legal pad and a tape recorder with a microphone. I handed the latter to Handy. After a few questions, I had to ask him to hold it up close to his mouth when he answered. He was, as I'd remembered, a quiet, soft-spoken person, and his present circumstances seemed to exacerbate that trait to the point where he was, at times, almost inaudible.

Handy offered his hand, told me he remembered me from his days with the Bulldogs. He asked where I lived now, what I was doing; when I told him I'd returned to New York, he raised his eyebrows a bit, as if to convey both understanding and envy. Then we began talking about him.

We went back as far as he could go—1971. He reminded me that he had been born in Greenwood; that his father, Sam Handy, had never married his mother and had left her when he was two years old; but that his mother, Hattie, had managed, through a combination of work and child support and government assistance, to feed and clothe Handy and his four younger siblings. "She basically provided for everything we wanted," he said. "Somehow she came up with the money."

A younger brother and three younger sisters plus Handy, his mother and his grandmother made seven people in all who lived in a three-room house on Taft Street in East Greenwood. In the tenth grade, the family moved to a three-bedroom apartment in the Snowden Jones housing project, the place Mike McNeill had pointed out with dread on my first day in Greenwood. Handy, though, was comfortable enough there to start tossing a football around with friends in the parking lot. Back on Taft Street, in sandlot games, Handy had always played the role of wide receiver, but after the move to Snowden Jones he started to try quarterbacking. As far as his new neighbors were concerned, he was a natural. They and his friends encouraged him to go out for the varsity team at Greenwood High School, and in the spring of his sophomore year, he did.

But Handy had never played on any kind of school team before, and his first attempt to join one did not get very far. "I came late for the physicals," he said, "and the coach wanted me to pay for the physicals, but it was $110 and I didn't have the cash."

The following fall, the Bulldogs won the North Mississippi Championship. A team that good might not have been looking for new talent, but Greenwood's quarterback graduated that spring, and Handy decided to try again. He had already finished his junior year of high school and had never really played organized football, but head coach David Bradberry recognized Handy's raw talent and took a chance on him. "He's a good coach," Handy said. "I got along with him real well."

"Were you surprised at how well you did?"

He shook his head. "No, I was sort of disappointed. I wanted to do better than I did, but overall it was O.K."

"Did you feel underrated at the time, like nobody outside of Greenwood knew who you were?"

"Yes."

"Why do you think that was?"

"I really couldn't tell."

He grew quiet, and I quickly steered the conversation back to Greenwood High School and his spectacular season. When we reminisced about the Tupelo game, he gave in to a slight smile, the only one of the day.

"When were you first contacted by college scouts?" I asked him.

"Around the middle of playoff time," he said, and even then, two years after most of the quarterbacks he'd beaten had first been scouted, there were only one or two who showed any interest at all in Handy Campbell, and they were from low-profile black colleges. It wasn't until after the Tupelo game that Southeastern Conference schools started to take notice, although the interest never seemed to be much more than casual—at least not in the SEC, the South's premier powerhouse football league. "Who went after you the hardest?" I asked.

"Alcorn State," he replied, a black college down in Lorman, Mississippi that was decidedly *not* in the SEC. I knew almost nothing about the school except that my former colleague, Margaret Dean, had gone there.

"Why didn't you go there?" I asked.

"I didn't like the location," he said. "In the middle of nowhere, really." But I sensed that he was being diplomatic, that the real reason he turned them down was that they were not in his league, that a person with his gift deserved a place in a much more prestigious program than Alcorn's. And I sensed, too, that he harbored the suspicion—as did I—that it was no coincidence that he was courted much more ardently by a relatively small black college than he was by schools like Ole Miss and Mississippi State, which had only started accepting black players onto their teams within his lifetime, and which regularly played their games before a national television audience.

Ultimately, though, the list of suitors grew to include Southern University, a black school in Baton Rouge, and then Ole Miss and Mississippi State. And then, he told me, the list grew to encompass "all of the colleges in Mississippi, except some of the Division 2 schools."

"And how did you settle on Mississippi State?"

"I decided to go with them first because I wanted to play in the SEC and play on TV, so I decided to go with them, and when I went there things didn't work out so I transferred to Ole Miss."

As he said this, his tone of voice was so matter-of-fact that for a moment I missed the significance of the statement. *Things didn't work out so I transferred to Ole Miss.* Like moving to another car on a train because in the one you're in the air conditioning isn't working. But in fact it was nothing so casual at all; this was where his entire train got derailed. In the movie, after the poor black kid becomes an overnight high school football hero and is drafted by a powerhouse school, he becomes a college football hero and sails into the National Football League as a first-round draft pick. He doesn't transfer out and try his luck elsewhere because "things don't work out." Things always work out, as a matter of course. The poor black kid who manages to rise up from the ghetto doesn't then get pushed back down; no one wants to see a movie like that.

"What happened at State?" I asked.

"Well," he said, "basically, they promised me a lot of things I didn't get, and then when I got there they weren't interested in me. They already had made up their mind about who was going to be the starting quarterback." Before I could ask who, Handy, anticipating the question, lifted his head, looked me right in the eye, and said, in an odd, low grumble: "Todd Jordan."

Todd Jordan: The golden boy of Tupelo's Golden Wave, the blond-haired wonder who was ranked as one of *Parade* magazine's top high school athletes, and was then decisively whipped by Handy Campbell and his Greenwood Bulldogs. I was stunned for a moment, but the truth was that it made perfect sense: Mississippi State had won only one game out of eleven the previous season, and they needed every good high school player they could get. And Rocky Felker wasn't about to gamble everything on either Handy Campbell or Todd Jordan. It was a smart move, at least for Coach Felker. I just wondered how he had pulled it off.

"Wait a minute," I said. "What did they promise you that they didn't deliver?"

"They promised money," Handy said. "Some of everything. But when I got there, it was totally opposite of what they said. When I got there, it seemed to me like they had already made up their mind about who they wanted to be the quarterback, and they wasn't really giving me a chance. Then they talked about moving me to defense, and I wasn't hearing none of that at the time."

"How did you know they had already decided to go with Jordan?"

"During practice sessions, you know, the number of reps they was giving me, and the number of reps they was giving him, and the number of reps they was giving the quarterbacks who had been there, and it was like totally in favor of Jordan. I wasn't having none of that."

I told him what I'd heard from Jack about Todd Jordan—that Jordan, too, had fared poorly at Mississippi State and was then snubbed by the NFL.

To my surprise, his reaction betrayed sympathy, not satisfaction, and a bit more erudition than I had expected. "It's unfortunate," he said. "I think a lot of guys out of Mississippi just get bad breaks. I don't know why, it just seem to be that way. There's a lot of talent here. It's just unfortunate people don't take the time out to give this talent a chance. A lot of guys make it, too, but there's a lot of those who don't make it that should."

"How did you get along with Rocky Felker?" I asked.

"I really didn't have time to get along with him," he said. He was at Mississippi State for a total of two weeks.

"How were you able to transfer to Ole Miss so quickly?"

"We had a couple alumnis come and took care of things, I guess," he said with a shrug. They had started wooing him while he was still at State.

"What did you think about that?"

"I really didn't have time to think about it. I know I wanted to stay in the SEC."

"So what happened at Ole Miss?"

"Ole Miss gave me a raw deal too, I guess," he said, without sounding particularly angry or bitter. "They told me a bunch of things that wasn't true also. They told me the first year I would sit out and be red-shirted [in accordance with NCAA rules regarding transfers], and when that year ended, they told me that I had to sit out that year, that I was automatically gonna lose it. They wanted to red-shirt me a second year because they already had two quarterbacks that was in my class with them. They was going to red-shirt me again. So . . ." His voice trailed off for a second or two. "It was just unfortunate."

"Why were they going to red-shirt you for a second season?"

Handy looked down at his shackled feet for a second, then back up at me, making eye contact for maybe the second time that day. "I think it was race," he said. "There was one other black quarterback that didn't play also. I thought, if I wasn't starting then maybe he should have been the one. The other guys—Russ Shows was O.K., but Tom Luke, he was like my backup quarterback in high school."

Shows and Luke had been Ole Miss's starting quarterbacks in the years Handy Campbell was there, and while they hadn't brought any championships home to Oxford, Mississippi, they were, as far as I knew, fairly well regarded by fans and alumni. I found it hard to believe that they were quite as undeserving as Handy Campbell was suggesting. I myself had seen Luke play, and I thought Handy's assessment of him was unfair. On the other hand, though, I couldn't conceive that anyone who knew the slightest bit about football, and who had seen all three of them play, would not come to the conclusion that Handy Campbell was, by far, the best quarterback. And the question of race had occurred to me, too. Ole Miss had never had a black starting quarterback; as far as I knew, they still held to the old line that blacks made fine running backs and wide receivers, being blessed with speed and the innate ability to take orders, but that they didn't have the brains or leadership abilities to quarterback a team. I didn't want to believe they still did, just as I hadn't wanted to believe that Carl Kelly, Jr. was being serious when he lectured me on the dangers of yellow niggers; I didn't want to believe that such a mindset could continue to flourish more than thirty years after desegregation, could flourish so close to the world in which I and Handy Campbell and everyone else still had to live. But how else could I explain the fact that Ole Miss had deliberately benched Handy Campbell for an unnecessary second season, and that, as he would soon tell me, they led him to believe at the end of that season that he would be red-shirted—not even allowed to suit up and sit on the bench, much less play—for a *third* one as well? After all, Billy Brewer, who had been Ole Miss's popular head football coach during Handy Campbell's years there, had said more than once that Handy Campbell had the best arm he'd ever seen. Why *wouldn't* they play him, or even make him eligible to play?

"How did you get along with Coach Brewer?" I asked.

"I got along well with him," he said. "He was a pretty good coach. He tried to help me keep my head up. He gave me some words of encouragement."

But, he told me, he was not so lucky with Jimmy "Red" Parker, the team's Offensive Coordinator and quarterback coach, and the man who was actually responsible for Handy Campbell. "It seems like he was constantly giving me the raw deal," he recalled. "He never gave me a chance."

"What do you mean? Could you give me an example?"

"In practice, I could do something good and he'd always look for the fault in it. When the other quarterbacks do something—Russ Shows, Tom Luke—he'd look for the good in what they do."

"Why do you think he didn't like you?"

"He always put it on a lack of experience, but I always thought, the only way you learn is to get out there and make your mistakes and learn from your mistakes."

"Do you think," I asked, "you would have gotten more chances if you were white?"

He thought about it for a few seconds, then nodded.

"And why did they kick you off the team?"

"I had a girl in the dorm," he said, seeming neither outraged nor proud, but simply resigned. "With some drinks and stuff."

It wasn't his first infraction; he confessed that in fact he'd had five or six. "A lot of the infractions I got had to do with drinking and stuff, partying, all that," he said. "Being wild, I guess." He was also, he told me later, arrested for driving under the influence while at Ole Miss.

"Why did you do it?" I asked.

"I don't know," he said. "Everybody in the whole dorm did it, so it really wasn't like it was that big of a deal, really. Like on the weekends, everybody'd go out, come back and have a party in the room." He fell silent for a moment, then added: "And I got caught."

"Were you the only one who got caught?"

"Other guys got caught, but I guess they handle different situations the way they wanted," he said. "They got busted, but you know they handle the situation different according to who it is."

He looked at me expectantly, hoping, perhaps, that I would finish the sentence for him and confirm his theory, that I would say yes, of course, they wouldn't have kicked a *white* player off the team for having a girl in his room. But I couldn't say it, because I didn't know for certain if it was true, and because I did know for certain that I didn't want it to be true. I had worked hard over the past few years to rebuild my sense of idealism, and I wasn't sure that it was yet strong enough to survive an encounter with the notion that someone like Handy Campbell, ambitious and supremely talented—someone who, more than anyone else I had ever even gotten close to, truly *deserved* to be a sports star—could not, in the end, overcome simple, crude prejudice and claim the glory that was rightfully his. If someone with his gifts could be knocked down so easily, I wondered, what hope was there for the rest of us?

"Tell me," I said, needing to change the subject and search for another explanation, anything that might fit. "How were your grades?"

"About a 2.3," he said. I had known football players at Penn with comparable grade point averages.

"Did you work hard?"

"I usually just did enough to get by. I knew I could have did a lot better, but grades wasn't really my concern at the time."

"What was your concern?"

"Partying," he said. "Football."

"So what did you do after you got kicked off the team?"

"I finished the semester," he said, making me wonder if perhaps he had really cared more about his studies than he had let on. "After the semester I went home, talked to a couple of coaches. I didn't have to leave Ole Miss, but I wanted to go somewhere I could play." I found it strange that he circumvented the obvious: Getting kicked off the team meant forfeiting his football scholarship, without which he couldn't afford to go to Ole Miss, or anywhere else. Perhaps, I thought, he prefers to believe that he actually had a choice in the matter, that he could have continued on at Ole Miss. He must have been more ashamed of his poverty than he was of his failure to adhere to the rules.

When he returned home, Handy considered his options: He was courted by Delta State, a Division 3 school; Southern University, Mississippi Valley State, and Alabama State, black schools; and junior colleges. The choices were much more limited than they had been back in the spring of 1989, and much less attractive. He chose Southern, the most competitive school in the lot, and upon arriving in Baton Rouge was automatically red-shirted for another year as a transfer. At the end of that season, though, he had a streak of bad luck, which started when the coach who had signed Handy got fired. When the new head coach came in, Handy remembered, "he brought in some new guys. But I ended up getting hurt before the season started—an old injury I had from Ole Miss, a rotator cuff. I was supposed to be starting."

"How'd you get hurt?"

"I got hit late [in practice] and I fell awkward and reinjured my rotator cuff on my throwing arm."

He would have to sit out at least another year, the doctors said. Handy couldn't take it anymore. "After I got hurt," he said, "I just got down on myself and I stopped going to classes. And I ended up dropping out." He left Southern in the fall of 1992. Four years had passed since his season of glory at Greenwood High School. He was now twenty-one years old, and he had yet to play a single down of college football. And it was becoming increasingly apparent that he never would.

After he dropped out, Handy moved into a girlfriend's apartment off-campus and got a job waiting tables at Shoney's. They stayed together about a year; then his girlfriend, DeVonna Evans, got pregnant and went home to have the baby at her parents' house in Crowley, Louisiana.

Eventually she had a daughter, Taylor Jania Campbell. For a while, Handy said, he visited them almost every weekend, but eventually the relationship faded. "I guess it's over with," he told me.

Handy continued to work at Shoney's, but in June 1993 he got into trouble with the police. "We was at a—like a little party that night," he recalled, "and they came in and they searched the house because of the noise. Then they said that some convenience store had just been robbed and this looked like the stuff that was taken, so they took me down to the store to be identified, and they pointed me out and some other guy and they took us to jail."

He didn't know the other guy and he didn't do it, he told me, but the police said they had enough to convict him, anyway. "I ended up going to court on it," he said, "and I took a bargain with them because I didn't have the time to keep going back and forth to the court so I tried to settle. So I could just pay for what was taken. And I ended up not paying for it, and when I came home I sort of just forgot about it."

"What kind of a plea bargain did you make?"

"The plea somehow was some type of guilty plea. I didn't know it was a guilty plea at the time. The lawyer told me this was a plea to just say I couldn't prove my innocence at the time because she said I was going to need some witnesses that I was at the house at the time of the robbery, and all the witnesses at that time, they was moved and gone from the area and I couldn't get in touch with them."

In December, 1993, Sam Handy died. Handy returned to Greenwood for his father's funeral, and stayed. There was nothing left for him in Baton Rouge but a judgment he could not afford to pay, and the specter of his failed ambition. So he moved back into Apartment 3-G at Snowden Jones and went to sleep in the same bed he had slept in as a child, with no idea of what he should, or could, do next.

He got a job at the local Shoney's, but that didn't last more than a few weeks. He tried to join the army, but they turned him away because of his football injury. He slept a lot, watched a lot of television, threw the football around the parking lot with kids who were increasingly young and whose memory of his former glory was increasingly faint. Rumors started circulating that he was doing drugs, and stealing to finance his habit.

There was some trouble, too. One night, he told me, "I was home like a month and I got, well, this chick came and pulled a gun on me, and I guess her sister's boyfriend or husband came and punched me and a friend of mine grabbed the chick that had the gun, me and the guy was fighting, and the police came, they was talking to us and I cursed and they arrested me for public profanity. They dismissed it somehow."

"Wait a minute," I said, bewildered and a bit suspicious. "Why did this woman pull a gun on you in the first place?"

"I don't know," he said. "She was claiming I had did something to her."

"Who was she?"

"I didn't know her." He dropped his head, signaling that the subject was closed.

Around the time of this incident an old friend of his returned home to Greenwood. Lanardo Myrick was a year older than Handy, but they had known each other since childhood. "We met playing basketball in the park," Handy recalled. "About the age of twelve, I guess."

"Did he play football, too?"

"He ran track. I think he ran the quarter, the 220. He was pretty good, he signed a scholarship with MVSU."

Handy presented the relationship as a normal friendship, but I had heard that it was much more than that. Jack had told me that Myrick had followed Handy Campbell, first to Mississippi State, then to Ole Miss. From the conversation, I gathered the impression that Lanardo Myrick was a groupie, a remora to Handy Campbell's shark.

Handy denied this. "He wasn't at State with me," he said, "but he was at Ole Miss with me for a semester. But I think he had to withdraw because they didn't sign him to a scholarship."

"Did you see him after that?"

"He occasionally came on the weekend to visit."

"How often did you see him while you were at Southern?"

"None."

"How come?"

"He had joined the army," Handy said. "And when I came back home, he somehow withdrew from the army, and he was staying with me [in Greenwood] for a couple of weeks before this happened."

Before this happened. I was intrigued by Myrick's "withdrawal" from the army and wanted to ask Handy more about it, but he had brought up something I wanted to talk about even more, something I had waited two hours for an opportunity to ask about—and the reason I was down here in the first place. "So tell me," I said, "about what happened."

But Handy just shrugged and fell silent again, and I feared that I was facing a scenario I had dreaded ever since we'd sat down—that he would be willing to discuss his childhood and family and football but not the trouble that had landed him in this jail. I had proceeded slowly, to make him comfortable, to get him in the habit of talking, to insure that, when the conversation turned to the most pressing of matters, he didn't just close down and refer me back to Lee Jones. Apparently, I thought, it hadn't worked. Beaten back, I retreated, regrouped, and tried again.

"How long did you know Freddie?" I asked.

Still, he remained silent. But then, after a few seconds, he spoke, softly: "I had known him for about three years."

"How did you know him?"

"From nightclubs and mutual friends, I guess."

"Did Lanardo know him, too?"

"Lanardo had known him for about a year and a half, I guess."

"What was your relationship with Freddie like?"

"Friends," he said. "Good friends. Hung out a lot."

That's not how I heard it, I thought. I wanted to press him further on that last question, but I worried it might shut him down before I heard the whole story. So I changed the subject.

"When was the last time you and Lanardo saw him?"

"It was on like a Friday. Friday night, I think."

I didn't have to think. I already knew that it was, in fact, a Friday night—Friday, August 26, 1994, to be exact. "What happened?" I asked.

"The three of us, we rode around and we drank beer," Handy recalled. "And we had been asking him, could we borrow the truck to go see our kids." Handy's daughter was still in Crowley; Myrick had a son down in Gulfport. "And that night he told us we could do it, he said he had some things to take care of anyway in Jackson, and he made a phone call and called this guy, and the guy came and met him, and he got in the car with him and told us to be careful."

"Who was this guy?"

"I don't know. I never saw him before."

"So, Freddie called this guy and asked him to come pick him up?" He nodded. "Where did he call him from?"

"He called from the Triple Stop convenience store on Main Street," he said. "The guy picked him up on the right side of KFC."

"And what time was this?"

"Five-thirty in the morning."

"And can you describe the guy who picked Freddie up?"

"I didn't get a good look at him," Handy said. "He stayed in the car."

"What kind of car was it?"

"Like a black Bonneville or something."

"Did Freddie tell you where he was going?"

"He said they was going to Jackson. That's all he said."

And that was Handy Campbell's story, the story he hoped would set him free: Freddie Williams, after spending the night with Handy and Lanardo Myrick, had loaned them his Pathfinder for a few days, called a man for a ride, got into a car that may or may not have been a black Pontiac Bonneville and which was being driven by a man Handy didn't know and couldn't see, and sped off, ostensibly toward Jackson. It didn't sound like much.

I sensed I wasn't going to get any more out of Handy Campbell that afternoon, but I had to ask him another question, a question I didn't really want to ask and didn't quite know how to ask: "Um," I said, "uh, when Freddie loaned you the truck . . . when he let you borrow the truck, did he, uh, did he ask you for anything in exchange?"

Handy looked a bit confused, but he didn't flinch, and didn't hesitate. "No," he mumbled.

I quickly changed the subject again, asking Handy where he and Myrick had gone. Down to Baton Rouge, he said, to visit some friends from Southern. But it was on the campus of Louisiana State University, also in Baton Rouge, where, on the night of August 29, 1995, they had been pulled over by police because, Handy said, they had made an illegal U-turn. When the police ran Handy's name through the computer, they found a bench warrant for him, stemming from his arrest for robbing a convenience store a year earlier: He had left the state without paying off the judgment. Then they ran the Pathfinder's plates. The computer responded: VEHICLE STOLEN. DRIVER MISSING.

"They asked where was he [the vehicle's owner] and we was like, 'He should be at home.' And the whole time he was missing and they was holding us in Baton Rouge, and then they found him dead and I guess they just said we did it."

The police held Handy Campbell and Lanardo Myrick in jail in Baton Rouge for two months on a charge of Grand Theft Auto before Freddie's body was found and the charge was upgraded to capital murder—capital because, according to the charges, they killed Freddie in the course of committing another felony, stealing his truck. Even before the body was found, though, the police strongly suspected Freddie was dead.

"They also had found a gun in the car," Handy told me, "that we had purchased for Freddie, in the truck."

"Where did you get it?"

"We purchased it off the street, because he said he already had one gun but he wanted another one. I bought it because he wanted one."

"What kind of gun?"

"It was a 9 millimeter."

"And you got it—"

"Here in Greenwood."

"Was this in exchange for lending you the truck?"

He shook his head. "That wasn't part of the deal. He had been asking about guns prior to that night I bought it, about two weeks before, I guess, and I just bought it because I figured I could buy it cheaper from the guy and sell it to Freddie for a little bit more and maybe get a couple of bucks in the process."

"When exactly did you get it for him?"

"I don't remember what day I bought it—I guess about two weeks before. I gave it to him the next night."

"Why did Freddie want another gun if he already had one?"

"He said he wanted one bigger than the one he had. He had a .22 and wanted something stronger, I guess."

I realized at that moment that I knew nothing about the state's case against Handy Campbell and Lanardo Myrick, that I would know nothing about it for another two months, and it occurred to me that this same gun, bought on the street by Handy Campbell and supposedly sold in turn to Freddie Williams, might very well have been the same gun that was used to kill Freddie. If it was, I thought, that's it; nothing will save him.

Once again I changed the subject, not wanting to dwell on what I perceived as his rapidly dimming prospects. I asked him about his involuntary two-month stay in Baton Rouge. I'd heard there was trouble; Handy quickly confirmed this, recalling that one night he was attacked by his cellmates, eight of them in all. "They put me in a cell with a bunch of guys, they were supposed to be gangsters or something," he explained. "And I wasn't a gangster, so I was reading the paper one night and they caught me off guard." They broke his jaw, he said. He raised a hand and rubbed it gingerly.

In October, after police in Greenwood found Freddie's body, Handy and Lanardo were extradited to Mississippi and placed in separate cells: Lanardo in the Greenwood city jail, behind the police station; Handy here, about a mile away. Not long thereafter, Handy was the target of another attack. "A bunch of guys in a gang again," he recalled. "I was arguing with a guy over a Spades game, and about eight of them, I guess, again, jumped in and jumped me." That time he'd suffered only a swollen jaw, but it was not the end of his troubles.

"I've been jumped by the guards a couple of times," he explained. The first time, in January 1995, six guards had been involved. "I had a bad nightmare or something and I was out of my mind, and they came and opened the door and the guard got me and took me to the bottom cell. And when we got down there he called some more deputies and they came in and they was less patient with me and demanded me to go with them. And I didn't want to go with them 'cause I was afraid of them, so they grabbed me and when I decided to go with them one of them hit me in the back of the head with a flashlight and the other sprayed me with mace. It made me hallucinate real bad," he said. "I was thinking awkward and breathing funny."

Another time, he said, they ordered him out of his cell so they could search it, and he refused to leave. "I've lost clothes, tapes, CDs that haven't been replaced," he explained. "I asked them could I stay while they searched my things because I've had so many things lost, and they jumped me, beat me again." This time, he said, there'd been three of them. After that, he left his cell immediately whenever a search was announced. Things continued to disappear.

Even so, Handy seemed to consider himself relatively fortunate. He knew that the next stop was Parchman. "They say things are a lot different over there," he said. "They have bigger gangs, meaner gangs. They're pretty tough on outsiders." He spoke these words in the same tone with which he'd related his life story: flat, seemingly uninterested, devoid of almost any emotion, betraying very little except for a sense of abject resignation.

It didn't change when I asked him what he would do if acquitted. "I'm gonna get out of Greenwood, probably," he said. "I'm gonna go back to Baton Rouge and see can I straighten out the bench warrant, see can I repay that and clear my name. This is one place I don't ever want to be again. I'd really like to patch things up with my baby's mom, probably get married with her, get back in school." As for playing football, though, he harbored no illusions. "I think that's history. I don't think I'm in as good shape as I need to be, and I really don't think I could get back to that level. I'd like to coach or something like that, though." He said he was nervous about the trial, had no idea how things might turn out, no idea who might have wanted to kill Freddie Williams, or why.

We spoke for a few more minutes, mostly about jail food and everyday life in his cell, where the prisoners could keep videogames, books, cards, and personal stereos, but were not allowed to leave except to meet with their attorneys. I told Handy that I planned to interview his mother the next day; he said that was fine. "She's real nervous," he warned. "She's very concerned."

I opened the door and called for the deputy. Handy stood up, extended his hand. I shook it. "Will you be there on Monday?" he asked. "Yes," I said, "I'll see you there." The deputy hooked his arm inside Handy's elbow and led him away, down the hall and around a corner. I heard a metal door open, then slam shut. The sound reminded me where I was and brought to mind a half-dozen questions I had forgotten to ask Handy, not to mention a few dozen more that the interview had raised—what had really happened at Mississippi State and Ole Miss and why, and who was this Lanardo Myrick, and what was the true nature of their relationship with each other and with Freddie Williams, and what kind of evidence did the prosecution have against Handy Campbell and how much of it, and how did someone as soft-spoken and phlegmatic as Handy Campbell manage to land in the middle of so much trouble wherever he went, and, circling over all of it like a pack of angry buzzards: Was I still certain that Handy Campbell did not kill Freddie Williams? I wanted, needed, really, for the answer to be yes; I needed to believe that someone I had admired so much was incapable of such an act, and that I was incapable of such a grave misjudgment of character. But in order to preserve that belief, I knew my mind would have to find a way around questions that seemed to have no answers save the obvious one: Guilty.

I wasn't sure my mind was that nimble.

ॐॐ

I stepped back into the Lawyer Room and began packing up my briefcase. And it occurred to me, as I did so, that no one had bothered to search me on the way in, or even to ask what was in my case. I was automatically above suspicion; I could have smuggled a gun or even a bomb into the jail without any trouble at all. Such are the benefits of being a white man in Greenwood, Mississippi. I let out a sharp breath, shook my head in profound disbelief, and walked out of there, unmolested, a free man.

As I left the courthouse, I shaded my eyes from the bright sunlight. I walked across the front lawn, past the front steps and a pair of towering magnolias, to the Confederate Memorial monument. It would be difficult to find a county courthouse anywhere in the South that doesn't have a Confederate monument on its front lawn, and perhaps, in the case of Mississippi, impossible. Over the years, I'd examined hundreds of them. But the one in Greenwood, the first one I'd ever seen up close, was one of the largest and most elaborate I had ever encountered, festooned with a half-dozen figures representing everything from the valiant Confederate soldier to the strong and resilient Southern woman who'd nursed his wounds and kept the cause alive in her heart. Years after I'd first laid eyes upon it, I came across a picture of this monument in the book *Powerful Days*, a collection of the photojournalist Charles Moore's portraits of the civil rights movement. In Moore's photograph, the monument towered over a line of neatly attired people marching in support of black voter registration; at the head of the line, comedian Dick Gregory, in a jacket and tie, stared down a half-dozen white policemen ordering him and the rest of the marchers to move away from the courthouse. Gregory refused; he was arrested and tossed into a cell in the jail I had just left. In the picture, the monument's inscription hovers just over Dick Gregory's head. The inscription was illegible in the photograph, and I was disturbed at the time to realize that I couldn't recall it anymore. Now, I pulled out my pad and wrote it down:

A TESTIMONIAL OF OUR AFFECTION AND REVERENCE FOR THE CONFEDERATE SOLDIER, THE MEMORY OF WHOSE BRAVE DEEDS AND HEROIC LIFE AND THE PRINCIPLES FOR WHICH HE SACRIFICED SO MUCH WE BEQUEATH TO OUR CHILDREN THROUGH ALL FUTURE GENERATIONS.

Behind me and around another corner, on the east side of the courthouse, I spotted a historic marker, standing near the entrance to the Fulton

Street bridge. I was certain I'd seen it before, too, but I couldn't quite remember what it had said. I walked over and read it again:

GREENWOOD

Founded by John Williams
as Williams Landing, 1834.
Chartered as Greenwood, 1844.
Since 1917 has been the world's largest
long staple cotton market.

That last sentence, I knew, was no longer true, had not been for quite some time; and as I wrote it down, I laughed to myself, thinking that the seemingly generic inscription on the Confederate Memorial monument was a more accurate—and insightful—description of Greenwood, Mississippi than was the town's own historic marker.

FIFTEEN

CONTAMINATED

The W. A. Snowden Jones Apartments
Greenwood, Mississippi
May 21, 1995

On Tuesday, October 25, 1994, Greenwood police pulled a partially decomposed body from a ditch near a railroad overpass, just a quarter-mile east of the *Greenwood Commonwealth*'s newsroom. The coroner had to rely on dental records for a positive ID, but everyone in town already knew it was Freddie Williams. For two months, the body had lain there, shielded only by a few weeds from the hot Delta sun, yet no one had found it—strange, since the ditch was only yards from a road, and just feet from a half-dozen concrete trestles covered with gang graffiti.

Seven months later, when Greenwood police officer Reginald Dean led me to the spot, I was transfixed by the spray-painted symbols, which looked so strange—bizarre, really—here in Greenwood, Mississippi: more than seven hundred miles from Chicago, a thousand from New York, two thousand from Los Angeles. "There were no gangs when I lived here," I said, trying to reassure myself that my memory of Greenwood was not overly idealized, and that I could not have missed something that big, no matter how young and naïve I might have been.

"They're here now," Officer Dean, the husband of my former colleague Margaret Dean, replied.

"Crack, too?"

Officer Dean (I just thought of him as "Dean," which was how

Margaret had always referred to him) stifled a chuckle. "Whatever you can get in New York, you can get here," he said. "Cheaper."

He watched wordlessly while I brushed the weeds aside and knelt on the ground, running my hand over the dirt, trying to appreciate fully the notion that a dead human form had lain on this very dirt, under these very weeds, for more than two months—and not just any dead human form, but one which had previously been so relentlessly *alive*, which in that life had warmly grasped my hand on my very first morning in Greenwood and welcomed me so colorfully to town. *If I can ever be of help, you just holler,* he'd offered. *I'll see you around, now.* And while I never got to know him very well, I did see him around, a lot, at the paper, at football games, in clubs and restaurants and Whittington Park, and always he was exactly the same, always at the center of a small crowd, loud and lively and a little bit ludicrous, his grin ever-present and bright as any of the half-dozen rings he was wearing at any given time, laughing and hooting and dancing and always addressing me as *Mister New York* or *stud* or *young stud* or *stud-hoss* or *Mister New York stud,* always as eager to make me feel at home in Greenwood—no, not just at home, but actually *happy* to be there—as he had been that first day in the newsroom. *I'll see you around, now.* I was glad I hadn't seen him here, lying in this dirt, in these weeds, lifeless. A sight so unthinkable, so absurd, might just have made me laugh horribly, or at the very least forced me to contemplate seriously the last few minutes of the life that ended here, when someone pointed a gun at this man who never failed to scrounge up a smile, and shot him dead. *If I can ever be of help, you just holler, now.* Who had been of help to him then, when even he must have hollered?

Eventually I rose to my feet and marveled aloud at the fact that the body had not been discovered sooner. "The newspaper's right over there," I said, still surprised at the spot's proximity to a place in which I had once spent a large chunk of nearly every day; I had imagined it had been dumped far out of town, maybe up in Carroll County, where, as Jack had once warned me, "They got places to bury a body, ain't *never* gon' find it." And weren't we very close to Handy Campbell's home?

"Where's Snowden Jones?" I asked.

"Right over there," Dean said, pointing to the east. "'Bout a quarter-mile."

I shook my head in bitter wonder. "So the body was right here for two months and nobody found it? They must not have looked very hard."

That remark could easily have been considered provocative, especially by a policeman, but Dean just stood there, impassive. He had always struck me as a man who did not say something unless it was absolutely necessary, a quality I had often tried to emulate when I had worked as a reporter here. Tried.

"Didn't it—" I said, then stopped for a second and tried again. "After all that time, didn't it start to *stink?*"

"People in Snowden Jones complained about a funny smell," he said. "Everybody just figured it was a dead dog or something."

❧❧

From across Main Street, Snowden Jones looks like an ordinary private apartment complex. It is only as you get closer that you start to notice details, like the age and condition of the cars in the parking lot, or the broken glass and crack vials spread out all over the grass and asphalt, or the men in their twenties and thirties who sit out on the buildings' front steps, doing nothing, all day and all night. The W. A. Snowden Jones Apartment complex is considered by most people in Greenwood, black and white, to be a rough place, and I had always regarded it warily, but it looked almost peaceful on that Sunday morning in May 1995 when I visited—quiet even, except for those men on the front steps who, seeing a white man walk by carrying a briefcase, called out: "You with the paper? You with the TV? You a *lawyer?*"

Back in 1988 and 1989, quite a few white men walked through this parking lot, looking for apartment 3-G, Hattie Campbell's place, where the wood-paneled wall in the living room is still covered with clippings and photos of Hattie's oldest son, the one the white men all came to see. "Coaches," Hattie recalled with a grimace as I looked around the wall of articles, many of which had been written by me. "They did him so bad. Dancing around and stuff, come in here, telling him this, telling him that."

It is the little things—the snowman on the red doormat, the wooden sign shaped like a white goose with "Welcome" spelled out on its belly—which make it apparent that Hattie Campbell's apartment is not just a hovel in the projects, that apartment 3-G is actually someone's *home*, as important and meaningful to them as John Emmerich's was to him, or mine to me. Handy's mother greeted me at the front door wearing a teal t-shirt, gray sweatpants, white socks and bedroom slippers. Despite the fact that her clothes were rumpled and she looked like she hadn't slept in a very long time, she was still a handsome woman—five feet six inches tall, her magenta hair in a stylish blunt cut, her teeth very straight and very white. She quickly ushered me into the living room, a twelve-by-twelve-foot space packed tight with two plush velour armchairs, a matching loveseat, a television, and dozens of large athletic trophies brought home by her five children. They seemed to block just about everything but a small window, through which I could see a narrow and overgrown lawn, then a clump of weeds and bushes, then a cotton field, and then Highway 49.

I was immediately drawn to Handy's wall, specifically to a familiar photograph of him, in uniform, raising an index finger in triumph. The cutline read, simply: "We're number one!" I tried to figure out when exactly the photo had been taken, but I couldn't. All I knew was that it must have been before he had left Mississippi State in frustration, before he had left Ole Miss in shame, before he'd had his jaw broken in a jail cell in Baton Rouge, before he'd been pepper-sprayed in the Leflore County jail. It was a picture of Handy Campbell as I'd remembered him, and as I still wanted to remember him but no longer could. Hattie walked over and looked at the photo with me. Neither of us said a word, but I knew we were both wishing that we could reset the game clock of her son's life, that we could start over again at the moment that picture had been taken and this time do things right. I turned to her and suggested we do the interview in another room. She readily agreed, and led me into the kitchen.

ঌৎক্ষ

Hattie Campbell had been born in Shuqualak, Mississippi, a small community eight or nine miles south of Macon, in Noxubee County, about halfway between Columbus and Meridian. Her father left her mother while she was pregnant with Hattie, her first and only child; Hattie did not meet her father until 1986, when she was thirty-three years old and already had five children of her own. When Hattie was four, her mother took her and moved to Greenwood, where she got a job in a grocery store on Broad Street. Thirteen years later, Hattie met Sam Handy, who worked at Dix Amusements on Main Street, where he repaired jukeboxes. Sam got her pregnant, but did not marry her. When her son was born, she refused to give him Sam's last name, but used it, instead, as a first name. She was eighteen at the time. Over the next thirteen years, she would have four more children by three more fathers. She never married any of them. She gave all of her children her last name, supported them by working as a maid. She earned so little that she also qualified for, and received, welfare and food stamps. When he was old enough, Handy started pitching in by working summers, cleaning up Whittington Park.

"What was Handy like as a child?" I asked her.

"Shy," she said. "Quiet. Whenever I had to go to work, he'd stay home and watch the kids. I ain't never had any problem with him, period. None of my kids."

"What kind of plans did you have for Handy?" I asked.

"I wanted him to be a lawyer," she said. Not a professional athlete.

In fact, she said, Handy was so timid as a child that for a long time she wouldn't let him participate in sports. "He wanted to play basketball," she recalled, "but I was just too scared to let him go. Cause they used to fight all the time. You know how children do, if they lose a game."

She couldn't keep him from throwing a football around with friends, though, and eventually she grew to recognize his gift and softened her attitude on sports. "He used to throw it so far," she recalled, "I used to always tell him he should be a quarterback." And when Handy went out for the Bulldogs and made the team, she went to every game.

Except one: Tupelo. "I didn't have any way up there," she explained, sadly. "I had a car, but the transmission was messed up at the time." And so she missed what would turn out to be the apex of her first-born son's very existence. She might just be the only person in Greenwood who will admit not having been there that night.

She listened to the game on the radio, though, and she was there to celebrate when he got home, well after midnight. "I was happy, real happy," she said. "We were just excited, you know, sitting around, talking."

"How did you feel about all of the colleges chasing after him?"

"I was very excited," she said, then added: "I let him make his own decision on that . . . I don't know that he went to the college he wanted to go to." The coaches, she said, threw so many wild promises at him so fast that he was just overwhelmed. I was curious about what she meant—where she imagined Handy would rather have gone if not Mississippi State. When I'd asked him about it, just the day before, he'd said that he had *wanted* to go to Mississippi State, that he had chosen them because he wanted to play in the SEC and on national television. I started to ask her more about it, then caught myself. I didn't want to get off on a tangent; I got the impression that she wasn't game for a long interview. Besides, I knew other people who could answer that question, people who were in a much better position to know just what Handy's options had been, and how he had arrived at his decision.

One thing, though, was clear: As soon as Handy arrived at Mississippi State, Ole Miss started trying to lure him away. And while they couldn't send recruiters to see Handy at Mississippi State, there were no rules about visiting his home in Greenwood, and making a strong pitch to Hattie. "They really had me believing," she recalled, "cause the man was coming here, talking 'bout how, you know, 'Education comes first, Miz Campbell,' and said 'Handy's not gonna be happy there, they got Todd Jordan.'"

"They said that?" I asked, incredulous. Even by the standards of the cutthroat world of competitive college football, this sounded very shady, to say the least. "Who was telling you this?"

"Jeff Taylor," she said. "A black alumni. He was here like every other day." Taylor was living in Greenwood at that time, working at the city jail.

"But how did this affect his playing at State?" I asked.

"'Cause they started influencing him in this and that," Hattie said, a little bitterly. "They were just telling him everything. And the coach at Mississippi State was telling me that he was not happy there. I think he called me one day, he was telling me that Handy wasn't performing right on the field, and this here and that, so he left, I went and picked him up."

"And then?"

"I brought him back home and they was here from Ole Miss," she said.

"You mean they were *waiting* for you?"

"I picked him up, and we made it back here about two o'clock, and they was out here. And they immediately took him up there, the same day."

"The very same day?"

"I'm telling you now, that's what they did."

I grimaced; this was beyond shady, and well into sleazy. And at Ole Miss, no less—Ole Miss, the crown jewel of the state's higher education system, the ivy-covered Southern belle that had to be protected from the likes of James Meredith. The lady, it turned out, was a tramp.

"So what happened at Ole Miss?" I asked.

"When he first left, he was doing good in practice," Hattie said, "and they were talking about how good he was doing, and took him to the Liberty Bowl. And one time, the quarterback got hurt and they was talking about putting him in the game, but they never did, I never did know why."

At that point, Handy's younger brother, Anthony, walked into the kitchen and started looking through the refrigerator. I greeted him, then turned back to Hattie and posed the question I'd been wanting to ask someone for the past twenty-four hours. "Why do you think they never played him? You must have some idea."

For the first time since she'd welcomed me into her apartment, she appeared uncomfortable. She turned and looked at Anthony, who raised his eyebrows and tipped his head to the side, signaling her to go ahead and say it.

"Before he got his shoulder hurt," she said, lowering her voice, "a coach from Delta Junior came over here and sat in my living room and told me they didn't have no intention of playing Handy at Ole Miss."

"Ever?"

"He said they didn't have no intention of playing him. He said they wanted Handy to keep everybody else from getting him."

"He would say that they recruited him for to get him from anybody else," Anthony said, walking over to the table and sitting down, "because they felt that Handy would be a threat with anybody else, stopping Ole Miss from succeeding during the next four years of him being in college, if he was going into the SEC."

"Wait a minute," I said. "If they thought Handy was so great a quarterback that they went to all that trouble to keep anyone else from playing him, why didn't they just play him themselves?"

"They were saying," Hattie said, her voice dropping further still, "Ole Miss had never played a black quarterback."

And there it was.

Sure, the thought had occurred to me; sure, I'd half-expected Handy Campbell or someone else to say it to me at some point. I knew that it had taken most white Southerners a long time to acclimate to the idea of a black quarterback, to accept the thought that blacks could do more than just run where they were told and catch a ball that was thrown to them, to come to terms with the fact that a black athlete could actually tell other players where to run, actually throw a ball to someone else—perhaps even to a white wide receiver. I knew that they hadn't liked the thought of a black quarterback captaining a team with whites on it, calling plays for white running backs, or even for black running backs, that the notion of a black man who could think and plan and strategize and issue orders, a black man who could *lead*, had been too threatening for some whites to bear.

But these things had been true in the Mississippi of 1959, perhaps 1969, and possibly even, among some small pockets of anachronistic resistance, in 1979. But Handy Campbell had gone to Ole Miss in the fall of *1989*. I felt like I had on my first morning in Greenwood, when I'd heard Carl Kelly, Jr. deliver his vile diatribe, and had thought to myself that the small old man before me must have been joking, that no one believed such things anymore. But he hadn't been joking; and this wasn't a joke, either. It was a man's life, the life of the son of the woman who was sitting across from me and had just become the first person to tell me what everyone else already knew: That Handy Campbell had been benched at Ole Miss because of the color of his skin, that they had never even considered playing him, not even as they were fervently wooing him away from Mississippi State. Their only concern had been keeping him from playing against them, that he never be allowed to play *anywhere*, that he be contained like a virus, bottled up and tucked away on some high shelf in a vault where no one could get at it. It didn't matter that they were taking from him something he deserved, and with it the only shot he might ever have at a life outside of a place like Snowden Jones; I doubted the thought had even occurred to them. My distaste for Ole Miss hardened into contempt, then disgust, and I found myself wishing that the riot sparked by James Meredith's arrival on campus had not been suppressed by National Guard troops, that it had been allowed to rage until it consumed the place, burning down the lovely old Lyceum building and all the rest of it, so that the ruins could be bulldozed away and a new University of Mississippi built on the same spot, one untainted by the rank hatred that had infused the old University of Mississippi and had infected so many of the people who had come into contact with it over the years—including, it now seemed, me.

I paused the tape recorder and pushed away from the table, asking Hattie if we could take a short break. I needed to clear my head, shake off the growing feeling that I was being contaminated by my involvement in this story, peripheral and after-the-fact as that involvement was. I asked Hattie if I could use the bathroom. She showed me where it was and I stepped inside, closed the door, ran the hot water and just stared in the mirror until the image before me blurred, faded, and disappeared.

When I returned to the kitchen, Hattie fixed me a glass of water, and we sat down again. I thought about asking her to repeat the story just told me about her conversation with the coach from Mississippi Delta Junior

College. Maybe the guy was just lying, I thought; maybe he was trying to lure Handy away from Ole Miss, just as Ole Miss had lured him away from Mississippi State. But surely, I reasoned, the guy couldn't have thought for a moment that Handy would have left an SEC school for any junior college—much less one as small and poor and low in prestige as MDJC—even if they would have allowed him to play both quarterback and linebacker and to coach the team besides. Besides, I had yet to hear or hypothesize another theory on why Ole Miss would bench someone as immensely gifted as Handy Campbell three seasons in a row—and not just bench him, but red-shirt him, so there could be no possibility of his playing, even if every other quarterback on the team were injured. I wanted to know more. But I sensed that Hattie Campbell had already told me all she knew about it, and again, I knew other people I could ask about it. I reached over to the tape recorder, released the pause button, and moved on to the subject of how her son had come to be kicked off the football team at Ole Miss.

According to the coaches, Hattie said, Handy had accumulated more than one infraction during his time on the team. "The coach told me that the first time, they had found some beer in his room," she said. "And the second time—this is after he got hurt—he found a girl in his room. Handy had got the key from the head coach's wife, cause he had locked the key in the room, and he [Coach Brewer] went for to pick the key up and discovered the girl was in Handy's room, and they booted him off the football team."

"And how did you find out about it?" I asked.

"You know how you sit in the living room watching the TV," she said, "and then the news come on and you see your boy throw the ball and hear *Handy Campbell got booted from Ole Miss.* I didn't know what to do." She paused for a second, looked down at her lap. "I didn't know what to do. I just started crying." She looked as if she might do so again.

"Were you angry?"

"I was most angry at them, the way they did him. Like the man said, they didn't have any intention of playing him no way. You got a good quarterback like Handy, you shouldn't be holding him up in the stands. If he did get caught with a girl in his room, he shoulda had a chance. They could have gave him a chance."

৵৽৽

We talked for another hour or so, about how Southern University had sent a recruiter to talk to Handy at Snowden Jones a week after he had dropped out of Ole Miss, how Handy had reinjured his shoulder down there and had an operation and had then grown discouraged, figuring he had just lost his last chance to play anywhere, how he had dropped out of Southern and hung around Baton Rouge for about a year and lived with his girlfriend and fathered a child and worked at Shoney's before his father died and Handy came home for the funeral and stayed. When I asked Hattie about Handy's first arrest in Baton Rouge, she looked surprised. "This is my first time hearing anything about that," she said. "He told me about some store or something, but he told me that they had him mixed up with somebody else. He told me they had him mixed up with another boy."

"What do you know about Lanardo?" I asked her.

"He had just come from the army," she said. "I been knowing him for quite a while. He used to come around. He all right."

"What do you think about the charges?"

"I just don't believe my son did anything like that," she said, especially not to Freddie. "He was a friend of Handy. He was a nice person."

"A lot of people here seem to think he did it," I said.

"It's hard to believe something like that, the way Tyrone grown up and stuff," she said, shaking her head in a way that was more sad than angry. "I know he couldn't have did anything like that." She told me that Anthony, too, had been falsely accused by the police.

"What happened?" I asked him.

"This was around January of '95, in Greenwood," Anthony said. "I was awaiting using the telephone, and a police officer told me to move for their privacy, and I told him I was waiting to use the telephone, he told me if I wanted to use the phone, wait out in the street. I told him I don't feel I have to wait out in the street to use no telephone. When I told him that he grabbed me, threw me to the ground, and tossed me in jail." This had happened, he said, at the Chevron station on Main Street. It was nine o'clock on a Thursday night.

"What were the charges?"

"They charged me with disorderly conduct, resisting arrest, and public drunkenness, but all of it got dismissed when I went to court. They threw it out."

"Why?"

"They didn't have no evidence."

"But the police beat you up?"

"Yes, sir," he said, calmly. "They beat me up in front of the store. One policeman—he was black. He threw me to the ground and he kneed me in the back. He just handled me real rough."

I could see that Hattie was starting to get upset, so I turned off the tape recorder and thanked her for her time. As I packed up, she told me that she went to visit her son every day she could, and that he had been attacked there by his cellmates and knocked around by the guards.

"He told me," I said. "Do you think he'd have trouble at Parchman?"

"I hope not," she said, "because Tyrone's kind of easygoing."

I closed up my briefcase and rose to leave. Anthony rose, too, and shook my hand, as did Hattie. As she walked me to the front door, she said something to me softly, but between her thick Southern accent and the vocal contortions she was putting herself through in an attempt not to cry, I couldn't quite make out what it was. What I thought she said was "What do you think will happen to my child?" Later, though, thinking back on it, I wondered if what she had really said was "What do you think will happen at the trial?"

Either way, my answer was the same: I don't know, but it doesn't look good. I spoke only the first half aloud.

Sixteen

The Delta Way

At 9:30 the following morning, I walked into a courtroom on the second floor of the Leflore County courthouse expecting to witness a trial. I walked back out an hour later without a trial to witness. I didn't know who was going to have to explain to Hattie Campbell that so many people in Greenwood had already judged her son guilty that the town could not even raise a jury to try him, that her son had to sit in a hot and overcrowded jail cell for another two months until another courtroom and another jury became available, sixty miles north. All I knew was that it wasn't going to be me, and for that much I was grateful.

So I stood there on the courthouse lawn for a while, talking to Corvette Walker and reading the inscriptions on the Confederate monument and the historic marker and jotting them down on the yellow legal pad I had thought I would be using to jot down opening statements and testimony and cross-examinations, and then I just stood there some more, not knowing what I was supposed to do next, and then I went and sat down at the base of the Confederate monument and watched people coming and going, all of them with some sense of purpose, while I suddenly had none. And then I went to see Jack.

He was out at Pillow Academy, where he'd been teaching and coaching for several years, having decided at some point that he really couldn't get by on what John Emmerich was willing to pay him, even with the extra cash he made by umpiring semipro baseball games and putting together a baseball camp every summer. So now Jack was teaching civics and coaching freshman and junior varsity baseball, and occasionally taking night classes at Delta State for a master's degree in education. I found him in his office at Pillow, a dark concrete space in the basement that looked to me like a storage room for athletic equipment.

"Hey, you old Yankee Jew!" he said, shaking my hand firmly while he gestured for me to sit down; then, as I pulled up a chair, he sank into his own and snatched a Styrofoam cup off his desktop, into which he presently spat some revolting brown slime extracted from the large lump in his left cheek. All of which is to say: Jack had changed not a bit.

"Hey, you redneck bastid," I said, imitating him as best I could. "Nice digs they gave you here. It's obvious they think very highly of you. It's just a matter of time before they make you principal."

"Is there somethin' I can do for you? Or did you just come down here so I could have the pleasure of kickin' y'Ivy League ass? And ain't you supposed to be covering a trial? A certain former football star you love so much?"

"What trial?" I said. "They had to move for a change of venue. It seems they can't scare up an impartial jury in Greenwood."

"And how long d'it take 'em to come to that brilliant conclusion?"

"About twenty minutes."

"That's about nineteen minutes and fifty-seven seconds longer'n it shoulda took. How you supposed to get an impartial jury here when everybody in town already knows damn well he did it? Oh, excuse me—everybody in town *but you*."

"And how exactly does everyone *know* this?"

"Well, let's see," he said, raising the cup to his mouth for another spit. "He and that Myrick was the last two to be seen with Freddie. They found 'em in Freddie's truck, and ev'body knows Freddie didn't lend that truck a his to nobody, whether they was suckin' his dick or not. Speakin' a which, Freddie wasn't wearin' any pants when they found him, I heard, and I'd already heard that your boy Handy Campbell was stealin' around town to get money to buy drugs, and it ain't that far a leap from stealin' to suckin' dick. And I also heard they had Freddie's jewelry on 'em when they got caught, and you know Freddie wasn't in the habit of passin' out his rings and stuff to nobody, even if they *was* suck—"

"Yeah, O.K., I get it."

"So what's that all look like to you?"

"I don't know," I said. "But it doesn't necessarily look like murder."

"Well," Jack said, spitting yet again, "Freddie's sho'nuff dead, I can tell you that. And if your boy didn't do it, then who did?"

I hadn't any idea; it was a question I had been asking myself for some time now, and my persistent inability to propose any answer at all was making me increasingly anxious, so I just changed the subject. "What happened to Handy Campbell at Ole Miss?" I asked.

"They kicked his ass off the team," he said. "Caught him with a girl in his room."

"I know that," I said. "But how come he never got to play?"

"What do you mean?"

"I mean, haven't you ever wondered why they never played him? They red-shirted him two seasons in a row, and they were already planning to do it for a third when he got caught with that girl in his room. I know they had to do it for his first season, but why the next two after that? Why would you bench somebody like Handy Campbell without even giving him a try first? Were Russ Shows and Tom Luke really better quarterbacks than he was?"

"They were all right," Jack said. "But they weren't in his league."

"Is it possible they just missed it somehow?"

"I doubt it. I can tell you, Billy Brewer has said more'n once that Handy Campbell had the best arm he ever saw."

"So why would he red-shirt him three years in a row?"

"I can tell you what I heard, and that was that he was just very undisciplined, that he needed a lot of work to get to the point where he woulda made a great college quarterback. You know, college ball is a lot more complicated than high school. A college quarterback cain't just call one play at a time and hope it works. He's gotta have a whole series of plays in mind, and after the snap he'll try for his first choice, and if that isn't possible at that moment he'll move on to number two, and then number three, and on until he finds something he can pull off. And your boy just didn't have any experience with anything like that. All he knew was to call one play and then try to execute it. That might work in high school, now, but it ain't gon' fly in the SEC."

"Fine," I said, "but how many high school quarterbacks enter college with that skill? Isn't that why college teams have trainers and coaches? And if Billy Brewer really thought Handy Campbell had the best arm he'd ever seen, wouldn't you think he'd make a serious effort to turn him into the finest quarterback he'd ever seen?"

Jack sat silent for a moment—a rare moment—and thought. "I reckon you'd have to ask him," he said, finally. "It does seem kinda strange, don't it?"

"Yes, it does," I said. "Do you think they didn't want to play a black quarterback?"

I expected Jack to recoil in defensive horror, to tell me how much he didn't appreciate a liberal pinko New Yorker putting down his state and its finest institution of higher learning, and why did I have to go on and make everything about race, anyway? But he surprised me. "Richit," he said, simply, "I don't know."

Emboldened by his response, I pressed further. "What about Mississippi State?" I asked. "What happened there?"

"You know as much about that as I do."

"But you were still sports editor back then. Surely you must have heard something."

"I'm tellin' you, Richit, all I know is that State drafted your boy and Todd Jordan, and when it looked like they were gon' go with Jordan your boy got pissed off and left."

"But he was only there for about two weeks. Could they have made that decision so quickly?"

"They could if Todd Jordan was clearly the superior quarterback."

"Uh, excuse me, but did you sleep through the entire second half of the Tupelo game?"

"Hell, no," Jack said, laughing. "I just pretended to so you wouldn't try to talk to me, you borin' Ivy League bastid. And I know what you're drivin' at here, too, so let me just tell you now I ain't got a clue. Maybe they went with Jordan because he was white, maybe they didn't, but I truly doubt Rocky Felker's gon' admit to it if he did. Why don't you talk to Melvin Smith about it? He's been out there for a few months, now."

"I know," I said. "I guess I should give him a call."

"You could do that," Jack said. "Or, you could just go talk to him in person. He's in town right now."

"Really?"

"I saw him myse'f about three hours ago. He's recruitin' for State. Prolly stayin' the same place you are. Why'nt you go bother him for a change and let me get some work done, Richit?"

"Yeah," I said, pointing to a dingy patch of floor off in the corner. "You missed a spot."

ॐ☞☜

Coach Smith didn't visit Greenwood very often anymore, and he didn't seem to miss it much. He had left town not long after I had, accepting a position coaching defensive backs at Delta State University. In the fall of 1990, his Army reserve unit got called up and sent over to participate in Operation Desert Shield, which soon became Desert Storm, the Gulf War. When he returned he resumed coaching at Delta State and was quickly promoted to the position of Defensive Coordinator, only to be lured away, soon thereafter, by Ole Miss, just as Ole Miss had lured Handy Campbell away from Mississippi State a few years before. He arrived shortly after Handy left and stayed there for three years, coaching tight ends and, later, wide receivers. Then Mississippi State lured him away to coach their wide receivers, although it wasn't clear that they had given him any more money or responsibility than Ole Miss had. Still, for a man who had never played pro football ("I was not athletic enough—I know that," he told me) and who in 1982 had gotten his first coaching job at Greenwood High School in part because "when they looked at me on paper, they thought I was white," his career trajectory was impressive. Even more impressive, at least to me, was the fact that Melvin Smith, who had grown up one of seven children on a farm in the small south Mississippi town of Magee, had been the first black man to play quarterback at both Magee High School and Millsaps, a private college in Jackson widely considered to be Mississippi's finest (and a school that remains almost entirely white, even today).

I didn't get a chance to talk to Coach Smith until about 10:30 that night, when he returned to his room at the Ramada, which was just a few doors down from mine. I caught him as he was returning from an alumni dinner; he'd had a bit to drink, and seemed to have aged a good bit since I'd last seen him—not that he looked older, exactly, but his short haircut, razor-straight mustache and chiseled facial features made him appear tougher, harder than he had seemed even while chewing out his players at Greenwood High School. Perhaps it was just that I was catching him at the end of a long day, so busy that he hadn't even had time to change out of his recruiter's outfit: black cowboy boots, black pants, white golf shirt with a logo sewn over the heart of the Mississippi State mascot—an angry-looking bulldog walking upright, teeth and fists clenched, chest thrust out. The image well-suited the man who wore it.

He had met that day with several prospects, and while most of them were talented enough as players to be of value to his team, he wondered whether they had what it took to be valuable members of society, as well. Not that they were at fault—they just hadn't been raised right. But Coach Smith was not willing to assign all the blame to their parents, either. In his mind, these kids were all but doomed at birth; Melvin Smith, I soon discovered, didn't particularly care for the Mississippi Delta.

"The Delta doesn't really give you a true picture of what the entire state is like," he explained. "This is a unique part of the world; this is a unique part of the United States, and you have people here . . . they have environmental problems. And once they're into the mainstream of society, a lot of times they don't fit well. They don't cope."

"Why do you think that is?" I asked.

"It's because of the dysfunctional upbringing," he answered, after thinking about it for a moment. "A lot of these children, their parents lived on a plantation. They left the plantation and they moved to town. They moved to town and the only place they had to live was the projects, and projects are simply jails, or penitentiaries, without fences." He spoke slowly, his voice even lower and raspier than usual. "There are some problems that have been perpetuated over the years—what I call a 'plantation mentality.'"

"What do you mean?"

"My daddy used to say the Delta was different," he recalled. "They used to say that blacks here were taught not to respect each other a long time ago. If they worked on your plantation, and on Friday when they got paid they went out to party and have a good time—if they killed somebody, they were told that 'if you make it back to my plantation, I will take care of you,' and consequently, those values are passed down . . . I think it's an animal we created a long time ago: slavery, enslaving people, conveying to people that they're less than human beings. It's okay when you protect those people and keep them, but when you bring them all to town and you turn them loose, who passed your values on? Where are these children getting values? That inferior complex is being passed along."

"How did you deal with that when you were here?" I asked.

"We took on the philosophy: Take what you got, and make what you want. Find what you have, and shape your system to fit them."

"How did you do that?"

"One thing we did at Greenwood High School, we took these kids and we competed well with kids outside the Delta. The first thing I tried to teach them is that they were important, they were somebody, they were special. And I think they would emulate us. They trusted us, they knew we cared about them, and consequently they were productive. They listened. It's amazing—I tell you, you can take those kids and you can win. You can do amazing things if you get them on your side."

"So that really worked out well."

Coach Smith kicked out his legs and leaned back in his chair. "It seemed like the Lord put us all here for a reason. Our school was really getting better, we were bringing blacks and whites together, and we were a mix of blacks and whites. It was an integrated staff, and there was mutual respect among that staff."

I nodded wistfully, thinking about how much worse things had gotten at Greenwood High School since the team I had covered, and the men who coached them, had all moved on. The tone of Coach Smith's voice, and the distant look on his face, told me that he knew it, too, that it saddened him to know that everything he and David Bradberry and the rest of the staff had worked so hard to build had since crumbled to dust and blown away with the wind, leaving nothing but memory to attest to the fact that it ever existed in the first place. I began to wonder if he'd had a bit to drink that evening because of where he was, and the memories the place held for him.

I changed the subject. "Had you seen Handy Campbell throw before he went out for the team?"

Coach Smith laughed—one short, loud outburst. "If I'd have seen him prior to his going out, he'd have been out for football, 'cause I'd have chased him. Anybody—if he looked like a ballplayer, we stayed after him. And then once he'd come out, we wasn't going to run him off. We'd coach him, and bring him along to the point where he was good enough to chew out." Mississippi State and Ole Miss had not been as patient, I thought, at least not with Handy Campbell.

"So Handy was a real find?" I asked.

He laughed again. "He was talented enough to play on Sunday."

"Do you think he had a gift?"

"Ain't no question. He was a natural. He did more than just play quarterback. He carried our team. He made big-time plays when he had to, to win games. It was just unreal."

And he and Coach Bradberry weren't the only ones to recognize Handy Campbell's gift. Coach Smith said that at least one coach at State, offensive coordinator Keith Daniels, wanted to start Handy over Todd Jordan. But Daniels was overruled, and later that season he was fired.

"Why?" I asked.

"There were differences between the offensive coordinator and the head coach," he said, "and Keith seems to feel like the reason he was let go that year was because he wanted to play Handy."

"So, when Handy told me that he left because he believed they'd already decided to start Todd Jordan and bench him—even though they'd both only been there about a week—he had it right?"

"His perception of the situation, from what I got later on, was exactly right," he said.

"Was Handy Campbell a better quarterback than Todd Jordan?"

"Yeah. Without a doubt."

"Then why did State choose to start Jordan?"

"It may have been because he was a hometown—he was from Tupelo, close by, and there were a lot of Tupelo alumni. Handy Campbell was a Delta kid; he wouldn't say anything, he wouldn't complain, he would go along. They had him; nobody else had him. He might say a few things but he didn't have a following that would really argue the situation, and it would just pass over."

"Do you think Handy's race was an issue at Mississippi State?"

Coach Smith hesitated. "Probably so," he said slowly, then quickly added, "but I'm not sittin' here calling Rocky a racist. I wasn't there."

I asked him about Ole Miss; I figured that, having worked there, he might have some ideas about why they never played Handy. He did: He said it was largely the decision of Ole Miss's offensive coordinator, Red Parker. "Red didn't want to play him," he explained.

"Why not?"

"He was black!" Coach Smith spat out, startling both of us, him even more than me, it seemed. He looked a bit unnerved, and moved quickly to clarify, possibly divert. "I don't think it was Red as much as his offensive line coach, Joe Wickline," he said. "I think Red listened to Joe a lot, and I know Joe didn't like Handy because of his demeanor."

"And his color?"

"That may have had a lot to do with it, too—but that in conjunction— I don't think Joe believed that they needed to play a black quarterback, and because of Handy's demeanor, it just supplemented Joe's point."

"What do you mean by Handy's *demeanor*?"

Melvin Smith shut his eyes for just a moment and searched his mind for the right metaphor. He found it in *The Andy Griffith Show*. "If he had been

Opie Taylor," he said, "he probably would have played. If he had been Opie at State, he probably would have played. Opie was ideal."

Coach Smith was doing some serious backpedaling now; I could tell that his former bluntness had made him nervous. After all, he still worked in this world, with some of these very same people. He had a family, and ambition. He had to protect his career. I knew that if I pushed him further on race right then, he would retreat yet further into the diversionary question of Handy's "demeanor." So I decided to get him to lower his guard by inviting him to tell me more about that demeanor.

"I know Bradberry used to tell me this all the time," he recalled, "he'd say, 'You know what worries me most? I worry about Notre Dame coming down here and signing Handy Campbell, and then he won't clean up his locker.' Handy wouldn't pick up. There were a lot of just plain basic things that Handy did not do that would make you mad as hell. I used to tell David, 'We know our kids stink, so we have to put deodorant on 'em, so when we present 'em to the public, they look right.' We had a lot of kids with problems, but we did a good job of shielding them." When I asked for an example, he told me a story about a teammate of Handy's: "Bennie Jackson—one time, David went looking for him, and he was over in one of those real rough juke joints, asleep—cause that was the only place he had to sleep. It's just a horrible lifestyle.

"We knew we had kids like that, and they appreciated what we did for them most of the time. So when you do a kid like Handy any injustice, the deep end might really be the deep end. You don't know how things are going to affect him. Things have to go right for them. They don't do very good with hurdles, barriers—especially something that's obvious, like race."

"Was he the best quarterback at Ole Miss?"

"There was not a better quarterback at Ole Miss than Handy Campbell," he said. "Russ Shows wasn't better than Handy Campbell. I was there. If I had gone to Ole Miss a little sooner, Handy probably would have stayed there. Handy needed special attention."

"Do you think he could have overcome the race thing?"

"He could have overcome it if he had the right supporting cast behind him: a traditional, functional family, strong mom and dad." Just the kind of family, I knew, that had produced a man like Melvin Smith, a man who had broken racial barriers at both his high school and college and who was, even now, one of only a few black coaches working at formerly all-white colleges in Mississippi.

And now, for reasons I couldn't fathom—perhaps he was starting to get really comfortable, or angry—Coach Smith turned and asked me a question: "No black quarterback has ever had success at Ole Miss. Why's that?"

I did not answer, but merely nodded my head, thoughtfully. It was not my question to answer.

"He has to be different," he said after a couple of seconds. "He has to be a special guy. I think he's judged a little bit different. It's just like—what are the chances of a black head football coach being there? What are the chances of a black athletic director being there? What are the chances of a black chancellor? I think the quarterback position is judged by the same standard as those positions are. And it's considered, quote, 'a white position.'"

"Still? Even today?"

"I think that's a stereotype that's starting to change, but that's not a problem at Mississippi State." They had already played a black quarterback, Coach Smith told me, named Derek Tate. "He started all last year. Did well, and I believe—to be honest with you—there are some people who still have their doubts. Because you wonder—people think that that person is not sharp enough intellectually—and Handy was a little bit before then. I don't know what went through their mind. But I know Handy Campbell."

I started to ask a question, but he cut me off. "Now, you can't blame what has happened to Handy—there's no excuse if, in fact, he's guilty—for what happened, whether he be a black quarterback, whatever kind," he said, and I could see he was getting nervous again, thinking he'd said too much. "He had opportunity—I think the reason he is not successful is that guy that looks in the mirror called Handy Campbell. Because he had all the talent, and he had opportunity, and you've got to be able to *overcome.* You've got to work hard. Anytime you're a pioneer, you've got to work hard."

I sensed that Melvin Smith was talking as much about himself as he was about Handy Campbell, about the things he'd had to overcome in the past, and the things he was still trying to overcome now. "When you think of Ole Miss," he asked me, "what comes to mind first?"

What came to my mind first was James Meredith and the bloody riot his presence there inspired, but I sensed Coach Smith was looking for a different answer. "Uh . . . the best school in the state?" I said.

"And it's 'too good' for most people—black and white," he said with a look of distaste. "I worked at Ole Miss three years—and I don't know how Handy was treated, but I would've liked for him to have followed the rules. And I know Coach Brewer liked Handy—he did." Suddenly, for the first time since I'd known him, Coach Melvin Smith looked sad.

"So why didn't he play him?" I asked.

"I always wondered why he didn't play—simply because I couldn't envision anybody being better. He was the best quarterback that I've ever been around."

"Some people have told me they think Handy just wasn't smart enough to quarterback an SEC team," I said, not adding that one of those people had been Jack Henderson.

For a second he looked angry, but he held his tongue; then, relaxing, he tried a laugh. "He was just as talented from the shoulders up as from the shoulders down," he said. "He had plenty of sense and savvy."

It was becoming apparent to me that fatigue and perhaps the effects of alcohol were overtaking Coach Smith; this inscrutably laconic man who had always struck me as a fortress of cold logic was now talking freely, emotionally, his thoughts skating here and there and back here again without much regard for order. I felt bad, catching him at such an unguarded moment, exploiting the breach in his defenses, getting him to answer questions he would have tactfully evaded any other time. But I needed those answers if I hoped to understand what had happened to Handy Campbell, and if this was my only chance to get them, I wasn't going to squander it.

"So Brewer didn't play Handy because Joe Wickline didn't like him?" I asked, steering the conversation back to specifics.

"I've gotten wind that Joe may have had some input," he said. "Parker made the final decision."

I sat silent for a moment, trying to grasp the full significance of what was happening at that moment: In a small, insular system where no one talked and everyone collaborated to obfuscate individual responsibility, Coach Smith was naming names. What, I wondered, had happened to him at Ole Miss to bring about such a remarkable conversion, to get a man whose every fiber was inclined toward circumspection to open his mouth and tell what he knew?

"How were you treated at Ole Miss," I asked, "as a black coach?"

"As a black coach, I felt I was treated . . ." His voice trailed off; and when he resumed speaking, it was different, softer, more deliberate. ". . . like a black coach," he said, finally. "I'm there because, in some ways, I'm worthy of being there, but I'm also there because *we need you here, because we have black athletes*. I don't know that I was ever taken serious as a coach. I think I was viewed as a black coach that's gonna coach a position, and he's gonna help us recruit, but he might not have the 'expertise' to come up with the plan."

"Did Coach Brewer feel that way, too?"

"Coach Brewer always treated me like a man," he said, quickly. "I don't know that I was viewed that way by everybody."

"Do you think Brewer would have minded seeing Handy Campbell play quarterback on his team?"

"No, because he wanted to win. But he empowered those coordinators to do their job, and the decision that they made, he went by it. He felt like they were gonna do what was best for the team."

"Do you think you could have risen to coordinator if you'd stayed there?"

"I don't think so."

"Could you handle the job?"

His eyes narrowed into cold, hard focus. "I know I can," he said, his voice dropping an octave. "I don't think. I *know*."

"Maybe at Mississippi State?"

"I don't know that that's going to happen," he said, returning to something near impassivity, as near as he could come while discussing this particular subject. "Because there is not an African-American that's a coordinator in the SEC. Florida doesn't have one. Georgia doesn't; LSU doesn't. I think all the schools have that perception that there's not anybody qualified, or that has the expertise to do that. I think that there are a number of people that are qualified. But first of all, you've got to have the willingness to empower somebody to do that, and you've got to dare to be different—to be the first. I believe you employ people and people get jobs based on merit and what they can do, but they have to be given an opportunity. If you're making this a race deal—racism still exists, and it's something that we just have to try and deal with and realize that it's there, and be able to handle it, and try and right wrongs. But it's not going to happen overnight."

It was something you heard all the time in Mississippi, from well-meaning whites as well as blacks: Yes, there needs to be a change, of course, but you can't rush these things. You have to take it slow. But what kind of comfort could that bring to someone like Handy Campbell, sitting in jail because *they* hadn't been quite ready yet to give him a fair shot at success? Just how much patience should he be expected to have, anyway? And shouldn't Melvin Smith, who had spent his life quietly breaking color lines, know better than anyone?

"So they just weren't ready for a Handy Campbell?" I asked.

"Handy Campbell was a black quarterback in Mississippi with a lot of talent," he said, his voice assuming its former philosophical tone, which I took as a sign that he was sobering up, and reclaiming his characteristic reserve. "And for some reason—whatever reason, whether it be his lack of ability—which is definitely not the problem—his poor attitude, or him being black—one of the three had something to do with him not making it anywhere. Lack of ability, poor attitude, or him being black. Now, which is it? What do I think? I think it was a combination: bad attitude, and him being black. He was a black kid with a poor attitude."

"What if he'd been a white kid with a poor attitude?"

"Probably would have worked out the same way. He would have fell apart. *Now,*" he said, leaning in close, "the chances are, him being a white kid with a poor attitude, there may have been more whites to take a special interest in him and that poor attitude than it was for Handy, because the racial balance at a predominantly white school is such that there are more whites that you come in contact with—maybe a white person in the admissions office, maybe a white person as an instructor, maybe a white academic counselor. There may have been one black coach on the staff at both schools at the time, but the support staff—they're probably white. So it might be more people that are like that individual to really see that and try and shape him."

"Were there other people looking out for him when you and Coach Bradberry had him at Greenwood High School?"

"Elizabeth Lewis," he said, and I immediately remembered Mrs. Lewis, a small, frail, white English teacher, not the kind of person I would have expected to show much concern about Handy Campbell's future. But according to Coach Smith, she had done that, and much more. "She took Handy under her wing," he recalled, "got close to the family, and she tutored him for that ACT. She took it personally—she knew he was smart. She recognized those qualities. That's the kind of person you have in Greenwood." It was the first positive thing he'd said about the town all night, and he quickly followed it by informing me that Mrs. Lewis no longer lived and taught in Greenwood, that she had since moved up to Batesville, Mississippi—the same town to which Handy's trial had been moved.

"It's too bad he didn't have you all in junior high school," I said. "Things might have worked out better for him."

"Had he been in a structured program from the seventh grade to the twelfth," Coach Smith said, "he'd probably be in the NFL. He had NFL potential, ain't no question. One of the best true passers I've ever seen in my life, and I've seen a lot of them."

"Do you think someone like Mrs. Lewis would have made a big difference at Ole Miss?" I asked.

He nodded his head emphatically. "I always felt like Handy needed somebody to constantly remind him, *This is wrong and that's right.*"

"Because . . ."

"I think he could be led astray real easily."

"But I thought you said he was smart, didn't you?"

"He was very clever, sharp," Coach Smith said. "He had a very good mind. And a very good mind that's poisoned, he can use that mind in the wrong way. And I think that may have happened to Handy."

I sensed that we were no longer talking about Handy Campbell's getting kicked off the team at Ole Miss, but rather, Handy Campbell's being thrown into the Leflore County jail. "What poisoned his mind?" I asked.

"His environment. His associates. The people he was around. Handy would not spend time around the people that you wanted him to be around. So, like my mother used to say, you play with trash and it'll get in your eyes and before you know it you'll be blind."

"So you weren't surprised when you first heard he was in jail?"

"No," he said, gravely. "And when somebody told me it was Handy Campbell and someone else—I said it was Lanardo Myrick."

"How did you know?"

"Because Lanardo Myrick clung to Handy. When Handy was an instant star, he hung around practice. He went up to State when Handy was there, and I would venture to say he hung around Ole Miss; they just maintained this relationship. Lanardo was kind of like—he kind of acted as Handy's confidante, advisor, kind of like an agent, so to speak, and I think that's what he called himself—*the brains of the outfit.* And I don't know as much about Lanardo as I should. I never knew Lanardo until Handy started playing. But I spent a lot of time going to Handy's house and visiting his mother, and dealing with him, period."

"So you think Myrick was a bad influence on Handy?"

"I think he was," Coach Smith said. "That amongst other things—his environment, being what he was around, what he saw. He had had a bad life, not a good life, and I don't think he had any fear of having a bad life. When you grow up having a good life, you have fear of living in the ghetto. But if you grow up in a junkpile—you go look at the projects, and then go look at

Parchman; the only difference is, Parchman has a fence. It's hard for me to envision what it's like growing up the way they did, because I didn't experience it. But I saw it for eight years working. I've seen it for six years as a college coach, because I recruit. I go into areas like that. I know, and I see. Mike Espy called the Mississippi Delta 'the Ethiopia of the United States.' I believe his assessment is absolutely correct. And that in itself leads to not caring, no remorse, no feeling, and the inability to decide what's right and what's wrong. Handy is just a product of the Delta and the Delta way. I can sum it all up with 'plantation mentality.' I don't know if you'll ever correct it."

I wanted to ask him directly if he thought Handy had done it, had murdered Freddie Williams, but I was pretty sure he'd just answered that question in his own indirect way. Besides, I could see that he was starting to squirm and look at the clock, and I knew at that point that I wasn't going to get much more out of Melvin Smith, or at least not much more that I could use, that wasn't calculated to be just vague enough to withstand any number of different interpretations. So instead I just thanked him for his time, told him how much I'd enjoyed seeing him again. He echoed the sentiment, reached out and gave my hand a firm shake. As we both stood up, I asked him what had become of the rest of the team that had beaten Tupelo that night.

He was blunt: Some had gone on to play at junior colleges, a few at four-year colleges, and one or two had even graduated. Antonious Bonner had actually tried out for a team in the Canadian Football League, though Coach Smith wasn't sure if he'd made it. But, he said, "Blue" Steel, the cocky little sparkplug of a running back, had gotten mixed up with drugs and had been forced to flee town. Still, he was relatively well off—several of his teammates were doing time at Parchman Penitentiary, and one, who had graduated a year ahead, had been shot dead on a Greenwood street after a stint at the University of Southern Mississippi.

As he was recounting what had happened to the kids who had once played for him—kids he'd worked so hard to guide toward a path like the one he had followed—he slowly, unconsciously, backed up and sat back down on the bed. And when he was through, he just continued to sit there, silent, looking at me and shaking his head.

"A lot of bad things have happened," he said after what seemed like a long time.

SEVENTEEN

A BAD PLACE TO BE

Billy Brewer was named head football coach at the University of Mississippi in 1983. He held that job for eleven seasons, compiling a record of sixty-seven wins, fifty-six losses and three ties for the Rebels. More than that, he personified Ole Miss football, and, to many, Southeastern Conference football, if not college football entirely. Brewer, a native of Columbus, Mississippi, had himself been a star player on the team in the 1950s, back before James Meredith, back when the team and the school it represented could still be said to have earned its nickname, rebelling, as they did then, against the Supreme Court and certain sections of the Constitution. Three decades later, Billy Brewer was arguably the most famous and beloved figure in the state of Mississippi, more famous than Trent Lott or Ray Mabus, more beloved than Eudora Welty or Willie Morris. He was an institution, so firmly ensconced at Ole Miss that it seemed he would still be coaching there long after the Lyceum crumbled to dust.

Then, on July 15, 1994—a day when Handy Campbell was still free and Freddie Williams still alive, a day when the two of them might very well have gone together to the public pool in Greenwood or sought some other way to dodge the terrible heat that descends upon the Delta in summertime—Ole Miss fired Billy Brewer.

He still had three years left on his contract. He still had a winning record. But a few months earlier, the NCAA had concluded an investigation and found that from November 1991 to February 1993, Ole Miss had "demonstrated a lack of appropriate institutional control" over its own football program; the program, it turned out, had broken all kinds of rules in the process of recruiting players, "providing entertainment, inducements, lodging and transportation to recruits." It was the second time in Brewer's tenure that the NCAA had leveled such charges against him, leading Ole Miss Chancellor Gerald Turner to terminate Brewer's contract. "Based upon the recommendations of the athletic committee," the chancellor explained in a formal statement, "my personal review of the facts gathered to date and my lack of confidence that the football program operates consistent with NCAA guidelines under the leadership of Coach Billy Brewer, Coach Brewer was today relieved of his responsibilities as head football coach at the University of Mississippi." In an interview with the campus newspaper, he added that the school's administration had conducted its own investigation into "the more-than-serious allegations and find that several allegations are essentially correct." Outraged Ole Miss boosters railed against the tyranny of the NCAA, claiming that it imposed rules so numerous and arcane that Billy Brewer couldn't possibly have known he was violating them. I didn't buy it; after all, he had known them well enough to kick Handy Campbell off the team for having a girl in his dorm room.

Brewer appealed his termination to his erstwhile boss, Warner Alford, Ole Miss's Director of Intercollegiate Athletics. Alford backed the school's decision. Brewer then went to Ole Miss's Public Action Review Board; they turned him down, too. On January 6, 1995, he filed suit in the Lafayette County Circuit Court against Turner and the Board of Trustees of State Institutions of Higher Learning, seeking "monetary damages for breach of contract, violation of his constitutional rights, and tortious interference with contract." Among other things, he claimed that the termination had "stigmatized" him in his profession, which may or may not have been why, when I managed to track him down six months later, he was working not as a college football coach but as Chief of Operations for the Tupelo Furniture Market.

Tupelo.

When I got him on the phone, Billy Brewer quickly told me he would not meet with me; perhaps he imagined I might be an investigator for the defendants in his lawsuit. He did, however, say I could ask him a few questions over the telephone.

I had no questions prepared; I had called Brewer merely to request an interview and make an appointment. When I blurted out that I was not interested in his suit but in Handy Campbell, he quickly cut me off. "Other than having a great arm, there's not much positive I can say about Handy," he told me, his voice tinged with bitterness. "So many people tried to help him. I won't say he refused the help or direction, but it just never took."

"What did you think of him?" I asked.

"He was a raw talent," he said. "What you're doing is gambling that this guy wants to better himself, get out of the environment he's in. He chose not to do that. It's a situation Handy made for himself."

"Did you think he'd work out when you signed him?"

"I had faith he still had the opportunities to make it. We red-shirted him and gambled on him, but he never made it. We had a difficult time with him. He had a difficult time in a structured environment."

A structured environment. Something about that phrase, and the way Brewer had used it, offended me, as if he were saying that Handy was a wild animal that had not done well in captivity. I wanted to ask him if he knew just how structured Handy's environment was these days.

I didn't. "Why did you kick him off the team?" I asked instead.

"I won't comment on infractions," he said.

"I know about the girl in his dorm room," I said. "But did you really have to kick him off for that? It seems a bit severe."

"I had no choice," he snapped. "SEC rules say, you get caught with a girl in your dorm room, you're off the team. That's it." His self-righteousness on this point—especially in light of his apparent disregard for other rules—made me almost angry enough to say something that would have ended the interview right then. But I didn't, and Brewer, perhaps sensing he had gone too far, changed his tone from indignant to concerned. "Now he's got a *real* problem facing him."

So he did know. "Were you surprised when you heard the news?" I asked.

"I would hope that no kid you're associated with would have those problems," he said. "I don't know if it's a sign of the times or what the heck it is."

He sounded truly sad, as if he could relate to the unfortunate turns Handy's life had taken—which, perhaps, he could; and I remembered what Melvin Smith had told me about Billy Brewer, that the head football coach might just have been the one person at Ole Miss who regarded him with something approaching color-blindness. "Tell me, Coach," I said, softening my tone. "How good a quarterback was he?"

He didn't hesitate. "He could have been as good a pure passer as anyone who's ever played the game," he declared, with perfect confidence. "He would have had the world by the belt."

⅌

David Bradberry, I'm quite sure, could have coached college ball in Mississippi, could even have replaced Billy Brewer, if he had capitalized on his success at Greenwood High School and taken his career up to the next level. But he didn't. I'm not sure why not—maybe he didn't want to make the kind of sacrifices he would have had to make in order to do so, or maybe he just cared about high school football and high school athletes more than he did his own ambition—but when Coach Bradberry left Greenwood High School, in 1991, it wasn't for Ole Miss or Mississippi State or Delta State, but for Clinton High School.

Clinton, Mississippi was a long way from Greenwood. In actual distance they were only about a hundred miles from one another, but there were, I imagined, no two more dissimilar towns in the entire state. Greenwood was poor, more than half black, sitting in the middle of the unfailingly rural Delta; Clinton was affluent, mostly white, and just a few miles from Jackson, the state's relatively civilized and populous capital, the largest city between New Orleans and Memphis. Their high schools reflected the difference: Greenwood's had been built in the 1960s and never touched again, left to slowly decompose with the passing years, while Clinton's, though probably the same age if not older, looked virtually new. Greenwood's gym was dark and dingy; even its football field and bleachers looked forlorn during the off-season, when the maintenance crew ignored them. Clinton's gym was bright and airy and smelled as clean as any I'd ever encountered, and its gridiron and grandstands would have done most colleges proud; the head football coach's office was in the school's brand-new field house, a solid building with bright white walls and large windows.

Coach Bradberry looked more compact than I'd remembered, and younger, too, his eyes a clear bright blue, his blond hair somehow more youthful for the patches of gray that were beginning to seep in. He sported a navy blue t-shirt, gray sweat shorts, bleached white socks and cross-trainers that looked as though they'd never been worn outside. As he greeted me

and shook my hand for the first time in six years, his easy polish reminded
me that he'd been dealing with reporters' questions on a daily basis since
Greenwood had first appointed him head football coach in 1987, promot-
ing him from the position of offensive coach, a post he'd held there for
four years. He looked and acted like a universal big brother, a bit distant
but warm, self-assured without a hint of arrogance or even immodesty, the
kind of guy for whom any man would have wanted his son to play, a man
whose mere presence could make you wish you were still in high school so
that you might be able to play for him, too. He was forty-two years old.

As he gestured for me to sit, he told me that he'd gotten a call from
Melvin Smith that very morning. I winced, wondering what Coach Smith
had said about the conversation we'd had the night before, and worried
that this interview would be a much more difficult and less revealing experience—at least for me. I tried to hide my discomfort by launching right
into a question. "Did you recognize Handy Campbell's talent the first time
you saw him?"

He smiled tersely, shook his head just a bit. "Looking at him, we pen-
ciled him in as a tight end," he recalled. "Big kid, we felt like he would possibly do something there." But, he said, "It didn't take you long to figure
out he could throw a football," then added: "You could see flashes of brilliance. When you saw some of the things he did, you could see him seeing
the whole field."

Flashes of brilliance. I had been leading up to asking Coach Bradberry if he
believed, contrary to what I'd heard around town the last few days, that
Handy had what it took—physically *and* mentally—to quarterback an
SEC team. But he'd just answered the question: Hell, yes. He had all that
and more, much more.

Then there was the question of Handy's "demeanor." I decided to ask
outright: "Did Handy have attitude problems?"

"I enjoyed Handy," Coach Bradberry said. "Of course, any football coach
would with a guy that's got the talent he's got, but Handy never was a bad
problem as far as our football team was concerned. I think all the coaches
could recognize the fact that he was a gifted athlete and the potential was
just unlimited. He did things like leaving his shoes on the floor, being
ragged, things like that. Those are the kinds of things that, because he had
never been involved in athletics before, that he had no conception of how it
was supposed to be. But those were little bitty things. I guess the one thing
I always admired about Handy and liked about him was that he was a

competitor. He was such a competitor that I never questioned when we went out on the field, was he going to play hard, or was he going to do the best he could. It never crossed my mind. In practice and in games, he was such a competitor."

"And off the field?"

"He was kind of quiet and stayed to himself a good bit. Even though he was a quarterback and had a fantastic season that year, I don't know that he took center stage at the school and all that. I remember watching a lot of colleges come through there to recruit him and he'd say very little, wouldn't respond much at all, probably because he didn't know what to ask or what to say in those situations. They'd come in there to recruit him and about the only thing he could say was 'yes sir, no sir.'"

"Was he uncomfortable?"

"I think that anytime you take somebody out of an environment and stick him in that type of world it's just a drastic change. He went through the recruiting process and boiled it down to State or Ole Miss, and he kind of drug his feet, I think because he didn't want to make a decision. He didn't want to hurt anybody's feelings at the time. Ole Miss kind of backed off of him on the last day, and I think he wanted to go to Ole Miss, then they backed off him and we called up there and they said 'I'm sorry, we've already offered that scholarship to somebody else.' So we called Mississippi State, and they had one or two left so they offered him one, so he signed with Mississippi State."

If I hadn't known that Ole Miss had started seriously wooing Handy almost immediately after he'd signed on with State, I might not have thought much about what Coach Bradberry had just told me, how Handy had really wanted to go to Ole Miss all along, how they had turned him down at the last minute. But I did know. I knew all about it—how Ole Miss had sent alumni around to see Handy at Snowden Jones after he had signed on with Rocky Felker, how they had sent alumni to talk to his *mother* after he had left for Starkville, how they had preyed upon his insecurities about competing with Todd Jordan and had finally succeeded in luring him away, even though he must have known he'd have to sit out for at least one season if he transferred out of Mississippi State. I knew it all, and though I resisted it, an image was starting to form in my mind of Ole Miss as the beautiful coquette who rejects an ardent suitor and then, when he finds another girl to settle down with, sets about to lure him away from her; and when she does lure him away, when she has succeeded in getting him to turn his back on his new love irrevocably, when she is sure that he is hers now for good, that he has nowhere else to go, that he has committed to her completely—she dumps him again. That was Ole Miss: the prettiest girl in class, the one every boy wants to date, no matter what it costs him. State was unglamorous, practical, blue-collar; Ole Miss was the shining, flawless diamond of the system, the one that, when threatened by the sullying interloper James Meredith, had summoned thousands of enraged white men with murder in their eyes to its defense. Of course Handy Campbell had wanted to go there. Everyone in Mississippi wanted to go to Ole Miss. In a state with little educational excellence and even less prestige, Ole Miss was the big prize. And they let him think, for a brief while, that he could actually have it.

⋙⋘

I told Coach Bradberry what Hattie and Anthony Campbell had told me, about the coach from Mississippi Delta Junior College at Moorhead, who told them that Ole Miss had no intention of playing a black quarterback, that they had only signed him to keep him away from the competition. Bradberry's eyes narrowed; his mouth turned down ever so slightly in a frown.

"That's recruiting talk," he said, "and it could be true, but I don't know if anybody has any proof that that's what happened. Moorhead was looking for Handy to be a great quarterback, and he coulda been. He woulda fit in great over there. I think in their mind, they were looking at it and saying Handy'll never play at Ole Miss. I don't know if Ole Miss ever told Moorhead that 'Handy's not gon' ever play here.' I think that's an assumption that a lot of people would make for different reasons."

Well, I thought, at least he acknowledged that it could be true. It was a lot more than I'd expected to get out of someone like David Bradberry, someone who was politic almost to a fault and who lived and worked in the middle of the world I was asking him to expose; hell, he was friends with most of these people.

"What's your understanding of why Handy got kicked off the team at Ole Miss?"

"I don't know a lot about it. I just know he got kicked off."

"But you do know the reason—he was caught with a girl in his dorm room, right?" He nodded. "Don't you think his teammates were doing it too?" I asked. "I mean, at least *some* of them?"

"If he was the only one at Ole Miss that had done that, I'd be surprised," he said, his voice now just a little bit softer. "I would imagine there was a lot of kids at Ole Miss that probably drank some. There was probably a lot of guys at Ole Miss that may have had a girl in the dorm at some point in time."

"So why did they choose to kick *him* off the team? It sounds like if they had kicked off everyone who'd done what he did, they would hardly be able to field a team at all."

Coach Bradberry thought for a second. "I think over the course of time he had done things that had caused them to lose faith in him," he said. "And I think that's a two-sided deal there. I think Handy was probably looking at it from a standpoint of *I'll never get a chance to play.* And he was not really interested in an education so much as he wanted to play football, and he never got a chance to play. I think that probably had something to do with him reaching a point where he may not have cared whether he got kicked out of school or not."

"Handy told me he thought Red Parker had it in for him, that he was particularly hard on him," I said. "He thought that might have been why he never got to play."

"I believe that Red Parker rides everybody hard," he said.

"But do you think Parker and the rest of them might have been especially hard on Handy because they didn't really want to play a black quarterback?"

Coach Bradberry furrowed his brow, as visibly uncomfortable as I'd ever seen him. "I don't think Red Parker was looking for a white quarterback," he said haltingly. "And I'll say this," he added, quickly and with conviction, "I don't believe Red Parker was totally at fault."

"Who else, then?"

"Joe Wickline. I think Red Parker was to the point at Ole Miss where he was in the second spring, and he said, 'We're fixin' to give Handy all the second snaps—Russ Shows is the number one guy and we're fixin' to give Handy all the second snaps.' And Joe made the comment—and Joe told me this after I got to Clinton—he said, 'I told him, Coach, I got a problem with that, here's a guy that we can't put any trust in or faith in, and you're fixin' to give him all the second snaps?' He said, 'What if Russ goes down next year, you're tellin' me that Handy Campbell is gonna be the quarterback?' He said, 'I don't agree with that.' And as a result, I think Handy was kind of shifted away."

I couldn't believe how much Coach Bradberry was giving me; it emboldened me to press him further. "Why did Wickline have such a problem with Handy?" I asked.

"I think it had something to do with a personality conflict of some type, but why I don't know. All I know is what he told me sitting here in this office. He said that he told Red that he had a problem with Handy being the guy that they were putting all their chips on behind Russ Shows at that point in time, and I think that had a lot to do with Handy not getting a lot of snaps that spring. And of course it was after that spring that he got kicked out."

After, that is, he had given up all hope of ever actually getting to play at Ole Miss. "Do you think he gave up too soon?" I asked.

"I think that Handy is a guy who didn't have a lot of patience with waiting. He couldn't see long-range on down the road that *I need to pay my dues, I need to play for a year or two and learn.*" And that, I sensed, was all David Bradberry was going to tell me about who had kept Handy from playing at Ole Miss, and why. But I had to imagine that he suspected, just as Handy did, that he was never going to get a chance to pay his dues, to play for a year or two and learn—at least not at Ole Miss. And if Hardy couldn't see long-range on down the road, it was only because there was no road before him at all. Just a hard wooden bench.

৵৽৶

But it wasn't enough for me to imagine what David Bradberry really believed; I had to know. "Do you think Ole Miss did the right thing in Handy's case?" I asked him.

Coach Bradberry shifted in his seat. "In my opinion, no," he said, "but I wasn't making the decisions. I would base it on—I told them when they were recruiting him out of high school, I said, 'He's the kind of guy you can take into Baton Rouge, Louisiana, and he can take you eighty yards in two minutes with the clock winding down and eighty thousand folks throwing whiskey bottles at you.' I think he's that kind of guy. I thought Handy was capable of leading them."

"But they didn't think so," I said. "Do you think Handy's race had anything to do with that?"

"I think race had a lot to do with a lot of peoples' thinking. Without a doubt. I think there's so many people that feel like that a black quarterback can't play at Ole Miss. Whether there was anybody on the coaching staff that felt that way, I don't know." He shifted uneasily in his seat again; I could tell Coach Bradberry was trying hard to walk a fine line between saying what he really thought and offending people he didn't want to—and maybe couldn't afford to—alienate. I changed the subject.

"Were you in touch with Handy back then?" I asked.

"I talked to him from time to time when he came home," he said.

"What did you think when you heard he'd left Ole Miss?"

"I thought it was a waste," he said, and I realized for the first time that David Bradberry had just told me so many things that should have saddened him terribly without betraying any real sadness, or much of any emotion at all. At the time I thought it nothing more than an indication of how smooth he was, how thoroughly professional; later, though, it would occur to me that he must have been very uncomfortable for most of the interview, that he was being asked questions he had no doubt asked himself more than once but which he had never before been asked, at least not on the record, and that he must have worked very hard to keep his tone as even as he had, that what seemed to me at the time to be unshakable impartiality was not natural for him at all, but something he had to put on to balance himself out.

"Do you think Handy could have gone pro someday, if things had worked out for him?" I asked.

"I think that talent-wise, he could throw it as well as some of those guys in the NFL. Without a doubt—he has the stature, he has everything that you look for. He has the toughness. He was a phenomenal talent." And, he added, Handy had high expectations for himself, too, and that Ole Miss played to his ambitions when they recruited him.

"How do you feel about that?" I asked.

"The bad part about the situation Handy's in right now," Coach Bradberry said, "is that it's not unique that he signed a scholarship out of high school, made it a year or two and then left, got kicked out of school, failed. Whatever the reasons, there's thousands of kids that are in the same situation across the nation. Handy's story has gone a little further, and that's the sad part of it. But as far as his particular situation, he's not unique. It happens every year, and it'll happen next year."

I shook my head, sat silent for a moment; I'd never heard anyone expose the dark underside of college athletics so quickly or clearly before. And I never have since.

ॐॐ

"Do you think he did it?" I asked David Bradberry, pretty sure I already
knew what the answer would be. After all, Melvin Smith thought Handy
did it; Jack thought he did it; and Margaret, and the entire jury pool in
Greenwood. I was pretty sure that even Lee Jones, Handy's attorney,
thought his client had shot Freddie Williams dead, or at least stood there
and watched Lanardo Myrick do it and then helped his friend dispose of
another friend's body. Everyone in town seemed to agree, except for
Handy's mother. And me.

"I would have thought that Handy would have been led into something
like that," he said. "I think Handy could be led in a lot of places. And I
think he and Lanardo were good friends. But on the other hand, it could
have been Handy doing the leading. I don't really know that relationship
well enough to know which one it is that leads the other one. But I would
think that Handy could be led into situations like that. I know going in
that he wouldn't lead him into murder, but lead him into—let's get this
guy's money. I'm not sure that you couldn't lead Handy into that."

"It's an awfully irrational path for him to take."

"When you feel hopeless, then nothing matters, and you're not thinking
rationally," he said with a sigh. "I think that anybody that would kill somebody is not rational."

"What do you think will happen?"

"In my heart, I hope to goodness something comes out where he is
found not guilty—more than they just don't have enough evidence. I'd like
to think that he's not guilty. I'd like to think that he's smarter than that; I'd
like to think that he can make better decisions than that."

I told Bradberry I'd heard he'd visited Handy in jail; he said yes, he'd
stopped by after Christmas while driving back to Clinton from his hometown of Sturgis, Mississippi, over in Oktibbeha County, near the Alabama
border. "I had not seen Handy in two or three years, and going into jail
and all that, it was kind of scary to me," he recalled. "I can see where that's
a bad place to be—there's not any daylight in there, it's all back in there
somewhere where you can hear something going on."

"What did you talk about?"

"Handy asked a lot of questions—how we did this year, how I liked
Clinton, how was our team, what's it gonna be like next year—I think, trying to get away from where he was."

"How *do* you like Clinton?" I asked. "How does it compare to Greenwood?"

"I don't feel near as useful in Clinton as I did in Greenwood," he said. "There, for two or three years in Greenwood I felt like I was making a difference, and I was helping kids to make a better life. Whether it was or not, that's the way we felt, and it gave you a tremendous feeling. You felt like you were making a difference. Here, these kids are gonna survive whether I'm here or not."

"Has what's happened to Handy changed the way you think about your job?"

"Back then I probably looked at getting a kid into college as a little more important than I do right now. Back then I thought that was the ultimate—*if I can work him enough and get him a college scholarship, boy, I have really done some good.* And it's evident that I didn't do much good."

"Why not?"

"I think that in Greenwood, to a certain degree, there's a feeling of hopelessness in a lot of cases, and that causes you to do certain things. A lot of those kids are supporting themselves when they're thirteen, fourteen years old. It's not like those kids are thinking, *I can't wait to grow up so I can get my education.* They don't think like that. That was one of the hardest things for me to understand when I went to Greenwood, in the first three years I was there—when kids would steal something out of the cafeteria, when they would break in line, and I couldn't comprehend why they would behave like that—and after I'd been there for a while and I'd back off and look at it, and those kids didn't know when they left school that they were gonna get fed that night. We're talking about survival; we're not talking about being polite in the cafeteria. And I've never been in that situation. I've never been hungry at night. So I began to change my views on what's right and what's wrong. And it's real easy for all us people that are eating three square meals a day and are living in a warm house, it's real easy for us to say, *Boy, those kids ought not to do that.* But you stick me out there on the street without a coat, and without being fed at night and getting up cold in the mornings, and see how I'm gonna react. That's the part that made a dent on me in Greenwood."

I had thought I'd known David Bradberry pretty well, that I'd had him figured out: a decent guy who did his job well, took good care of his family, and tried as best he could to avoid controversy. But the man sitting across the desk from me was someone I didn't recognize, someone who spoke more like a social worker than a high school football coach. I had just assumed that he had left Greenwood for Clinton because his life would be easier down there, but in fact it seemed he was more concerned with how easy life would be for the kids he coached. After eight years in Greenwood, eight years spent working with kids who were poor and frustrated and who knew that life would present them with many opportunities to lose and few, if any, to win, Coach Bradberry was probably just burned out. And now he sounded disillusioned, too.

"Coach Smith said that he saw a lot of hopelessness in Greenwood. He said it's a product of what he calls a 'plantation mentality.'"

"To me, there's two different groups of people in Greenwood. You have two extremes. Whether it's a plantation mentality or whatever, it goes back a long way, and it's an uphill fight for those young 'uns when they're coming through, to grow up and not have a whole lot of things or a whole lot of people to fend for them."

"And that's what pulled Handy back down?" I asked.

Coach Bradberry started to nod, then tipped his head to the side and reconsidered for a moment. "Somewhere along the line," he said, "Handy needed to grow up and accept responsibility and make decisions, and the things that he decided were going to affect his life . . ." His voice trailed off for a second. "I just wish there was a way out of the situation," he said, and looked down at the palms of his hands. "That's the only thing—I wish there was a way out of the situation."

❧❧

The next morning I drove from Greenwood up to Tupelo. I followed a boring route of mostly four-lane highways that didn't lead through town squares or convenience store parking lots; I didn't pick up any pretty girls, or eat any Slim Jims, or sample any chewing tobacco. I didn't listen to the same song eighteen times, or even twice. It was a grim trip, one that took about three hours less to make than it had taken Jack and Snuffy and Bubba Ruscoe and me almost seven years earlier.

I stopped by the Tupelo Furniture Market and asked to see Billy Brewer. I hoped to grab a few unscheduled minutes with him so that I might ask him more questions. If he wasn't expecting me, I figured he might not have time to catalogue about all the things he didn't want to discuss, which might in turn render him a bit more forthcoming than he had been on the phone. But he wasn't in. He wasn't even in town, I was told, wouldn't be back for several days. No matter; I hadn't come up here to see him. I left the Furniture Market and drove to my planned destination—the Tupelo Coliseum.

Despite its name, the Tupelo Coliseum wasn't, I soon discovered, terribly exciting. It wasn't a whole lot more than the Greenwood-Leflore Civic Center built on a slightly larger scale, a big open space surrounded by retractable seating and thick, dull concrete walls. The Civic Center in Greenwood was chronically underused, hosting high school basketball games, mostly, and the occasional party or dance or show or professional wrestling match; the Tupelo Coliseum probably saw a little more action, but not much. In all likelihood the most glamorous thing about it was that one of its employees, a jack-of-all-trades who did maintenance work and heavy lifting and moving and setup and cleanup, was a former star quarterback at the local high school who'd once been written up in *Parade* magazine.

Todd Jordan had turned twenty-five just the week before; the features of his face made him look a good bit younger than that, his expression a good bit older. Like Handy Campbell, he appeared to me at once larger and smaller than I'd remembered him. He'd seemed like a giant when he'd first strode out onto the gridiron that night, a blond Goliath stomping out to crush Greenwood's black David. But up close now I could see that he was in fact a couple of inches shorter than Handy, and his blond mane, that regal golden fleece, was darker now and limp and flopped down lazily over the collar of his shirt, sprawling out over his shoulders as if it were just plain tired. He looked just plain tired, too—tired of moving heavy objects and sweeping dirty floors, tired of a job that didn't begin to utilize his intellect or his considerable physical gifts, tired of people like me who had seen him back when he had been *Todd Jordan* and now came to gawk at him in his defeat and obscurity, to see the All-American Hero laid low and wanting. Why he agreed to meet with me, I do not know; but he did, and as I walked into the Coliseum set aside some crates he was moving and greeted me as heartily as if I were Tom Landry coming by to sign him up. He was game, no doubt about it, and no matter how much I had resented him for taking what I believed should have been Handy's, I had to admire him now.

He escorted me back to the star dressing room—it actually had a star, and the word "star," on the door—and offered me a hard plastic chair. There was only one; he sat on the vanity. He wore an "Icehouse Beer" cap (backward, of course), a yellow "SEC Basketball '93" t-shirt, blue shorts and battered old hightop sneakers; he sported a scraggly, reddish goatee and mustache, and hadn't shaved the rest of his face in several days. If someone had come up to me before the Tupelo game and handed me a photograph of what Todd Jordan would look like in seven years' time, I would have laughed in his face. This was no icon, but merely an everyman, out of luck and just trying to get through life, or at least the next day or two.

He was born and raised in Tupelo, he told me, and had started playing organized competitive football in the fifth grade, quarterbacking in the sixth. "When I was eight and nine years old, I won the punt, pass and kick," he said, a sort of pee-wee football triathlon in which the competition can rise up to the national level. Tupelo High School's head football coach, Ricky Black, made sure Todd joined his varsity squad just as soon as he was eligible.

In the ninth grade, his parents split up. In the tenth grade, when he was still the backup quarterback for the varsity squad, he got his first college letter, from Florida State. "I'm not sure how they found out about me," he said. "Maybe they asked Coach Black."

By the time he finished tenth grade, he was getting lots of letters; he had also moved up to starting quarterback. He started every game in his junior year, won ten and lost only two, an eleventh-grade record. He was profiled in recruiting magazines. "You don't see a lot of quarterbacks my size coming out of high school," is how he explained it to me. In winter, he was a starting forward for the basketball team; in spring, the starting third baseman for the baseball team, where he batted .400 and made the All State squad. When that season ended, he attended Florida State's football camp, at the invitation of the school.

Then came his senior year, the year he led the Golden Wave through an undefeated regular season and two post-season victories, the year just about every college in the South with a serious football program sent scouts to see him play, wooed him, made him big promises. They all said they wanted him to start right away, that they would restructure their entire offense to suit his style of play, that they would provide him with the best showcase for his talents, the best chance to be drafted into the NFL. They pushed hard.

"At one game," he told me, laughing, "Coach Arch from LSU came up to me and said, 'Todd, I've never talked to you, I've never seen you play, but

I just want you to know you've got a scholarship if you want to come to LSU.'" But they all said that, more or less: Ole Miss and State and Southern Mississippi, Miami, Tennessee, Texas A&M, Florida, Colorado, Louisville. Alabama sent eight football coaches to chat him up after a game—a *basketball* game. Being bested by Handy Campbell, it seems, didn't dull his prospects a bit. The schools kept calling. "It never slowed up," he said.

"Why did you choose State?" I asked.

"State was down," he explained. "You could only go up. They'd had a 1–10 season. I thought I'd go in and contribute right away, and that was really what looked good—I could go in and battle for the job, get some playing time."

"Did you know they were signing Handy Campbell, too?"

"Matter of fact, Handy had called me, asked me what I was gonna do. I said, 'I'm not sure.' Then he called me and I said, 'I'm gonna sign with State,' and he said, 'I am, too.' I said, 'All right.' Then we got into two-a-days, and I think Handy lasted about a week."

"How did you get along with him?"

"We got along well. Handy was a funny person, I guess you could say. He made everybody laugh. But he was a little bit quiet, and I could see where people might not like him 'cause they might think he's a snob or something, which he really wasn't. He was just a little quiet around strangers."

The first week there, he said, was the toughest for all of them. "It's really a lonely week," he explained, "'cause you go through two-a-days, you got meetings every morning and every night, and that's all you do is live football. Then the next week, when the veterans come in, you live football for another week. So really, it's just football, nobody on campus, for two weeks. You're used to going to practice in high school, then going home, and et cetera, and just doing what you want to do. Here, you go to practice, you come home, you sleep, you get up, you go to practice, you go eat, you meet, and you go to sleep. There's no real social life during two-a-days. It's a big change, and a lot of people can't handle that change. It's real rough—two, two-and-a-half hours each session. It's hot."

"Handy told me that they had already decided after a few days that they weren't going to start him at quarterback," I said. "He told me that they were actually talking about moving him to defense, and that's when he decided to leave. Is that how you remember it?"

"The first week and a half, when you're a freshman, you go offense *and* defense," he told me. "So they're looking to where you can help them the most. And that weeds some people out, 'cause you know, you've been a quarterback all your life, now all of a sudden you're working defensive back some, they say, *Well, heck with this, I can go somewhere and just be a quarterback instead of having to do all this.*"

"What would you have done," I asked him, "if they'd wanted to put you on defense?"

"I'd probably have been looking somewhere else," he said without hesitating. Once again, he impressed me.

"Were you surprised when Handy turned up at Ole Miss?"

"I thought maybe he'd go to Jackson State or Mississippi Valley, a place he could go in and play right away." I didn't point out that the colleges he'd just named were both black schools, and far less competitive than places like Ole Miss and State. I thought about doing it, or at least saying something, but Todd Jordan didn't strike me as racist, not at all; and I quickly came to understand that *everyone* who was there then probably figured that Handy would turn up at a place like Valley or Jackson State. That was just how they saw things, how they had always seen things. Black quarterbacks played at black schools. Not at Ole Miss.

As for Todd Jordan: They did start him at quarterback. His freshman year, he played in six games, and won three. At the end of that season, State got a new offensive coordinator; the following season, Jordan was redshirted.

"How did you feel about that?" I asked him.

"Frustrated," he said. "I was tempted, really tempted, to transfer. I talked to a few people about transferring, but I stuck it out that year."

The following season he was back off the bench. But he didn't start a single game—at least not as quarterback. "I played in eight or nine games, mostly as a short punter," he said. "I did what they call a 'pooch punt.' I played in maybe nine games, but very sparingly." He did get a little game time at quarterback, but not much, and never when it really mattered. "I hardly got to throw," he said. "After that season, I thought about transferring to a Division II school. Because I'd already had my red-shirt year. I didn't want to sit out another year in Division I, and then have only one year to play. I took an unofficial visit to Delta State."

"What was your top priority?" I asked.

"Getting looked at by pro scouts," he said.

But he grew increasingly frustrated, and at one point was even tempted to give up football altogether. But he didn't, he said, "'cause for one thing, I didn't have the money to put myself through school, and my parents didn't, either. That was about the only way I could get through school." Still, he couldn't seem to get any playing time, and he was starting to despair.

Then, the following season, he started in a game against South Carolina—his first start in three years—but only as a punter. For the next year he did nothing but punt. By the season's end, he had an average of forty-six yards per punt, the third highest in the NCAA. State didn't fare nearly as well; their record that year was 4–6.

The next season's opening game was against Memphis State. Jordan was a senior, in his fifth year at State; he hadn't started a game as quarterback in four years. But then, in a turnabout worthy of an old movie, Coach Felker decided to give him one more try. Jordan played a spectacular game, throwing for 370 yards and three touchdowns. He would go on to start every game that season.

But this was not an old movie, at least not the kind that ends with the protagonist's glorious redemption. Despite his performance in that first game, Memphis State beat Mississippi State, 45–35; and at the end of the season, his record was three wins, six losses, and two ties. "I had a good first of the year, and a good last of the year," he explained. The rest of it didn't go so well.

That was in 1993. That year, even though he was eligible, Todd Jordan didn't get picked up in the NFL draft. The following summer, he went to the Indianapolis Colts' training camp after signing on as a free agent. "Basically, you go in just like the draftees go in," he explained, "but they can drop you anytime, and that's it." Shortly after he arrived, the Colts signed quarterback Jim Harbaugh; after that, Jordan recalled, "I didn't have a prayer."

They cut him after three weeks.

In December, he graduated from Mississippi State.

"What was your degree in?" I asked him.

"Fitness Management," he replied, raising his eyebrows and nodding dolefully.

"How were your grades?"

"I got through," he said.

He came home to Tupelo, looked for work, and after a few fruitless months landed the job at the Coliseum. "It was just something until I can find something else," he said.

That something else, he now hoped, had turned up the following spring, just a few weeks before I met with him: He signed a free agent contract with the San Antonio Texans of the Canadian Football League. It was the same deal he had with the Colts—the contract meant only that he could come and try out for the team, which he was planning to do later that summer. He said they were looking at him as a quarterback and as a punter.

"I think I've got a real good chance," he told me. "I had about given up on football." He had gotten some calls from the Arena League, but he didn't really want to play there if he didn't have to. "Canadian League rules are crazy," he told me, "but Arena League rules are *really* crazy."

I told him why I had come to see him, the real reason I had come back to Mississippi now. He nodded, knowingly.

"Were you surprised when you first heard about it?" I asked him.

"I was surprised to hear he was there for murder," he said. "As far as being in trouble, no, because of the trouble he had had staying places, schools and all. But he didn't seem like a guy who'd kill somebody."

As we shook hands and said good-bye that afternoon, I thanked Todd Jordan for taking the time to meet with me, and for being so candid. I wished him luck in trying out for the San Antonio Texans, and I read later that they did sign him that summer, as a punter. He played for one season, at the end of which the team folded. I don't know where he is today.

EIGHTEEN

HE WHO STANDS FIRM

By the time I returned from Tupelo, I had driven so many miles around north Mississippi that I decided to spend the following day just sitting in my hotel room, making telephone calls.

First I called Keith Daniels, who had been the Offensive Coordinator at Mississippi State when Handy arrived there, but who left after that season and was now the Head Football Coach at Pearl River Junior College in Poplarville, Mississippi. Melvin Smith had told me that Daniels had been Handy's greatest advocate at State, and had lobbied strongly for him, and not Todd Jordan, to be starting quarterback—so strongly that it may have cost Daniels his job. I asked him if he was surprised when Handy left State. "Yeah," he said, "because it was very obvious he had a lot of potential. I was surprised, and didn't want that to happen."

"Who was a better quarterback," I asked, "Handy Campbell or Todd Jordan?"

There was a silence on the line for a moment. "What difference would that make at this point in time?" Daniels said. "I don't have anything to gain by hurting either one of their feelings."

I respected that.

Next I called Tom Luke, one of two starting quarterbacks at Ole Miss when Handy was there, who was now assistant football and baseball coach at Jackson Academy in Jackson, Mississippi. I asked what his impressions of Handy Campbell had been. "Great attitude," he said. "Super nice guy. I think everybody liked him."

"Does it surprise you to learn about the trouble he's in now?" I asked.

"Yeah, it does," he said. "It really does. He didn't seem like the type at all. I'd never seen him in a bad mood, you know. Never. Coach Parker, in practice, would run him to death, and he'd come in joking about it."

After that, I knew my next call would have to be to Jimmy "Red" Parker, who had been the Offensive Coordinator at Ole Miss when Handy had been there. I found him now at Fordyce High School in Rison, Arkansas, where he was the Head Football Coach. "I liked Handy," he said as soon as I mentioned Campbell's name, "I sure did. I just thought he was a real good kid."

"Why did you red-shirt him and put him on the scout team," I asked, "rather than give him a chance to play?"

"It's not unusual for a quarterback, particularly one who grew so fast, like Happy did," he said, making me wonder if he had coined a nickname for Handy that no one else had ever used, or had just forgotten his name. "You know, a kid who grew as fast as he did, it's gonna take a while for his body to mature. So I would say that would not be the least bit unusual for a situation like that."

"I heard that you wanted to make Handy your first backup quarterback," I said, "but Joe Wickline objected very strongly, so he was red-shirted instead."

"I don't recall that," Parker said after a moment. "I'm not saying he did not say it—but I don't remember it."

"Some people think Joe Wickline might not have been crazy about the thought of playing a black quarterback."

"I don't care what anybody thinks, I think Joe Wickline—" he paused for a moment "—Joe never thought about anything but the good of the team. Any reservations he may have voiced would have been the reservations of his offensive linemen. And my policy was to let everybody run their own department."

Parker sounded a bit defensive; I wondered if he didn't feel a little guilty about listening to Joe Wickline. If he did, though, he certainly wasn't going to tell me so—not if I asked him, anyway. I tried a different approach. "Handy's told me that the two of you didn't get along," I said.

"That's a complete shock to me," he said, his tone softening, "because I never had a cross word with Happy. I never, *ever* had a cross word with him. The only thing I did was fuss at him for not going to class. You want your quarterback to be a model. I wanted Handy to be something special."

"He said you rode him pretty hard."

"I ride *everybody* pretty hard. I expect all of 'em to be the best they can. Now, if I hadn't *cared* about him, I would never say a word to him."

"So you cared about him?"

"Dadgum right I cared about him!" he said. "I care about him right now, too."

"Do you think he could have made it on the team?"

"I thought he had the potential, and I haven't changed my mind about that yet."

"How do you feel about what's happening to him now?"

"I am devastated," he said. "It really does hurt me a lot, 'cause I thought a lot of him. I think a lot of him right this minute."

Somehow, I believed him.

❧

Before I made the next phone call, I took care to write out the questions I wanted to ask and then rewrite them. I didn't expect it to be an easy interview. Finally, after steeling myself for a few minutes, I picked up the telephone and called Joe Wickline. Like Handy and Tom Luke and Red Parker, he was no longer at Ole Miss; now he was the offensive coordinator at Pearl River Junior College—working under Keith Daniels.

Wickline seemed friendly enough as he took my call, but his tone grew wary as soon as I raised the subject of Handy Campbell. "What was he like?" I asked.

"Very quiet," he said. "He's a very quiet guy and kept to himself as far as I was concerned, and I never had any dealings with him one way or the other."

Incredible. My first impulse was to challenge him on that very statement—"I never had any dealings with him"—but that, I imagined, would shut the interview down before it could begin. And I had a lot more questions to ask him yet.

"Why is it that he never got to play?" I asked.

He was silent for a moment—did he sense what was coming? "There may have been things that Joe Wickline doesn't know about," he said, finally. "There may have been things that were personal."

"Like maybe some friction between Handy and Coach Parker?" I said, hoping to ease his guard down a bit.

"I don't remember any of that," he said. "Even if it was friction, I don't think that would have had the first thing to do with why Handy Campbell was [only] on the scout team. Because Red Parker and myself, and most any coach out there that's worth a shit and has any sense at all, leaves the personal shit behind, because the rest of it don't matter if you win football games."

"So, are you saying that Handy wasn't as good as Russ Shows or Tom Luke? Because I've heard otherwise from several people who saw all of them, and even Billy Brewer said that Handy Campbell had the best arm he'd ever seen."

"From what I understand, with the quarterbacks at the time, he wasn't as good as those two guys. He wasn't as seasoned. He wasn't there long enough. So to put your whole season in the hands of a guy who hasn't been there, and take it out of the hands of some guys that have a chance to help you win—and we did—that'd be ignorant."

Something about his use of that word—*ignorant*—made me angry; I don't know if it was his tone, or if I sensed somehow that he might have used that same word to describe someone like Handy Campbell, but I decided that I didn't much care anymore about not making him uncomfortable.

"More than one person has told me," I said, "that Red Parker wanted to make Handy his first backup quarterback after Russ Shows, but that *you* strongly objected, so he red-shirted Handy instead."

"I don't advise him," Wickline said quickly. "I never advised him on who to play at any point in time. He may have asked my opinion, and I may have gave it to him."

"One person told me that you stood in his office and told him just what I've told you—that Parker wanted to give Handy all the second snaps, but that you told Parker you had a big problem with making Handy the guy you put all your chips on after Russ Shows, that you didn't trust Handy or have any faith in him, and you didn't like the thought that, if Shows went down, Handy would become starting quarterback."

"I'll say this: I can honestly say that I do not recall making any suggestions about Handy Campbell to do anything, O.K.? I'll say this: I'll always stick by the individuals who are proven players, who have been there before and have produced, before I go with a player who's unproven, who has not shown that he's able to play yet. Now, whether I said that about Handy Campbell, I don't have any idea."

"What's your understanding of why Handy was kicked off the team?" I asked.

"There were some personal reasons involved, and some discipline."

"Can you be more specific?"

But Wickline ignored my question, and took the offensive. "Let me ask *you* this," he said, his tone becoming sharp. "Who told you about my conversation with Red? It's hard to believe that someone would say that—I didn't even coach quarterbacks."

"David Bradberry told me," I replied. "He said the conversation took place in his office down in Clinton."

There was a long silence on the line—so long I began to wonder if Wickline had hung up on me. Then he spoke: "I don't mind telling you," he said, audibly straining to sound calm, "there've been some guys I've said, well I don't think he's ready yet. I can remember very distinctly, remember situations. But I can never, ever remember saying anything about Handy Campbell. I wasn't around him—when I coach I've got fifteen, twenty guys I'm constantly around."

"But you must have had your opinions of him."

"He was a transfer freshman, and it was a bunch of things I didn't think he was ready for. I don't want to get into it any deeper. But he just didn't show some of the things as far as work ethic, maturity, leadership—there were some things that he lacked that wasn't altogether his fault because, hell, he was still a freshman. I don't want to say anything about a guy who's still eighteen years old who didn't have a chance to learn yet."

"But you did offer Red Parker some input on whether or not Handy should have been given all the second snaps."

Now he became angry. "That's a discussion that takes place," he barked. "I've got some situations that went on the table, I've made comments about some guys, yea or nay on, that was my opinion, which don't amount to anything. I don't make any damn decision on who plays or who doesn't play. I can recall those, and if I can recall those, then I know I can recall if I made a comment of that nature about Handy Campbell."

And that, I knew, was it: Wickline was backed against a wall, and he wasn't going to retreat any further.

"Were you surprised," I asked, "when he got kicked off the team?"

"I wasn't one way or the other," Wickline said, trying again to sound calm, "'cause it happens from time to time."

"Are you surprised that he's been accused of murder?"

"I wasn't around him enough to really get a feel," he claimed. "I wasn't exposed to him enough to get a read."

꙳꙳

After that, I called Jeff Tatum and Jay Miller, the coaches from Mississippi Delta Junior College who visited Hattie Campbell at Snowden Jones after Handy left State for Ole Miss and, according to Hattie and her son Anthony, told them that Ole Miss had no intention of playing a black quarterback, that they had only signed him to keep him from signing with a competitor. They both admitted, in separate conversations, that they'd tried to lure Handy away from Ole Miss. "I thought he was the best quarterback in the state," Miller told me.

"We were hoping he'd come to us instead of sitting out that year," Tatum said. "We'd heard he was going to be red-shirted."

But they both denied saying anything about Ole Miss's intentions. "None of us would have told her that," Tatum asserted. "I can definitely tell you it wasn't nobody on our staff. As long as I've been at MDJC, nobody on our staff has ever negative recruited. Nobody on *our* staff ever said that."

"I think the time that they're talking about is when he was a senior in high school," Miller speculated. "Before he ever signed with State. I believe what I told Handy was that . . ." He thought for a few seconds. "At that time, Ole Miss had a quarterback. And State had a quarterback."

There were obvious inconsistencies: Miller claimed the conversation had taken place back when Handy was still in high school, while Tatum placed it later, after Handy had already left State for Ole Miss; Tatum insisted that no one at MDJC had ever or would ever "negative recruit"— a term I'd never heard before, although the fact that such a term even existed told me that it was a phenomenon that couldn't have been all that rare—but Miller said that he, at least, had told Handy that his prospects at State and Ole Miss were not good. But his reasoning—that those schools already had quarterbacks—struck me as absurd. Schools *always* already had quarterbacks, and yet they always recruited new ones anyway, and started them if they were better than the veterans. Handy knew this as well as anyone, and was counting on it; and if Miller really believed that Handy was the best quarterback in the state, he would also have believed that Ole Miss or State would, in fact, play him, no matter who else they had on their roster—unless, that is, there were other factors involved, like the color of the new quarterback. Miller and Tatum, native Mississippians who had been involved in competitive football most of their lives, would have known that, too. And I was pretty sure they would have shared that knowledge with Handy and his family if they thought it might help lure him away, despite their claims to the contrary.

Their stories, though, were solid compared to Joe Wickline's: He had started out claiming that, contrary to the story I'd heard, he didn't know anything about why Handy had been benched instead of promoted to backup quarterback, and that he had no memory of opposing Handy's promotion to Red Parker. Then, when confronted with my confirmation of the story by someone whose reputation for veracity was above reproach, Wickline grew angry and snapped that he'd had no authority over who played at Ole Miss and who didn't—despite Red Parker's policy of letting everyone run his own department; and besides, he added, Handy Campbell just wasn't good enough to play. That last statement ran counter to what everyone else had said, and it confirmed my impression, gleaned during our phone call, that unlike Red Parker and Tom Luke and Keith Daniels and Todd Jordan and just about everyone else I'd spoken to, Joe Wickline didn't much care for Handy Campbell.

Whether or not that lack of regard was due in part to Handy's race, and whether or not it had motivated him to blackball Handy, I could not say for sure; I had my suspicions, of course, but I hadn't been able to verify them definitively, and I knew that I never would. That didn't surprise me, really. After all, none of these men had any interest in exposing a colleague's malfeasance, and certainly none of them had any interest in confessing to their own. Like Melvin Smith and David Bradberry, they were all still a part of Mississippi's football community, and they didn't want to have to leave that community prematurely. But unlike Handy's old high school coaches, these men didn't know me, and didn't have any reason to tell me much of anything. I knew I should have felt grateful to have gotten as much out of them as I had.

But I didn't. Handy Campbell, a "talented athlete" and "super nice guy," was sharing a cramped jail cell with five other men and awaiting trial for murder. He was almost certainly going to prison for the rest of his life, maybe even to the death chamber, and the one thing I knew for sure at that moment was this: He wouldn't be in jail at all if someone at Ole Miss had given him a chance to suit up and get into the game. All of them knew exactly why Handy hadn't been given that chance. But none of them would jeopardize their own careers by talking; and as much as I appreciated the precariousness of their situations, none of those situations seemed terribly precarious at all when compared with Handy Campbell's.

✂✎

I made one more phone call that day, to Elizabeth Lewis, Handy's English teacher at Greenwood High School. I had never met Mrs. Lewis, or if I did I had no memory of it, but several people had described her to me as a kind, caring woman who took a great interest in Handy's welfare—remarkable, considering that Handy was not a particularly good student, and shy besides. Even more remarkable, I thought, was that she was white. I hadn't heard too many stories of white teachers in Mississippi taking a special interest in black students.

But Mrs. Lewis went beyond that when it came to Handy Campbell; it seemed to me as if she regarded him as her own son. Certainly, she took his recent misfortune as personally as anyone I'd spoken with, breaking into sobs several times during our conversation.

"If he'd had the self-discipline, he would have made it," she said. "He didn't have anybody that would ride roughshod over him. Coach Smith could have done it, but he was in Saudi Arabia. Kids that age need that."

"What was Handy's biggest problem?" I asked.

"He just was not channeled at all," she said. "If he had gotten ahold of himself he could have passed his classes—he had the ability. He was very bright. He just didn't have the spark to do it on his own."

I thought about mentioning that Handy's problem at Ole Miss hadn't been academic—that he had passed most of his classes, in fact—but I didn't want to have to tell Mrs. Lewis that I thought the real problem there had been the color of Handy's skin. "Did you try to help him when he was up at Ole Miss?" I asked.

"I'm afraid I did some fussing," she said. "But it didn't work. I guess I'm just not strong enough."

"Still," I said, "it's quite a leap from being kicked out of college to being charged with capital murder. How do you think something like that could have happened?"

"How could it have happened? *Lanardo* is how it could have happened!" she exclaimed. "He was a leech. He was just trouble."

"How so?"

"Lanardo was a bad penny—he just kept turning up. He was a pill. He's a born liar; you can't believe a word he says. He was *definitely* a bad influence."

Lanardo Myrick.

Hearing that name again was like getting hit in the face with a glassful of ice water. I hadn't heard it since I'd talked to Coach Smith, nearly a week before; no one else had brought him up, and I hadn't asked. I didn't know very much about him, and, truth be told, didn't want to know much more than that. Like Coach Smith, I had already designated Lanardo Myrick the scapegoat in this ugly affair, and I needed to keep him there, needed to use him to fill in the gaps in the story. Otherwise, none of it made any sense: How else could someone like Handy Campbell, the shy, humble kid who eagerly shared the glory of victory with his teammates and coaches; who dealt with bitter defeat by quietly withdrawing; who wasn't even aggressive enough to maintain eye contact with another person for more than a second or two—how could someone like him even be *suspected* of murder? It had to be Myrick's fault, somehow. He had to be the catalyst. Maybe the police were already after him for something else, and when they finally snagged him Handy got caught in the net, too. Maybe he had turned Handy on to drugs, and to stealing as a way to pay for them. Maybe Myrick had even killed Freddie Williams, took his Pathfinder, picked Handy up, told him Freddie had loaned it to them for a few days—the recruiters from Ole Miss had already proven that Handy could be lied to, that much was certain—and drove down to Louisiana. That would make Handy an accessory after the fact—assuming he had learned, at some point before his arrest, that Freddie was dead. It was a stretch, but I could conceive something like that happening. What I couldn't conceive was that anyone could warp Handy Campbell into a killer, not even this Myrick.

Then again, I didn't know Lanardo Myrick, had never met him. He could be some sick kind of wizard, a reverse alchemist who worked with people instead of metal. He could be anything, for all I knew. But I did know, now, that I would have to interview him, and soon, much as I dreaded the prospect. I had never really considered seriously the possibility of *not* interviewing Myrick—he was just too important to the story for that—but I had put it off as much as I could, setting up other interviews, making phone calls, dropping in on old friends. But by now I had interviewed and called and visited everyone I could think of, and there was nothing left to do but the one thing I didn't really want to do at all.

I thanked Mrs. Lewis for her time, told her I would let her know how things worked out; and then, just before I hung up, I remembered one more question I wanted to ask her.

"Tell me," I said, "did you see much of Handy after he came back to Greenwood?"

The anger that had hijacked her voice when she spoke about Lanardo Myrick let go of Elizabeth Lewis, and once more she wept. "He avoided me," she recalled. "He was disappointed in the way things worked out."

꒰꒷꒱

The Greenwood City Jail is located in the same building as the headquarters of the town's Police Department. It's a plain, modern brick edifice, as different from the proud old Leflore County Courthouse as Lanardo Myrick was from Handy Campbell.

I don't doubt that my opinions concerning the relative merits of the two defendants colored the way I viewed their places of internment. The Leflore County Jail, Handy Campbell's home for the past eight months, was bleak, but it was a dignified bleak, muted white walls (at least in the corridors), tight little concrete cells and steely gray bars. A mile away, Lanardo Myrick's quarters in the Greenwood city jail resembled more closely a cage in some underfunded zoo—large and messy and even more overcrowded than Handy's, a dingy space where there was no direct light, just a pallid green shimmer that darted around the walls and floor and made the place look like a shabby public bath. The guards who escorted me to their version of a "lawyer room"—really just an empty cell, and no more private than any other in the place—were shorter and pudgier and more dour than those who worked at the courthouse. Still, like their counterparts across town, they didn't bother to check my briefcase or knapsack before letting me enter their jail in order to meet with a man accused of murder.

One of them, a woman who seemed almost catatonically bored, gestured for me to sit and then disappeared with her partner. A few minutes later she returned with the prisoner, walked him into the cell, and quickly turned to leave, locking the door behind her. I thought about asking her to remove his handcuffs; hearing the deadbolt clank into place, though, I decided against it.

And here in front of me, now, was Lanardo Myrick: Six feet two inches tall, one hundred and seventy pounds, as thin as a person can be without appearing malnourished. Hair so short I often wasn't sure, in that light, whether it was really there. Oversized, black-framed, thick-lensed glasses that sat awkwardly on his face, perpetually sliding down the slope of his nose until he pushed them back up to the bridge, where they would teeter for a few seconds before once again beginning their descent. A white "World Cup USA '94" t-shirt, green-and-blue-striped knee-length shorts, tube socks and cheap plastic sandals and expensive leg-irons and a huge red book, the same one I had seen him carry into the courtroom on the day his trial was supposed to have begun. And that grin. It faded once or twice over the course of our conversation but never disappeared entirely, not even for a moment.

He shuffled in and sat down directly in front of me, on an ancient, battered folding metal chair. One of its rubber feet was missing, causing it to wobble incessantly throughout the interview; at times, when Myrick would grow excited about something, the naked metal leg would tap-tap-tap against the cold cement floor like a hammer on a chisel, a sound that did nothing to make me feel more at ease in there.

Myrick, though, went out of his way to be a gracious host. When I asked him, for instance, what that book was—he'd carried it in only with great effort, balanced on his bent forearms, then held it on his lap, pinned firmly under his crossed hands, throughout the interview—he leapt up to hand it to me; but the shackles on his wrists and ankles thwarted the gesture and he plunged forward, falling against the table with such a racket that a guard came by (eventually) to see what was going on. In the meantime I was able to get a good look at the cover, and read the fat letters etched in gold leaf on puffy red leatherette: *The New International Bible.* He told me proudly that he read from it several times a day, and from time to time, when trying to add a little more emphasis to what he was saying, he would tap on its cover and smile knowingly, maybe even wink.

He did not wait for me to ask him an opening question, but simply started talking about how poorly the police had handled things, how unfairly they had treated him and Handy. "From the day one," he said, "we tried to tell them, I tried to cooperate with them, tell them all the circumstances around it, and they ignored us. They ignored me, I know, they told me, 'We don't wanna hear your side, we just want to know how this happened and this happened.' Well, they're not listening to all the other things. And jury selection was a joke. They had a lot of people there said, 'We already formed our opinion.' How you form an opinion if you don't have no evidence—what evidence do you have? At my preliminary hearing they asked this detective, Stafford, they asked him, 'Did you check out any other leads?' And he said, 'Well, no, I thought we had 'em.' You know, you *thought*, with *my* life is on the line. But it'll be all right," he said, settling into a broad grin, patting his Bible and nodding, knowingly. "It'll work its way out. I know so. I'm praying, hoping." His voice was higher than Handy's and more nasal, and yet infused with a certain warmth, even charm, that his friend's self-effacing mumbles somehow lacked. Myrick's voice reflected an infallible confidence; he spoke loud and sharp and very quickly, too quickly for me to ask him anything at first.

Finally, after a few minutes, I managed to squeeze in a question about his background. He was born in Kansas City, he said, on September 14, 1970. His parents split up when he was five, and his mother, Dorothy Weathers, took her children and moved to Greenwood. His father, Charlie Myrick, stayed in Kansas City. When Lanardo was in the seventh grade they moved again, to Kenner, Louisiana, but returned to Greenwood three years later.

"When did you and Handy become friends?" I asked.

"We started hangin' out in high school," he said. At the time, they both lived in Snowden Jones, Handy in 3-G, Lanardo in 8-F. Lanardo was a year ahead of Handy in school, and ran for the track team, even making it to the North Mississippi championship in his senior year. "I ran the 330 hurdles," he said.

"How'd you do?" I asked.

He shook his head. "Came in fifth place," he said. "Doing something silly." It was around this time, too, that he and Handy staged their "Fastest Man in Snowden Jones" competition, in which Handy, who did not run track, beat him.

"What did you guys do outside of sports?" I asked.

He laughed. "That's all we did. There was no 'outside of sports,'" he said, then segued seamlessly into a tale of how Valley gave him a track scholarship and how later he went down to Texas to run at the Houston Track Club with Carl Lewis in 1991. After a couple of minutes I forced my way into his soliloquy and tried to steer the conversation back to his friend.

"Me and him kinda butt head-to-head on a lot of things, especially football," he explained. "He thinks he knows everything. He had the football ability, athletic, but nobody ever said, hey, when are you gon' go to class? School? Books? Nobody ever said that. His mom didn't know. Who else ever went to college in that family? They built Handy up to be an athlete. Nobody said anything about being a man. Being 'class.' *Well, we'll give you money but we're not gonna teach you what to do with it.* Hey, you got a woman, but you don't know anything about marriage or responsibility or nothing, you're just—*You're an athlete, you're Handy Campbell, throw the ball.* I was trying to tell him, 'Hey, man, we got to study.' It's something new. Ain't nobody said, 'study.' Ain't nobody tell you to go to college for academics. They just said to go for ball. That was what I call the killer. He'd never work. There was no work ethic. Like me. It just never was. I had a little bit more than him, but not enough. Not enough to survive in this world full of racism and prejudice and all that stuff."

By this time, I had no idea what he was talking about anymore; he was just chattering faster and faster, zigzagging between subjects and tenses and places and years and mixing it all up. But from what I could pick out here and there, I sensed that what he was really doing in all of this was presenting his defense, which seemed to come down to: Look what society made *Handy* do.

I had to marvel at his shrewdness, starting off with the usual "We didn't do anything," and then, in case you didn't buy that, setting up a foundation for: "They made him do it—and I said *him*, you'll note, not *me*." I wondered if I hadn't underestimated him, taking my cues from Coach Smith and Mrs. Lewis, who had presented Lanardo as a remora to Handy's shark, devoted, loyal, in awe of his friend and always in tow. But the Lanardo Myrick I was speaking with—or, in any event, listening to—clearly saw himself as the star, the conscience, the leader, and Handy as a supporting player, a moral weakling, a follower. Worse, Myrick appeared ready to sacrifice Handy on a moment's notice if he thought that doing so might give him a chance to save himself, or even to get a slightly better deal. I perceived him as grossly self-important, incapable of feeling remorse or questioning his own rectitude. I figured he was a sociopath, and probably manic, too—and maybe, under the right circumstances, capable of murder.

⚜

After high school, Lanardo Myrick enrolled at Mississippi Valley State University in Itta Bena—attending, he said, on a track scholarship. But he didn't last two semesters there before dropping out, and after a couple of short-lived jobs—Jackie's Food Mart, Shoney's—he left town and enlisted in the army.

"That must have been a big change for you," I said. "Why did you do it?"

"I was looking for some—what you call it?—discipline shit, but I should have been looking at myself. I was looking for somebody else to make something out of me. I should have been looking for it myself. You see, that's the thing with Handy—he never had any. Who was going to discipline him—his mom?" He laughed. "You could get over a mom. He didn't have no father. I didn't have a father."

He enlisted, he said, at Fort Leonard Wood, Missouri, in November 1993, and trained to be a truck driver, "which was silly—it was all a part of my plan to get some discipline."

"Did you see Handy at all during this time?"

"I came home for Christmas and in March, I saw him both times. He had just come back from Baton Rouge and he wasn't doing too well. He just wasn't—he wanted to go to school. I could tell he wanted—he wanted to do the things everybody wanted him to do. And between both of us, it was kind of like—failure. That was a big thing."

And then, Myrick recalled, he got into trouble with the army, breaking his hand when he punched a wall during an argument.

"Over what?" I asked.

"Just silly pressures," he said. "And then this woman filed sexual harassment charges against me. It was totally false. It was all racial. They wanted me out."

Myrick returned to Greenwood in early August 1994. "Me, I came home to get me a job," he explained, "'cause I got a trade now, truck driving, get me a job and do the things I wanted to do, 'cause I kinda wanted to try for the Olympics, or get close enough to the—just to some of the dreams I wanted."

"What happened?" I asked.

"I stayed out two weeks," he said, grinning broadly, "and here I am!" Which is to say: Within two weeks of his return to Greenwood, he and Handy were arrested while driving Freddie's truck in Baton Rouge.

"Tell me," I said. "Where did Freddie Williams fit into all this?"

He smiled. "Nobody's talking about the facts," he said, and I could see something creep into his eyes, a sharp glint that hinted at conspiracy. "The other things, what I call 'the touchy subjects.' It's like, a lot about 'gay activity' with the victim . . . it's even the way they're treatin' our relationship with the man, with Freddie, it's kinda like we didn't know him, like we were some deuces. We practically grew up knowing him. It's a trip how they're doing it. It's a weird thing, now, 'cause they put him up on a pedestal as far as who he is, who he was, when a lot of people really didn't know who he was."

"Who was he?"

"Like us, you know, kinda lost in life. He had a wife, but he never slept in bed with her. She slept in the bedroom, he slept on the couch. They never had sex. They had not had any sex for weeks, months. They didn't like each other. But, it was like, they were staying at the house for the sake of the kids, which, Freddie was saying, he was hurting. When his older son saw him, he was kind of learning that he was, you know . . ."

Myrick left the sentence hanging, just closed his mouth and smirked.

"Gay?" I said. "Was he gay?"

Myrick tipped his head to one side, rolled his eyes. "Well, I never seen it," he said, "but I figure, you know, from what everybody said, he had to have been. You know, he never made no advance at us. You know, he kinda made, you know, like, 'I'm gonna get me a *man*,' you know. He would say those things, like, you know, 'I need a lover.' You know, that type thing . . . it was Freddie. Like your friend confiding. He's not taking nothing from you, so you just listen. He never said 'I want you,' you know. Never."

"I've heard that when you came back from the army you were living with Handy and his mother at Snowden Jones. Why was that?"

"There was some trouble between my mother and her boyfriend. I didn't want to stay at a stranger's house—how that sound? Plus, I'm looking for a job in Greenwood. I went to Snowden Jones with the intention of staying with my grandma, but then I start hangin' with Handy. The second or third day, we met Freddie—he came over in the Pathfinder, we're talkin', chit-chattin', and me and Handy started hangin' with him." He leaned in closer. "Touchy subject. It's a weird thing. His wife—I know she couldn't have known him. The last six or seven days before I got locked up were the real ones, because every day had a significant meaning to it, like—it was a *bond*."

"So what happened on Freddie's last night?"

He drew back again, sat upright in his chair, and flashed a smile that said: You dog, trying to put one past me, eh? "I can't talk much about that, now," he said, still smiling. "I don't want this to come back and haunt me."

"How so?" I asked.

"To me, I believe it's bigger than I think it is, and I don't have enough money or patience to handle it," he responded, cryptically.

"Handle what?"

"Let me tell you, this is something weird in Greenwood. They have an injunction—there's only one bond agent in Greenwood, they have an injunction for no other ones to come in this town. Why did they hold me two months in Baton Rouge? I have a paper in this room that says to release me! Another funny thing: During that week, Freddie was making references to money—you know, people put him on a pedestal—as far as, we got money, you know, we got a blue Maxima and a Pathfinder, big gold, big rings, and all this. Now, because he had a job, no one ever wondered, how'd he get all that money? You know, this Pathfinder's pretty expensive, that's maybe six, seven hundred a month. How'd he get this money? And that goes to some of the things he was saying, which I didn't even know the truth about—just, you know. This is my bombshell. I'm gonna have to keep this one. It's all funny. It'll all work out."

He was spiraling out of control, now, and it was all I could do just to hang on and not lose him entirely. He was trying, near as I could tell, to set Freddie up as this great enigma, at once more benevolent and more sinister than anyone knew—anyone but his good friend Lanardo, that is—the kind of guy who loans out his truck and then just disappears all the time, as a matter of course. At the same time, Myrick was busily sketching out a huge conspiracy, with only one bail bondsman in town, and a mysterious document in his cell—which he couldn't show me, no, not today—that decreed he should be set free immediately, and lots of money of obscure origin flowing through Freddie Williams, who was at the center of every-thing, only now that Freddie was gone they were trying to blame it on a couple of hapless college dropouts who just wanted to hang out and have a good time, drink a little, maybe smoke some. Was Myrick trying to fash-ion some grand red herring? Or did he really believe this stuff, crazy as it was? Whatever the case, I figured I didn't have much left to lose by being direct with him.

"Come on," I said, trying on a conspiratorial smile. "Tell me about that last night."

But he just smiled back, a perfect mimic of mine. "Can't talk about that night," he said, "because that's what I'm here for."

"Why did you want to borrow Freddie's truck?"

"I can't answer that one. I'll wait till I get to court to answer that one. That's too much of the case, 'cause those are some of the things they're talking about."

"I've heard that Freddie said you could borrow the truck in exchange for sexual favors. Is that true?"

"I don't know about that one—is it?" His grin broke into a laugh. I wasn't sure if he was trying to charm or frustrate or frighten me, but he managed to do all three.

"I'm gon' tell you this," he said. "I know one thing: It's not like, 'Gimme your truck.' You see, what people say is another thing. I wanna ask his wife what it's all about—that's another thing."

"So who killed him?"

"I know one thing—whoever it is, they're not playing fair. It's not a setup—I believe somebody took advantage of the situation."

I was about to make a crack—A murderer not playing fair? Shocking!—when it occurred to me how much what Lanardo Myrick had just said reminded me of another criminal case that was being tried at that very moment, two thousand miles away; I just couldn't figure out if Myrick thought he was O. J. Simpson or Johnnie Cochran, or maybe both.

"Uh, could you be a little more specific?" I said.

"That's just too much," he said, chuckling and waving me off. "I done gave you too much already."

"Did Freddie ask you for anything in exchange for lending you his truck?"

"Ask for what? Talking 'bout sex or something? Naah. Matter fact, I'm gon' leave that one alone. People don't even wanna talk about who he was—just keep him on a pedestal. Same thing, you take two kids to court, everybody says they're guilty. You convict them two, you still ain't solved who broke your window, because, if you don't have the evidence . . ." He stopped, lowered the microphone for a second, pointed to my tape recorder, smirked and shook his head. "You know," he said, "I'm paranoid about tapes."

"I also heard you fired your first lawyer," I said.

"If I give you enough ammunition to blow a hole in the ship and you don't even fire the gun, something's wrong. Everytime he came to me, it was like he had seen a ghost."

"What do you think of Willie Perkins?"

"He kinda disappoints me." He looked down at his lap and drummed his hands against the cover of his massive Bible. "I been reading it all my life," he said, "but you know, you read but you never heed."

"When did you start heeding?"

"When I got in the jail in Baton Rouge."

"What was that like?"

"Baton Rouge was a learning experience. We stayed there about two days; we were going to find some guy he loaned money to, just kickin' around the campus. For me, I just wanted to relax. To me it was a vacation."

"No, I meant what was it like for you in the jail in Baton Rouge, but since you brought it up, which campus were you hanging around?"

"Southern."

"So why were you arrested on the LSU campus?"

"They pulled us over in connection with the stolen vehicle. Things started trippin' me out—it really tripped me out. I know why they picked us up: two black men, at LSU, at night . . ."

"But what were you doing *at LSU?*" I asked him.

"We'd been drinkin', hangin' out," he said. "We just wanted to ride."

"So what happened when they stopped you?"

"They said, 'How did you get this man's vehicle? What'd y'all do to him?' I said, What do you mean, 'What'd you do to him?' He said, 'Come on, come on, nigger, talk. That's all you black people do is lie. Tell me the truth.' I said, 'I'm not talkin', you gettin' mad.' He gets out of the car, lieutenant says, 'I'm gonna hold y'all 'cause this vehicle has been stolen, and the man who owns it hasn't showed up.' I said, 'What do you mean? Freddie's missing?' And the Greenwood police said, he said, 'You ain't no punk, but you gon' be one when you get to Parchman.'"

"What did he mean by 'punk'?"

"You know, faggot, homosexual. He said, 'If you ain't one now, you gon' be one when you get to Parchman. You know what they gon' do to you?' All this hollering."

"Have you had any problems in jail?"

"No, I don't have any problems. Handy's had a few, but not me."

For some reason, that didn't surprise me. Myrick was a survivor, I could tell, someone who could talk or charm or smile his way out of almost any threatening situation, and if that wouldn't do it he could always find a way to deflect it onto someone else. I did not doubt that at least one of the beatings Handy had endured in jail had originally been meant for his friend, instead. No wonder he seemed so confident everything would work out just fine; still, I asked him to tell me why he was.

" 'Cause I'm innocent," he said, looking as earnest as he had all morning. "He's innocent."

"So, do you have any idea who did it, then?"

"Not an idea. I used to have a picture, an image. But nobody ever asked me. I know the man who Freddie left with." I asked him who that was, what he looked like, but Myrick just grinned and shook his finger at me and said something about how his memory has faded after so many months in jail.

I just stared at him, out of questions at last. "Anything else?" I said, tired after a long psychological chess game and hoping his answer would be a simple no.

But now the grin returned. "Do *you* have anything else?"

It was an invitation I couldn't decline, and so I drew myself up in my chair and said: "You want to tell me what happened that night?"

"No," he muttered. "I just . . ." He raised an index finger to his lips, and pointed the other one at my tape recorder.

"If I turn off the tape, you want to tell me?" I offered, surprising myself. It was a serious compromise—I taped all of my interviews from start to finish, just to make sure I didn't miss anything or misquote anyone—but I really wanted to hear what he would say, and if this was the only way I could get him to talk, I would just have to do it.

"Yeah," he said, his smile spreading into a grin. "I could tell you then."

I turned it off.

And as soon as I did Myrick was transformed, as if he had unlocked his handcuffs and kicked off his leg irons and revealed himself to be not an inmate but in fact the chief of police. He started talking fast, very fast, his voice dropping down a few decibels in the process. Leaning in conspiratorially, he spun a tale of three friends cruising around Greenwood on a hot August night, stopping by nightclubs and bars and, when they had all closed, cruising several convenience stores, buying beer and malt liquor and drinking it in the parking lot before moving on. They were in the Pathfinder, of course, and Freddie let each of them drive it in turns while he partied in the backseat with whoever wasn't driving. At one point, Myrick said, he drove for a long time while Freddie and Handy hunkered down in the back, speaking in hushed tones and bumping around and making odd noises; when I asked him what they were doing back there, he just smirked and shrugged, then offered that Handy was probably trying to convince Freddie to let them borrow the truck so that they could visit their kids, whom they hadn't seen in months, and to pay calls on friends in Baton Rouge, some of whom, Myrick said, owed Handy money. I told him I'd heard that Freddie never loaned his truck to anyone, rarely even let anyone else drive it; he agreed. How, then, I asked, did they get Freddie to lend it to them at all, much less two kids who planned to drive it hundreds of miles and out of state, who might reasonably be expected to be gone with it for at least a week?

Myrick just smiled, smiled exactly as he had so many times in the past couple of hours, only now, for some reason, that smile failed to charm me. Now, for some reason, that smile antagonized me. "Come on," I said. "There's something you're not telling me." Again he just smiled, and again it antagonized me, and I started to feel annoyed and then irritated and then angry, and I said: "You know what everyone's saying, don't you? You know that everyone says Freddie told you he'd let you and Handy borrow the truck if you both sucked his dick, and you did, and then maybe he said O.K. you can have it, or maybe he changed his mind and said no, but that either way you killed him then, either because you were pissed at him for breaking his word, or you were afraid he'd tell everyone what the two of you had done."

And the smile faded, very nearly evaporated, and Myrick said: "No, no, no. People say a lot of things. They say what they want; they put Freddie up on a pedestal. But that's not how it was. That's not how it happened. No. No way. That never happened. No."

"What never happened?" I asked.

"None of it," he said.

"Freddie didn't ask you to suck his dick in exchange for letting you borrow his truck?" I said.

"No," he said, "no, no, no, no, nothin' like that, he didn't ask us for nothin'. He just let us borrow it."

"Why?" I said.

"Just because," he said, "he really liked us. He really liked us." And now the smile returned in force, and I knew that was it, he was back in control again, he wasn't going to let anything slip.

"So what happened then," I asked, "after he said you could have the truck, just because *he really liked you?*"

"We just drove around some more," Myrick said, "drinking here and there."

"Until when?"

"What happened was we went to the Double Quick, and—"

"Which Double Quick?"

"On Main Street, and we went there and we're hanging out and then Freddie said he needs to call this guy to come pick him up so he can go out some more and we can have the truck, and he goes to the payphone and calls him, and we stay there and wait, and in a few minutes this car comes by and stops, and Freddie gets out of the truck and gives us the keys and gets into the car and drives off, and that's the last I saw him."

"The last?"

"That's the last."

"And where was this?"

"I told you, we were at the Double Quick."

"And this car pulled up next to you?"

"Yes."

"In the parking lot?"

"Right."

"By the pumps?"

"Right."

"And what kind of car was it?"

"You know," he said, grinning, "I don't remember that."

"What color was it?"

"It was dark."

"Dark what?"

"I don't know. I don't remember exactly. It was dark."

"And how many people were in it before Freddie got in?"

"There was one guy."

"What did he look like?"

"I don't know."

"But you said you could describe him."

"I said I *used to* could describe him."

"But not now?"

"Not now."

"You said you knew who he was."

"I did?"

"You told me you knew who the guy was."

"Maybe I used to."

"But not now?"

"Not now."

"Did you get the license plate number?"

"No, I didn't see that."

"Was it a Mississippi tag?"

"Probably, yeah."

"Leflore County?"

"I didn't see that."

"And Freddie got into the car?"

"Yes."

"Front or back?"

"I don't remember. The front, probably."

"And they just drove off and left you and Handy with the Pathfinder?"

"That's right."

"Where did Freddie say he was going?"

"He didn't say where, just going off to party some more."

"In Greenwood?"

"I guess. He didn't say."

"But no one reported seeing him in Greenwood after that," I said.

"I don't know," he said. "Maybe that's just what they say, you know?"

"And what time was this?"

"About three."

"Three?"

"Three, three-thirty."

"And that was the last time you saw him?"

"That was the last."

While we spoke I scribbled and scratched on my yellow legal pad until my hand started to hurt. Luckily I ran out of things to ask about that time, too, and so I stood up and thanked him, told him we were through. He scrambled up out of his chair and reached out to shake my hand. I offered him my hand and he clasped it in between both of his and smiled and laughed and said he guessed he'd see me again soon, and don't worry, now, it'll all be all right. I told him I wasn't worried.

I wasn't. Not about him.

⚜

I stopped by the *Commonwealth* later that afternoon to look up a few stories about Freddie's disappearance, the discovery of his remains two months later, and the arrest and arraignment of the two men suspected of murdering him. While I was there I ran into Tim Kalich, the former general manager who had taken over the paper after John Emmerich's death. I asked him what he knew about Lanardo Myrick.

"Not much," he said. "He sends us a lot of letters, though."

"Really? What does he say?"

"Nothing about the case. Just preachy stuff about community and society, mostly."

"Do you publish them?"

"I think we did publish one." He walked over to the table near the front door where the huge books of *Commonwealth* tear sheets were kept, and started to flip through them.

"Here it is," he said after a few minutes, tore out a page and handed it to me. It was dated December 27, 1994—four months after Freddie disappeared, two days after his family's first Christmas without him. I scanned down and read:

> We must convert a culture of violence which defeats and destroys into a culture of character which uplifts and empowers.
>
> We need strong families who spend time together and families who attend a church, mosque or synagogue together.
>
> The Holy Bible states in Matthew 24:10 and 13, "Many will turn away from faith and will betray and hate each other . . . But he who stands firm in the end will be saved.
>
> —Lanardo Myrick, Greenwood

Editor's Note: *The writer of this letter is in the Greenwood City Jail charged with Capital murder in the August shooting death of United Parcel Service driver Freddie Williams.*

Later I would conclude that Myrick had almost certainly not written this letter himself, that he was probably on the mailing list of some religious organization, perhaps one that specialized in ministering to prisoners, and that most likely they had sent him the letter with a request that he sign his name to it and mail it in to the local newspaper.

At the time, though, I just laughed—at the bizarre juxtaposition of the letter and that editor's note, of course, but even more at the absurdity of such a lofty, idealistic epistle coming from a man who had murdered a friend and then stole his truck.

And I realized, as I laughed, the chilling significance of the notion I had found so humorous: I had at last decided that Lanardo Myrick had murdered Freddie Williams.

I did not know, yet, what role Handy Campbell had played in the killing. But I intended to find out, and to do so I would have to pay Handy another visit at the Leflore County jail.

NINETEEN

DIORAMA

*T*o my surprise, Lee Jones had no problem at all with my request to meet with and interview his client again. "Why the hell not?" was his exact response, and though I could have offered him a half-dozen convincing reasons, I said only: "Thanks."

And so it was that once again I found myself at the Leflore County courthouse on a Saturday morning, exactly one week after my first visit. There was no waiting this time; as I walked through the side door I caught Sheriff Banks's eye, and he signaled a deputy to escort me upstairs. Yet again no one asked to see my briefcase, and I started to feel exalted and powerful and to understand, for the first time, really, how the enormous privileges accorded to white skin could prove terribly intoxicating, and how some white people might grow so addicted to those privileges that they would fight ferociously to keep them, no matter the cost. How strange, I thought, that I never saw it that way when I lived here; back then the same treatment only made me feel nauseated with guilt. I must have been stronger then, better. I have to get out of here soon.

Only a week had passed since I had last seen Handy Campbell, but a lot had changed in that week, at least for him. His trial had been postponed, moved to another town where no one knew who he was, much less who he had been; his hope for imminent freedom, or at least an end to the uncertainty of his fate, had been defeated. As he once again shuffled slowly into the lawyer room, he looked different to me. Was he more tired than the last time I'd seen him, more anxious, depressed? Or was he in fact different at all? Was the difference really in me, in the way I looked at him now? The last time I saw him I knew he had to be innocent; now I wasn't so sure. That look on his face, the one that I used to take for thoughtful humility—was it really a subtle shade of malevolence? Guilt? Utter obliviousness? Could I really have misjudged him all these years? Or was this a new and degraded Handy Campbell, a product of the frustration and bitterness that his dealings with Ole Miss and Mississippi State and the law would have instilled in almost anyone? Was there even a Handy Campbell there at all? My belief that I really knew him was, I now understood, an illusion. He was a mystery to me.

As I sat there in the lawyer room and watched him make his way to the empty chair, I realized that I didn't *want* to interview him again, not at all; and when the deputy who led him in—the same one as last week—stopped on his way out of the room to ask me if I wanted to have the prisoner unshackled again, I almost said no. I resented the officer for his consideration, for putting the matter in my hands and forcing me to choose between the prisoner's discomfort and my own, especially since there was really no choice at all. Of course I had to request that the prisoner be unshackled. To say or do anything else would surely make him suspicious, and far less inclined to answer even the most innocuous of my questions. And seeing that few of today's questions would be innocuous, and that the only reason I had come back to this jail—indeed, the only reason I was still in Mississippi at all—was to get some answers, I couldn't very well spoil the interview before it had even begun. Yes, I said aloud, please remove the prisoner's handcuffs; and said to myself at the same time, just another hour or two, just get through this last one and you can go back home for a few months.

The prisoner raised his arms to the guard, who quickly unfastened the cuffs and left the room. I tried on a smile, thanked Handy for meeting with me again, told him I had only a few questions this time and handed him the microphone. He took it and, remembering what I'd told him last time, held it close to his mouth.

I pressed the Record button on my tape recorder and started talking. I told him I'd met with and spoken to a lot of people since I'd last seen him—his mother and brother, Coach Bradberry and Coach Smith, some people at State and Ole Miss and a couple of guys from Moorhead; even

Mrs. Lewis and Todd Jordan. He raised his eyebrows at the mention of his old rival, but I smiled and nodded, and he did the same, and the tension immediately dissipated. I did not tell him I'd met with Lanardo Myrick, and was relieved when he didn't mention it, either. If he didn't know about my visit to the Greenwood City Jail, I figured, it meant that no one had considered my meeting with Myrick to be a matter of any concern, not even Myrick or his lawyer, Willie Perkins. It also meant that Handy wouldn't know just why I was asking him certain questions. "I just want to clear a couple of things up," I said.

He nodded. "Tell me again," I continued, "what's your understanding of why they never played you at Ole Miss?"

"The first year I had to be red-shirted," he said, "and they said they'd be able to use that as a red-shirt year. But when it came the second year they said they couldn't red-shirt me because of some SEC ruling that if you transfer to another school within that conference you had to lose that year and they red-shirted me my second year."

He hadn't really answered my question; instead of telling me why he thought they had never given him a chance to get off the bench, he told me, as best he could, what they had told *him,* and it was clear that he didn't understand it at all. Neither, for that matter, did I, and I suspected that they didn't, either.

"Was there ever a time when you thought they were going to give you a shot?" I asked.

"I remember this one time," he said, "the first-string quarterback got hurt and the second-string quarterback got hurt and it was only three quarterbacks, that week I got a lot of reps, I did real well and they moved me up to second-string. But when the other guys got back, it was like I didn't get any more reps, they just overlooked me."

That settled it: Even with Russ Shows and Tom Luke out of the picture, Handy never got any closer than second-string; a third quarterback, so insignificant that no one ever mentioned him—to this day I don't know his name—was deemed more fit to play in an actual game than was Handy. That meant that of five quarterbacks on the Ole Miss roster, Handy Campbell, who had "the best arm" the team's head coach had ever seen, was ranked fourth. I did not doubt that, had number three gotten injured, too, Handy would have been pushed back to fifth. He was not going to play at Ole Miss, not under any circumstances, and the fact that they saw fit to spark his hopes every once in a while only made them that much more cruel. I was seized in turn by anger and then pity, and I felt myself growing sympathetic to Handy once again. This was no killer. This was a victim.

"A couple of people have suggested you might have been a little impatient," I said, "both at State and Ole Miss. What do you think?"

"Impatient?" He laughed. "Well, my thinking is, the only way you get experience is through being out there. You can't sit back and watch somebody do something and learn from that. The only way you learn is you get out there and make your mistakes and then learn from your mistakes." I nodded, knowing it had worked just that way for me when I first came to Greenwood, seven years earlier; that was the reason I had come to Greenwood in the first place. Why hadn't Handy Campbell been given the same chance up at Ole Miss?

"Do you think you gave up too early?" I asked.

He shrugged. "I really don't know."

"If you thought you would get to play, do you think you would have done the things that got you kicked off the team?"

"I doubt it. I believe that, because of the reason I wasn't playing, I believe that led me to do a lot of the dumb things I did. I goofed off."

"I spoke to Jay Miller on the phone," I said. "He was one of the coaches who came to see you from Moorhead."

"That's right."

"He says that all he said to you about Ole Miss is that they already had a quarterback. Is that how you remember it?"

He shook his head hard. "What he said was, he didn't think I'd ever get a chance to play at Ole Miss because of something."

"Something? What?"

"Racism is what he was hinting at. He was just saying that, because I was a black quarterback, that I wouldn't get a fair shake at Ole Miss."

That sounded like more than a hint. "When did he say this to you?"

"I had just signed with Ole Miss, just coming from State."

"He told me he only visited you in high school."

He shook his head harder. Had Miller just blatantly lied to me?

"Did you ever talk to Coach Brewer about it?" I asked.

"I did at the beginning of the second season, when he told me again I would be red-shirted. I asked him what would he think about me transferring to Delta Junior; at least over there I would get to play and I wouldn't just sit up like stale potato chips or something, and he told me that he hadn't made up his mind really that I was gonna be red-shirted. And he said he wanted me to stick around just in case one of those guys go down, they might get hurt. He told me I would get looked at, and let it go from there. But I never really got looked at."

His voice was deepening in frustration with every sentence; I figured I'd better change the subject fast if I wanted to get him to open up about other, more recent matters. "Coach Bradberry told me he had advised you to use your time in college to focus on landing a good job afterward, not just on playing football."

"I took that in," he said, sighing. "It was good words of advice, but mainly I wanted to play in the NFL. To be the very best, I guess you could say." He folded his arms on his chest and let his head hang down, limp.

O.K., I thought, that didn't work too well. Time to try something else. "Did you used to drink a lot?" I asked. "Before you got arrested?"

"Not really," he said. "I guess you could call me, um, what I was, uh, like a weekend alcoholic or something, on the weekends. On the weekends, you know, at a party or something, just drink a lot then. I didn't really get drunk, you know, but it was a lot of beers I drunk."

"How about drugs?"

"I tried marijuana, I guess my eleventh-grade year in high school."

"How often?"

"A couple of times. I didn't get hooked."

"And when did you start drinking?"

"My tenth-grade year."

"Did you drink a lot on that last night with Freddie?"

"Yes."

Now came a question that I imagined he, like Myrick, would evade or ignore. I'd spent the past half hour or so trying to figure out a way to pose it so that he might just answer it before he fully realized the significance of the question, but I couldn't come up with anything. And so, in desperation, I was just blunt: "Was Freddie gay?"

And he was blunt, too. "Yes," he said, and that was it. No hesitation, no squirming, no snickering. Just: "Yes." I wondered why I wasn't just blunt all the time.

"Do you know for sure?" I asked.

"Yes."

"How?"

"Well . . ." He laughed. "He was gay."

"Did he tell you about it?"

"Yes."

"And what did he tell you?"

"He tell me he was gay."

"Did he ever fool around with men in Greenwood?"

"He said he had before."

"Did he say with whom?"

Handy looked away for a moment. "He named some guys."

"Did he ever hit on you?" I asked.

"He did."

"What happened?"

"He's hit on me a couple times. When I first knew him, when he hit on me, I told him I wasn't, you know, with that. So, I liked one of his friends, and he hooked us up, and I guess we just started hanging from there."

"Who was the friend?"

"A girl named Bertha Williams."

"You said he hit on you a couple of times. What did he do the first time?"

"He was just making statements, I guess."

"And the second time?"

"We all spent the night over at one of my friend's house stayin' at Snowden Jones, named Kooky. And he was making statements then."

"So what'd you do that time?"

"Mmm, nothing, really."

"Did it make you uncomfortable?"

"Not really. He was a fun guy to be around, he didn't never go out the way to hit on you. He would just crack wise statements about it."

And now came the question I had wanted to ask him since the last interview, when I'd tried to but had lost my nerve in the process. "Uh, Handy," I said, choosing, for some reason, not to go with blunt, though it had always served me well. "You know, uh, one of the rumors floating around town is that when you asked to borrow the truck, he said you could have it, you know, if you would do something for him."

"All right."

"Is that true?"

"Yes."

"What did he say?"

"Um, he said he would let us borrow it, if . . . we would do him a favor."

"And what was that?"

He belched out a chuckle—nervous? embarrassed?—and looked down at his hands. "Uh, the favor was," he said, just above a mumble, "he wanted to suck our penis."

And there it was. True, it wasn't quite what I'd heard all along from several different sources, which was that Freddie's request had been for Campbell and Myrick to perform fellatio on *him*, not the other way around—a version of events that seemed to be backed up by the fact that Freddie's body had, according to the same rumor, been found clad in a shirt but no pants. But I could think of several reasons why Handy might want to recount things a little differently: In his version, only Freddie was *really* performing a homosexual act; Handy and Lanardo were merely *receiving* blow jobs, not giving them, and hey, there's nothing really *gay* about that, now, is there? It's all the same if you close your eyes, they could say. In this new version, too, they weren't kneeling, subservient, in front of Freddie the queer, but standing before him, in control; and yet, at the same time, they could also be the victims, getting sodomized by this perverted old UPS driver. It was a warped, twisted, self-serving sort of disclosure, I knew. But it was something.

"He wanted to suck *your* penis," I repeated.

"Yes," Handy said.

"Lanardo's too?"

"Yes."

"Did you let him?"

"Yes."

"Both of you?"

"Yes."

"And then," I said, "you borrowed the truck?"

"Yes," he replied.

"But you're not gay."

He laughed again. "No."

"Why'd you let him do that?"

Another laugh. "We really wanted to go somewhere really bad, and, um, I guess that was the only way he was gonna let us borrow it."

"Did it get you off?"

"No, not me. I don't know about Lanardo."

"How long was it for—a while, or just a second, or what?"

"Mm, I guess five, ten minutes."

"So, is that the only time you've ever done anything like that with any-body?"

A chuckle. "Yeah."

"Had he hit on Lanardo, too?"

"He had before."

"And how did Lanardo react?"

"The same way, like. We laughed it off."

"Lanardo's not gay either?"

"No."

"He never had any encounter like that before?"

"I don't know about him."

"But you never did?"

"No."

"Just that one time?"

"Yeah."

"Isn't that kind of strange?" I said. "I mean, if I really wanted to borrow somebody's truck, and he said to me, you know, 'I'll let you have it if you let me suck your penis,' I don't care how badly I wanted that truck, I wouldn't let him do it. So, uh . . . what were you *thinking?*"

Yet another laugh. "I don't know," he said. "We was just, we was think-ing about going to see, um, our kids, I guess."

"At what point in the evening did this happen?"

"It was later, after we had been drinking, I guess."

"So then, he did it and then he said, 'O.K., now you can have the truck?'"

"Yes."

"And then how long after that did you leave him?"

"Um, I left right away. Him and Lanardo went, they kept riding out. I wanted to go home and pack, 'cause he was gonna give us the truck that night."

"So they dropped you off at home?"

"Yes."

"And then he and Lanardo drove off?"

"Mm-hm."

I paused for a moment, took a deep breath, and, shielding my right hand with my left arm so that Handy might not see what I was doing, jot-ted a few notes down on my big yellow legal pad.

"What time was this?" I asked.

"I can't remember any times, really," he said. "I guess it was about twelve they dropped me off."

"And then what time did they come back and pick you up?"

"About two-thirty, I guess."

"So you went home and packed, and then they came back."

"Mm-hm."

"Where did this happen, the whole, you know, uh, favor exchange?"

"I think it was on the road in Carrollton."

I remembered a little piece of the story, a rumor I had heard from Jack. "Did you stop at Mims that night?" I asked.

He looked confused. "Mims One-Stop," I said, "up in the hills?"

"Oh. Yes."

"And the favor, was this after you went there?"

"Umm . . . yes."

"So how long did he let you have the truck for?"

"We were supposed to bring it back Friday."

"And what night of the week was it when he let you have it? Saturday?"

He thought for a moment. "It was Friday night, Saturday morning."

"So he let you have it for a week."

"Yes."

"And what was he going to do all that time?"

"He said he was going to, um, Jackson, or something like that."

"This was a new truck, wasn't it?"

"Mm-hm."

"Freddie took care of it?"

"Yes."

"What was his jewelry doing in the back of the truck?" That was another rumor I'd heard.

"Umm," he said, "I don't know, I didn't see any jewelry."

"But you said the gun that you got for him was in the back there—isn't that what you told me?"

"Yes."

"O.K., so he comes and picks you up again at your place at 2:30. Then where did you go?"

"Umm . . . we rode around. I guess this is about—I guess, you know, I'm twistin' it. I guess it was about two when they dropped me off, and when they came back it was about four I guess, and we rode for about

another hour. And that's when he called the guy, and he picked him up."

"What kind of car was the guy in?"

"It was a dark-colored car. I guess it was a Bonneville or something."

"Like a blue?"

"Black. Dark blue, maybe."

"You didn't see where the tag was from?"

"No."

"You don't know if it was Leflore or Carroll or whatever?"

"No."

"You'd never seen the guy before?"

"No."

"You got a look at him, though."

"I really didn't see his face too good, no."

"Was he black, or was he white?"

"It was a black guy."

"Any idea how old he was?"

"No, I didn't see him that good."

"Freddie didn't tell you who he was?"

"Um, he may have said his name, but I don't remember."

"Did he say where he and that guy were going to go?"

"They said they was—he said they was going to Jackson."

"Was that guy somebody he fooled around with?"

"I really don't know."

With every sentence he slumped over further in his chair, and slowly raised his loosely clenched hands to the sides of his head like a boxer trying to shield himself from a slow barrage of jabs and roundhouses. If I had thought there was a chance that he might drop those tired fists and expose himself for a second, I would have kept the questions coming, repeating them five, ten times if I had to in order to get him to tell me the whole story. But I could tell that I wasn't going to get him to give me any more, no matter what I did. The Greenwood Police Department hadn't been able to, and I was sure they'd made quite an effort.

"Why did you try to join the army?" I asked.

"I was thinking about maybe going for a couple of years," he said, "and then getting back in school."

"But why?" I said. "Was it because Lanardo had enlisted?"

He looked at me for just a second—a half-second, really, but it was long enough to make me worry: Did Handy ever tell me that? Or did I just reveal that I'd spoken to Myrick, too?

Luckily, he didn't seem to notice. "I don't think it was because Lanardo was in the army," he said. "I think it was because, if I had never played football, that probably would have been the route I took."

"What about it appealed to you?"

"Stability. They teach you how to be really disciplined, and I had known a couple of guys that went into the service, and they was doing really well."

"Did you talk about it with Lanardo?"

"He told me he didn't like it at all. He said it was the usual—they're prejudiced, a lot of stuff."

"Is that why he left?"

"I don't know. He didn't tell me."

There was a single knock on the door and it swung open, startling me a bit. Another deputy, a tall black man named Albert King, came in as far as he could, which, since he was built like a linebacker, was no more than a couple of steps. He asked if everything was all right, and how much more time I would need. Fine, I said, and only a few more minutes. All right, he said, nodded at me, glowered at Handy for a second or two, and left.

"I think him and Freddie was friends," Handy said after another second or two had passed in silence. "I guess he's takin' a lot out on me."

"How?"

"He just—he's on me hard. He doesn't allow me things other people get. When my stuff comes up missing he doesn't try to find them. I got some pens, and they came and took them."

"Are you having any other problems in here?"

"You don't get to exercise, you don't get to go outside. I've been asking to go to the law library, you know, to get me some help with the case—I've been denied that. It's crooked. It's not supposed to be like this. It's not supposed to be like home, I know that, but they treat you like animals here."

"Did they set bail for you?"

"Five hundred thousand dollars." Whoever set that amount wanted to make sure they stayed locked up until they were tried, since there was no chance their families could hope to post the 10 percent a bondsman would require.

"Did they offer you a plea bargain?"

He shook his head.

"Were you surprised," I asked, "when they couldn't get a jury here?"

"Not really," he said. "I sort of expected the views would be like that. I really wanted to have the trial here. I really wanted the jury to be from here also."

"Why?"

"I just thought maybe it would be better if it was from here. The way they trying to make things look is that Freddie didn't let anybody use his truck, but I'm sure some of the people around these neighborhoods know he did let people use his car."

"That's not what I heard."

He looked away and shrugged. Lanardo Myrick had been manic and supremely confident he would be acquitted; Handy Campbell was depressed and just an inch away from giving up entirely, the antithesis of the seventeen-year-old kid who had charged back onto the field after half-time in Tupelo.

"He was a great guy, wasn't he," I said.

"Yes," Handy said. "He was."

"Why would someone want to kill him?"

Again he looked away and shrugged, exactly as he did before, not ten seconds earlier.

"I really don't know," he muttered.

❧❧❧

When we were through, Albert King came in and snapped the cuffs back on Handy's wrists and led him back to his cell and locked him in, and then escorted me back down to the sheriff's office. I thanked him and Sheriff Banks and stepped back into a normal Saturday morning, sunny and warm, free of steel doors and iron bars and packed cells and inmates and officers; free of people altogether, in fact. From where I stood, on the front lawn of the Leflore County Courthouse, Greenwood looked like a diorama—perfect little buildings and streets and magnolia trees arranged in clean lines and angles, and not a person in sight, unless you counted the stone figures crowded onto the Confederate monument. It was a Greenwood I had seen only very rarely, and, pretty as it was, I didn't like it very much. I missed the people, black and white—the friendly ones and the surly ones, the harmless ones and the menacing ones, the clean-cut middle-classers and the rednecks. I missed the friends, with whom I had been too busy to spend much time, and the strangers, whom I had been too busy to observe. I missed the little oasis of humanity in the middle of a vast and empty Delta. I missed Greenwood, the Greenwood I had known, the one that had taken in a twenty-one-year-old refugee from a heartless job market and worked tirelessly to make him feel welcomed and valued, even as he eyed it warily and often critically. I was just now coming to comprehend what I had discovered a week earlier: My Greenwood was gone, as gone as the Greenwood that Vic and Jack had mourned at that Christmas parade we'd all attended, as gone as the lonely swamp outpost deep in the interior of the Confederate States of America, as gone as Point Leflore and Williams Landing, as gone as that twenty-one-year-old kid was gone, irretrievably and forever.

I walked over to Washington Street, toward the library, and passed the house where Marshall Levitt lived, the house in which his feisty old mother, Nancy, had been born in 1893. She was gone now, too, just as Greenwood's entire Jewish community would be, someday. I wondered if there would come a day when Greenwood itself would just cease to exist, if the emptiness of the Delta would eventually creep over the town like kudzu and reclaim it, if maybe people weren't meant to live so far out and isolated from other settlements, if that kind of isolation might not engender a society so insular and intradependent that it would ultimately consume itself in tribalism and suspicion. Maybe, I thought, and maybe not; but one thing was clear: They were either going to live together, or die together. I only hoped they still had a choice.

As for me: Once again, I found myself with nowhere to go. I had done what I had come here to do, or as much of it as could be done now, anyway. But something was vexing me yet, and I needed to sit down and figure it out. The library was closed for some reason, so I crossed the street and settled down on the steps of the old Confederate Memorial Hall; since I had never seen anyone enter or exit the place, I figured it was as good a place as any to sit and think undisturbed.

I opened my case, pulled out two legal pads, and laid them side by side on my lap. On my left knee I balanced the pad on which I had written notes from my interview with Lanardo Myrick, while on my right knee I placed the pad with my notes from the two interviews with Handy Campbell. I tore out an empty page to jot things down on, as necessary, and started flipping through the two pads. I already knew that Handy and Lanardo had given me different stories about why Freddie had supposedly loaned them his truck—Lanardo said it was just because "he really liked us," while Handy admitted that Freddie had done it only after they let him perform oral sex on them. But I had marked a spot in today's notes where I thought I might find another discrepancy. And sure enough, there it was: Lanardo had said they'd all driven around together all night, while Handy claimed that they had dropped him off at home for a couple of hours so he could pack for the trip.

And now I found another discrepancy: Handy said Freddie called his friend from a payphone at the Triple-Stop convenience store and then waited with Handy and Lanardo at the Kentucky Fried Chicken, but Myrick said Freddie called from the Double-Quick gas station and then waited there for his friend to pick him up.

And another: Lanardo said Freddie's friend picked him up at the Double-Quick between three and three-thirty in the morning; Handy said it happened at the Kentucky Fried Chicken at five-thirty.

And another: Handy claimed Freddie told him he and his other friend were heading down to Jackson, while Myrick had told me Freddie and his new friend were going partying in Greenwood.

I combed through the two pads again and again, but it always came up the same. The only things they seemed to agree on were that Freddie had loaned them his truck, that he drove off with a friend in a dark-colored car, and that they didn't kill him. The police were smart to keep them apart, I thought. These stories will never hold up in court.

I sat there for a long time, watching the occasional car or person pass by, staring into the library and trying to discern a faint little shimmer I saw there, until I realized it was only my reflection in the darkened glass.

And then I sat there some more, knowing all along that I would have to accept the conclusion I was trying desperately, stupidly, to avoid.

The stories won't hold up in court because they are . . . just stories.

They did it.

TWENTY

IN EVERY MAN

The Mississippi State Penitentiary at Parchman is the worst prison in America. Any Mississippian will tell you so.

The place looms so large in the collective consciousness of Mississippi that "Parchman" is probably the only word that can stop almost any conversation there cold. It's just one of many correctional facilities operated and maintained by the Hospitality State, but it is very much its own entity. In Mississippi, you either go to prison or you go to Parchman. No one who is serving out a sentence at Parchman is ever referred to as being "in prison." They are always, without exception, said to be "at Parchman." No Mississippian needs to have the distinction explained to them. That knowledge, it seems, is part of their birthright.

I didn't have to hear the word too many times before I understood that Parchman was a place to fear, and fear gravely. No one at the *Commonwealth* or anywhere else ever said such a thing to me explicitly, but I could tell, just by the way people uttered the word, that *Parchman* was a place one didn't speak of lightly. It was the monster in the cellar: Best not to open the door and look at it, even at a safe distance. You never know.

The few times I had visited Parchman as a reporter, I'd never ventured past the welcome center, a small wooden cabin just inside the main gate, or the warden's office in a modern brick building just up the road. I knew then that I was a reporter and not a criminal, that I had called and made an appointment, that I was a guest, just visiting, on a specific mission, on official business, and that when I was finished—or when I just decided I didn't want to be in there anymore—that gate would open up and let me back out into the world outside. But still, I got in and out of there as quickly as I could. I never made idle chitchat, never asked an unnecessary question, never challenged an assertion from my hosts. It was probably the only place in Mississippi that I did not regard with fascination. Just dread.

Now, seven years after I'd visited it last, I knew I would have to go back to Parchman.

⁊ᡣᡝ

As I drove up to the guard post, a sentry stepped out in front of my car while another briskly walked over to my window and directed me to tell him who I was. When I told him, he searched the list on his clipboard, made a check next to my name and asked me somewhat more politely to step out of the car and open the trunk. He climbed into the car and checked the glove compartment and the pouches behind the front seats and the flap behind the visor and, lastly, underneath the seats, calmly explaining to me that he would have to hold onto my camera and tape recorder for the duration of my visit. He let me keep my pen and notebook.

And then he stepped aside, told his partner to open the gate, and welcomed me to Parchman.

As soon as I was through the gate I looked down at the car's odometer: I was exactly thirty-six miles from Greenwood. Thirty-six miles from Greenwood High School and Bulldog Stadium; thirty-six miles from the Leflore County Jail. Thirty-six miles from the Snowden Jones apartments, the place Melvin Smith had called Parchman without a fence. I doubted even he appreciated just how close the place Handy Campbell had grown up was to the place he would, in all likelihood, die. And close in more ways than one: Parchman didn't have a fence, either.

"Parchman sits on seventeen thousand acres of this flat Delta farmland," Hugh Ferguson, the prison's director of public affairs, told me that afternoon. "And almost no trees. If you try to run, where you gon' go?" In fact, the place is naturally so inhospitable to escape that when prisoners work in the fields, which they do every single day, they are not even chained to one another, and each loose gang is supervised by only one guard with a shotgun. Very few prisoners ever even attempt to break out.

I met Hugh Ferguson that day at the welcome center, a bizarrely quaint little house that doubles as a museum. Ferguson looked out of place in Parchman, too: He was a short, stocky, white-haired man whose cheeks always seemed to be in full blush—not the kind of guy I expected to find working a job that consisted largely of leading the "scared straight" tours of Parchman that most Mississippi children experience at least once during their school years. Then again, he didn't have to put the fear of God into those kids. There were plenty of other people there to do that.

A lot of kids never even got past the museum, with its expansive display of knives and homemade weapons that have been taken from prisoners over the years, including a huge machete and a shiv fashioned from a plastic toothbrush. "We do have gangs, and gang violence," Ferguson told me. "Prisoners here are under the gun at all times."

In keeping with the welcome center's theme of really weird juxtapositions, the display of confiscated weapons was situated near a cozy fireplace complete with mantelpiece, over which were hung more than a dozen old black-and-white photographs tracing Parchman's history. Most were sterile pictures of various cell-blocks which had long since been razed, but there were a few chilling shots, too, including one of the gas chamber, and another of a convict in stripes who looked to be about twelve years old.

He was. But that, Ferguson explained to me, was back in the thirties; children that young were no longer sent to Parchman. Then, as I slouched a bit with relief, he added: "We do have fourteen-year-olds here right now. And old men, too." Once again I stood up straight as a yardstick.

Ferguson mercifully directed my attention away from the old photos and the weapons and led me across the room to a rack upon which hung several uniforms, each a different color. "Most prisoners wear these," he said, pointing to a pair of white trousers with a blue stripe up the leg. "Trusties wear the blue pants with the white stripe, and they both wear these." He handed me a powder blue work shirt, on the back of which was stenciled MDOC CONVICT in giant black letters; clearly, prisoners who did hope to escape would need a change of clothing once they made it outside. "And over here," Ferguson said, "we have the jumpsuits, yellow for protective custody and red for death row." I wondered if the colors had been chosen for the obvious reasons: red for blood, yellow for cowardice. As insensitive as the former choice seemed, I was even more offended that the prison's most threatened inmates were forced to wear an outfit that anyone could spot at a distance of half a mile. It was much more effective, I thought, than a simple bull's-eye would have been.

Hugh Ferguson led me outside, and we hiked up the road to a group of low concrete administrative buildings. We walked through the halls, past several men mopping the floor; these, Ferguson told me, loud enough for them to hear, were trusties, prisoners who were considered relatively low risk and well behaved. As a reward for their years of incarceration without infractions, they were allowed the privilege of cleaning up these buildings. It didn't seem like much of a reward to me, but, as I would soon learn, everything in Parchman was relative. In this world, these men were the kings of good fortune.

Ferguson led me into an office which contained, among other things, the first women I had seen at Parchman; one of them handed him a set of keys. We walked back out again, past the mopping trusties—some of whom waved and greeted my host formally—down the hall and back out to the parking lot, where we made our way to a white cargo van and climbed inside.

Almost as soon as we pulled out onto the road I spotted several gangs of convicts working in the fields. Their arms and necks baked in the sun; the air around them shimmered in the heat. It was still May, but already the temperature was in the nineties. "It'll stay like this through September," Ferguson said. "July and August get even hotter." It made sense to me: This was hell. I understood, now, why the trusties cherished those janitorial jobs in the offices.

"Are the cell blocks air-conditioned?" I asked, immensely grateful at that moment that the van was.

He laughed. "No, and they never will be. I don't guess the prison system will ever allow it. The only prisoners who get a taste of air conditioning are those trusties who get to work in the offices."

"But you give the prisoners fans," I said. "Don't you?"

"They can buy a fan, if they want. We sell them."

"Buy them? How?"

"Prisoners here have bank accounts. They can draw up to twenty dollars a week if they want, to buy cigarettes and candy, soap and toothbrushes, things like that."

"Where does the money come from?"

"Family members and friends on the outside put the money into their accounts for them."

"And how much do they make working out there?"

"Not the first dime," he said.

"Really?" I said, startled. "Do they have to work?"

"Every day," he said. "Seven days a week, eight to ten hours a day. Everyone except the inmates in lockdown, and believe me, them fellas'd rather be workin' out here, tell you what."

"What are they all doing out there?"

"Some clean-up. Mostly they work on the crops, planting and picking, all that stuff."

"And what do you do with the crops after they're harvested?"

"We sell 'em down in Jackson."

"And who gets the money?"

"The Mississippi Department of Corrections," he said. It sounded to me an awful lot like slavery, but I wasn't about to say so, at least not while I was still inside the place.

"There must be inmates who don't have anyone out there who can put money in their account, aren't there?"

"Sure, lots of 'em."

"What do they do?"

"They don't," he said, and I understood from the tone of his voice that we weren't going to discuss that subject anymore. I wondered what those inmates did, sweltering in their cells, unable to wash themselves off or brush their teeth. It was an ugly image and I tried to chase it out of my mind, without much success.

At the time of my visit, Parchman was home to sixty-eight hundred prisoners, meaning that roughly one Mississippian in thirty was imprisoned there. The prison's population had exploded over the past decade, growing so fast the MDOC couldn't keep up with it. By 1995, some sections of Parchman were overcrowded by a factor of two or even three; every gymnasium they had there had long ago been converted into inmate housing, and still the bodies kept coming in, more upon more upon more. The MDOC did what it could—that is, they constructed more cells at Parchman, and more prisons throughout the state—but the more cells they built, the more inmates showed up to overfill them. "We cannot build prisons fast enough," Ferguson told me with a sigh. "They're not talking about building children more schools. They're talking about building more prisons." Indeed, as we drove around those seventeen thousand acres, I saw several construction sites.

Parchman, Hugh Ferguson explained, was not a prison like Alcatraz; it was not centralized in one or even a few buildings. It was, in fact, many different camps, spread out and euphemistically titled "units," each of which served a different segment of the inmate population, and each of which was surrounded by walls topped with two spirals of razor-wire. Unit 29 is the main maximum-security camp for the general prison population; it houses fifteen hundred prisoners at any given time. Most prisoners start out in Unit 29, and almost everyone passes through it at one time or another. "You don't know who you're sleeping by," Ferguson said of life in Unit 29, though I imagined that was probably true for the rest of the place, too.

There were units for trusties and elderly inmates, a unit for sick inmates and another set aside just for those who had AIDS. Unit 27, Ferguson explained as we passed it, was for Protective Custody; its yard was packed with yellow jumpsuits. I noticed almost immediately that a very large percentage of the inmates in Unit 27 were white, as opposed to the blue-and-white clad gangs roasting out in the fields, almost all of whom, it seemed to me, were black. "Eighty-five percent of our inmates are black," Ferguson told me when I asked him about it. "A white man catches hell if he comes here. You don't want to be white and go to prison," he said. "Not just here, but the world over. Most of the white men here have to go into protective custody pretty soon." I tried to think about what he was saying about race relations in prison, but I kept returning to that figure: 85 percent. Only 45 percent of Mississippi's entire population was black, I knew, and no one would claim that they were responsible for anything near 85 percent of its crime. I wondered how the MDOC—how anyone in the law enforcement community, from policemen to judges to the state's Attorney General—could possibly justify those statistics; then again, I thought, they probably don't have to. I doubted many people ever challenged them on the matter.

Nor did I; before I could say much of anything, Hugh Ferguson was pointing out another cell block, one that looked different from all the others. For one thing, it didn't have any windows—just narrow little slats pointing sharply toward the ground. "For the prisoners in there," he told me, "it's a privilege to look up at the sky." This was Unit 32: Death Row.

It's also the lockdown unit. Prisoners get sent to Unit 32 for escape attempts, acts of violence, and general troublemaking. Here they live alone in a seven-by-nine-foot cell furnished only with a small concrete bed and a thin foam mattress. They are not permitted to have radios, are not granted access to telephones; they do not work. Once a day, for an hour or less, they are allowed out of their cells to exercise, which they do in a twelve-by-twelve-foot square of asphalt with one basketball hoop, and surrounded by its own high fence, also topped with razor wire. When I passed there was one prisoner in it, stark and isolated in his red jump suit. He really was looking up at the sky.

Prisoners suspected of an offense are sent immediately to Unit 32; they stay in there for twenty days before they get a hearing. If the hearing doesn't go well for the inmate—and often it doesn't—he might well be sentenced to serve out the rest of his term in lockdown. Depending on the sentence, that can be a very long time. "If he's sentenced here for life," Ferguson explained, "he's here for life." Mississippi, it seems, doesn't care much for the notion of parole, except in the case of death, a prospect that I imagine must grow increasingly appealing to the men entombed in Unit 32.

I asked Ferguson if he really thought it was appropriate to show these things to young children. "I think it's a necessity," he said. "It's easy for these kids to get weapons. When I was coming up, if we wanted to fight we would ball up our fists. No more. Young people this day and time need to learn about this place. It's real, it ain't no joke."

As we pulled away from Unit 32 I turned for one last look, and noticed that the lone prisoner in its "exercise yard" was just standing there in his red jumpsuit, staring at the van with his arms hanging slack at his sides. I'm sure he thought, if only for an instant, about the two people sitting in that van, men who could get in and out of it as often and easily as they pleased, could if it suited them drive it up to the Yukon or down to Tierra Del Fuego while he passed at least twenty-three hours of every day in a seven-by-nine-foot windowless chamber, with maybe an hour a day in a twelve-by-twelve-foot cage if he was lucky and behaved himself—two men who, unlike him, lived their lives utterly, blissfully unaware of when or where or how those lives would end. That inmate's existence and mine were so dissimilar that we might as well be on different planets; and yet, here we were, separated only by about sixty yards and one terrible act of violence. Sixty yards. From where I sat, Handy Campbell could have thrown a football to this guy—or at least to the fence that penned him in.

Handy Campbell: In the course of the tour I had all but forgotten him, but he was the reason I had come here today. I had spent the better part of two weeks interviewing his former coaches and teachers, his family and his friends and his codefendant and him. I had examined every aspect of his life, mapped out every facet of his career on the gridiron, charted every degree of his rise and fall. I figured I knew his story inside and out, from every angle. But I was wrong.

I hadn't known just what was at stake, hadn't really understood what it was that those friends and relatives and teachers and coaches were thinking, and seeing, when they sighed and shook their heads and called the whole thing a terrible shame and even cried about it. I hadn't known any of it, until now. In Mississippi, convicted murderers aren't sent to prison. They're sent to Parchman. Every single person I'd interviewed knew exactly what that meant. Now I did, too.

And I also knew, as they all did, that in all probability Handy Campbell would be spending the rest of his life in this place. The only question seemed to be how long that life would last, and where, exactly, it would end—in a bed at the infirmary, or on the floor of a shower room, or strapped to a gurney in Unit 32. We had started out together, Handy and I, back in the fall of 1988, a supremely gifted high school quarterback and a cocky cub reporter; I had fancied a notion that our fortunes might rise in parallel trajectories, but it hadn't worked out that way. Instead, our paths had diverged, leading to places neither of us could have predicted, or would have cared to. Now I knew where his ended.

And I had seen enough of it. I wanted to tell Hugh Ferguson to swing the van around and take me back to my car, but when I turned to him I saw that he was gazing out at the horizon, and looking strangely pained. I wondered what could have so affected this man who just minutes earlier had described to me the lockdown unit and death row with a stoicism I found almost inhuman. All I could see out there was a tiny grove of pecan trees—the only foliage I had spotted since we'd left the office—and, behind them, several battered old trailers.

"We let some of the better-behaved inmates, trusties and such, use those for conjugal visits once in a while," he said, pointing to them. He let out a long breath, drove on in silence for a minute or two, and then uttered something that shocked me more than anything I'd heard or seen all day: "I believe there's some good in every man."

I turned and stared at him in stunned silence. How could this man, who witnessed every single day the very worst side of humanity, who saw it wherever he turned in the form of brutal inmates convicted of brutal crimes, kept in check by brutal guards and a brutal corrections system—

how could he, of all people, retain even a tiny shard of such an idealistic notion? And what had made him, just now, dig out that shard and hold it up to the light?

It was those trailers, those rusted little boxes. They reminded Hugh Ferguson that even a convict, even a man who could take another man's life, was capable of loving somebody, and worthy of that person's love in return. And Hugh Ferguson, in turn, reminded me of the reason I had left Mississippi in the first place: my own inability to deal with such extremes of good and bad existing in the same person, in many people, in the many people in Greenwood who had been at once so good to me and so bad to some of the people they had known all their lives. If Hugh Ferguson could believe such a thing, I knew it must be true; and if it was true, if there really was some good in everyone, even the vilest of criminals, then the paradox I had left Mississippi to escape was ubiquitous, and I had better just accept it, and find a way to deal with it. Handy Campbell had been a good kid; Handy Campbell had murdered a good friend. As much as I had clung, in the past couple of days, to the hope that it was Myrick, and not Handy, who had actually pulled the trigger, I saw now that it didn't really matter. Handy was guilty, and he was coming here, and as much as I hated that thought, I knew he deserved it.

Still, I couldn't help wondering: Who did pull that trigger—Myrick or Handy? Whoever it was, he sure wasn't about to tell me, not now. Nothing else would happen, I knew, without the passage of time. How much time, I didn't know; all I knew was that I wasn't going to get any more out of this trip.

I flew home the next day.

Two weeks later, Handy Campbell confessed.

PART THREE

THE DEATH OF MY GREENWOOD

TWENTY-ONE

ONE MORE MISSISSIPPI MYSTERY

This is how I heard about it:

I didn't, at least not until six weeks after it happened, when I returned to Mississippi to witness the trial and, walking into the Panola County Courthouse, encountered Lee Jones. For the first time since I'd known him, he actually looked worried as he ushered me over to a quiet corner and signaled me to lean down and cupped a hand over his mouth and said:

"Uh, we got us a bit of a problem."

"What kind of problem?" I asked, thinking that maybe he'd had to ask for another change of venue, this time to Alabama.

"He, uh," Lee Jones said in a loud whisper, "he kinda confessed."

"He *what?*"

"He told a couple of deputies he did it."

"He did? When?"

"Last month."

"Jesus," I said. "Why didn't you tell me this when I called you? And why are we here now?"

"He didn't plead guilty," he explained. "He just told 'em he done it. And I didn't tell you because I reckoned I could get it thrown out before it got this far. Hell, he was outta his mind, it was late at night, and—anyway, like I said, I figured it'd get thrown out before we got to trial."

"But it didn't?"

327

"I'ma try one more time," he said. "Right now." He beckoned me to follow him into the courtroom and take a seat up front. Judge Evans was already sitting on the bench, chatting with Frank Carlton, the District Attorney for Leflore, Sunflower, and Washington counties. A bad sign, I thought, and I was right: Judge Evans quickly ruled that the confession was admissible. And then, without pausing, he banged his gavel and ordered the jury pool into the courtroom.

They walked through the door quietly, single file; every last one of them, young and old, black and white, appeared tired and hot and eager for nothing but to get out of there and go somewhere else. Why, I wondered anxiously, had Handy not plea-bargained? And then I remembered Ronnie Ray Strong, who hadn't plea-bargained, either, because the prosecution hadn't offered him the opportunity. I wondered if that was how things were in this case, too—if Frank Carlton was so sure of his case that he hadn't made any overtures to the defense. Lee Jones hadn't told me about any such offer, and I had to believe that, as nervous as he'd appeared that morning, he would have taken just about anything Frank Carlton would have given him.

But Carlton apparently hadn't offered, and now, after a delay of ten weeks and a move of sixty miles, the case of *Mississippi vs. Handy T. Campbell and Lanardo Myrick* was going to trial at last.

⅋⅋

There is nothing stately or quaint or charming or even attractive about the Panola County Courthouse. It was built in the 1960s and exemplifies all of the worst architectural impulses of that era, which is to say that it is a big bland bunker of a building, bereft not just of decoration but of design itself. Inside, the courtroom lacks even the charm of the one I'd visited that day in Vaiden, which was then splintering and sagging and so degraded that it soon had to be razed, lest it collapse in the midst of a trial and kill everyone in it. Worse than that, the courtroom at Batesville is just sterile, a cavernous space lacking a gallery and ceiling fans and filled instead with rows and rows and rows of long polished benches. I sat in one of them and thought about another courtroom, two thousand miles west in Los Angeles, that at that very moment was teeming with lawyers and reporters and cameramen and artists and well-connected members of the public, all of them there to witness another murder trial of a former football star. But two thousand miles east of that carnival, in Batesville, Mississippi, this murder trial of a former football star was opening in a courtroom packed with nothing but empty seats. Fewer than three dozen people sat in this courtroom, including a judge, two defendants, two prosecutors, two defense attorneys, twelve jurors and four alternates. On the right side of the courtroom—the defense side—sat Hattie and Anthony and April and Tracy Campbell and a family friend I did not recognize. On the left side, the prosecution side, sat Freddie Williams's widow, and his mother, Iola, and a half dozen of his friends. I sat on the aisle, directly behind the defense table, and studied the jurors during the opening statements. As a group, they were on the youngish side; there were seven women and five men, eight blacks and four whites. I pulled out a pen and my legal pad and drew a diagram of the jury box:

WW	BM	WM	WW	BM	BW
BW	WW	BW	BM	BM	BM

And the alternates:

BM	WW
WW	BM

I jotted all of this down while both sides prepared for their opening statements, and then, while they continued to prepare, I studied it again and again, trying to divine some meaning in the numbers, the ratios, the order of seating. Ordinarily, I would imagine that the presence of only one white male on the panel would benefit the defense; but in this case, both the victim and the accused were black, and the fact that blacks outnumbered whites on the panel by two-to-one could easily work in the prosecution's favor. And those seven women . . . were women more likely to convict, or less? And their relative youth—which way would that play? And who was better at picking a jury, Frank Carlton or Lee Jones? I didn't know, of course, and couldn't even guess any of the answers, but that didn't stop me from flailing around for a theorem that would predict, before the trial began, how it would end.

And then it began, with Judge Evans calling upon the prosecution to make its opening statement. I looked over at Frank Carlton. He didn't move. Instead, his assistant, Cheryl Griffin, a woman who looked like she could have been Carlton's daughter, rose and addressed the jury. That's bad news for Lee Jones, I thought; Carlton is so sure of his case he's leaving the opening to a young ADA.

"This is not a television show," Griffin said by way of opening. "It's not scripted. Nobody has written out what everybody's going to say. These are live witnesses, and they're going to say things their own way." And if this is any indication, I thought, so are the lawyers.

"This is a circumstantial evidence case," Griffin continued. "I don't anticipate putting a witness up on the witness stand who's going to tell you, *I saw those two men rob and murder Freddie Williams.* But I am going to put witnesses up there to tell you that Freddie was last seen with these two men; they were in possession of a vehicle that he loved, that he cared for, that he was proud of; that they were in possession of his jewelry that he wore regularly; and that the items that he would have normally used every day—his driver's license, his checkbook, his ATM card—were still in his vehicle. And I submit to you, at the end of this case, there's not going to be any doubt in your mind that Handy Campbell and Lanardo Myrick murdered and robbed Freddie Williams, a man who he thought was their friend."

I understood Carlton's confidence.

"You've heard what they expect to prove," Lee Jones said, rising from his chair. "What I expect to come out—and quite frankly, we, the defense is not going to have a lot of testimony, a lot of proof. I expect the bulk of our case will be through the cross-examination of the witnesses that the State will put on, because, as was indicated, the defendant doesn't have to prove anything."

I winced. Lee Jones was already on the defensive, and the State had yet to put up a single witness.

"I mean," he continued, "they're leading you down a path, okay? And I'm cautioning you to be watching where you're going and don't step in a hole." I looked over at the jury; they didn't seem particularly concerned, except maybe about the competence of the attorney standing before them.

"With respect to whether the defendant will testify or not, that decision just has not been made. Just haven't decided that. But I submit to you, the fact that he's demanded a trial, he's told you he's not guilty. And basically, that's all a defendant can say, *I didn't do it, I'm not guilty.* Then after he says that, what else can he say? *I don't know anything about it.* That's it. He's out of bullets."

I actually flinched at that one: "Out of bullets." Bad choice of metaphor.

"These things and these circumstances—the State's going to put on witnesses to try to show you things about the driver's license, the check-book in the vehicle. I submit to you, a lot of people will leave their—a checkbook or their driver's license in the vehicle, because that's when you need your driver's license, is when you're in your vehicle. Ladies and gentlemen, for these reasons—these are some of the things I'm pointing out to you."

I wondered if the jury was making better sense of this statement then I was. I searched their faces: They weren't.

"Additionally, I would expect this evidence to come out—and I ask you to realize and understand that Mr. Campbell has been—he's been incarcerated, he's been jailed, from the time he was stopped in Louisiana until now, over ten months. Not surprising, he did not adapt well to being incarcerated, to being in jail. It didn't set well with him. It upset him, depressed him. He had some problems with it. Because of this, he sought some assistance from the mental health people. Just like you do if you have a problem with your foot, you go see a medical doctor. If you've got problems in your head, you go see a mental health specialist."

It's official, I mused—I'm not in New York anymore.

"That was done for Handy after he'd been locked up about ten months. He didn't sleep for three or four days, four or five days, didn't eat, these type things that will let you know that something is not right. He was taken to the mental health facility there in Greenwood that's called 'Life Help,' or Region VI Mental Health. And while they were waiting to see the doctor—and there's some dispute about what was said, but I expect they'll put some deputy sheriffs on that Mr. Campbell said something about, *Well I shot*—or something along those lines. You're going to hear something about that. And I ask you to keep an open mind on that. I ask you to keep an open mind with respect to the circumstance when that comment was made, the fact that he was there about mental health."

Was he, I wondered, pleading insanity here? Wasn't he supposed to be arguing that his client didn't do it at all? Or was he planning to do both? Or neither? Or anything?

"Pay attention to these things," he said in conclusion. "These are some of these obstacles out there I want you to—I'm warning you about to be looking for, because although I'm concerned about it for my client because I know the jury's going to hear it, but for that one comment, there is not one iota of evidence against him."

"But for that one comment"? As Lee Jones took his seat again, I couldn't help but think: Thank God he's done with that.

When he sat down, Willie Perkins rose and strode over to the jury box. He was much more succinct.

"Where is the eyewitness?" he said. "Where is the evidence that would show murder or armed robbery, other than scratches and pieces that we think that the testimony of the State would show? We'll ask you at the end of the trial to return a verdict of not guilty."

And he was done.

☙❧

"State may proceed to call your witnesses," Judge Evans declared.

"The State will call Lavonna Williams, Your Honor," Cheryl Griffin said.

As far as I could remember I'd never met Freddie's wife, had never even seen her before. I hadn't had any luck in getting her to return my phone calls, either, although I couldn't blame her for that—she didn't know me, didn't know anything about me, and stood to gain exactly nothing from speaking to me. Now that I thought about it, it occurred to me that none of the people who had spoken to me on my last trip had anything to gain, either, and yet they all did anyway. That was Mississippi for you.

Lavonna Williams stood and made her way to the witness stand. She was in her midthirties, younger than I'd pictured, and she did not appear to doubt for a moment that she was still an attractive woman. Her hair was carefully coiffed; she wore a low-cut, sleeveless denim dress, two gold necklaces, large gold earrings and long, bright-green fingernails.

"State your name, please," Cheryl Griffin said.

"Lavonna Denise Williams."

"Mrs. Williams, where do you live?"

"In Greenwood, 606 Montjoy."

"And are you married?"

"Well, I'm a widow now."

There was an uncomfortable pause; it seemed to me that Griffin had, for just a moment, forgotten why all of them were there that day. "And who were you married to?"

"Mr. Freddie Williams, Jr."

"How long were you and Freddie married?"

"It would have been fifteen years the twenty-third of August."

"Have any children?"

"Two."

"What was marriage with Freddie like?"

"Everything. We was happy."

"Have problems like most married people do?"

"We was all right."

"And where did Freddie work?"

"At UPS."

"And how long had Freddie worked there?"

"About maybe thirteen, fourteen years."

"What was his work record like?"

"Every day, Monday through Friday."

"Was he known to miss work?"

"No."

"Had he ever received any awards or commendations from his place of employment?"

"Yes."

"What were those for?"

"Working every day, and perfect driver."

"Was his job important to him?"

"Yes."

"How did Freddie get back and forth to work?"

"In his vehicle."

In his vehicle? This was starting to sound a bit rehearsed.

"What kind of vehicle did Freddie have during the period of time— that period of time right before he was reported missing?"

"1994 Nissan Pathfinder."

"How long had Freddie had the Pathfinder?"

"About coming up to two months."

"Had any payments been made on it yet?"

"Like, one."

"One payment? What happened to the Pathfinder after it was found in Baton Rouge and returned to you?"

"Had to let it go back."

"The bank had to take it back because payments couldn't be made? Is that—"

"Yeah."

Rehearsed *and* coached.

"What did Freddie think of his truck?"

"Everything. He liked it."

"How did he take care of it?"

"By driving it hisself."

"Did he wash it and—"

"Wash it, yeah."

Rehearsed *and* coached *and* directed.

"Did he let a lot of people drive it?"

"No, not to my knowledge."

"Did he let you drive it?"

"Very seldom I drove it."

"Did you ever drive it by yourself?"

"Maybe once or twice."

"Once or twice in a month or two?"

"Yeah."

"Why didn't you drive it more often?"

"Because I was working a lot. I just didn't get to drive it a lot."

Griffin looked confused. "Did he *want* you to drive it?"

"Yeah, he let me drive it."

Now the prosecutor's face flushed red; she looked down at her clipboard, her eyes working back and forth, back and forth.

"Let you drive it?" she repeated haltingly.

"Yeah," Lavonna Williams said, without hesitating.

Ah, I thought. Now *that* was neither rehearsed nor coached, and it certainly wasn't directed; the prosecutor had been trying to get the witness to say just the opposite, that her husband *never* let her, or anyone else, drive his car. I was eager to see how Griffin would try to recover after that.

She didn't seem to have a plan. "What days of the week did Freddie work?" she asked again.

"Every day."

"But," she said, flustered, "I mean—"

"Monday through Friday," the witness said, deadpan.

"Monday through Friday. Okay. What did he do on the weekends?"

"Go out."

"Freddie liked to go out and have a good time?"

"Yeah."

"And if he went out, did he go out on Sunday night?"

"No."

"Why not?"

"Because he was getting ready for work Monday."

"Do you know Handy Campbell?"

Whoa, I thought. That was abrupt.

"No, not really."

"Had you ever seen him before?"

"Yeah, maybe once or twice."

"How about Lanardo Myrick, do you know him?"

"No."

"Did Freddie ever mention either one of those two people to you?"

"No."

"Before Freddie disappeared, when was the last time that you saw him, what day of the week?"

"Friday night."

"Okay. Can you tell us about the last few hours or the last time you saw Freddie?"

I was starting to wonder just how well organized Griffin was; she seemed to be all over the place.

Fortunately for her, Lavonna Williams didn't seem to notice. "He came home, like, I guess maybe about six or seven o'clock that evening," the witness recalled, "and he just sat around, you know, and then he got ready to go out, like, maybe after ten o'clock when he left, something like that."

"Okay. When you say 'he left,' do you have any idea where he was going?"

"He say out to Itta Bena."

"To a club in Itta Bena?"

"To the club."

"Do you know if he was going with anyone?"

"No, not really."

"Would it be unusual for him to go out with his friends on a Friday night?"

"No."

"Do you happen to remember what he was wearing when he went out?"

"A royal blue short pants outfit."

I had to swallow a chuckle; Freddie Williams might just have been the only man in Greenwood who would have worn such a thing.

"When did you start worrying that something might be wrong?"

"Like, that Saturday, that Saturday evening. I really got worried, like, Saturday."

"And why did you start getting worried?"

"Because it's not normal for him not to call home or come by."

And even though Lavonna Williams betrayed almost no emotion at all when she said this, her words smacked me like a hard slap in the face. Here I was, sitting back lazily, shooting silent barbs at just about everyone else in the courtroom, when it suddenly hit me: She was worried because Freddie hadn't called, because he *couldn't* call—because he was dead, lying half-naked in a shallow ditch beside the railroad tracks. This may seem to me like a farce, I realized, but it is a *trial*, a *murder* trial, a trial of two young men accused of murdering *that woman's husband*, that woman sitting *right there*, twenty feet from where I sit with a yellow legal pad on my knee, and no matter how amusing I find it all, no matter how badly everyone does or doesn't do their job here today, the one thing that's already decided forever is that, as Jack said, Freddie Williams is sho' nuff dead.

I sat up straight.

"So his normal routine," Cheryl Griffin said, "if he had gone out, would have been to either come home the next morning or to call you?"

"Yeah," Lavonna Williams answered.

"Would he have stayed out without having a change of clothes like that?"

"No."

"Was he particular about his clothes and his grooming habits?"

"Yes."

"So when he didn't come home Saturday, you started getting worried. What did you do?"

"Just called around and asked friends and things if they'd seen him."

"And to your knowledge, had anybody seen him?"

"Well, Kimberly Billups had said she had seen him, like, that night. And nobody else hadn't seen him."

"Did Freddie wear any jewelry?"

"Rings and necklace. And he had a bracelet."

"Okay. What kind of rings did he wear?"

"He had a wedding band and, like, four—maybe three or four diamonds."

"Okay. What other kind of rings did he wear?"

"He had a class ring he wear all the time."

"What school was this class ring from?"

"Amanda Elzy."

"Did Freddie go to Amanda Elzy?"

"No. That was a ring my son had found and gave him."

"How long had Freddie been wearing that ring?"

"For numerous of years."

"Did he wear a watch?"

"Yes."

"Do you recall what kind of watch it was?"

"A Bulova."

"Do you know where he got the watch?"

"I bought it for him at JCPenney's for his birthday."

"The week before Freddie disappeared, had he been to work?"

"No, he was on vacation."

"When was he supposed to go back to work?"

"That following Monday."

"Had he—had he gotten paid? Do you know whether or not he had a paycheck waiting for him?"

"Yes, he did."

"And did you talk with his supervisor at UPS about that check?"

"Yes, ma'am."

"Because Freddie never picked it up?"

"Yes."

"Do you know anyone with a big Buick Roadmaster car?"

For a moment, the witness looked confused by the sharp transition. "No," she said.

"Did you hear anything that Freddie might be planning on going out of town anywhere?"

"No."

"May I approach the witness, Your Honor?"

"You may," Judge Evans said.

Griffin stepped up to the dock and handed Lavonna Williams a photograph. "Ms. Williams," she said, "can you tell me who that's a picture of?"

"My husband, Freddie Williams."

"And about how long ago was that picture taken?"

"Maybe about four, about four or five years, I think."

"Your Honor," Griffin said, turning toward the bench, "I move at this time to have this picture marked for identification."

Lee Jones slowly rose to his feet. "I have an objection to relevancy," he said.

"State the reason," the judge said; then, without waiting for a response, he added: "You're overruled. It may be received and marked."

Lee Jones stared at the judge for a second. "It's not relevant!" he insisted. "It's obviously to invoke the passion and prejudice of the jury and sympathies of the jury. That's its only purpose."

"All right, sir," Evans said, his patience visibly wearing thin. "The objection of the defendant is noted."

Jones sat back down, and Griffin held up the picture at an angle that allowed me to catch a glimpse it. As I did, I wondered what it could be that Lee Jones found so objectionable; it was nothing, really, just an old photo of Freddie Williams, his lips parted in a familiar smile.

"Your Honor," Griffin said, "may I pass it to the jury?"

"You may," Judge Evans said. "You may proceed while it's being passed."

"Ms. Williams," Griffin said, turning back to the witness, "you testified that normally Freddie wore some jewelry. I believe you said it was a Bulova watch?"

"Yes," the witness replied.

"A wedding ring and a class ring?"

"Yes."

Griffin passed several small plastic bags to the witness, each containing a piece of jewelry. One by one, Lavonna Williams identified them: Freddie's wedding ring, his watch, his Amanda Elzy class ring. He always wore his wedding ring, she said, and wore the watch whenever he went out, especially on weekends. Griffin asked that they be marked and entered as evidence; this time, Lee Jones didn't bother to object, and Judge Evans granted the request. Griffin asked if she could pass them to the jury; the judge said she could. She did so, then turned back to the witness for one final question.

"Ms. Williams," she said, "what's it been like at home without Freddie?"

"Lonesome," Lavonna Williams replied. "Depressing."

"Object to relevancy," Lee Jones barked, springing up from his chair.

"Sustained," the judge declared. Jones nodded, smiled faintly and took his seat again.

"Your Honor," Griffin said, "we tender this witness."

ॐॐ

"Ms. Williams," Lee Jones said as he rose to begin his cross-examination, "it's my understanding that Mr. Williams had a nickname, *Itty*. Is that correct?"

"Yes," the witness said.

"So if somebody talks about *Itty*, we're talking about the same person as Freddie Williams?"

"Yes."

Jones nodded thoughtfully and paced around in silence for a few seconds. "Freddie was gay, was he not?"

The question achieved its objective: Every member of the jury, even those who had looked ready to doze off, now sat up straight and focused their attention on the defense attorney.

Except the witness, that is; she didn't seem to have much interest in what the short, bearded man standing before her had to say. She kept her reply brief.

"No."

Now Jones became flustered. He shuffled over to the defense table, looked over his notes for a few seconds, composed himself and paced back to the witness. "Ms. Williams," he said slowly, "were you aware that Mr. Williams knew Handy Campbell?"

"I assume he knew of him," the witness answered.

"What's the basis of that assumption? What are you basing that on?"

"Because I don't know him. I—they say they was friends. I don't know."

"Well, did Mr. Campbell visit in your home?"

"Not to my knowledge. I don't know if he was there. I don't know, I wasn't there."

Jones digressed for a bit into questions about Freddie's vacation and the witness' work schedule and when exactly it was that she last saw her husband, but apparently his efforts were fruitless, because he soon returned to the subject of his client.

"Did you ever hear Mr. Williams make any comments or acknowledge that he knew Handy Campbell?"

"Yes, he would talk—he talked about him, I think, once, because he was trying to get a job or something."

"During the week prior to your husband's disappearance, while he was on vacation, did you know that he was running or keeping company with Handy Campbell?"

"I heard some friends and things say he were."

"But you never saw it yourself?"

"No."

"How long prior to the disappearance was it that Mr. Williams made some comment about, I think you said, helping Handy get a job or talking about Handy and a job?"

"Maybe, like, a week or so before."

Jones raised his hand and opened his mouth to ask another question, then apparently thought better of it, turned and paced around for a few more seconds before turning to the judge. "Tender," he said.

Willie Perkins stood up. "May I proceed, Your Honor?" he said.

"Yes," Judge Evans replied.

Perkins slowly strolled over to the witness stand. "Ms. Williams," he said when he got there, "I represent Lanardo Myrick, and I want to ask you some questions about your testimony. First, counsel that preceded me asked you whether or not Freddie was gay, and you denied that today under oath."

"Say what, now?" Lavonna Williams replied, visibly confused.

"Mr. Jones, the lawyer who just finished asking you questions, asked you whether or not your husband was gay. And you denied that under oath today. Is that correct?"

"Yep."

"Okay. Now, I don't know if this is a change of words or miscommunication of words, but I'm going to ask you another question. Was your husband bisexual?"

"No, not to my knowledge, no."

"No, not to your knowledge?"

"I don't really know what that means."

Perkins cocked his head to one side and stared at the witness.

"She said she didn't know what that meant, Mr. Perkins," Judge Evans interjected.

"Bisexual," Perkins said to the witness, "means that he engaged in sexual activities and conduct with males as well as females."

"No."

Lavonna Williams had succeeded in frustrating every attorney she faced that day, and now it was Willie Perkins's turn. He didn't seem any better prepared for it than Cheryl Griffin and Lee Jones had been, but he recovered more quickly. "Was he not described as being a flashy dresser?"

"No," the witness said, once again looking confused. "Flashy dresser?"

"Yes," Perkins said. "When he went out."

"He dressed neatly."

"And he went out and he was with females and males that he met at different clubs?"

"Yes."

"Danced a lot?"

"Yes."

"And I believe you said that—on your direct examination you stated that if he stayed out all night, he would call you."

"Yes."

"And how often did he stay out all night?"

"It wasn't regular."

"But he did stay out all night?"

"He would stay."

"Did you ever inquire where he was when he was staying out all night?"

"He would just be, like, at a friend's house."

"But any of these friends happen to be males?"

"No."

"Ma'am?"

"No."

Willie Perkins paused for a moment and looked at his notes. "Now, in Greenwood," he resumed, "correct me if I'm wrong, night clubs are required to close up about 1 A.M. Is that correct?"

"Yes."

"On these incidents when Mr. Williams stayed out all night, generally what time would you see him the next day?"

"Early in the morning. Like, seven, eight o'clock."

Again Perkins paused for a moment. It looked like he was trying to figure out his next move; he didn't seem terribly organized to me, and I suspected he wasn't sure what he was trying to get the witness to say.

"That wedding band," he said, finally. "Did Mr. Williams wear that band?"

"Yes, he wore it."

"Did he ever take it off?"

"Maybe sometimes when he go to work, he didn't wear it."

"Let me ask you this: If he was in his vehicle and he was out partying and drinking, if he took it off, was it logically that he would leave it in his vehicle?"

"He ain't going to take it off."

"Okay," Perkins said, looking as if he had a bad taste in his mouth.

"Of course, you wasn't there on the night in question or the morning."
   "No."

There was a caustic edge to Perkins's statement, and apparently he decided to tender the witness before he let it develop further. Cheryl Griffin declined to redirect the witness, and Lavonna Williams stepped down from the witness stand looking exactly as she had when she'd first been called up to testify—exactly, in fact, as she had throughout her testimony, which is to say: utterly blasé. I wondered how someone could be as detached in discussing the murder of her husband as she might be in describing a fender bender she witnessed in the parking lot of Wal-Mart. Hadn't she loved Freddie? Perhaps not, I thought; I certainly didn't believe her when she said that if Freddie were gay or bisexual, she wasn't aware of it. If that was true, she was the only person in Greenwood who wasn't. Still, would that knowledge have been enough to kill whatever affection they must have once had for each other? Surely, if that had been the case, she would have divorced him, since divorce was as common in Greenwood as anywhere else, and she wouldn't have lost much by doing so, at least not in terms of money or social status. So how could she have been so cold up there? And who comes to court dressed like that, especially if they're expected to fulfill the role of the grieving widow? I couldn't figure it out, and as Frank Carlton rose to call the prosecution's next witness, I resigned myself to the notion that Lavonna Williams was just one more Mississippi mystery.

It was a notion that was only bolstered by my memory of what had happened when I had tried to contact her back in Greenwood two months earlier. Returning to my hotel room that Sunday afternoon after interviewing Handy's mother and brother at Snowden Jones, I had picked up the phone and called Lavonna Williams to ask if I could come over and interview her, too. The girl who answered said Lavonna wasn't home, so I asked her to take down my name and number and ask Mrs. Williams to please call me. I couldn't tell if the child on the phone was Freddie's daughter or not, and I didn't ask.

When I hadn't heard back from Lavonna after a couple of days, I called again. This time a woman answered the phone. "Mrs. Williams?" I said.

"She's not home," the voice said. "She'll be back later." Again I left my name and number.

And again, I heard nothing, and again, after a couple of days, I tried again. This time the phone rang and rang, until finally a machine picked up. Loud party music blared through the earpiece for a few seconds, and then a voice said giddily, as if delivering the punchline of a joke: "Leave a message at the beep!"

I recognized the voice immediately. It was Freddie's.

҉

"We call Mr. Sanders, please," Frank Carlton said. "Xavier Sanders."

Frank Carlton was a slight man with a very large head of white hair; he spoke with a gracious and occasionally folksy accent, wore conservative gray suits that were always pressed just right and steely gray wire-rim glasses. By contrast, his current witness, Xavier Sanders, was a tall black man in his midtwenties dressed in a blue basketball t-shirt, blue shorts, and sneakers; I half-expected Judge Evans to express disgust over the casual dress of the witnesses appearing in his court, but instead he simply directed Xavier Sanders to take a seat on the stand.

Carlton quickly established his witness' age and address and employment and marital status and then launched into his questions. "Do you know either of the two defendants here today?" he asked.

"Yes, I do, sir," Xavier Sanders answered.

"Do you know both of them?"

"Yes, I do."

"How long have you known them?"

"Approximately eight years, sir."

I confess: I was impressed with his manners.

"Did you see either of these two men that we've just described around the time—do you remember when—uh, did you know Freddie Williams?"

"Yes, I do, sir."

"Do you remember when Mr. Williams came up missing?"

"Sir," Xavier Sanders said, "I remember when he came up missing. It had to have been that Sunday when I read the newspaper."

"Had you seen either Campbell or Myrick shortly before Mr. Williams came up missing?"

"Yes, sir, I did."

"Tell us the occasion you saw him and what he was doing."

"I saw Handy and Lanardo Myrick. They was in the park that Tuesday. We was playing ball, twenty-one. Lanardo came on the court. He was already pissed off or mad or something. So Lanardo was talking about what he going to do Friday. He didn't exactly say what he going to do, but

344   RICHARD RUBIN

he said he going to do something Friday. And when he said that, Handy went across the street. When he went across the street, I'd say it had to been around fifteen, ten minutes later, Lanardo was right behind him. When Lanardo was right behind him, Handy was watching for him. Well, when Handy was watching out for him, that's when Lanardo came from behind the—McLaurin, across the street. It had to been ten or fifteen feet from where the park was. So he came behind the outhouse. And when he came behind it, Lanardo had whatever. It was black. I couldn't see that far then. But when he had it, he had put it up in his pants and covered it over with his shirt. And when he had did that, Handy was the first one that came across the street. When Handy came across the street, then Lanardo came.

"And when Lanardo came, he gave Handy the pistol. I spotted what it was. And when he had gave him the pistol, then Lanardo gave the pistol to Handy and put it up in a white towel. And that's when I had left, sir."

"All right," Frank Carlton said. "And can you describe this gun other than it being a black pistol? Know any more about the caliber, perhaps, or the size and shape of it?"

"No, I don't, sir."

"Okay. But you saw the two defendants exchange a pistol on this occasion that you've just described—is that right?"

"Yes, I did, sir."

Carlton turned to the judge. "I believe that's all, Your Honor," he said.

"You may cross-examine," Evans said to Lee Jones.

"No questions," Jones said without standing.

"Any questions, Mr. Perkins?"

Willie Perkins did stand. "No, Your Honor," he said, and promptly sat back down.

ॐ❦

The next few witnesses served mainly to chart the course of Freddie Williams's last night alive. Earnestine Sanders, a friend of Freddie's for more than a decade, testified that Freddie had picked her up in his Pathfinder at about 10:15 and had taken her to the VIP club, a nightspot they frequented in Itta Bena. He was wearing, she recalled, a blue short pants set, a necklace, a chain, and a couple of rings, including his Elzy ring. At the club they had a few drinks, she said, and stayed until a little before one in the morning, at which point he drove her home. As he was dropping her off he told her that he was hungry and tired, that he was going to get something to eat and go home, and that he'd call her in the morning; the two of them, she testified, usually went shopping together on Saturdays. When Sanders was finished, another friend of Freddie's, Kimberly Billups, took the stand and testified that she and a friend had run into Freddie later that same night, at around two-fifteen or two-thirty A.M., in the parking lot of the Double-Quick convenience store on Main Street. He told her he'd been out with Earnestine, and that he was fixing to go home. She admired his blue shoes, she recalled, and asked if she could borrow them; he said that was fine, and told her to stop by his house the next day so he could give them to her. About fifteen to thirty minutes later, when she and her friend were driving home, they spotted Freddie again, heading east on McLaurin, then turning left on Avenue F and pulling over to park, across the street from a park; Billups didn't stop, but continued driving on home. Lee Jones and Willie Perkins tried hard to shake their stories, especially their claims that Freddie had made plans with them for the next day. Lee Jones asked Earnestine Sanders if she'd had sex with Freddie that night; when she said no, Willie Perkins asked her if Freddie had been gay. Not that I ever saw, she said, and when Perkins later posed the same question to Kimberly Billups, he got the same answer. Was Freddie drunk? Was he high? Isn't that park, the one at McLaurin and Avenue F where you said you saw Freddie stop that night, a den of homo-sexual and drug-related activity? Perkins fired question after question at them relentlessly, but whatever answers he and Jones were hoping to elicit eluded them. Sanders and Billups never wavered in their stories. As far as the prosecution was concerned, they were two fine witnesses.

The next two, though, were trouble.

Larry McCrary and Clarence Meeks, both middle-aged black men, had been working at Mims One Stop on Highway 82, up in the hills in between Greenwood and Carrollton, on the night in question; McCrary had been working the cash register, while Meeks—who was Freddie Williams's uncle—was sweeping up. The prosecution expected them to testify that at some point between one and three in the morning, Freddie's Pathfinder had pulled into the parking lot, and that at least one of the defendants had gotten out and come into the store to buy cigarettes or alcohol or both; but when Cheryl Griffin put them on the stand, both would say only that they saw a truck that *looked like* Freddie's, and that nobody had gotten out of it, at least as far as they could recall. At first,

Griffin was merely stunned, although she quickly became flustered, too, then argumentative, and finally just crestfallen. Frank Carlton, on the other hand, just sat there silent, smiling vacantly as if all was right with the world, and especially with his case.

A few yards away, Jones and Perkins hid their delight behind sober expressions as they waited for the State to call its next witness; Handy Campbell merely stared down at the ground, dejected, as he had all day. But Lanardo Myrick turned his head around, looked at his mother and smiled; then he looked right at me and nodded his head, and I knew he was thinking: *See, I told you everything was gonna work out all right.* Much as I was sure he secretly wanted to, though, Myrick couldn't take credit for what had happened up there with Larry McCrary and Clarence Meeks. No one at the defense table could. It was just a windfall, an unexpected gift from the prosecution. What had happened? Had the prosecutors been sloppy or merely cocky, believing their case was so strong that they didn't need to know in advance what exactly their witnesses were going to say? Or had they somehow been ambushed? I didn't know enough about their case to decide; I only hoped they knew more about it than I did.

Cheryl Griffin, still looking somewhat disoriented, whispered something in the ear of Frank Carlton, who, for the first time in more than an hour, indicated that he was, in fact, still there, slowly rising to his feet and saying: "May we approach the bench, Your Honor?"

Judge Evans nodded, and once again all four lawyers walked up and crowded around him. "We have two more witnesses, Your Honor," Carlton said, too softly for the jury to hear, "both of whom Ms. Griffin tells me she's talked to, and they have changed their story substantially since they've talked to police, similar to the last two, and we're not going to put them on." Jones asked who they were; Carlton told him—Pattie Lewis and Jeannette Summerville, both of them from Greenwood—and then they all conferred for a few moments more. Finally, Judge Evans told them to return to their seats, then turned and addressed the jury.

"Ladies and gentlemen," he said, "the next witnesses are on their way. They have not gotten here. They're from Baton Rouge, and they were expected here before this time, but they're not here and we don't have anywhere to go right now except home. I know it's going to disappoint me to let you off this early, but we're going to take a recess until nine o'clock in the morning."

Early? It felt like midnight in that immense, windowless courtroom. I looked at my watch: It was a quarter after four.

"Please remember, now," the judge continued, "no discussion of the case with any person whatsoever, and be very careful not to let any person discuss this with you. And if anyone approaches you, then begin to get away from them and report it to me. I don't think we have any local news in here—"

He scanned over the crowd and stopped to stare at me for a second (instinctively, I slumped down in my seat), then remembered, I suppose, that I wasn't local anymore.

"—but don't read any newspaper accounts of this proceeding today. You decide the case on what you hear here in the courtroom, and not anyone else's turn or twist on it. And if anything comes over the five-thirty or six o'clock news regarding this, turn your TV off. Will you do that?"

The jurors were quick to say to yes; they were eager to leave. The lawyers were, too, but Evans told them that there was another matter that needed to be dealt with first. Jones and Perkins, Carlton and Griffin, all looked at each other, confused, as the jury filed out of the courtroom; then, when they had all left, the bailiff called in two young black men, Ronald Caid and Lawrence Williams, and swore them in. Instead of taking the witness stand, though, Caid and Williams stood before the bench and were questioned directly by Judge Evans.

"I understand," the judge began, "that you have both informed the Court that during the noon recess, you observed Sheila Lavon Roberson, juror number nine, seated over there in the black checked dress, seated next to some relative of one of the defendants and having a conversation—is that correct?"

The two men said yes, it was, although they did not overhear what was said. Did they understand, Judge Evans asked, that juror number nine has denied this? They understood, they replied, but they know what they saw, and they both saw it.

And who, the judge asked, did they see her talking to?

Hattie Campbell, they both said. The mother of defendant Handy Campbell.

I looked over at the defense table. Handy Campbell sat there as he had all day, mute and lethargic, seemingly unaware of what had been going on all around him, even though what had been going on all around him was a contest to determine whether his next address would be apartment 3-G at

Snowden Jones or Unit 32 at Parchman. His presence in the courtroom had been so understated that for long stretches of time I had actually forgotten he was there. In the eight hours I'd been sitting there, I'd studied everyone so closely—the judge and the prosecutors and the defense attorneys and the jurors, Freddie's widow and his mother and his friends or cousins or whoever they were, and Myrick's mother and Myrick himself, and Hattie Campbell and April and Anthony and Tracy—everyone but the person I was there to see, to watch, witness. I hadn't talked to him; I'd tried not to even look at him. I was distancing myself, I suspect, from a condemned man.

Evans turned to the defense lawyers. "Any questions you gentlemen want to ask?"

"Yes, sir," Lee Jones said emphatically, and turned to Caid and Williams. "Gentlemen," he said to them, "this took place during the noon recess?"

"That's correct," they said.

"Y'all were both subpoenaed as witnesses?"

"Yes, sir."

"All right. Y'all were sequestered and not here during the picking of the jury or the naming of the jury, is that correct?"

"No, sir, we were not here."

"Then how was it you knew this woman was a member of the jury panel?"

"She had a 'Juror' button on her dress," Williams said.

Jones froze. "Uh, okay," he muttered after a long moment of silence. "That's all I have."

Judge Evans dismissed juror number nine, Sheila Roberson, replacing her with alternate juror number one, an older black man named Carl Dugger. Cheryl Griffin pointed out that she had overheard a conversation between Lee Jones and Hattie Campbell that led her to believe that Hattie was also, during breaks, walking out into the hallway, where the witnesses who had yet to testify were waiting, and filling them in on what the other witnesses were saying in their testimony; and I remembered, as she told this to the judge, that I had witnessed such a conversation myself, between Hattie Campbell and Larry McCrary. At the time I hadn't thought too much of it, since I didn't yet know who McCrary was, much less that he was going to testify for the prosecution later that afternoon.

Now, though, I stared at Handy's mother, the woman who had welcomed me into her house, who had nearly cried several times during our interview, who had asked me if I knew what would happen to her child. Had she somehow managed to get McCrary and maybe even Clarence Meeks to change their testimony, to "forget" that they had seen her son at Mims Truck Stop that night, sitting in Freddie Williams's Pathfinder? I didn't know, but that fact didn't surprise me anymore; I was starting to come to the conclusion that I didn't know a damn thing about this whole ugly affair. Maybe Handy Campbell really had been the one to pull the trigger; maybe his mother had used me, had exploited my sympathy for her son and my fervent desire to believe that he couldn't have killed anyone, much less Freddie Williams. Maybe she was more ruthless than pathetic; maybe Lavonna Williams was more afraid than aloof. Maybe Lanardo Myrick really did have a fixer in his camp. Maybe Cheryl Griffin and Frank Carlton really had been ambushed. All I really knew for sure at that moment was that thinking about it was really starting to make me feel really sick—and really angry.

Apparently, I wasn't alone. Up on the bench, Judge Evans was clearly struggling to contain his fearsome temper, and for the first time, I found myself wishing he would just let it loose. "I want to make a statement here," he said, as loud as he could without actually yelling. "I didn't caution the spectators here. If, per chance, this were to happen again, I'm going to warn you now that if you even approach one of these jurors and I get wind of it, I'm going to take some action. And you won't like what that action will be when I take it. So you've been warned."

And he sent everyone home.

❦

I drove back to my motel, walked across the highway to the nearest Waffle House, ate dinner and shuffled back to my room, exhausted. I took a long, hot shower and then collapsed onto my bed, trying so hard to cast out the bits and pieces of testimony that buzzed around in my head like horseflies that I pushed myself into a deep sleep. At some point I was awakened by the ringing telephone; as I picked it up, I looked at the clock on the nightstand. It was a quarter to eight in the evening.

"Hi, Richard!" trumpeted a voice barely cloaked in a shabby knockoff of a Southern accent. "How are *you?*"

It was Tim Kalich, back at the *Commonwealth*. He wanted to know what had happened at the trial that day.

I was annoyed at the prospect of having to think about something I had worked so hard to chase out of my mind, and more annoyed that he was trying to get me to do his work for him. "Are you asking me to string for the paper?" I mumbled.

"Sure!" he said, and added, with a forced laugh: "Can't pay you, though!" Tim, I'd heard, was vigorously perpetuating John Emmerich's tradition of parsimony.

"Why didn't you send up a reporter?" I asked.

"Couldn't spare one," he said. "Didn't think it was important enough."

"Well," I replied, starting to wake up, "if it wasn't important enough for you to cover, why are you calling me now?"

"Just in case," he said, "something happened."

I thought about hanging up, but I didn't really have the energy; I didn't have the energy to do anything but what I did, which was to lie there, mute, for about thirty seconds.

"Well," Tim said, finally, "*did* anything happen?"

"Nothing *you'd* want to waste inches on," I said.

"All right," he said, oblivious to the edge in my voice. Or maybe just apathetic. "Thanks!"

I went to hang up, then stopped myself. "Uh, Tim," I said.

"Yeah?"

"How did you find me?"

He chuckled. "You forget," he said. "My wife's from Batesville."

I didn't ask what he meant by that. I didn't want to know.

Twenty-Two

Something Blue

$\mathcal{F}$rank Carlton wasn't tall or burly. He didn't gesticulate wildly when he spoke, didn't dramatically contort his face when making a point, didn't favor seersucker suits or bowties or suspenders, didn't perpetually wipe his brow with a starched handkerchief or fan it with a straw hat. But if you had sat in a courtroom and closed your eyes and listened to him cross-examine a witness or raise an objection or deliver a closing statement, that's how you would have pictured him.

You would have, that is, if you had been in such a courtroom in 1988. I was, and I did.

By 1995, though, he was in a gentle decline, or so it appeared to me. It was hard to spot—though his cheeks may have sunk a bit, and his thick head of iron-gray hair had edged somewhat closer to white, for the most part he looked the same as he had when I'd first met him. But frequently, during the first day of the trial, I thought I'd spotted on his face a wistful, absent look, as if the capital murder trial he was prosecuting just didn't engage him at all, as if he were daydreaming about walking his dog or mowing the lawn. I didn't know exactly how old he was, but I did know that he'd been prosecuting cases in court for a long time, so long that he certainly didn't have to be doing it anymore, so long that he was very nearly at the point where it would seem undignified for him to still be doing it, rather than passing those responsibilities on to younger staffers and retiring to his office and presiding over everything at a much greater remove. Frankly, I couldn't understand why he hadn't, unless maybe it was because he believed that the public, in electing him to the post again and again and again, expected him to protect it from becoming largely ceremonial. That was the answer I expected him to give me when I asked him the question in the corridor of the Panola County Courthouse shortly before the second day of testimony was scheduled to begin. But he surprised me.

"Believe it or not," he said, "this is Cheryl Griffin's first murder trial."

"Really!" I said, neglecting to add that I most certainly did believe it.

"But I'll tell you what," he said, "even if it wasn't, I'd be here anyway. To tell you the honest truth, this is the only part of the goddamned job that I like."

I couldn't hide my astonishment—at the sentiment, yes, but even more at the fact that he would say such a thing to me. After all, he knew who I was and why I was there; at several points during the previous day's testimony, he had turned and posed a provocative question not to the witness or the jury or even the judge but to me, the only white man in the crowd, sitting on the aisle and scribbling steadily on my big yellow legal pad. And once or twice, after a witness furnished an answer that was exactly what he was looking for, he glanced at me and raised his eyebrows, as if to say, "Did you get that?"

"Uh, Frank," I said, embarrassed by his candor and the sentiment and eager to change the subject, "I'm not sure I understand why you put up some of those witnesses yesterday. Especially those last two. I mean, even if they had given you the answers you'd expected, I don't know what that would have added to your case. There's no way the defendants will try to deny that they saw Freddie that night. They did have his truck, after all."

Carlton didn't say anything, and after a few seconds of silence, I realized why. I hadn't actually asked him a question.

"I guess," I blurted, "what I'm trying to say is—Frank, what's your *strategy* here?"

The district attorney smiled and threw his arm around my shoulder. "Richard," he said, his voice infused with avuncular warmth, "tryin' a case is a little like fuckin'. You put in all you got, and basically, there's not much else you can do!"

⁂

I wasn't sure how Mrs. Carlton would have felt about that philosophy, especially as it did not pertain to her husband's job, but I didn't have too much time to speculate. A minute later the bailiff announced Judge Evans's arrival; a minute after that the judge banged his gavel and called the court to order; and a minute after that Frank Carlton stepped up and proceeded to put in all he had.

He started with Eddie Lee Brooks, a clerk at Mims Truck Stop and Auto Service on Highway 82—not to be confused with Mims One Stop, which was also on Highway 82, up in the hills near Carrollton. Eddie Brooks's Mims was down in the Delta, a mile or two east of Greenwood, a mile or two west of the other Mims'. Brooks testified that sometime between three and four in the morning, as he was cleaning up and getting ready to go home, a brown Nissan Pathfinder—he recognized it, without a doubt, as Freddie Williams's—pulled up in front. Three people were inside; one of them, a thin black man unknown to Brooks, emerged from the front passenger door, came inside, bought a pack of cigarettes, left for a moment, came back in for some matches, and left again.

Lee Jones declined to cross-examine, and Willie Perkins's brief efforts to shake Brooks's identification of the vehicle as Freddie's Pathfinder were unsuccessful. That went much better, I thought as Eddie Brooks stepped down off the witness stand; but then Cheryl Griffin jumped up and asked Judge Evans if she could approach the bench. After conferring with her for a moment, the judge ordered the jury out of the courtroom. Griffin walked back to the prosecution's table, turned around to face the judge once again, and spoke loud enough for everyone left in the courtroom to hear.

"Your Honor," she said, "I would ask you to remind the spectators to stay out of the witness room."

Evans grunted and looked—or so I thought, anyway—right at me. I slumped down in my seat and tried not to look guilty. Then I remembered: *I* hadn't been in the witness room. I didn't even know where it was.

"I believe," Griffin continued, "Ms. Myrick has been in the witness room this morning talking with Eddie Brooks."

Now the judge was angry. "I don't want—" he said with a growl, then stopped himself and began again, clearly struggling to contain his temper. "Mister Sheriff, can you get us a bailiff to put around there?"

"Yes, sir," the sheriff said, no doubt glad he wasn't the object of Judge Evans's anger.

"And I don't want *nobody* but the witnesses in and out of the witness room under any circumstances."

"Yes, sir."

"She made a false statement, sir," declared a voice somewhere behind me. I turned around and saw a wiry black woman standing tall, her face betraying a mixture of indignation and fear, her finger pointed at Cheryl Griffin. It was Lanardo Myrick's mother, speaking in court for the first time.

Even the judge looked stunned. "Well," he said, "that's all right."

That wasn't enough for Myrick's mother. "I do not know Eddie Brooks," she said, adamantly.

"That's all right," Evans repeated.

"In other words, she lied."

"No, ma'am," Griffin said, shaking her head so vigorously that large strands of light brown hair wriggled loose from her coiffure. "We can get somebody to—"

"No," the judge cut her off.

"I do not know Eddie Brooks," Myrick's mother reiterated.

"Well," Judge Evans said, cutting her off, too, "I'm telling you now, don't go in that witness room, because any further—"

"Never *been* in there, sir."

"Your Honor," Griffin interjected, "it was—talking with a witness, I believe, was the instruction yesterday, not to talk with the witnesses anymore."

"Don't talk with the witnesses," Evans said, and sighed.

"I never talked to him, sir," Mrs. Myrick said. "I promise to God." And she sat down.

Judge Evans looked relieved, and instructed the prosecution to call their next witness. A stocky man with a mustache and graying hair stepped up and was sworn in. His appearance startled me, although it would take me a minute to figure out why: He was the first white person to testify in this trial. And he was a policeman, in uniform

Sergeant Lawrence Rabalais, Jr., of the Louisiana State University Police, was the next person, after Eddie Lee Brooks, to have spotted Freddie Williams's Pathfinder. It was five days later—Wednesday, August 31, 1994.

"I was westbound on West Lakeshore, which runs in front of the sorority houses," he recalled from the witness stand, "and I observed a vehicle exiting a dorm lot. And we'd had quite a few burglaries within the last two weeks, so I was going to go ahead and run a license check on the vehicle as a suspicious vehicle in case we had any burglaries."

What, I wondered, had made Sergeant Rabalais regard this particular vehicle with suspicion? It could have been that it was a truck, I supposed, or the fact that it looked pretty new or had an out-of-state license plate. But I couldn't help but assume the obvious: Two black men were cruising sorority row, late at night. That was enough.

"I was stopping at a stop sign," the witness continued, "and they were stopped about a block behind me at a stop sign. And once they turned left on West Lakeshore, I made a U-turn and followed in behind them to get a license plate number. Once I got the license plate number, before dispatch could read it back to me, the vehicle turned in an abandoned alumni center that's got, like, a horseshoe drive. They turned in there, and I kept on going straight. And just right after that, the dispatcher read the information back to me as a vehicle being stolen with the registered owner being missing and in danger."

Missing and in danger. I shuddered a bit at the sound of those words, just like I imagined Sergeant Rabalais must have shuddered when he'd heard them come in over his radio that dark night. It wasn't a vague phrase; it didn't contain the words *possibly* or *potentially* or *reportedly.* There was no room in there for an explanation that wasn't sinister. At the very least, the occupants of that vehicle he'd followed were car thieves. They might be kidnappers, or murderers. They did not belong in that vehicle, and there was no explanation for their being there that could result in anything less than an arrest—or an attempt at one, anyway.

Sergeant Rabalais explained that two other LSU policemen, Lieutenant Timothy Henderson and Lieutenant Robert Jones, were on patrol at the same time and heard the dispatcher's report over their own radios. The three of them proceeded to close in on the Pathfinder, intercepting it at a stoplight at the corner of Highland and Parker. "We ran a license check," Rabalais continued, "and it came back the owner being a Freddie Williams, Jr. And once we stopped the vehicle, we then had both subjects exit the vehicle, and they were handcuffed. And Lieutenant Jones then read them their rights and they were placed into units"—that is, squad cars— "at which time our dispatch teletyped the Greenwood P.D. to confirm that the vehicle was stolen."

"Were they placed in the same unit or in different units?" Griffin asked. Frank Carlton, apparently confident that the police officer would not change his testimony at the last minute, let his junior prosecutor handle Sergeant Rabalais's direct examination.

"Mr. Campbell, the driver, was placed in Lieutenant Jones's unit," Rabalais recalled, "and Mr. Myrick was placed in Officer Henderson's unit."

"What happened after they were placed in separate patrol units?"

"Once we got confirmation the vehicle was stolen, we then called a wrecker company to tow the vehicle for impound. Myself and Lieutenant Jones, once the wrecker got there, we began inventorying the vehicle, at which point, in the glove box, we found Mr. Williams's driver's license, a checkbook and an ATM card. There were other things, like sunglasses, found and stuff. Once we went to the back of the vehicle, Lieutenant Jones opened the back hatch, at which point a Blue Steel Stallard Arms 9 millimeter fell out onto the roadway." As he spoke, I could picture the scene: two police officers standing on a lonely road in the middle of the night, inspecting a vehicle that had been stolen from a man who was now missing, jerking open the tailgate and there's a flash and something coming at them and then it falls at their feet and hits the pavement with a tremendous clatter that rips through the darkness and then . . .

"Was the weapon in any type of holster or device?" Willie Perkins would later ask Lieutenant Jones on cross-examination. "It was just in the open?"

"It scared me when it fell out," Jones would offer in reply, seeming at first to not answer the question at all, until I realized that he was, in fact, furnishing much more of an answer than Perkins had wanted. "I thought it might have got me."

And, just as they had during Sergeant Rabalais's testimony, everyone in the jury listened intently and flinched in sympathy—everyone, that is, but juror number three, a young, heavyset black man named Richard Pittman, Jr. He was fast asleep.

☙❧

In all, the prosecution put up five LSU police officers. After Sergeant Rabalais came Lieutenant Jones, who testified that after the 9 millimeter pistol was secured he and Rabalais inspected the rest of the vehicle, and discovered that the entire rear cargo area was piled eighteen inches high with clothing and shoes and Sega game gear. At this point, Handy Campbell and Lanardo Myrick were being held down on the hood of one of the patrol cars; Lieutenant Jones handcuffed them, read them their rights, and separated them. Jones put Campbell into the backseat of his unit, and instructed officer Timothy Henderson to take custody of Myrick. While the officers waited for the wrecker to come and impound the Pathfinder, Jones searched Handy Campbell's pockets, and found, in addition to some change and a used bus ticket, two 9 millimeter bullets. He then told Campbell that he had verified that the truck was still considered missing without the owner's permission. "I asked him how he got the vehicle, and he said they got it from Freddie, that they were at a party together in Greenwood on the twenty-sixth, I think it was a Friday night, and that when they got ready to leave, they told Freddie that they needed the truck because they wanted to come down to Baton Rouge or south Louisiana or somewhere in that area, that they were going to be gone about a week, and that Freddie said they could use the truck and that it would be okay for them to do that. And they said that—he said that Freddie then left this party in another car. He couldn't describe it, but that he was with several other people who were at the party, they left together, and Freddie gave him the truck."

"Did Mr. Campbell say anything about calling Greenwood to confirm this story that you've just told me?" Carlton asked him.

"Yes," Lieutenant Jones replied. "He gave me the phone number and said that we could call that phone number and Freddie would verify that it was okay, that he gave them the truck, and everything was okay. I had my radio operator call the phone number, and he radioed me back and said that—"

"Object to hearsay," Lee Jones called out from his seat at the defense table. Judge Evans and Frank Carlton both ignored him.

"Well," Carlton asked the witness, "did you make an attempt to verify his statement?"

"It could not be verified," Jones replied. In fact, as they would eventually discover, the phone number Handy had given the officer was not Freddie Williams's—it was Hattie Campbell's.

Next up on the witness stand was Officer Timothy Henderson. While helping Lieutenant Jones handcuff Lanardo Myrick, Henderson testified, he had noticed that Myrick was wearing a large high school class ring and a gold-colored wristwatch. He then put the handcuffed Myrick in the backseat of his patrol car—Unit 112—locked the door, and walked away for a minute or two to talk to the other officers on the scene. When he returned to the car and climbed into the driver's seat, Myrick, sitting directly behind him, asked: "What's wrong? Is Freddie missing?"

"Had you said anything previously to him about the whereabouts of Freddie Williams?" Carlton asked him.

"No," Henderson replied. "I had not."

I looked over at the jury box; they were all focused intently on the witness' testimony, even juror number three.

Henderson drove Myrick back to the police station. There he and Campbell were booked and transferred to a local jail, where they were held, in separate cells, on a charge of grand theft auto.

Two weeks later, on the night of September 15, 1994, LSU police officer Michelle Reese was cleaning out Unit 112 when she found, stuffed underneath the rear seat on the driver's side, a plain gold wedding band, a high school class ring, and a gold-colored wristwatch. She took them, she testified, back to the station and logged them in as evidence, according the department protocol. Cheryl Griffin, who was examining Officer Reese, held up a plastic baggie containing three shiny objects and handed it to the witness. Reese identified them as the three items—gold wedding band, large high school class ring, and wristwatch—she had dug out from under the backseat of Unit 112 that night; they were then passed around, first to opposing counsel and then to the jury, just as a baggie containing the Blue Steel Stallard Arms 9 millimeter pistol had been passed around during Sergeant Rabalais's testimony.

After logging the three items into evidence, Reese testified, she handed them over to the Evidence Custodian on duty that night, Sergeant Jesse Sandifer, who took the stand next and testified that he examined all three items carefully, and was most puzzled by the class ring, as it was from a high school he'd never heard of—Amanda Elzy. It took some looking, but he was finally able to locate the school, and was so surprised by what he found that he cried out: "I'll be damned—Greenwood, Mississippi!" Sergeant Rabalais, who was in the police station at the time, overheard him and came running, shouting, "What? What? What?" And so it was that they discovered a crucial link between the victim, who was still missing, and the defendants, who were still in custody.

If Larry McCrary and Clarence Meeks had cost the prosecution some momentum, the five LSU police officers helped them regain it, and then some. Every one of them delivered his or her testimony flawlessly, affording Lee Jones and Willie Perkins so little room for questioning that they gave up trying to cross-examine them altogether after Officer Henderson was through. The jury was receptive, too; clearly, most of them were impressed with the amount of circumstantial evidence the prosecution had collected. I know I was, never having heard most of it before. Frank Carlton, I thought, certainly had a lot to put in: The gun; Handy's fake phone number and the 9 millimeter bullets in his pocket; Myrick's premature expression of concern for Freddie's welfare, and his attempt to dispose of the evidence; Freddie's vehicle, his checkbook, his ATM card, his wristwatch, his wedding band, his Elzy ring. All that was missing was his body.

That came next.

⬥⬥⬥

In all the time I spent in Vaiden, Mississippi, I met dozens of people, but none of them had ever introduced me to a lifelong resident named Morris Austin. I shouldn't have been surprised, really, because Morris Austin's ancestors were buried on the other side of that chain-link fence from the ancestors of all the people I met there, and to my great shame I never got around to climbing that fence in Vaiden, either in the cemetery or in the town itself. What should have surprised me was that I managed to meet him at all—and in, of all places, the Panola County Courthouse in Batesville, seventy-five miles north of Vaiden.

Morris Austin had spent the past thirty years working as a machine operator for the Illinois Central Railroad. On October 24, 1994, a machine broke down on a track in Greenwood, and he and his crew were sent down there to work on it. While working there they smelled something strange, but they didn't pay much attention to it. The next day, while still working on that machine, Austin went to his car to fetch a wrench. "I decided to walk across the track," he testified, "and go down that side, and I discovered something blue over there, kind of down beside the track in the weeds there. And I'm a funny guy—if I see something, I'm going to check it out, you know. And it was wrapped up. I said it must be something somebody threw away, an animal or something in a sack or something.

"And I walked over there and looked, and I seen this—" Austin faltered for a second "—his head and his eyes and his teeth and—" he cleared his throat, took a breath "—but his tongue and eyes was gone."

I heard a faint cry and looked across the aisle. Iola Williams, Freddie's mother, was sitting there, twenty feet away, her eyes shut tight.

"And I looked to my right there," Austin continued, "and I seen his legs and his feets, and I was kind of stunned a few minutes. I didn't know what to do, and I started back across the track. And I seen an officer coming, they're usually riding through there. And I flagged him down and told him I had something to show him. He came on over there and looked, and he got a little upset, too. He said, 'We been looking for this guy,' I guess he said a month, a month and a half, something like that, and he called his name. I had heard about it on the news."

"Did you note whether or not any of the bushes or any item around the body had been disturbed in any manner?" Willie Perkins asked Morris Austin.

"Not that I can remember," the witness replied. "No."

"And you were—to your knowledge, you're the first person who found and saw the body in that area?"

"I guess I was."

"You don't know how the body got there or how long it had been there?" Lee Jones asked.

"I sure don't."

"Don't know who put it there?"

"I don't," Austin said. "I wish I knew."

"Tender," Jones said, and Morris Austin stepped down and went home to Vaiden. I envied him.

⹂⹊

The Greenwood police officer Morris Austin had flagged down that day was named Richard Johnson. After Austin led him to the body, Johnson returned to his squad car, radioed headquarters, and passed the news on to Detective Ronald Caid. Caid, who had been with the department for six years and bore the rank of sergeant, had assisted two other detectives, Lieutenant Lester Martin and Sergeant Lawrence Williams, in their investigation of the disappearance of Freddie Williams; now he was called to the crime scene as the primary detective. He quickly secured the area and requested assistance from the state crime lab. While he waited for them to arrive, he took nearly a dozen photographs, all of which were now entered as evidence. The first few, shots of the crime scene, seemed sterile enough. Then things got ugly.

"This is a picture of four men with shovels attempting to lift the remains," Caid said, pointing to one of the pictures. "They were in a very decayed state. We had trouble getting the body up and trying to keep it all

together." I turned my head so as not to see the people on the other side of the aisle, and did everything I could to not hear them, too.

"These are the remains," Caid said, pointing to another photo. "We're putting them into a plastic bag before putting them into a body bag." And another: "This is what I saw when I first walked up. It was very hard to see the body. What caught my attention first were the teeth. Once I spotted the teeth, I could spot the outline of some facial characteristics and was able to identify that as a person."

There was nothing I could do to avoid hearing the sharp wail that erupted across the aisle that time. My stomach tightened; I wished I had skipped breakfast that morning.

"At the time that you were called out and first viewed the body," Griffin asked him, "did you have any suspicion as to who this body may have belonged to?"

"Keeping in mind that we'd been working on the Freddie Williams case for several months at that time," Caid said, "and I knew that what Mr. Williams was supposed to have had on the last time he was seen was a royal blue shirt and shorts set, when I saw the remains there in the ditch and I saw the clothing that matched what he was supposed to have had on, I believed at that time it was going to be that of Freddie Williams."

"Mister Caid," Lee Jones said to the witness, "it's my understanding that as part of your investigation, you requested a trace on a 9 millimeter Stallard Arms model JS handgun?"

"Yes, sir," Sergeant Caid replied.

"Did you get a result on that?"

"No, sir, not to my knowledge."

"During the investigation, did you ascertain the type of area that Church Street in Jackson, Mississippi, was?"

"It was an area known for drugs, prostitution, and gay activity."

It took me a moment to realize that Lee Jones had just slipped that question in there, seamlessly, and another moment to realize that it had nothing to do with the case as it had been presented so far. Apparently it took the prosecution even longer than that, as they didn't object to the question when Jones asked it. And Jones shrewdly dropped the subject as soon as he got his answer, denying the prosecution another chance to do it. He just dropped it—or rather, left it hanging there, no doubt counting on the notion that "drugs," "prostitution," and "gay activity" were the kind of words a jury would chew on long after they had been issued forth from the witness stand.

"Your report," Jones continued, "indicates two weapons were sent to the crime lab. Do you know the caliber of either of those weapons?"

"One was a 9 millimeter, and the other was a .22 caliber."

"What was the purpose of sending these to the crime lab?"

"To see if we could get a ballistics comparison between either of the weapons and a piece of copper jacketing that had been recovered from the victim's chest cavity."

"And did you get any report?"

"Yes, sir," Sergeant Caid replied, "and the results were inconclusive."

"Just couldn't make a determination?"

"Correct."

"You indicate there was a piece of copper jacketing. How was that found?"

"During the autopsy."

"Although it was with the body, you didn't find it at the scene. It was sent with the remains to Jackson?"

"Yes, sir." Caid shifted in his seat. He looked annoyed. Or uncomfortable. Or both.

"Other than the remains themselves, did you find any other physical evidence at the scene?"

"No," Caid said, then reconsidered for a moment. "Well, other than his clothing, no, sir. That was it."

"I assume the thought was, the copper jacketing or whatever, the projectile, that that was a portion of bullet that was used?"

"Yes, sir."

"A copper projectile is—those are associated with a .22 caliber sometimes?"

"Several calibers use jacketing."

"What calibers would those be, to your knowledge?"

"Just about any caliber."

".22?"

"I can't recall seeing a .22 jacket bullet, no, sir."

Jones tried again. "Well," he said, "not jacketed, but copper projectile?"

"Possibly," Caid said.

"What about a .22 magnum?"

"Possibly."

".25 auto?"

"Possibly."

".380?"

"Possibly."

Judge Evans leaned forward to the microphone. "What's a .380 and a .25 got to do with—go ahead and get to the 9 millimeter!"

Lee Jones tried on an embarrassed smile, but Judge Evans merely glared at him, and he quickly dropped it. "9 millimeter?" he said to the witness, his voice cracking.

"Yeah," Caid said. "It's possible."

".38?"

"Yes, sir, possibly."

".44?"

"Yes, sir, possibly."

"So it's not just a 9 millimeter, it could be basically any handgun?"

"Yes, sir."

Jones turned to the judge and smiled again, this time with a little more confidence. "Tender this witness," he said.

"Mr. Perkins, do you have any questions?" Evans asked.

"Yes, sir, Your Honor," Willie Perkins said, then rose and approached the witness. "Detective Caid," he said, "you assisted Detective Martin and Detective Williams in investigating this matter?"

"Yes, sir," Caid said. "The entire detective division was involved in it."

"Were there any other suspects or leads that you followed other than the two defendants in this matter?"

"Me personally? No, sir."

"Were there any other allegations pertaining to other persons who may have been involved with Mr. Williams that may have caused his death?"

"No, sir."

"Did you receive an allegation or information pertaining to Mr. Williams getting into a blue Roadmaster-looking type car with a Louisiana plate on the night that he became missing?"

"According to Lieutenant Martin," Sergeant Caid replied, "the two defendants said that they had let him off at a store and he'd climbed into a big car, possibly a Buick Roadmaster with Louisiana plates."

"But wasn't there at least one witness unconnected with the family or with any defendant that verified some type of blue-looking car that Mr. Williams had conversation with a person in it?"

"I did not talk to anybody like that, that I can recall."

Perkins studied his notes for a moment. "Do you know a Fitzgerald?" he asked.

"No, sir, I don't know him."

"I believe his name was Scott Fitzgerald?"

I chuckled at the thought of the author of *The Great Gatsby* involved in an affair like this one. We were a long, long way from East Egg.

Caid just shook his head.

Perkins shuffled back to the defense table and conferred in whispers with Lee Jones for a few seconds. He nodded his head and returned to the witness.

"I believe," he said, "the correct name was a Fisher Stevenson?"

"Yes, Fisher Stevenson," Caid replied. "Lieutenant Andrews is the one that spoke with him."

"Does your report reveal anything about a car?"

"Mr. Stevenson stated that the car was a brand-new–looking four-door car with dark tinted windows and bearing a Louisiana tag. He said it might be either a Buick Roadmaster or a Lincoln, he's not sure which. He said he noticed three heads inside the vehicle, all black males, and said that he'd spoke to Freddie Williams, and then he, Stevenson, went walking down Weeks Lane. I don't see—"

"I guess my question, Detective Caid, is whether or not your department just focused in on two individuals that was found in the vehicle, or did you seek other leads that you may have had that could have led to the death of Freddie Williams?"

"Yes, sir, we followed each lead we got."

I took a moment to savor the spectacle before me: In a Mississippi courtroom, a black lawyer was grilling a white police officer who persistently addressed him, in turn, as "sir." Thirty years earlier, it would have been the black lawyer calling the white policeman "sir," with the officer, no doubt, addressing the lawyer as "Willie"; certainly, a black lawyer who interrogated a white witness so aggressively would have been endangering his health, professionally and physically. Then again, a black lawyer probably wouldn't have been appearing in court in the first place.

"So you, in fact, did follow up on the information Fisher Stevenson furnished?" Perkins asked.

"As far as I know," Caid answered, "Lieutenant Andrews did follow up on that, yes, sir."

"And you know of no results?"

"No, sir."

"Okay," Perkins said, and continued without pausing. "Correct me if I'm wrong, that at or about this time, there was a scam going with the United Parcel Service about money orders—is that correct?"

"I'm not familiar with that investigation," Caid replied.

"You're not familiar about a UPS scam about the employees and money orders?"

"There was an investigation going on in Jackson at that time that I remember reading about."

"But wasn't one of the individuals a Mr. Sherwin Stewart, a former resident of Greenwood, Mississippi?"

"I do not know that."

"You know a Mr. Sherwin Stewart, sir?"

"No, sir."

"Did you do any follow-up to see whether or not Mr. Williams, a UPS employee, was involved with that?"

"I spoke to Mr. Thompson, who is the hub supervisor for UPS. And from all indication, there was no connection between Freddie Williams and any ongoing investigation with UPS."

I was starting to understand just how much of a break the defense had caught when the trial was moved from Greenwood to Batesville. A Greenwood jury, I figured, would have known something about Lee Jones and Willie Perkins and Freddie Williams, would have known that all this talk of Fisher Stevenson and Sherwin Stewart and Church Street and UPS money order scams was just a dodge. A Greenwood jury would not have been distracted by any of that, and certainly not by Willie Perkins's next line of questioning.

"During the time when Mr. Williams was missing," Perkins began, "can you give me a general description of what information was sent out in your homicide missing person unidentified body form?"

"Are you talking about the one that we sent out to different departments?" Caid asked. I was glad he did, having no idea what a "missing person unidentified body form" was supposed to be.

"Yes," Perkins replied.

"It had a picture of Freddie Williams," Caid recalled, "a close-up shot of his face. And also, it gave a physical description and numbers to call in the event that anyone saw him."

"Did you describe other information, like social activities and et cetera?"

"It just had his physical description—I think it was what he last had on."

"Let me ask you this, Detective: In your information that you sent out, did you not describe the victim as being 'bisexual' and a 'frequent outgoing socializer'?"

"I don't recall that, no, sir."

Perkins asked the judge for permission to approach the witness. "Detective," he said, walking up to the stand and presenting him with a piece of paper, "are you familiar with that form as being information sent out by the Greenwood Police Department during the time that Mr. Williams was missing?"

Detective Caid looked at the form for a second or two. "I'm familiar with these," he said. "I have not gone through this. I'm not the one who did this."

Perkins ignored his disclaimer. "Under 'Lifestyle,' what block has been checked?"

"Okay. It's got 'bisexual.'"

"What about—"

"And 'socializes frequently.'"

"Okay. And further, you have a general description of—"

"Yes, sir. It says, 'Victim is bisexual and a frequent outgoing socializer.'"

No, I thought, a Greenwood jury wouldn't have been distracted by this. They wouldn't even know what a "frequent outgoing socializer" was, much less suspect that it was of any account at all. I know I didn't. But none of that seemed to matter to this jury. They were transfixed.

"And that was sent out when you was trying to find Mr. Williams?" Perkins asked, waving the form in the air.

"As far as I know, yes, sir."

"Was there pressure on the Greenwood Police Department to hurry up and solve this case?"

"Well, with any murder, we like to get to the bottom of it and get the case wrapped up, yes, sir."

"There was pressure?"

"No more than any other case, no, sir."

"Officer, you know where McLaurin Street is?"

"Yes, sir."

"Describe that area."

"It's a low-income area. It's got numerous juke joints and dilapidated housing. Railroad tracks run close by."

"Describe the area of Avenue F and McLaurin," Perkins said, straying far from the simple yes or no format of a standard cross-examination. I looked over at Frank Carlton, expecting he would rise any second to object. But he just sat there, smiling vacantly. "Talk about the activities that transpire there."

"We have numerous drug sales go on in that area, sidewalk drinking, loitering, standing around, fights."

"Male and female prostitution, do you have that problem in that area?"

"At times, yes, sir."

What, I wondered, would Perkins have done if the trial hadn't been moved, if everyone in the jury knew exactly where McLaurin Street was and what it was like, if they all drove by it two or three times a week and probably knew a few people who lived on it or right off it and could tell you that it wasn't an unfathomable bedlam of sordid vice, a sneaky little corner of hell that could and would entrap and destroy even the most righteous of men, that Detective Caid spoke the truth when he said that there were problems there *at times*. But this wasn't Greenwood. Perkins knew that no one on this jury would have ever seen McLaurin Street, and that the worse his description of it was, the more likely the jury was to accept it. He knew they would relish the notion that, as bad as parts of Batesville were, there was nothing in their town that could approach the kind of sin and squalor they had in Greenwood. He gave them what they wanted. And then he left them with it.

"Nothing further, Your Honor."

On redirect, Cheryl Griffin asked Detective Caid if he had contacted the Jackson Police Department, and why. He explained that, "in an interview that one of the defendants gave, I can't remember which one, they state that Freddie had told them as he was getting out of the car that he was going to church. And I didn't know if 'church' was possibly a name for something else, if they meant Church as in a Church Street or Church as in a sanctuary. So keeping that in mind, I called Jackson just to see if they had a bar by the name of Church, or a Church Street area."

"So that was a lead you followed up from a story given to you, a statement given to someone by the defendants in the case?"

"Yes, ma'am."

"And was Freddie ever seen in Jackson, Mississippi, on August—when he disappeared?"

"No, ma'am, we've never had any information given to us by the Jackson Police Department or from anybody in Jackson."

"When you were investigating this case, who did your investigation reveal as being the last people known to be with Freddie Williams before his disappearance and murder?"

"Last ones that were known were Lanardo Myrick and Handy Campbell."

"Who did your investigation reveal were found in Freddie Williams's vehicle with his driver's license, checkbook, identification?"

"Lanardo Myrick and Handy Campbell."

Griffin turned to the judge. "Nothing further," she said, and, looking pleased with herself, sat down. She had set out to steer the testimony away from sullying rumors and insinuations and back toward the damning evidence, and, judging by the expressions on the faces of Lee Jones and Willie Perkins and Handy Campbell, she had succeeded (Myrick's cocky grin never wavered, no matter what was being said about him). But looking at the jury, I wasn't so sure; evidence didn't seem to engage them as much as tales of McLaurin Street. And if I could see that, I was sure Lee Jones and Willie Perkins could, too.

❧❦

To identify the body, the Greenwood Police Department called upon Dr. Sigurds Otto Krolls, a tall, distinguished-looking gentleman with a head of straight white hair and a slight German accent. Dr. Krolls, a dental pathologist and forensic dental specialist—what he called a "forensic odontologist"—at the University Medical Center in Jackson, compared the corpse's teeth with existing dental records, and declared, as he recalled on the witness stand: "It is my belief that the body is that of Freddie Williams." No one argued with him.

Once identified, the remains were transported to the office of the state medical examiner in Jackson, where Dr. Emily Ward, a forensic pathologist, examined them for an autopsy on October 31. Dr. Ward, a slight woman in her early forties, testified that by the time it reached her, "The body of Mr. Williams was in a state of advanced postmortem decomposition. In other words, most of the tissue was no longer present on the body. The skeleton was there and some of the tissue, but the majority of it had begun to decompose."

"And did you find any remnants of a gunshot wound in the remains of Mr. Williams?" Frank Carlton asked her.

"Yes, sir, I did," she replied.

Carlton produced a sealed box, which Dr. Ward had previously marked with Freddie Williams's case number, the date, and her initials. Opening it in front of the jury, he handed the box to the witness and asked her to identify its contents. "There are two pieces of metal here," she said, looking into the box. "One of them is a flattened piece of what looks like a lead projectile. And then the other piece is a separate piece which looks like, in my opinion, a piece of copper jacketing from a bullet."

"And where did you recover these two items?"

"From the left shoulder of the remains of Freddie Williams."

"And did you find any indication of other gunshot wounds to the body?"

"There was a round hole on the right cheek just below the cheekbone which looked like a gunshot entrance wound, and a corresponding large defect on the left side of his skull, including the left ear, where there's just a vacant place where nothing was there. So it appeared that a bullet had entered the right side of his face and exited the left side of his head or in the area of his ear."

Someone on the other side of the aisle muttered something angrily; someone else shushed him, and let out what sounded like a quiet sob. It occurred to me that, like me, Freddie's friends and family were probably hearing these kinds of details for the very first time.

"Do you have an opinion, Doctor, as to the cause of the death of Freddie Williams?"

"In my opinion, Freddie Williams died of multiple gunshot wounds."

"Particularly the one to the head?"

"Yes, sir, that's right."

"In your experience and training, do you have an opinion as to the caliber of the wound in Freddie's head?"

"It's difficult to be absolutely certain about the caliber of the bullet because it's so deformed, as it's traveled through the body. But the amount of lead that is there—"

"Excuse me, Your Honor," Willie Perkins interjected. "I'm going to object to any opinion given. It appears to be outside of her expertise. It would be more in the field of ballistics, and she has not been qualified."

"Well," Judge Evans said impatiently, "she may state if she knows from her expertise and training." Perkins started to say something else, then stopped himself and sat down.

"Please continue, Doctor," Carlton said to the witness.

"Mr. Carlton," Dr. Ward said, "I've removed hundreds of bullets from bodies, and I can't tell you the exact caliber, as I said. But I can tell you that it's not a small caliber bullet and it didn't come from a shotgun or a rifle."

"In your opinion, is it larger than, say, a .22?"

"Yes, sir, it is."

"Is it consistent with a 9 millimeter?"

"Object to leading, Your Honor," Perkins called out from his seat.

"Overruled," Judge Evans replied with a sigh.

"It is consistent with a 9 millimeter," Dr. Ward said. "Yes, sir."

"Thank you very much," Carlton said. "We tender."

"Dr. Ward," Lee Jones began his cross-examination, "what other sized projectiles or caliber would it also be consistent with?"

"I guess," the witness replied, "it could be from a .357 magnum or possibly a .38. But it's a pretty large chunk of lead, so it's not from a small caliber bullet, in my opinion."

"Talking about a .38 or .357, 9 millimeter, in that range?"

"Yes, sir. I guess your question was could it possibly be one of those others. It could if we remember that there's a piece of copper jacketing there, too. I think that's important."

"So it could be either of these three or others?"

"I guess it could be a, possibly, .44, .45, something like that."

"The wound to the head, there was no projectile found?"

"That's correct. There's a hole where the bullet went in, and another hole where the bullet came out of his head."

"As far as a piece of lead or jacketing, we don't have anything for that wound?"

"No, sir, we do not."

"The jacketing and the lead that's been introduced is associating with the left shoulder?"

"That's correct."

"Where was that located on the body, what part of the shoulder?"

"I think it came from more toward the front of the body than the back."

"I guess I'm more interested in how high up it was," Jones explained.

"Well, it's hard to tell," the witness explained, "because, see, most of the soft tissue is not present there anymore. We just have his skeleton bones sticking there. And there's a little bit of muscle here in the region of the shoulder, and we recovered the bullet from that. But once a body's been that much decomposed, it's hard to be very precise about the exact anatomic spot that we removed the bullet. About as good as I can tell you is that it's from the front of the left shoulder."

"Do you have an opinion whether that wound would have been fatal?"

"It certainly could have been fatal."

Jones paused for a second, then asked Dr. Ward if she was familiar with the Greenwood area, and if she was familiar with the climate in the area around August and September. She was, she said, having grown up there. Jones then asked her if she had an opinion regarding how long the body had been dead before it was found.

"I can tell you certainly the body's been there for more than two or three days," she said. "Once you get past three or four days, something like that, it's really hard to be specific about it because it's so dependent on the environmental exposure the body has had, whether it was in a sunny area or shady area, whether it was humid or not. And there are just too many environmental variabilities to say anything more than that."

I thought back to the afternoon, a couple of months earlier, when Officer Dean had shown me the spot where Freddie's body had been found, and how surprised I was at how close it was to the road—not to mention Snowden Jones and the offices of the *Greenwood Commonwealth*. How could the police have missed it for two months? And why wasn't it they who finally discovered it, but a railroad worker from Vaiden who wasn't even looking for it? Why couldn't they have found it in time for it to be much more useful to someone like Dr. Ward?

For his part, Willie Perkins wasn't inclined to question something that worked so well in his favor; he only wanted to exploit it further. "The body had been decomposed—is that correct?" he asked the witness.

"It was in the process of decomposing, yes," she replied.

"Okay. And you didn't have blood, you didn't have tissue—is that correct?"

"There is tissue still present on the body. It's just that some of it's gone, and some of it has changed from the state that it would be shortly after he died because of the decomposition. So it's a little flabbier and softer than it would have been right after death."

"And when you get a body in that condition—I guess my question to you is, what evidence do you have to determine the cause of death?"

"Well," Dr. Ward explained, "there's a very round, precise hole on his right cheek that measures three-eighths of an inch in diameter. And I don't know of anything other than a bullet that would leave a hole like that on somebody's cheek and leave a corresponding large defect on the left side of his head."

"How reliable is that determination, Doctor, given the condition of the body?"

"Well, I—certainly, my opinion is within reasonable medical certainty."

"Could other pathologists share a different opinion?"

"I suppose so, yes, sir."

"Okay. So wouldn't that be mere speculation, given that the body has been decomposed?"

"No, sir. And I would hate to mislead the jury to think that I'm speculating about every—everything I've said is based on medical evidence and is within reasonable medical certainty."

Perkins walked back to the table, studied his notes for a second. "Now," he said, returning to face the witness, "I believe there was two fragments of a copper piece of a bullet found in the left shoulder?"

"Yes, sir, in the chest in the region of the left shoulder."

"Could that have been from an old gunshot wound to the victim?"

"Well," Dr. Ward said, starting to sound more relaxed, "now that you mention it, I don't think it was an old gunshot wound, because if the bullet had been there for a long time, it would have developed scar tissue around it and that copper would have degenerated in the body, and we would have expected to see a lot of scar tissue around there. And since there's no scar tissue around these two fragments that are easily removed from the tissue there, it is a recent wound."

As soon as Dr. Ward had said no, it could not have been an old wound, a look flashed across Willie Perkins's face, equal parts surprise and embarrassment and panic; and as she went on, making her point more clearly and forcefully, I could see that he wanted nothing more at that point than for her to just stop talking. He had committed a fatal error for a courtroom lawyer—asking a witness a question without first knowing the answer. He tried, clumsily, to recover. "The, uh—could other experts show different views on that?"

"I can't answer that question," Dr. Ward said. She wasn't giving him any more.

And that was it for this witness. Willie Perkins knew, I suspect, that he should have let Lee Jones's cross-examination stand as it was, and not try to improve upon it; as it was, he had managed only to undermine it. He quickly wrapped things up, and the witness was dismissed. The defense could only have been glad to see her go.

⤞⤝

When the cause of death was determined, the charge against Handy Campbell and Lanardo Myrick was upgraded from grand-theft auto to murder. The Greenwood Police Department sent two officers down to Baton Rouge to pick them up and carry them back to Mississippi, in separate cars, to be indicted on the more serious charge. When they arrived in Greenwood, Campbell and Myrick were ushered into police headquarters, where they encountered Lieutenant Melvin Andrews, another detective who had worked the case. Andrews had been with the department for nearly twenty years; he was highly regarded in both the police department and Greenwood itself, in part because he had once been shot in the hand in the line of duty. Lieutenant Andrews greeted the new arrivals, advised them again of their rights, and asked them if they wanted to say anything. They did not. At that point, Campbell was led away, and Myrick, who remained behind in Andrews's office, asked where they were taking him.

"And I made the statement," Andrews recalled on the witness stand, "that I was going to have to put Campbell in the county jail to keep them separated because I didn't want them getting their stories together. And when I said that, Myrick made the statement, he says, 'We already have our story together.' I said, 'Oh, well,' and he said, 'Well, not like you think.'"

"And that was made in the presence of another detective?" Cheryl Griffin asked.

"Detective Shirley Terry was sitting in the office when Myrick said that," he replied.

There wasn't anything Lee Jones could do with that testimony, so he focused instead on the mysterious Fisher Stevenson, who claimed to have seen Freddie Williams on the night in question, standing in the parking lot of a club called Mitchell's Lounge, "talking to a young, black male he described as wearing a round-shaped black hat, white shirt, baggy pants. The young guy sounded, to Stevenson, to be gay. The guy and Freddie were standing beside a light blue four-door car, dark tinted windows, bearing Louisiana plates, possibly a Roadmaster or a Lincoln," and that he "noticed three people inside this vehicle, all black males." Jones asked

Detective Andrews if he'd investigated that report; Andrews said he had.

"And where did that lead?" Jones asked.

"That led nowhere," Andrews replied.

"Did you develop information that he was with someone else?"

"No, sir. That, that Mr. Stevenson told me right there, I could not find anything else to back up that."

Jones looked frustrated. "But, uh, in talking with Mr. Stevenson, you were led to believe or understand what?"

"That he was just out there talking to somebody in the parking lot of Mitchell's Lounge."

There was nothing else Lee Jones could do with that. "Tender," he said.

೩ೕ

Ken Spencer had spent more than a decade in law enforcement, starting out as a sheriff's deputy in Sunflower County, Mississippi, then becoming a policeman in nearby Greenville, until, on April 1, 1995, he started work as a deputy with the Leflore County Sheriff's Department. He looked the part, too—a big, beefy man with dark blond hair and a mustache and a sharp mouth and eyes that wordlessly conveyed the sense that he was not a man to be trifled with, an aura that served him well in his job, part of which entailed guarding the prisoners being held in the Leflore County Jail.

On the morning of June 22, 1995, he was assigned to transport prisoner Handy Campbell to the Life Help Center in Greenwood, also known as the Region VI Mental Health Center. It wasn't an easy assignment, as Deputy Spencer recalled: "On that morning when I brought Mr. Campbell down from the jail and entered the interior door of the courthouse to the sheriff's office, Mr. Campbell became somewhat agitated and began making loud barking noises and trying to attempt to keep from walking through the sheriff's office, and also talking in a loud tone of voice stating he wanted to see Ricky Banks," the sheriff of Leflore County.

"What happened at that point?" Griffin asked the witness.

"Sergeant Charles Cooley came out of the deputy's office," Spencer recalled, "which is just to the back of the sheriff's office, came out to investigate and accompanied me to Life Help with Mr. Campbell."

"Was anyone else present at Life Help besides you, Sergeant Cooley and Handy Campbell?"

"Yes, Hattie Campbell, Mr. Campbell's mother."

"Did Ms. Campbell ride with you to the Mental Health Center?"

"No, she didn't."

"Do you have any knowledge of how she got there?"

"No, ma'am, I don't. She was there when we arrived."

"Was she waiting for you, or did you just happen to run into her?"

"It appeared she was waiting on us. She was standing in front of the door, in front of the building on the outside when we arrived."

"When you got to Life Help, did you see a doctor right away?"

"No, we didn't."

"What happened?"

"We went into the Life Help Center and told them that we were there. We were shown to a waiting room just alongside of the main waiting room there, and Ms. Campbell, Sergeant Cooley, Handy and myself were placed in the room to wait on the doctor."

"Do you recall approximately how long you were there, total?"

"Overall, we were there approximately two and a half hours, maybe, from the time we came in until the time the doctor saw Mr. Campbell."

"While there, did Handy Campbell make any statements to you or in your presence regarding this case?"

"Yes, he did."

"Can you tell us what led up to that and then what the statements were?"

"As I stated, the four of us were sitting in the waiting room. Sergeant Cooley and I were talking to Ms. Campbell and to Handy about the fact that Sergeant Cooley had known Handy's mother, father, and family in general, for several years. During this conversation, the conversation turned to football; we began talking about football. And suddenly, out of—Mr. Campbell stopped talking and said, 'Wait a minute, wait a minute. I need to tell you something. Can I tell you something?' At which time I told him he could.

"At that point, Mr. Campbell said, 'You know, me and that other guy, we were looking for some—we were wanting to get some more money,' or, 'to get some money, and I didn't mean to do it. I didn't mean to hit him.'

"And at that point, I interrupted Mr. Campbell and advised him that anything he said concerning his case could be used against him in a court of law, and did he understand this? He nodded 'yes.' And upon nodding 'yes,' he turned his hand. He said, 'I just shot like this,' turned his wrist in to the left like this, 'but I didn't mean to hit him.'"

I didn't want to look at Handy Campbell then, didn't want to see the look on his face, his posture, the cast of his eyes as his confession was being shared for the first time with twelve jurors and three alternates and a dozen spectators; there was no expression of sorrow or contrition or helplessness that could redeem him or even save him at this point, and I didn't want to see him try anyway and fail. But I couldn't help myself: I did look, and the expression I saw was just nothing, just a dull, vacant stare focused on the floor in front of him. It was as if he had nothing to do with any of this, as if he were trapped in a theater where a movie that didn't particularly engage him was showing.

"Was he free from restraints at that time?" Griffin asked.

"No, ma'am," Spencer replied. "He had a waist belt on with handcuffs and leg irons."

"So he raised up his hand partway, and—"

"Right, as far as the restraints would let him."

"Prior to Mr. Campbell making this statement, what was his demeanor? You said at the jail he was agitated. Did he calm down at some point?"

"Mr. Campbell appeared to be pretty much calm by the time we got to the Life Help Center. Of course, by the time we got into the waiting room, he was—as I stated, we were talking about football, Sergeant Cooley was talking to him about his family, you know, and this and the like."

"Were these conversations coherent?"

"Yes."

"Did they make sense?"

"Yes."

"And were they made of his own free will?"

"They were."

"And they were made in the presence of his mother?"

"That is correct."

"Did Handy Campbell say anything about what kind of relationship he had with Freddie Williams?"

"He stated that Freddie was a friend of his."

"Deputy Spencer," Lee Jones said, beginning his cross, "you're trained in law enforcement, is that correct?"

"That's correct," Spencer replied.

"You don't pretend to have any degree of expertise in psychology or psychiatry?"

"No, sir, I do not."

"Were you advised or did you understand that Mr. Campbell did not adjust well to the jail environment?"

"No, sir. Until that morning was the first time I had ever seen Handy Campbell."

"So you hadn't heard any conversation with any other deputies about Handy not doing well in jail?"

"No, sir."

"You indicate that when you brought Mr. Campbell down from the jail, he was in an agitated state?"

"Coming down from the jail, Mr. Campbell was pretty well calm. This only occurred as we were walking out of the hallway of the courthouse."

"How long did this episode go on? Being agitated."

"I would say just a few minutes."

"In addition to becoming agitated, you indicate in your report and you've testified Mr. Campbell was making loud barking noises. Could you imitate those for me?"

Deputy Spencer looked a bit uneasy, but he was game. "Yes," he said, "it was imitated as, say, the barking of a dog, going 'Woof! Woof! Woof!' Like that."

It was all I could do to keep from laughing; to suppress the urge, I looked over at Handy Campbell. The sight of him, slumped down like a marionette dropped on the floor, was enough to squelch any laughter I might have had inside me.

"During your discussions," Jones continued, "Mr. Campbell told you, did he not, that he'd been out with Freddie Williams shooting the gun?"

"No, sir," Spencer replied. "He did not."

Jones thought for a second and tried again. "Do you recall Handy telling his mother in your presence, 'I didn't do it'?"

"No, sir."

"That 'He was my friend'?"

"He did say that Freddie Williams was his friend."

And that was it for Lee Jones. Willie Perkins declined to examine the witness; Handy Campbell wasn't *his* client.

☙ ❧

Like Ken Spencer, Sergeant Charlie Cooley of the Leflore County Sheriff's Department was a big man, tall and broad-shouldered, middle-aged and balding but still quite imposing in his uniform. Unlike Ken Spencer, though, there was a subtle kindness in his face, and a gentleness to his manner; he looked like the kind of man who could, if necessary, use force to bend an uncooperative inmate to his will, but would invariably try almost anything else first—a soft tone of voice, a smile, a joke, an offer of gratitude, even the word "please." This distinguished him, in my imagination, from the policemen who had testified before him that day, and that may very well have had to do with a much more obvious trait that set him apart from them: Sergeant Cooley was black. Perhaps that distinguishing feature led me to ascribe a certain benevolence to him; or perhaps it was the fact that he reminded me somehow of the man who, six years earlier, had pushed my car out of the mud that night outside of Webster's, and had then had to decline my offer of a drink because he wouldn't have felt welcome inside the restaurant. As the witness made his way to the witness stand, I wondered if I weren't giving him too much credit. His testimony soon affirmed that I wasn't.

"How long have you worked for the sheriff's department?" Cheryl Griffin asked him.

"Twenty-three years, seven months, and almost one day."

At that precise moment, a natural phenomenon I could never have imagined possible occurred, right there, in that courtroom: Judge Gray Evans *smiled*.

"Reckon you gon' finish out your day?" the judge asked the witness.

"Hope so, Judge," Cooley replied coolly. "Hope so."

"Sergeant Cooley," Griffin asked, "do you know the defendant Handy Campbell?"

"Yes, ma'am," Cooley said. "I do."

"And do you know Handy Campbell's family?"

"Yes, ma'am, I do."

"How long have you known the Campbell family?"

"In the neighborhood about, I'd say, thirty-odd years, something like that. Around thirty years."

"And how long have you known Handy Campbell?"

"He was small, quite small. In fact, I knew the family before he was born."

"Did you have occasion to be involved in the transportation of Handy Campbell to the Life Help Center on June twenty-second of this year?"

"Yes, ma'am. Officer Bowie and myself, we was sitting in one of the deputy rooms discussing another case. At that time, I heard somebody barking real loud like a dog. They kept hollering 'Ricky Banks! Ricky Banks!' So we walked out of the room, because we thought they were coming toward the sheriff's office. At that time, Deputy Spencer was struggling with Handy, trying to get him around the counter and get him outside and put him in the car to take him to mental health. So I walked up, and he told me he needed some help. I said, 'Okay.' I said, 'Let's go, Handy.'

"So he just grabbed my hands, squeezed my hands and said, 'I want you to go with me.' I told him, I say, 'Okay, I'll go with you.' So we walked him out and put him in the car, proceeded to mental health with him."

"What happened when you got in the patrol car?"

"We were riding along headed to mental health, and I told Handy that I knowed his family, his mother and his father, for a long time, they were good friends of mine. So we got to talking, and I asked him did he know my sister. My sister retired from Greenwood High in 1990, and she taught school over there. So he told me he knew my sister and that she was a good lady."

"So you had a conversation with Handy Campbell?" Griffin asked.

"Yes, ma'am, we did," Sergeant Cooley replied.

"And did the conversation that Handy Campbell had with you make sense?"

"Yes, ma'am, it did."

"What happened when you got to the mental health center—did you meet up with anyone?"

"Yes, ma'am. We met his mother, Hattie, at the door. And she wanted to know could she go in the waiting room with us, and I told her she could. So she went inside the waiting room with us."

"Did Ms. Campbell leave at some point?"

"She left and went over to the Wheels restaurant and got him some food."

"And did he eventually eat that food?"

"Yes, ma'am, he did."

"Did the subject of football come up?"

"Yes, ma'am."

"Why would that be significant to Handy Campbell?"

"Well, Handy played quarterback at Greenwood High. Handy started talking about Tupelo, the Tupelo game, and that's why the conversation came up."

"And did his conversation about football make sense?"

"Yes, ma'am. Sure."

"It wasn't off-the-wall?"

"No, ma'am."

"And do you recall what his demeanor was at that time? Was he still barking and whatnot?"

"No, ma'am. The barking quit when he squeezed my hand and he wanted me to go with him."

"Did he give you any trouble after that?"

"No, ma'am, no trouble."

"What was his demeanor?"

"He was calm, real calm."

"At some point while you were in the mental health center, the Life Help Center, did Handy Campbell make a comment in your presence regarding what happened in the Freddie Williams case?"

"We were talking about football, mostly it was football. And he said, he said, 'Hold it a minute.' He said, 'I want to tell you something,' like that. And then he said, 'I need to tell you something,' you know. Those are the words. So Spencer told him, 'Go ahead.'

"So he said that 'Freddie Williams was a friend of mine,' and he and the other wanted some money or need some money, in that words. At that time that's when Spencer cut him off and said, 'Hold it a minute, Handy,' said, 'Let me advise you of your rights.' So he advised him of his rights. He nodded his head and say he understood his rights.

"So I—we had the cuffs on him, chain, you know, back then. He turned his hand sideways. He said, 'I didn't mean to shoot him.' He said, 'I shot like this,' his hand turned sideways." Sergeant Cooley reached out his own hand to mimic the gesture, just as Deputy Spencer had during his testimony. As he did, I turned and looked at Handy. He was now seated upright in his chair, no longer slumped over as he had been throughout most of the trial; I imagined Lee Jones had prevailed upon him to improve his posture so that he might more resemble a man who wasn't bent under the weight of a guilty conscience. His expression, though, was no more focused than before, and his forearms rested on the table, useless, dead weight. I found it impossible at that moment to summon up an image of those arms in action, poised like a catapult to shoot a football into the sky forever, as I had seen them do so many times; they were gone now, vestigial appendages, their only saving grace the fact that they were not bound by a steel chain, as they had been the last two times I had encountered him. It occurred to me that this trial might very well be the last time I would ever see them unshackled.

"And that time, he started crying," Cooley continued, lowering his arm. "I said, 'Well, go ahead on and get it off your chest,' just like that. And I kept looking at his mother, just seeing what—you know, what kind of action she was going to take, but she never did flinch no kind of way whatsoever.

"But he finally cut off, you know. After he—I told him to get it off his chest, he finally cut off. So then, she told Deputy Spencer and myself, she said, 'Well, y'all are two good men.'"

"I'm going to object to hearsay," Lee Jones called out from his seat, and all twelve jurors—even juror number three, who had napped on and off throughout the day—turned and glared at him, obviously as taken with Sergeant Cooley and his story as I was.

"Sustained," Judge Evans said.

Griffin, not wanting to lose her momentum, led Cooley through the episode one more time, beginning with Ken Spencer stopping Handy and reading him his rights, and asking the witness to mimic one more time Handy's hand gestures as he reenacted the shooting there in the waiting room at the Life Help Center; this time, Cooley raised both arms, to illustrate exactly how Handy would have done it with his arms chained together, and reiterated: "I shot like this. I didn't mean to hit him."

"And then he started crying?" Griffin asked.

"Started crying," Cooley replied. "So I told him, I said, 'Go ahead on and get it off your chest.'" And hearing it again, I wondered if maybe, just maybe, Sergeant Cooley hadn't been acting purely out of sympathy.

"Did he see the mental health people?"

"Yes, ma'am, he did. One nurse came in, and a short time later, a doctor came in, and she asked myself and Deputy Spencer to step on the outside. So we left out, and we stayed on the outside until they got through with him. Then we brought him back to the jailhouse."

"Tender this witness," Griffin said, and confidently strolled back to her seat. As it happened, her most compelling and sympathetic witness brought with him the best tale to tell, the State's best evidence—a heartfelt confession of guilt. And he, like two-thirds of the jury, was black. I didn't envy Lee Jones as he stood up to begin his cross.

"Deputy Cooley," he said, forcing a smile, which only made him look more nervous. "It's hard for me not to call you Charlie."

"Go ahead, now," the witness said, mercifully. "Go ahead. That's all right."

"Deputy Cooley," Jones said, anyway. "As you indicated, you've been at the Leflore County Sheriff's Department twenty some-odd years."

"Correct," the witness answered.

"Handy Campbell, I believe, he first became incarcerated in your jail November eleventh, when he came back from—or came from Louisiana. He had been continuously in y'all's jail?"

"As far as I know, attorney. I don't—I don't know."

"Mr. Campbell did not adjust well to jail, did he?"

"He had problems in jail. He had problems at one time."

"One time or several times, deputy?"

"It may have been several times he had problems. I never was there when it happened."

"But we know how the deputies and the reputation get around the jail that he wasn't adjusting well," Jones said, haltingly. "You had that under-standing, didn't you?"

"Yeah, I know that's true," Cooley replied.

"Do you recall any conversation about him hallucinating?"

"Recall? No, I can't recall."

"Did he get so disturbed on some occasion you had to call Sheriff Banks on the weekends?"

"I knew they had a bunch of problems. Every time they had a problem, I wasn't on either time that they had problems with him, you know, during that time."

"But you're aware that the sheriff had to become involved?"

"I'm aware of—that the jailor and things did, yeah."

"The thing about his momma going to get the food, Deputy Cooley, were you aware that he was saying he hadn't eaten in four days, Handy hadn't eaten?"

"The conversation came up. She asked him would he—would he eat some food if she go and get him some food. And he told her he would." Cooley nodded his head once; Lee Jones opened his mouth to pose another question, but before he could Cooley spoke up again: "Now, let me go a little further. After he got through and got it off his chest, he was a different person. I can say that. Everything went downhill. Yep."

Jones looked lost. What could he possibly say to discredit testimony like that? "Well," he said, "it's, uh, my understanding your report indicates that, uh, after that, he went to crying."

"Yeah," Sergeant Cooley said. "He was crying."

"And he never said anything else about it?"

"No. But he was a changed person." Cooley paused for a moment, searching for another way to explain it. "You know," he said, "you can look at things and tell, like when it rain, you know, and the sun come out, you can tell a difference. He was a changed person."

"But, after he started crying, he didn't talk about it anymore?" Jones asked.

"I told him to get it off his chest, go ahead and get it off his chest. He didn't talk about it no more. He said that he was going to do better in jail, and he was going to start reading the Bible." Cooley was telling the story for the third or fourth time, now, but he never varied in the details, and his calm never broke; I started to believe again that his main concern at the time really was his prisoner's peace of mind. "Now," he continued, "he made that statement, that he was going to read his Bible, you know, and the fact being, as far as I know, we haven't had any more trouble out of him since then."

"But when you carried him back to the jail," Jones asked, "you sent him—he was sent back with three prescriptions of medication drugs, is that correct?"

"They gave him some medicine," Cooley replied. "I can't recall exactly how much. Something for rest and something else, I think it was. They told him what he needed it for, told him for his nerves or something another. I don't know what it was. But he hadn't been no trouble since."

"Since he had the medicine, he hasn't been any problem?"

"Since he had the medicine," Cooley said, *"and* got it off his chest, too."

Jones stared at his notepad for a moment, plotting his next course. "Do you recall Handy saying that Freddie Williams was a friend of his?"

"I did, yes, sir."

"And that he was upset about what happened to Freddie Williams?"

"Well, he said that he shot him like this," Cooley stated, and once again held out his hand and turned it to the side. "He said, 'I wasn't intending to hit him.' He said that. That's when he started crying. Volunteered it hisself. I didn't ask him nothing. I didn't—I was shocked myself. I didn't know."

"But he never actually said, 'I shot him.' What he said was, 'I didn't mean to hit him.' That's what your report says."

"He said, 'I shot like this, but I didn't mean to hit him.' Like I said—"

"But he never said he shot him?" Jones repeated, starting to sound a bit mean. Or desperate.

"Well—"

"Now did he?"

"I'm telling you like what he said. I don't know what he—" Cooley shook his head. "Whatever."

"He never said he shot him?"

I looked over at the prosecution's table, expecting someone to announce an objection already. Griffin looked like she wanted to call out but just couldn't bring herself to, while Frank Carlton just nodded his head obliviously, thinking again about his lawn.

"He said, 'I shot like this,'" Cooley stated, refusing to allow Lee Jones's growing agitation to infect him. "He leaned toward his arm this way, said, 'I didn't mean to hit him.' That's all he said. That's *it*."

"Once—one more time," Jones said, his voice growing louder. "He never said he shot him?"

I looked at Frank Carlton again: He really was acting like a man who believed that he had just put in all he had, and could do nothing else.

"Mr. Jones," the judge growled. "He's answered the question."

"I've answered," Cooley concurred.

"Judge," Jones cried, "it calls for a 'yes' or 'no'!"

"No, sir," Evans said, obviously working to retain his control. "He's answered the question in the manner in which he said it. You may move ahead."

Jones stood absolutely still for a moment, then took a deep breath and turned back toward the witness. "Then after that comment he made," he said, softly, "he never said anything else about it?"

"No more than he said he was going to do better in jail, which he has," Sergeant Cooley answered, "and that was going to read his Bible. I don't know whether he's reading his Bible or not, but I know he's doing better in jail." I was quite sure Myrick, who had somehow managed to maintain his grin throughout this ordeal, was reading enough Bible for the both of them.

"You talked about your sister, I believe, that taught at school," Jones said. "Is that correct? You talked about that?"

"I asked him did he know my sister. And he told me he knew my sister. Which, I knew if he was out there, he knew her because she ran study hall. If you got in any kind of trouble or anything, you had to go by her."

"Well, it wasn't all Mr. Campbell talking about football. You were talking about it and Deputy Spencer was talking about it—is that correct?"

"Deputy Spencer told him that he played tight end, and he wish the time that he was in school that he had a quarterback like Handy Campbell. They were just discussing, you know, just about football, is what it was, and left there and went to Freddie; left there and went to him."

And there they were, the two extremes of Handy Campbell's brief life in one brief conversation, from football glory to a confession of murder. Lee Jones couldn't have encapsulated the tragedy of this trial any better if he had planned it all out.

But he had also backed himself into a corner: By forcing Charlie Cooley to repeat it so many times, he was ensuring that the story of Handy Campbell's confession would be deeply imprinted on the consciousness of the jury. It was a formidable setback to the defense; to overcome it, Lee Jones would try a gambit that, repulsive as it was, had worked well for him in the past.

TWENTY-THREE

CONFEDERACY OF SILENCE

*E*very day of the trial, when Judge Evans called recess for lunch, I left the courthouse and walked several blocks through downtown Batesville, Mississippi, to a restaurant that was apparently favored by the town's business community. It was new and clean and no doubt conceived to be a terribly charming place, self-consciously quaint and Southern—Batesville was on the interstate, after all—with old farm implements and license plates and cotton paraphernalia and sepia-toned photographs of people who may or may not have had any connection to Panola County hanging on its walls, and waitresses who were invariably young and pretty and innocently flirtatious.

Over the course of the trial I got to know one of them a little bit, a fresh-faced girl who had never yet left the South but who entertained fantasies of moving to New York and becoming an actress or maybe a dancer. She readily admitted that she knew nothing about New York, couldn't even locate it on a map, but she had seen enough of it in movies and on television to know it was where she wanted to be. As I talked to her, it slowly dawned on me that this girl was to New York what I had once been to Mississippi: an utter stranger drawn to a strange place not so much for what it was or even what she or I perceived it to be, but because it was so very different from the world in which we had grown up that it could, if we let it, reconfigure us into entirely new people, unfettered by

386

our old identities and everything that came with them. She wanted to shed the mantle of the small-town Mississippi girl and start all over again as an off-off-off-Broadway ingénue, just as I had sought to relieve myself of the burden of being a good Jewish boy from New York who went to a good school and got good grades so he could someday become a good lawyer, and instead start all over again as a reporter in a small town in Mississippi. I wondered if I should tell her what I had eventually discovered: You can never reinvent yourself completely; at your core you'll always retain some critical elements of your old self and you won't get to choose them and won't even know what they are until they reveal themselves to you and whoever you happen to be around at the time, coworkers or dinner companions or a couple of ladies leading you on a tour of their town's old cemetery.

But I didn't. I didn't tell her a thing.

෪෨෪

The trial of *The State of Mississippi vs. Handy Campbell and Lanardo Myrick* lasted three days. The prosecution spent two days presenting their case, entered more than a dozen items and documents into evidence, and put up nineteen witnesses.

The defense put up four. Two of them were accused of murder.

If the other two defense witnesses had been stronger, the defendants probably wouldn't have testified at all. As Lee Jones had made clear—at least to me—in his opening statement, he didn't want to put his client up on the stand, didn't want to subject him to a cross-examination at the hands of Frank Carlton or anyone else. But he had no choice; things weren't going well for the defense at that point.

It started when Judge Evans declined to call it a day at a quarter to four in the afternoon—much to the dismay of juror number three, who was already whining, "I want to go ho-o-ome!" Instead, when Charlie Cooley stepped down off the witness stand and Frank Carlton declared that the state had finished presenting its case, the judge ordered the defense to begin presenting its case right away. Jones, still shaken from his encounter with Charlie Cooley and obviously even more disappointed than juror number three by the judge's work ethic, had his associate, a young lawyer named Elizabeth Davis, conduct the direct examination of his first witness.

She was Dr. Mary Lane Burks Wheatley, a psychiatrist in her sixties whose hair nevertheless clung tenaciously to its last traces of blond; perhaps to offset this, she wore it in an exceedingly sensible cut, and sported enormous steel-framed eyeglasses, the kind that automatically add ten years and one postgraduate degree to the face they adorn. Dr. Wheatley worked part time as a consulting psychiatrist at Life Help, the Region VI Mental Health Center in Greenwood. She didn't spend much time there— three days every other week, to be precise—but she did happen to be working on the morning of June 22, 1995, when an inmate at the Leflore County Jail named Handy Campbell was brought in by two sheriff's deputies. "Ms. Lula Randall, a nurse at the center, informed me that we have what we call an ICE, which is an in-center emergency, and she had seen an individual and needed for me to see him also and to evaluate him and see if he needed any treatment," Dr. Wheatley recalled. "I actually left my office and went up to a small waiting room that they have where they keep people who come in on uncomfortable circumstances. And he was, because he was in shackles. And when I saw him, I realized that he had a poor posture. He looked very dejected."

And he still does, I thought as I turned and glanced over at him seated next to the recuperating Lee Jones. Every time I looked at Handy, in fact, he appeared exactly the same, no matter what was transpiring around him. It didn't strike me as being particularly strange, really; if I were on trial for murder, and it seemed likely I was going to be convicted and possibly even sentenced to death, I suppose I'd look dejected, too. But Handy's was a flat dejection, inanimate, stagnant, bereft of shame and remorse no matter what was being discussed—the 9 millimeter bullets found in his pockets, the misleading phone number he gave the police, the grotesque state of Freddie's remains when they were finally discovered, even the imitation of the way he had barked like a dog. None of it appeared to move him at all.

"What do you mean?" Davis asked the witness.

"Well," Dr. Wheatley replied, "he was slumped over and had what, in our business, we call a depressed affect. That means that you really have a real extremely sad look on your face. And I'd already been informed that he had not been eating and sleeping, and that he reportedly heard voices, which immediately makes me think of someone who is what I call clini-cally depressed, and not just ordinarily sad about his circumstances, but much more than that. And after I asked my questions and did my observa-tions, I made the decision that he did have a serious mental illness and was basically psychotic.

"Now, the diagnosis that we use—and you just take it out of a textbook—is major depression with psychosis. Basically, the symptoms of that are not sleeping, not eating more than—more than several days. And we had at least a week on him. You need two weeks, technically, but we also had a history in our chart that he'd had a serious episode of illness for a few days in January. And that was enough, that plus a week of not eating and sleeping. He was unkempt, he was disheveled, he wasn't bathed, and he was hearing—reported—it was reported that he was hearing voices. And I believe his mother said that he was hearing—that she had told—he had told her he was hearing voices. But he told the nurse and he told me. A lot of remorse or sadness. All of these, you put them together when you— someone like I, who's seen a lot of major depression, and you put them together in a symptom we call major depression, which means they need medicine. And so this is what we basically did. We started—I started. We didn't—it's not 'we.' I did. I started—"

"Doctor," Elizabeth Davis said, "can I stop you for a moment?"

Please, I thought. I was having some difficulty keeping up with the witness, although I was trying pretty hard—much harder than, say, the jury, who all seemed to be following number three's lead by fidgeting and looking at their watches. (Number three, meanwhile, having set the example, had contentedly drifted off into another nap; I sincerely hoped he wasn't the foreman.)

"Dr. Wheatley," Davis continued, "could you explain what you mean by the term 'psychosis'?"

"Well," Wheatley said, "'psychosis' is a term that we use a whole lot in our business, and a lot of people have it. This basically means a loss of contact with reality, a person who's hallucinating when there's nobody there, or who's hearing things, voices or noises. And I have people that hear bells, and there's no bells there or nobody outside or nobody around that's saying something. That's an abnormality. Now, I did not pick up any delusions." Nevertheless, she gave Handy some Mellaril, an antipsychotic. She also gave him Cogentin, she said, to combat muscle stiffness, a common side effect of Mellaril; and Paxil, an antidepressant.

"All right," Davis said. "Is there anything further you would use to describe his condition?"

"Well," Dr. Wheatley said, "he had what we call 'psychomotor retardation,' which is another symptom of depression. And this is a person who's moving slowly. Not—of course, I didn't have him walk; he was in shackles. But he didn't move, he just sat there. And people who are very depressed don't. And they talk slowly, they talk hesitantly." Of course, I thought, Handy Campbell *always* moved and talked slowly, even when he was elated. That was just his style, his personality. A Greenwood jury would have known that. But we were in Batesville.

"All right," Davis said. "Would you describe him as having a nervous breakdown at that point?"

"Well," Dr. Wheatley said—she liked to say "well"—"when I make the diagnosis of major depression with psychosis, that's my textbook term. But people that I've worked with all my life and living in the state of Mississippi and elsewhere, they can understand when I say 'nervous break- down.' And, of course, there can be a lot of different kinds of nervous breakdowns, but that's basically what we're talking about."

"All right," Davis said—she liked to say "all right"—"would you describe anything he said at that time as being trustworthy?"

"Well, people that are talking at that time can say things that are truth- ful or that are not quite truthful, and they're not meaning to say truthful or not truthful. What they're basically doing is saying things that are a rela- tionship to how they feel, usually, or—well, how they—how bad they feel at the time. You know, a person who is depressed like that will start talk- ing about how terrible he feels because he stole a nickel candy bar when he was five years old. And—"

"All right," Davis interjected, obviously uncomfortable with the answer she received and eager to move on. "Dr. Wheatley, on the twenty-second of June when you saw Mr. Campbell, was he in touch with reality?"

"In some—in some ways he was. But he was—when you have a person who has hallucinations, that is a loss of contact with reality."

"In other words, they've kind of lost the boundary between real and what's not real, correct?"

"That is right."

"And he was at that point because his diagnosis at that—on that day was with psychosis, correct?"

"That's right."

"All right. And when he came back on July fifth, you described him as being improved?"

"Right."

"And basically he was—had—he had improved because of the medica- tions, correct?"

"Well, we'd like to think it was because of the medications. And I said in my notes he's as improved as what we'd expect at this particular time. Now, his depression was not gone. I didn't consider him well from the depression. I just considered he was—"

"But it had improved?" Davis said, cutting the doctor off again. She was having as much trouble controlling her witness as the deputies had had controlling their prisoner.

"His symptoms had improved. He was eating better, sleeping better, some hallucinations were gone."

"In other words, Dr. Wheatley, Mr. Campbell had responded to your treatment?"

"Yes, he had."

"Tender the witness," Davis said, looking quite relieved. She wasn't the only one. At times during Dr. Wheatley's testimony, Lee Jones had looked like he might be having a bit of a nervous breakdown himself. I couldn't blame him; if Dr. Wheatley's goal had been to convince the jury that Handy Campbell was delusional when he confessed, I wasn't sure she'd really succeeded. The jury didn't look all that convinced, or even interested. Mostly, they looked tired.

On the other hand, so did Frank Carlton, who didn't seem to know what to ask Dr. Wheatley on cross-examination.

"Dr. Wheatley," he began, "I don't believe you personally saw Handy Campbell but two occasions. Is that correct?"

"That's correct," the doctor responded.

"And the decisions you made concerning his condition were based on what he told you concerning his condition and what you saw about his appearance on the two occasions you saw him—is that correct?"

"Well, yes. We go by history and information gained from the patient in their behavior."

"We've had other people testify here today, Doctor, that there were four people in the waiting room prior to you or the nurse's arrival—that would be two deputies, Mr. Campbell, and his mother. Does your recollection reflect that?"

"Well, I don't know that I have a recollection of exactly how many people were there, but I will say that the waiting room was full. There were several relatives."

"Okay. The testimony by others was that they stayed there some two or two and a half hours prior to seeing you. Does that correspond to your recollection?"

If Carlton's intention was to put Dr. Wheatley on the defensive, he succeeded. "Well," she huffed, "I don't have any idea about the time frame
involved because I'm back in the back seeing patients rather than—one
after the other, and then I discover that because I have seen several emer-
gencies, my patients that are scheduled for the day have been put off. But
usually, my delay on seeing patients—either I'll see them immediately up
to about three hours, because I am the only psychiatrist there."

"Well, I understand," Carlton said in a soothing tone of voice intended
more to contrast himself from the witness than to comfort her. "I certainly
didn't mean to interpret any neglect. I simply wanted to know if your recollection of the time frame was the same as other people's recollection."

"Well, I wasn't trying to imply that I felt like I neglected," Dr. Wheatley
blurted. "But at the same time, I'm back in the back working, and I don't
usually bother to ask how long they've been waiting, because honestly, I
don't really want to know. It embarrasses me."

"It might depress you to know how long they had to wait?" Carlton
offered with a smile. I wasn't sure if he was trying to get Dr. Wheatley to
admit that "depressed" was a vague term that could mean many different
things, or simply to defuse the tension with a joke. Whatever his intentions were, the effort was wasted.

"That's right," the witness replied, neither smiling nor elaborating.

"All right," Carlton said.

"I really admire people that do have the strength to wait that long," Dr.
Wheatley offered, revealing her bias. Carlton smiled; Lee Jones grimaced.

"The testimony was also to the effect that he ate some food from
Wheels during this two and a half hours," Carlton said. "Did you see any
indication of that?"

"No, that would be something that I would not have information
about."

"Well, it may have been a box sitting there is all I'm saying, or—"

"No."

"Okay."

"That would have been something that I would not have needed to
know."

Jones winced.

"So you didn't ask any questions about had he just eaten almost immediately prior to seeing you?"

"No."

"Okay. You don't have any way of knowing whether he did that or not?"

"That's correct."

Jones looked like he couldn't decide whether to jump up and object or slump down in his chair until he was under the table. I knew what worried him: Dr. Wheatley had testified that her diagnosis was based, in part, on her belief that Handy hadn't eaten in a week; now, Frank Carlton had gotten her to admit that she hadn't been aware that Campbell had eaten that very day, while waiting to see her, and that she hadn't even bothered to ask. I sat up and waited for Carlton to destroy Wheatley's credibility in a manner that would make even the somnolent jury take notice.

But Carlton didn't do anything like that; he just moved on. "Okay," he said, employing his own favorite verbal tic, "now, you gave Ms. Davis a number of descriptions and symptoms, I think, of depression and other things. I believe what you said, you didn't pick up any indication of delusions in Mr. Campbell. Delusions are sometimes a symptom of depression. Is that—have I misquoted you?"

"Well," Wheatley said, "in a way, you have."

"Please correct me," Carlton offered.

"The point I was trying to get across was that when we diagnose major depression, we don't have to have psychotic symptoms. When we do find delusions and hallucinations, then we say 'major depression,' and we just add the tag 'with psychosis.' If we say 'major depression,' we don't actually write down 'without psychosis.'"

Now I was confused: Dr. Wheatley had testified that she'd diagnosed Handy as suffering from major depression with psychosis, even though she also testified that she hadn't "picked up" any delusions in examining him, and didn't really describe any hallucinations, either. But once again, Frank Carlton failed to exploit the situation. He just moved on.

"So you find it unusual that someone who is charged with murder and who has been in jail for several months would be depressed?"

"Well, to be honest, my experience with people who had been in jail—every time I've ever seen somebody, they have been depressed. But at the same time, I'm a psychiatrist."

"Could someone who was clinically depressed commit murder?"

"Well, someone who is clinically depressed could commit murder," Dr. Wheatley said. "Someone who's *not* clinically depressed could commit murder."

"So," Carlton said, "your answer is 'yes'?"

"That's right."

"Do you have any information concerning the death of a man named Freddie Williams?"

"No, sir, I don't."

"Thank you very much," Carlton said, and was about to tender the witness when Cheryl Griffin caught his eye and summoned him over. She whispered into Carlton's ear for a moment, and Carlton returned.

"Doctor," he said, "I thought I got an answer. Cocounsel is not sure. Did you testify that you determined Handy Campbell had hallucinated because he said he had?"

For the first time, I was glad Cheryl Griffin was a part of the state's team. At least she was still awake.

"Right," Wheatley said. "When I asked him about hearing voices—well, first—wait. No, let me back up. One thing we did have—I had when I walked into the room is a history made available to me by the nurse that he had been hearing voices. But I did not observe him. You know, he didn't cock his head or act like—act like he was hearing something when I was talking. So I asked him if he heard voices and was hearing voices and there wasn't anybody there or it didn't come—it—I—what I remember asking him was if—did he hear voices and there wasn't anybody in the jail cell talking and it wasn't their voice, and he said yes. And in this culture in the Mississippi Delta, I can ask that—I feel pretty comfortable about asking that question because I do get an answer. Of course, you know, I did not see him move his body or act as if he were actively listening."

Was that a yes, or a no, or what? I didn't know, and I suspected that Frank Carlton didn't, either. And if we didn't, I strongly doubted that anyone in the jury did. I sensed that somewhere in there, Wheatley had conceded that her diagnosis of psychosis was based largely on Handy Campbell's say-so, but that admission had been mixed in with so much doublespeak and so many qualifications and half-finished sentences that someone would have had to really want to ferret it out in order to do so. And from what I'd seen of the jury, they just didn't want it all that badly.

Neither, apparently, did Frank Carlton. "Thank you very much" was all he said.

⁂

After that Judge Evans sent everyone home for the day. The police officers went home to Baton Rouge; the detectives and deputies went home to

Greenwood. The jurors went home and slept (except for number three, I'm sure; he'd slept quite enough during the day). Frank Carlton and Cheryl Griffin and Lee Jones and Willie Perkins and Gray Evans and Iola Williams and Hattie Campbell all went home and prepared themselves for the last day of trial. Handy Campbell and Lanardo Myrick went back to jail and waited. I went back to my motel room and reviewed my notes.

The state had a strong enough case. They had the defendants, of course, had found them driving around in the victim's truck, along with the victim's checkbook and ATM card and wedding ring and school ring and wristwatch, less than a week after the victim had disappeared. They had the 9 millimeter pistol that had fallen out of the victim's truck when they'd searched it, and the two 9 millimeter bullets they'd found in one of the defendant's pockets when they'd searched him. They had one defendant who'd been seen purchasing a pistol just three days before the victim had disappeared, and had clumsily tried to dispose of the victim's jewelry after getting caught, and had made statements in the presence of police officers that indicated he had personal knowledge of the victim's fate and had already concocted a cover story; and they had another defendant who'd confessed.

A strong case.

It would have been stronger, of course, if they'd had an eyewitness, but few murder cases do; as a class, murderers are surely not the most intelligent of people, but they generally know enough to understand that murder is an act best performed out of sight. And it would have been a stronger case, of course, if the police had found the body while it could still have been of great use to a coroner—that is, while it was still a *body*, rather than just a skeleton and some teeth and a little tissue here and there. Why they hadn't found it sooner—before it had decomposed, while there still might very well have been a bullet in there, a bullet that could have been connected to a gun that could have been connected to one of the defendants—remained, to me, one of the great mysteries of this case. I'd puzzled over it for months now, ever since that afternoon when my old colleague Margaret Dean's husband showed me to the spot where Morris Austin had stumbled upon the remains of Freddie Williams, two months after the latter had disappeared and long after most of the physical evidence, like the bullet that killed him and the very blood he shed as he died, had vanished. It was so close to the road, to the Bypass, to Main Street and Snowden Jones, and the *Greenwood Commonwealth;* how, I'd asked

Margaret that same afternoon, could they possibly have missed it?

"If it had been someone important, instead of Freddie," she'd responded, "they'd have found that body. They'd have found that bullet. They'd have found that blood."

By *important*, I knew, she'd meant: white. And of course, Freddie was not white. He may have been well known and well liked, but he was not, by any means, white.

But did that mean that investigating the matter of his disappearance was assigned a relatively low priority within the Greenwood Police Department? Did it mean that the best detectives hadn't been assigned to the case, or if they had been they weren't pushed terribly hard, didn't work around the clock to solve the mystery, didn't do everything they could to find his dead body and gather every piece of evidence out there as quickly as possible? I didn't want to think so; as well as I knew Greenwood, knew what it was and how things worked there and tried not to blind myself to any of it, I did not want to believe it could be the kind of place where the police would consider the color of a missing man's skin before deciding how much of an effort they would make to find him. All right, so a black man couldn't live wherever he wanted to in Greenwood, couldn't send his children to any school he wanted, couldn't work anywhere he wanted or eat anywhere he wanted or swim anywhere he wanted or get his hair cut anywhere he wanted or worship anywhere he wanted, couldn't go to any doctor he wanted or be buried by any undertaker he wanted in any cemetery he wanted. That was Greenwood; hell, that was most of America, north and south. Separate but equal might not be technically legal anymore, but it was still the law of the land. I knew that. I could see it. I even accepted it, to the extent that it was mine to accept. But I guess I'd gotten tired of deploring it, decrying it, detesting it, too. Or maybe I'd just gotten used to it. It's easy to get used to things that work in your favor. It's easy to focus on the "equal" part of the archaic principle, and overlook the "separate."

But to do that and still maintain the belief that you are a good and fair person, you have to be able to forget that Chief Justice Earl Warren exposed the old principle as a fraud when he wrote, in the *Brown* decision, that separate facilities are inherently unequal. You have to be capable of ignoring the fact that at the heart of the old principle is the notion that all men are *not* created equal, and that, as Justice Henry B. Brown wrote in *Plessy v. Ferguson*, "If one race be inferior to the other socially, the

Constitution of the United States cannot put them upon the same plane." You have to find a way to blind yourself to the truth, which is that our entire social order is still constructed upon the belief that a black life is worth less than a white one.

And maybe I could have done that, could have closed my eyes to all of it, if I hadn't sat in on a trial of two people accused of murdering a man that I knew, a black man, and heard with my own ears about how a largely white police department made only a half-hearted effort to find his body and build a case against his killers, and saw with my own eyes how two white prosecutors made only a half-hearted effort to try that case and convict those killers and secure justice for the family of that dead black man.

But I did sit in on that trial. I did hear about how sloppy and lackadaisical the Greenwood Police Department was in building that case. I did see how unenthused and uninspired Frank Carlton and Cheryl Griffin were in trying it. And as much as I wished to, I could not blind myself to the fact that Margaret had spoken the truth: If Freddie had been white, the police would have found that body, that bullet, that blood; if he'd been white, Griffin and Carlton would have gone after his killers with righteous and relentless zeal. If Freddie Williams had been white, the police and the prosecutors would have cared enough about this case.

But he wasn't. And they didn't. And if they didn't, I was starting to realize, it was too much to expect that the jury would.

On the other hand, both the defendants were black, too—which meant that, all other things being fairly equal, the trial would come down to this: Whom did the jury care about less—the defendants, or the victim? To win, Lee Jones would have to make the jury care less about the late Freddie Williams, and simultaneously give them a reason to acquit his client. I had no idea whether or not Lee Jones could pull it off. But I was sure he had a plan, and pretty sure I knew what it was.

His first witness on day three proved me right.

&

"Your Honor, the defense calls Paul Jones."

Paul Jones, a slightly built black man, approached the witness stand still carrying the book he was reading while waiting to be called—John Grisham's *The Chamber.*

As the witness was sworn in, Lee Jones slowly rose from his chair and strutted up to the stand. Somewhere between the previous afternoon and this morning, Jones had clearly recovered a good part of the confidence he had lost while cross-examining Charlie Cooley.

"Mr. Jones," he began, "do you know an individual—or *did* you know an individual—named Freddie Williams?"

"Yes," the witness replied.

"How was it you came to know Mr. Williams?"

"Through a girl named Jeannette Summerville."

"And for what length or period of time did you know Mr. Williams?"

"It was off and on. Whenever, you know, they came around me, I knew him. I didn't really know him as a friend or nothing like that."

"But for what length of time did you know him?"

"I imagine a year, two years."

"And during this period of time, how frequently would you see Mr. Williams?"

"Not that often. Whenever they would see me in a club or something, they'll come around me, something like that."

"When you say 'they,' who are you referring to?"

"Jeannette—it was numerous of girls that used to be with him. I can't recall all of them's name, but one was named Nickie, Nick. Bert. He kept a group of girls around."

"Were you aware," Lee Jones asked, "or do you have any personal knowledge of Mr. Williams's sexual preferences?"

Here it comes, I thought. I looked over at Frank Carlton, thinking he just might rise in objection this time, on grounds of relevancy. But he didn't, of course. He wouldn't.

"Well," Paul Jones said, "at first I thought he was straight, until he came up on me, he made little gestures toward me. At first, you know, I—you know, I didn't think too much of him, because, you know, he looked like a straight guy. He dressed well and everything."

On Paul Jones's planet, I mused, gay men don't dress as well as straight men.

"But one particular night," the witness continued, "it was on a Thursday, we were playing cards. And I used to wear a lot of jewelry, and he wore a lot of jewelry. I had a ring similar to his, and he used to talk about how nice my ring looked and that I should keep my nails groomed for my hands to look good and everything. And he used to tell me how nice of a man I looked, how fine I was and stuff like that. But, you know, I never did think he was gay or nothing like that.

"So he went on later that night, he—you know, they were giving me booze—you know, every time my cup get emptied, him or either Jeannette would fill my cup up. So I guess they thought I was, you know, high. And he just started rubbing on my hand right where the ring was. And you know, I kind of got uneasy about that. And he—I guess he sensed it."

At that moment, something utterly unexpected occurred in that courtroom. Frank Carlton stood up and said:

"Your Honor, I'm going to object. I've been waiting for a point in all this, and I don't seem to see it. I object to the relevance of this testimony."

Finally.

"Mr. Jones," Judge Evans said, "step up and tell me what you're after here."

Lee Jones thought about it for a moment. "I've gotten what I need on that point," he said, a bit uneasily.

"All right," the judge said.

The lawyer turned back toward his witness. "Mr. Jones," he said, "with respect to his vehicles and personal property, how was Mr. Williams?"

"How was he?" Paul Jones repeated. "I don't understand."

"Was he particular about his vehicles and things?" Lee Jones asked.

"Oh, he kept his vehicle—everything he had was up. He kept it nice. He kept himself nice. Everything he did was, you know, top of the line."

"How was he with, I guess, sharing or letting people use his vehicle?"

"Well, he was very open with his vehicle to certain people, I guess. I don't understand why he—you know, he told me I could get it anytime I want it. He even let me have it. He let me—he used to have a Maxima, top-of-the-line Maxima, and he would let me get the Maxima all the time. I'd just have to bring it back to him at a certain time."

The witness stopped talking. Lee Jones didn't ask him another question, though, just nodded, silently coaching the witness to continue, to give him the full answer that he was, apparently, anticipating.

It took a moment, but Paul Jones eventually figured it out. "He even offered me money," he said, finally. 'You know,' he said, 'You ever need some money, you can come to me for money.'"

Again the witness fell silent; again, the lawyer signaled for him to continue.

"And I said, 'No, that's all right,'" Paul Jones continued. "He said, 'Well, you know, a thousand, three thousand, four thousand, anything you want, don't be ashamed to ask for it.'"

"Do you have any personal knowledge of whether or not Mr. Williams liked for his wife to operate or ride in his vehicle?" Lee Jones asked.

"Well," the witness said, "this is what he told me. He told me—"

"I'm going to object to that, Your Honor, to some conversation that he had with a man who's dead." It was Frank Carlton again; he was almost like a new man.

"Sustained," Judge Evans ruled.

"Did he, uh, permit his wife to drive the vehicle?" Lee Jones asked.

"No," the witness replied.

"Do you know why?"

"Because she had a wreck in one of his vehicles that he had. A numerous of wrecks is what he told me."

I wondered why Frank Carlton wasn't objecting to this conversation with a man who was dead. Perhaps he felt he'd done enough.

"Were people other than yourself able to operate Mr. Williams's vehicle?"

"Yes."

"The testimony has been, at the time of his death, Mr. Williams had a Pathfinder. Were you aware of that?"

"Yes."

"Did you ever operate that vehicle?"

"No."

"Why was it that you did not?"

"Because the way he came up on me, you know, I didn't agree with that. I told—as a matter of fact, I told him my sexual preference was with a female. I didn't—I didn't want to be around him, so I stopped. And when I see him, I used to go the other way."

"So once he got the vehicle, you just wasn't around him?"

"Right."

Lee Jones looked at the judge. "We tender," he said.

"Mr. Jones," Frank Carlton said, rising for his cross, "I have just a couple of questions. I gather from what you said that you subscribe Mr. Williams's conduct toward you as a result of his physical attraction for you—talked about your nails and what a nice-looking man you were and so forth."

"Right."

"Until today, have you been incarcerated in the Leflore County jail?"

Lee Jones leapt up; I saw panic in his eyes. "Your Honor," he shouted, "object to the relevancy!"

Frank Carlton smiled at the judge. "I was going to ask if, in that portion of time, if he knew either of the two defendants."

"All right," Judge Evans said. "You may proceed."

Carlton turned back to the witness. "Do you know either of the two defendants here?" he asked.

"I met—I met—I met Handy and heard about him," Paul Jones said shakily. "But no, I don't know him personally."

"Where did you meet him?"

Paul Jones looked at Lee Jones. Lee Jones looked away.

"In the county jail."

"How long have you spent in the county jail with Handy?"

"I wasn't with him."

"Well, I don't mean *with him,* but in the same jail with him."

"In the same cell? Probably four days."

"Mr. Jones, in the charge against you, who was your attorney?"

"Mr. Perkins."

Willie Perkins! I looked over at Lanardo Myrick's attorney; he had cast his gaze downward and kept it there, as if something terribly fascinating were happening in the vicinity of his shoes. Myrick, his grin gone for a moment, turned and stared at Perkins. No doubt he was trying to convey the impression that he was shocked—shocked!—that his lawyer would have had anything to do with this. I expected a murmur to spread through the crowd, like it always does in the movies at moments like this one; but there was no murmur. There was no crowd. There were just a dozen or so spectators and a dozen or so jurors, only half of whom really seemed to be paying attention.

"The same Mr. Perkins here today?" Frank Carlton asked, trying to prolong the drama a bit.

"Yes," Paul Jones answered.

"Thank you very much," Carlton said.

"Your Honor," Willie Perkins called out, "I would like to ask a few questions in light of the D.A.'s questions."

Judge Evans nodded.

"Mr. Jones," Perkins asked Paul Jones, "who was the judge in that case that I represented you?"

"Gray Evans," the witness replied.

"And have I talked to you at all about being a witness in this case?"

"No."

Of course not, I thought. Paul Jones wasn't Willie Perkins's witness. He was Lee Jones's witness. And I was quite sure Willie Perkins had spoken to Lee Jones about the matter beforehand. But Perkins, of course, wasn't about to volunteer that information.

"Nothing further," was all he said.

Judge Evans dismissed Paul Jones and turned to the lawyer who had called him to testify. "We'll have your next witness," he said.

And then Lee Jones said: "We call Handy Campbell."

⤙✦⤚

He wore a dark suit, the same one Lee Jones had cut the tags off that day two months earlier when his trial was supposed to have begun in Greenwood, the same suit he'd worn on the first day of this trial, and the second; and a bright red tie. He had shaved. His hair was cut clean, almost to the scalp. He stood up straight as he approached the witness stand, raised his hand up straight as he was sworn in, sat up straight as he prepared to testify. His eyes, which had been opaque and dead throughout the trial, were now focused, alert. He spoke clearly and loud, nothing like the mumbling he so often affected. He did everything Lee Jones told him to do to make himself look like a confident defendant, confident of his innocence, confident he would be acquitted. To the jury, I'm sure, he appeared somewhat self-assured. But they didn't see, as he strode up to the stand, his hands, hanging at his sides, slowly clench and unclench, clench and unclench. They didn't see it, and they certainly didn't know what it meant. They didn't know Handy Campbell. But I did. And I knew that he was anxious. He was nervous. Afraid.

"State your name, please," Lee Jones said.

"Handy Tyrone Campbell," the witness replied.

"Mr. Campbell, where do you live?"

"1620 Main Street, Apartment 3-G, Greenwood, Mississippi."

"Where did you attend school?"

"Greenwood High."

"Did you go to college?"

"Well, I signed a scholarship to play football for Ole Miss." The jury, of course, had no inkling of the long and grueling story behind that simple statement.

"Did you complete your college education?"

"No. I had transferred to Southern University in Baton Rouge for a year. So I have three years of college experience."

Lee Jones paced around for a moment, then turned back to his witness. "Mr. Campbell," he said, "you have been present and heard the testimony. There's some matters I'd like you to clear up for the jury. With respect to—do you recall when you were stopped by the police officers on the campus of LSU University? One of the officers testified that you gave a phone number, telephone number." Jones recited the number in question. "Did you, in fact, do that?"

"I did."

"And why did you give the officer that number?"

"Because that was my home number, and I figured I could get in touch with Freddie through my folks. I knew my folks would try and do everything they could to get in touch with him."

"Did you ever tell the police officer that that was Freddie's phone number?"

"No. I told them that they could reach him through that number because I figured my folks would call him and get in touch with him." That, of course, was not the way Lieutenant Robert Jones of the LSU Police Department had remembered it, and Jones, a solid and credible witness, had given the jury his version of the incident from the witness stand just the day before. Handy Campbell's version didn't ring true; even he sounded like he didn't quite believe it. And the jury didn't appear to, either.

But one or two of them, Lee Jones knew, might. And if that one or two might also, later, be looking for reasons to discount some of the evidence against his client, he was going to give them as many as he could.

"Also," Jones said, "with respect to—you heard the two deputies testify with respect to you being at Life Help in a waiting room and making some statements about, if I recall correctly, 'I didn't mean to shoot him,' I think, was the quote. Tell me what you recall of that day."

"I'd been—I'd been incarcerated for eleven months," Handy said. "And through that time, I've been—I've been attacked four times, twice by deputies, twice by gang members at the jail. And I've had a lot of weird thoughts to be wandering through my mind about everything. And—"

"And as a result of these assaults," Jones interjected, apparently concerned about where Handy might be headed with his story, "have you suffered any physical injuries?"

"Right," Handy said. "I have three broken bones in my face. I've been heavily maced by the security guards and the police department. It's just done messed my face all up. And I've just been worried and trying to piece together how could—how could all this be happening. And I don't—I just—I can't explain why."

Handy started to slump over in his seat; his voice grew softer. I wondered if Jones hadn't coached him on this, too, if he hadn't thought maybe Handy should deflate a bit on the stand, for effect. But then I saw him look at Handy and jerk his head back, just a bit, and Handy sat straight up again.

"And the day I was—I was taken from my cell to go to the mental health center, Officer Spencer was really shoving me. I didn't want to go because I didn't know why would I—why would I be—where I'm going, you know. And he was shoving me, and I feared that he was fixin' to attack me. So I called out for Ricky Banks. I called out for him to come. And since he's the sheriff, I figure he's the person I need to talk to."

At this point, a Greenwood jury would have begun to question Handy Campbell's veracity; they would have known that no prisoner at the Leflore County jail would expect Sheriff Ricky Banks to take their side against one of his own deputies. But we weren't in Greenwood.

"And Officer Spencer kept shoving me," he continued. "So I think Cooley came up, and I asked him to go with me, and he did. And when I got to the Life Help Center, I was trying to explain myself to them, but they didn't really want to hear it. They kept cutting me off, talking about football. And I was saying I was sorry for Freddie's death. I never told them that I shot him, because I didn't."

It seemed to me that those last two sentences contradicted each other. But Lee Jones didn't seem worried, and Frank Carlton didn't seem to notice. And Handy just kept on answering, long after all of us, no doubt, had forgotten the original question.

"We was out shooting one day, that I recall," he said, without pausing, "and I had dreams about that, that when we was shooting, maybe I accidentally hit him. But in reality, that couldn't have happened because that was two weeks before he let me use his truck, and I was—I was just disillusioned."

That struck me as an interesting choice of words, not only because it was a malapropism, but because at that moment I was feeling the same way. I, too, was feeling disillusioned—about Handy Campbell, whom I had once considered such a good kid, humble and soft-spoken and even gentle, underclass and underappreciated and possibly underfed and probably undereducated and certainly an underdog in every sense of the word, one of those who will be first in the next world because they have been last in this one, have been fed hope and then had it cruelly snatched away from them time and time again and have borne it all in silence, the very opposite of the kind of creature who would kill his own friend for a truck and some cash and jewelry or maybe just to keep him quiet, and then get up on the witness stand and lie about all of it in front of a judge and twelve jurors. But I'd been wrong; it seemed Handy was just that kind of creature. And that wasn't even the worst of it. The worst of it was that he was also capable, when it served his purpose, of playing the underdog. And it sure served his purpose now.

"I can't explain it because I'm not a psychiatrist," he said. "But I've been really sad about everything. I just can't piece together why all this is happening. He was my friend, true enough, but I feel like I've been the victim here. I haven't had time to really show remorse for my friend's death or anything. And seem like everybody's just been out to get me, and I don't—I can't understand why."

I was only there to observe, to objectively witness the event, but at that moment I wanted to stand up and shout at him: You're the victim here? *You?* Walk over there and tell that to Freddie's mother! Go back to Greenwood and tell it to his children!

But of course, I didn't say a word. In all the time I'd spent in Mississippi, then and now, I could scarcely remember a time when I'd had to work harder just to keep my mouth shut.

Now Lee Jones spoke. "Back to the part about—the deputies illustrated about your trying to pull your hand up and turn it to the side and shoot," he said.

"I was illustrating how I shot on that day that we was out shooting his pistol," the defendant testified. "He had a .22, and we were shooting that one. And he told me that he wanted something bigger and stronger, stronger than a .22, and—"

"So you and Freddie had been out weeks before you got the gun—uh, the vehicle?"

"The vehicle, right. We—that was about—I say about two weeks before that time."

"What did y'all do?"

"The normal, every day—every time we hook up, we always go out and drink, and drink beers and just ride around and talk."

"And on this day, y'all decided to stop and shoot the .22 pistol?"

"Right."

"I believe you told me previously," Jones said, "about while y'all were shooting, Freddie made some comment about—"

"Excuse me?" Handy leaned forward and narrowed his eyes.

"He made a comment about your shooting?"

That didn't seem like a proper question for direct examination, at least not to me. Frank Carlton apparently disagreed, because he just sat there, silent.

"Oh," Handy said. "He said, 'Damn, I felt the fire from that shot,' and that was that."

Clearly, this was a dialogue Jones and his client had worked out beforehand; it was supposed to explain how Campbell could have, even in a deluded state, "recalled" shooting Freddie. They must have practiced it a lot, I thought, because Handy was delivering his answers even before Jones finished asking the questions:

"And is that what you were talking about to the—"

"Right."

"When you were talking to the deputies?"

"I was hallucinating on that day. I don't know why I was—I was just tremendously depressed, and I was down on myself. And I just don't—I don't know why it got to this point."

"Deputy Cooley insinuated, or stated for a fact, that once you got this burden off your chest, the statement you made—"

"I never got anything off my chest because they didn't listen to me. As soon as I tried to illustrate what happened, they kept cutting me off and they kept referring back to my football days. And I didn't want to talk about that because I guess that got me down, too, thinking about what might have been."

"Well," Jones asked, "has your condition improved since that day, June twenty-second?"

"Yes, it has," Handy said. "I've been—I've been taking heavy medication. I think the medicine has helped a lot. But it's affecting my vision a little bit."

"Mr. Campbell," Jones said, "another matter that, if I was on the jury, I'd want to know about. The police officers indicate that when they got you to the station, they emptied your personal belongings out, and there were two 9 millimeter bullets——"

"Right."

"——in your trouser pockets or pants pockets that——along with some other items. I believe you said a bus ticket and some change or something like that."

"Right. I never——"

"Is there any explanation or do you have a remark about that?"

"I do," Campbell said. "I never really been comfortable around loaded guns, so I unloaded the gun. And I guess I kept the two bullets in my pocket."

"How was it that you came to be in possession of and operating his motor vehicle?"

"Freddie let me borrow it."

"Tell us about that. Give us the details of that, where you met up with him, what happened, what transpired and how you ended up with it, where you were going——those type things."

"I was sitting on the park, I think Saturday night, and he rode by and he picked me up, and we went riding, drinking as usual. And I asked him for the truck. At first he said no."

"Was anyone with you?" Jones couldn't afford to let Handy leave out any critical details of his story. I was surprised he didn't try to correct Handy's gaffe about the timing——Freddie had disappeared on a Friday night, not Saturday——but perhaps he didn't want to risk calling the jury's attention to it.

"Mr. Myrick," Handy said, then immediately reverted to his script. "At first he said no. But after riding around a little bit and drinking a lot, he began to say, 'Well, I'll do it for you, but you've got to do something for me.'"

This was it. This was Handy's defense. More accurately, this was Lee Jones's defense. The same one he used with Donnie Gene Silcox. I wish I could say I hadn't seen it coming.

"And I asked him what he was talking about. He said, 'Well,' you know, 'You know I been liking you a long time.' And I laid back, and we just kept drinking and riding for a while. And later on, he brought up the conversation again. He asked me did I want to borrow the vehicle. I said yes. He said, 'Well, y'all guys going to have to do something for me.'"

I remembered the first time I had asked him about it, how he had looked squarely at me and denied it without hesitating; and the second time I'd asked him about it, when he chuckled, nervous, embarrassed, stared down at his hands and softly told me the story he now declaimed loud and clear in front of a dozen people he didn't know, and a dozen more he knew too well. Which of those three Handy Campbells was the real one? None of them, I imagined; I was starting to suspect that there was no real Handy Campbell anymore, that these days he was whoever he needed to be at any particular moment. Had he always been that way, I wondered, and I had just terribly misjudged him all along? Or was Handy the chameleon a more recent development, the product of his frustration and degradation in the world of college football? I hoped it was the latter, although I found both options very depressing.

"And I asked him what. And he was—he was talking about some sexual—some sexual things."

"And after you figured out what he was talking about," Lee Jones said, "what transpired, what occurred?"

"I told him I would do it," Campbell said. "He wanted to suck our—suck our penis."

So, I thought, he's sticking with *this* version of the story.

"What happened?"

"I let him do it to borrow the truck." His face betrayed no emotion, just earnestness.

"Where did this occur?"

"We pulled over in Carrollton somewhere off the road. I don't—I can't explain the exact location."

"And after this occurred, what did the three of y'all do?"

"Rode around for a little while. And we came back to Greenwood, and he made a telephone call. He said he had things to do anyway and that he was going to Jackson. He made a phone call to some guy, and the guy came to pick him up, and he left. I don't—I don't know where they went."

"Where did you leave Freddie Williams?"

"We parked—well, you know where KFC at in Greenwood, next to Scottane? The Kentucky Fried Chicken. We parked there, and the car pulled in behind us. And he got in, and they left."

That part of his story had always been the same: that the vehicle exchange, as it were, had occurred in the parking lot of the KFC on Main Street. The problem was, no one alive—except the defendants—could corroborate the story. No one else had seen it happen, had seen either the defendants or Freddie Williams anywhere near that KFC on the night in question. And that struck me as very strange, and incredible. To make sure, I had run the whole thing past Margaret, who, like me, had been known to frequent that establishment, from time to time, late at night. "Are you joking?" she'd said. "That place is so crowded on Friday night, a mosquito couldn't get in and out of there without being seen."

"What was your understanding," Jones asked his client, "with regard to how long you could use the vehicle?"

"It was understood to be for a week," the defendant answered. "But we was going to come back Thursday. And I believe it was Tuesday night we got stopped and they locked us up."

"What was the purpose of you needing the vehicle?"

"We was going to see Lanardo's kid and my kid."

"Where are they located?"

"Gulfport and Crowley, Louisiana."

"And did y'all do that?"

"Right."

"When you were interviewed by a detective from Greenwood, did they—usually before a police officer will talk to you, they'll advise you of your rights and ask you to sign a form. Did you do that?"

"I did."

"And did you have a conversation with the officers?"

"I did."

"How close did that conversation with the detective occur to when you were initially stopped by the police officers?"

"I think maybe ten, twelve hours, maybe."

"And your testimony about how you obtained the vehicle and what you did to get the vehicle and when you were returning, those type things, and your last contact with Freddie, was that what you told the police on that day?"

"Yes."

"How long did this first conversation, or the recorded conversation, last with the police officer?"

"I'd say about an hour and a half."

Jones paused, paced around for a second or two to try to create some drama. "On TV," he said, "we'll see detectives, and they'll play—one of them will be the heavy, and the other one will be the light one, you know, telling—one of them's your—trying to befriend you, and the other one is going to be the hard one. Did they use any police tactics like that on you?"

Frank Carlton stood up. Again! "If Mr. Jones wants to testify," he said, "he ought to take the stand. I object to this dialogue." The judge agreed.

Lee Jones took a breath, then another. "Did the officers use any—did you recognize any tactics the officers used in interrogating you?" he asked the witness.

"They were trying to scare me," Campbell replied. "They was threatening me and telling me I could get life, the needle, electric chair, and—I don't know."

"Did that scare you?"

"It didn't scare me at that moment because I was innocent. I believed Freddie was going to come and clear this matter up. But after being in the jail so long, I thought about that and thought about everything that was going on, and I—eventually I became afraid."

I looked over at the jury. They didn't appear to be particularly sympathetic, or disgusted, or outraged, or engaged. They did appear to be unhappy about being forced to sit through all of this; it was quite clear, by this time, that most of them resented having to be there. Lee Jones must have noticed, too, because he dropped that line of questioning and moved to wrap things up quickly.

"Mr. Campbell," Jones said, "there's been introduced as Exhibit 4 some items, which are a driver's license, a checkbook, and a bankcard. The testimony is that these came out of the vehicle, out of the glovebox. Do you recall them being there?"

"No," the witness said. "He took a bag with him. I thought he had took all of his personal things. I never checked the glove box."

"Did you use this card to try to get any money?"

"No."

"Did you use this license for identification or anything?"

"No."

"What did you steal of Freddie Williams's?"

"Nothing."

"Did you rob Freddie Williams?"

"No, I did not."

"Did you shoot him?"

"No."

"Did you kill him?"

"No."

Cheryl Griffin had warned the jury, in her opening statement, that the trial they were about to experience would be nothing like those they'd seen on television shows; if they'd doubted her before, they couldn't now. There was no passion in Handy Campbell's responses to these most important questions—no passion, and no conviction, and no feeling. It didn't sound much like he was telling the truth, but it didn't sound much like he was lying, either. It sounded like he was reading a script—just reading it aloud, running through it merely to make sure there were no typographical errors in it. No doubt Lee Jones had expected, or at least hoped, that his client would answer his questions fervently, that he would stare into the jurors' eyes and say "No!" in such a way that they would have to believe him, not just believe him but believe that to accuse him of such a crime and then put him on trial for it was the grossest miscarriage of justice in the history of American jurisprudence. No doubt Lee Jones had hoped to end his direct examination on such a note. But Handy Campbell hadn't looked at the jury at all. He had barely looked at his own lawyer. He didn't say "No!" He just said "No," as if the question were "Do you want to go get some ice cream?" And what else, then, could Lee Jones do?

"Tender," he said, leaving the jury stranded far from the place he'd really wanted them to dwell.

Luckily for him, Frank Carlton started his cross by offering them a ride back.

❧❦

"Mr. Campbell," Carlton drawled as he opened his cross-examination, "if I understand what you're telling us, in return for sexual favors, Mr. Williams loaned you his vehicle—is that correct?"

Campbell forced a nod. "That is correct," he said mechanically.

"And I believe you told us that you and Mr. Williams had been friends for some time."

"About three years."

"And during that three years he never loaned you his vehicle?"

Handy looked puzzled, unsure of which answer would serve him best. Finally, he decided upon: "He has on numbers of occasions."

"Oh?" Carlton said, raising his eyebrows. "He *had* loaned it to you?"

Handy squirmed in his seat. Too late to change his story. "Right," he mumbled.

"Did you have sexual relations with him on those occasions?"

"Uh, no."

"So this occasion was different in that he wouldn't let you use the vehicle on this occasion unless you consented to sexual favors with him, is that correct?"

"That's what he wanted to do."

"Well, is that correct?"

"That's correct."

"Okay," Carlton said. "What about Mr. Myrick? Did he have sex with him also?"

Campbell looked over, briefly, at Myrick; Myrick looked away, then turned his eyes down and studied the red leather cover of his enormous Bible. "Yes," the witness said.

"So in return for these two sexual favors, he let the two of you use the vehicle?"

"Right."

Handy tried to look confident, but he only succeeded in looking nervous, and a bit nauseated. Carlton looked poised to tear apart the witness' story; but then, without explanation, he just dropped the subject entirely, and started asking Handy questions about the gun he was seen purchasing at the playground, three days before Freddie Williams disappeared. He got several of the facts wrong—who had bought the gun and handed it off to whom, and other important details—but, luckily for him, the witness didn't seem to notice. When Handy stuck to his story, that he had bought the gun for Freddie, the prosecutor declined to challenge it. Instead, he just changed the subject again. I marveled at his apparent fickleness. Only this time, the problem wasn't that he lacked a strategy for prosecuting this case; rather, he seemed to lack the desire to make much of an effort to prosecute it. Or even to remember it very well.

"Did you get to Crowley to see your child in Louisiana?" Carlton asked. The witness looked confused, and Carlton repeated: "Crowley, Louisiana?"

"Yes," Handy said, "I did."

"And did you get to Gulfport to see Mr. Myrick's child in Gulfport?" Carlton's delivery was considerably less smooth than that of those other prosecutors I had seen recently, the ones in that courtroom in Los Angeles. But they *were* on television.

"Yes."

"So y'all made the trip from Greenwood down to Gulfport, I guess, and over to Louisiana, is that right?"

"Right."

"How long did you stay in Crowley?"

"Three, maybe four hours."

Wait a minute, I expected Carlton to say. *You're telling me that you let Freddie Williams sodomize you just so he would lend you his truck for a week because you wanted to go see your kids, and then you only go visit with them for three or four hours? Do you really expect these twelve men and women to believe that, Mr. Campbell?*

But Carlton didn't say that. He didn't say anything like that. He just paced around dramatically, an exaggerated look of astonishment on his face, and asked: "And left?"

"Excuse me?" Campbell said.

"You left there?"

"Right. We went to Baton Rouge, Louisiana. I had a couple of guys there who owed me some money. I was trying to get in touch with them."

Carlton furrowed his brow and nodded in a way that was meant to indicate—to everyone but the defendant, I suppose—that he didn't believe a word the witness was saying. "Is that what you were doing riding around the campus at four o'clock in the morning?" he asked.

"No," Handy said. "I was drinking then." He did not crack a smile.

"So you were riding around campus drinking at four o'clock in the morning?"

"Not around campus. We spotted a couple of girls we wanted to meet, and we followed them onto the LSU campus, and we got stopped there."

There were so many flaws in Campbell's story that I didn't know where to begin picking it apart. Apparently Frank Carlton didn't, either, because he didn't even try. Perhaps he believed himself such an effective district attorney that he didn't even need to grill a defendant like Handy Campbell, that a mere scowl on his prosecutorial lips was sufficient. In any event, he just changed the subject again.

"Okay," he said. "Well, you heard the police officers from LSU testify. Is what they said correct, that they did stop you after driving around for some time and converging on you, as they said? That happened, did it not?"

"It did happen," the witness replied.

"And you heard the police officer say that you told him to call that number, and Freddie would clear it up?"

"I told him he could get in touch with Freddie through that number."

"I understand. But you heard him say that you said call the number, and Freddie—that this is Freddie's number. That's what he said, is it not?"

No, I thought, that is not what he said.

"He may have said that," Handy said.

Lee Jones jumped to his feet. "That's not what the officer said!" he declared.

"Well," Frank Carlton said to the witness, "what did you understand him to say?"

"To be honest," Campbell replied, "I wasn't really listening to him. I know what I told him. I don't know what he said I said."

"Okay. So yesterday you were not paying any attention, is that it?"

"I paid attention. I just don't know what—I can't recall what I said."

"Okay. But you don't deny here today that the number you gave the police officer was your mother's number in Greenwood?"

"Right."

"You didn't expect to find Freddie at that number, did you?"

"I didn't dial the number."

"I'm sorry?"

"I didn't dial the number."

"That's not my question. You didn't expect the police officer to find Freddie at that number, did you?"

"I expected them to get in touch with him through that number," Handy said.

"I see," Carlton said. "Do you know what Freddie's number is?"

"I'm not sure, but I think it's—" He looked at the ceiling for a moment. "No, I don't. I can't—"

"But you didn't give them Freddie's phone number," Carlton said, "or you didn't give them Freddie's name or even the fact that they lived in Itta Bena. You didn't tell him that, did you?"

I should hope not, I thought. Freddie didn't live in Itta Bena.

"He don't live in Itta Bena," Campbell said.

Carlton didn't even bother to look embarrassed. "Well, did you tell them where he lived?"

"No, I did not. They didn't ask me."

"Did you tell him what his name and number was?"

"I gave them a number to get in touch with him."

"And that number was your mother's phone number?"

"Right."

"And that is your explanation for why you gave them that number, is that correct?"

"That's correct."

Once again, Handy Campbell had offered a story that left him vulnerable to exposure. And once again, Frank Carlton declined to pick that story apart. Once again, he merely changed the subject.

"Do—did—do you tell us now," he said, "that Freddie Williams understood that you and your friend, Mr. Myrick, were going to use that vehicle for a week; is that correct?"

"That's correct."

"And he knew that?"

"Right."

"And you parked the vehicle, I think you said, at KFC, and he got out and left—is that correct?"

"He got in the vehicle with another guy."

Yesterday, there were three men in the other vehicle. Today it was down to one. Never mind; Frank Carlton didn't seem to notice.

"I believe you told me just a minute ago that he even took a little bag with him."

"Right."

"Is that right?"

"That's correct."

"But he managed to leave his watch and his class ring that he always wore and his wedding ring and his bankbook and his ATM card and his driver's license. He left those things with you. That's a fact, isn't it?"

"Yes, sir, it is."

"And you knew you were going to be gone for a week when he packed his little bag and got out?"

"Right."

And, despite what I'd seen so far, I expected, or at least hoped, that Frank Carlton would call Handy Campbell on this, the most ludicrous part of the defendants' story. I hoped he would say he just didn't believe Handy, didn't imagine the jury could believe him. I hoped he would say that Handy's entire story was unbelievable, that anyone with the sense God gave a chicken could see right through it, could see it for what it was, which was a pack of lies, and a flimsy one at that, a fable so shoddy that to offer it as a counter to the charge of murdering your own friend just so you could take his truck was an insult to everyone in that courtroom, to everyone in the state of Mississippi. I hoped he would then set in and undertake to unravel that flimsy pack of lies, lie by lie, until the defendant, naked and exposed, would break down on the stand, just like he had in that mental health clinic's waiting room, and confess everything all over again.

But Frank Carlton didn't say or do any of that. And what he did say and do next made me question whether Frank Carlton had stopped paying attention to what Handy Campbell was saying. Then again, to say that he'd *stopped* doing it implies that he had, at some point, been doing it, and I was starting to suspect that even *that* wasn't true. In fact, I wondered, right then, if Frank Carlton had been paying much attention to *anything* that had been going on in this courtroom over the past three days.

And if he hadn't been, why not? Was he no longer up to the job? Or was he so confident of his own skill, and of the strength of his case, that he figured his mere presence in court was enough to secure convictions? Or was it, I wondered, that he simply didn't give a damn about this case at all, didn't give a damn about these two niggers on trial here or the queer nigger they killed for his truck after letting him suck their dicks, and damn it, just didn't give a damn about any of it, gave so little a damn about it, in fact, that even though this was the only part of the goddamned job he liked, he wasn't even going to bother to do it today, just like he hadn't yesterday, and the day before that, and what difference did it make, really, whether or not these two niggers here killed that queer nigger there, and whether or not he proved it in court, and whether or not they went to prison or back to the projects and got their asses smoked there?

I shuddered; my own thoughts shocked me. They shock me now, too, as I write them here. I didn't want any of it to be true, not of Frank Carlton or Greenwood or the Delta or Mississippi or the South or America. I would have given anything to come up with a likelier explanation for what I was seeing in that courtroom. But I couldn't.

What Frank Carlton said next was this:

"Thank you very much. That's all."

Frank Carlton had put in all he had.

❧❧

The next and last witness, Lanardo Myrick, pretty much mimicked his codefendant's testimony. Naturally, he embellished it in parts, saying, for instance, that his first thought after Freddie had offered to lend them his truck in exchange for oral sex was, "Well, anything for Freddie, you know. I mean he—as much as he's done for us, you know, being a friend talking to us, you know, giving us good advice. I didn't really think anything was wrong with it that much, as some people may think." Or when he hinted that Freddie's plans for the rest of the weekend, after he loaned them his truck, were not quite wholesome: "You know, he had been talking all week about going to Jackson, which—and it was a lot of unrelated, you know, comments about Jackson, money, stuff like that, that he wanted to make— you know, he had a way of making money, that, you know—me, I thought personally, he was talking about male prostitution." Or when he tried to present certain officers in the LSU police department in the same light that a certain group of lawyers were, at that very moment, presenting certain detectives in the Los Angeles Police Department: "Henderson, big kind of guy, that was the one that put me in the back of the car. He was pretty rough with me. . . . He said, 'Well, that's what's wrong with you people. You niggers don't never want to fess up to what's going on. Y'all always act like you don't know nothing.'" And of course, Myrick denied making any of the incriminating statements the police said he had, and claimed he had no idea how Freddie's jewelry had gotten into the backseat of Unit 112.

Frank Carlton didn't challenge the defendant too hard on that strange bit of obliviousness—or, for that matter, anything else. He wasn't any more aggressive in his cross-examination of Myrick than he had been with Campbell—no more aggressive, no more organized, no more attentive, no more concerned. He'd put in all he had on the first two days; now, it appeared, he was just passing time until he could go home.

We all were, I suppose. Cheryl Griffin gave an uninspired and uninspiring closing argument in which she summoned up, without any passion or even emphasis, all of the state's witnesses and evidence. "I told you at the beginning of this trial," she said in conclusion, "that we would prove this case to you beyond a reasonable doubt that these men murdered Freddie Williams, and that's exactly what we've done. Ladies and gentlemen, I stand up here with a clear conscience, and I ask you to find Handy Campbell and Lanardo Myrick guilty; guilty of murdering Freddie Williams, guilty of armed robbery."

Lee Jones began his closing by reminding the jury that the burden of proof rested with the prosecution. "I submit to you that I don't know what happened to Freddie Williams," he said. "These men don't know. It's not our job. We don't have to do that to walk away from this not guilty. But what has been shown, has come out, was that Freddie Williams chose a lifestyle that he chose, and he paid with his life for."

I looked at the jury: Were they actually buying this theory? I couldn't tell; as always, they were inscrutable, although at least now they also looked somewhat alert.

"I will submit to you that Mr. Campbell has errored in his judgment in some things that he has done," he continued. "But he's not on trial for those things, whether he traded sex for a vehicle or something like that. I can't condone it, but that's not what he's being charged with. That's not why he's before you today." Jones ran through his own list of counterpoints to the state's evidence, in no particular order and without any emphasis of his own, and then alighted back on the notion of the state having the burden of proof, lamenting the fact that, in exchange for that burden, the district attorney would get the last word that day. "And when Mr. Carlton gets up here," Jones intoned, "and waxes fine over what I've said and talks bad about Mr. Campbell and about how they have done such a great job and proved their case, I ask that when you retire to deliberate, say: I wonder what Lawyer Jones would have said had he had an opportunity to get back up. Because I won't have one. This, ladies and gentlemen, is the last voice you will hear speak for Handy Campbell. From here on, it's going to be downhill."

"My client and I can't look into your hearts and into your minds," Willie Perkins said. "We believe and we know that you will live up to your oath, for the State has not proven Lanardo guilty. So when you go to your separate homes and you turn out your lights, your conscience will be clear, for you would have lived up to your oath as jurors, for you would have found Lanardo Myrick not guilty of murder, not guilty of armed robbery. And I submit to you, very sincerely, that your verdict ought to be not guilty."

"As a young boy," Frank Carlton said, alive again and folksier than ever, "I grew up on a farm over in Calhoun County, lived there till the fourth grade and moved to the Delta. While I was a tyke over there, we didn't have a lot of toys, and certainly no TV. In fact, I remember when electricity come down the rock road to our house, I was proud to have a light.

"I used to play out in the fields with my cousins and brothers. And one of the things that I did in the springtime was walk the turn rows and look at the land and marvel at nature. One of the things that used to happen to me with some regularity in the springtime was I'd stumble up on a crippled killdeer. And that bird would have a broken wing, and I would chase her. And she'd stay three or four steps ahead of me for a good ways. And all of a sudden, that wing would heal and she'd fly off.

"As a tyke, I didn't understand this. I couldn't really fathom what was happening until I got a little older and a little wiser and a little more experienced. And what I found out was, whenever I stumbled close to that bird's nest, she started being crippled and tricking me away from the important things. And as soon as I got far enough away from what was important, pop! She's gone.

"They've run some killdeers on you, ladies and gentlemen. Think about it. Did you see in the law that Judge Evans read to you any evidence that said it's all right if the guy's homosexual to kill him? That ain't the law. So what difference does it make what his lifestyle was?"

It's about time *someone* here said that, I thought.

"It has nothing to do with this case," Carlton continued, "because you can't kill Freddie Williams, legally, no matter what his lifestyle is because there are a lot of people who have different lifestyles. That's not the law. Don't follow that killdeer. Don't fall for that."

"Man, I tell you what," Lee Jones would say to me later, "I've heard that damn killdeer closing so many times I could deliver it m'se'f, word for word."

At the time, though, I was impressed—not with Frank Carlton's gift for metaphor, but for the simple fact that he seemed to understand what the defense was up to, at last. And then he impressed me further by going back over the testimony and making all the points I had expected him to make during his cross-examinations. But he had to rush through that part— Judge Evans had imposed a strict time limit on all closing arguments—and his organizational skills were still wanting, and I doubted the jury was getting much of it—especially juror number three, who was, once again, asleep in his chair.

"The fragments and the bullets made it possible," Carlton said, winding down. "Get a little further on down the line, and the ring and the chains missing, they make it probable. And you get a little further down the line, and the other items, the checkbook and the driver's license and the ATM card, make it beyond a reasonable doubt. And let me just tell you that when you get all the way down to the watch and the two rings, including the wedding ring, you have passed all doubt. You're as far as you can go, because this case has all the elements, everything you need to find them guilty.

"These two young men killed Freddie Williams with that pistol and took his goods. They took his truck. They took his gold chain. They took his other items, including his wedding ring, his Amanda Elzy ring and his watch. And that's armed robbery. They should be found guilty for a very simple reason: They did it."

⁂

These are the facts:

The trial of *The State of Mississippi vs. Handy Campbell and Lanardo Myrick* began promptly at 9:00 A.M. on July 31, 1995.

On August 2, at 2:20 P.M., Judge Gray Evans discharged the jury to deliberate, instructing them that they would have to return four separate verdicts, one for each charge of murder, and one for each charge of armed robbery.

At 3:50 P.M., the jury sent Judge Evans a note: "What happens when there's two to ten?" The judge sent back instructions that the jury must do their best to reach a unanimous verdict.

At 4:10, I asked Lee Jones why he had put up the victim's sexuality as the keystone of his defense. "Hell," he said with a nervous laugh, "we had to put up *something*."

"Do you think he did it?" I asked.

Jones smiled conspiratorially. "I think Campbell's innocent," he said. "I think the other guy pulled the trigger."

At 4:35, I encountered Judge Evans in the corridor outside the courtroom, and asked him if he thought the defendants were innocent or guilty. "I think they're guilty," he said curtly. "And I think the Greenwood Police Department fucked up."

At 5:00, Frank Carlton left the courthouse and went to Memphis to visit his grandchildren.

At 6:00, the jury returned their verdict—just in time for dinner.

⁂

When word came down that the jury had reached a verdict, Judge Evans was working on a cheekful of chewing tobacco. He didn't bother to remove it as he addressed the gallery.

"I want everybody to understand," he said, speaking in turn to each side of the aisle, favoring neither, "if you don't think you can control your emotions, regardless of what the verdict is, I want you to leave now. Because I want *no* display of any kind made in praise or condemnation of this jury's verdicts, regardless of what they are. So if there's *any* comments made, or any squealing going on, I'm going to lock somebody up."

And it was strange, very strange, but at that moment, so close to the revelation of the verdict I'd fretted over since the previous Thanksgiving, I wasn't trying to figure out which side of the aisle the judge was worried might react which way. I was thinking about a couple of conversations I'd had on my first day in Greenwood—September 9, 1988—with men who were now dead: Carl Kelly, Jr., and John Emmerich.

When my former boss had died, the *Commonwealth* had devoted almost an entire edition to his memory, lionizing him as one of the most remarkable men ever to settle in Leflore County. When Carl Kelly, Jr., had died, his passing had barely rated a standard obituary. He wasn't famous, or even well known; he wasn't a man about town. I met him only once, for maybe twenty minutes, during which time he'd tried to suss out my politics and my religion and my opinion of my new boss and then ranted at length about the dangers of yella niggers and the necessity of keeping the white race pure for the yet unsired namesakes he had already included on his elaborate letterhead. It was such a bizarre encounter that in the seven years since it had happened I had told almost no one about it.

But I thought about it often. I thought about it because I'd never had an experience like it before, nor another like it since. Not that Carl Kelly was the only unregenerate racist I'd ever met; I'd met quite a few of them—in Greenwood and Tuscaloosa and Memphis, and Los Angeles and Chicago and New York. But Carl Kelly was the first, and I suspect he knew it. He was eighty-seven years old and frail and couldn't see or hear very well, but somehow he had divined that no one before him had ever shared with me that which he so fervently believed to be The Truth. So he did, and then left me to figure out what to do about it.

Of course, I had no idea. But I didn't have a lot of time to think about it, either; he was there, and I was there, and while I was trying hard to get the hell away from him as quickly as possible, I wasn't planning to leave Greenwood anytime in the near future, and who knew how soon, and how frequently, I might encounter this kind of thing again? And so I, right there on Carl Kelly's front lawn, devised my great compromise, my confederacy of silence, in which I would erect a solid wall between what I thought about people like Carl Kelly and how I acted toward them. I thought it would enable me to have it both ways, to be at once agreeable and outraged, to avoid both standing out and caving in, to hang on to both my job and my self-respect. I thought, simply, that it would enable me to stay and live and work in Mississippi.

And it did. It worked.

For a while.

And then it didn't. And I had to leave.

Of course, I didn't know that morning how it would succeed and then fail; I didn't know yet if I could even do it, and that worried me. It worried me so much that I suppose it must have showed. Which, I now understand, is what led to that second conversation.

This was hours later, after I had looked at several other apartments and had a few more uncomfortable landlord encounters and then went to the *Commonwealth*'s offices for the first time and met my coworkers and sat through an uncomfortable staff meeting and met Freddie Williams and then went on an uncomfortable drive through Greenwood with Mike McNeill. This was after all that, after I'd returned back to the Emmerichs' house and had cocktails and dinner and sat around visiting with my hosts until Celia excused herself and went somewhere to do something, leaving me alone with my new boss and a sudden silence that was, well, uncomfortable.

But then he broke it. "Richard," he said, "I know you did some writing for your high school paper and your college paper, but I think you're going to find out that you really don't know anything about journalism."

Suddenly, the silence didn't seem so uncomfortable anymore. "What I mean to say," he continued, sounding not at all apologetic, "is that our little paper here is not anything like your high school paper, not even your college paper."

"I'm sure it's not," I said.

"Let me finish," he said—in the months to come, he would say that to me more times than either of us would care to count—"I'm not done. I'm trying to tell you that even though you may have gotten all kinds of experience at those papers, they didn't teach you a whole lot that you can use here. I know you think they did. But I can tell you, I've had a lot of kids right out of college come down and work for me, some of them with a lot more experience than you, even, and not one of them knew the first thing about putting out a real daily newspaper."

He stopped talking, signaled that now was the time for me to speak.

I had nothing to say.

"Right," he offered, after more silence. "Like I told you on the phone, I don't care about that. I assume when I hire someone like you that they have no experience whatsoever, no matter what they *tell* me." He looked squarely at me; I tried not to appear guilty, although I was starting to figure out that both of us knew he wasn't just talking about someone *like* me. "And that's all right. Like I said to you then, I consider it a trade-off: You get real work experience, I get an Ivy League graduate for two hundred and forty dollars a week," he said with a smile but not a laugh. "I know you're a bright kid. We'll teach you everything you need to know on the job, and you'll learn it and you'll do fine. You'll figure it all out as you go along, I'm not worried about that. But there's something you need to understand going in."

"What's that?"

"I'm glad you asked. Now, our little paper here, it's the only one in town. It's the only daily in the area. It's the only one for fifty miles. And it's a *real* newspaper. People here read it to find out what's going on. That's what it's for, as far as you're concerned. And there's no room in there for your opinion. There's only one person at the *Commonwealth* who gets to put his opinion in the paper, and that's me, on the editorial page. You don't get to. Mike doesn't get to. Nobody gets to but me. That's not your job. Your job is to tell people what happened, and that's it. I don't expect you to not have opinions about things. You can *have* all the opinions you want. Hell, I probably agree with most of them. But you don't share them with the readers. You keep 'em to yourself. I don't want to see the word 'I' in anything with your byline on it. Once in a while, somebody might ask you to write a column, and then you can tell everybody what you think about the subject at hand. But other than that, I don't want to know when I read my newspaper what Richard Rubin is thinking, and I don't want to be able to figure it out. Call it 'objectivity' or 'journalistic integrity' or whatever you want, but that's the way things are at my paper, and that's the way they have to be, and that's the way they will be. Do you understand me?"

"Yes," I said. "I do."

"Good," he spat, then cast aside his stern persona and reassumed the warm and paternal one he'd greeted me with the previous night at the bus station and that morning at the breakfast table. "That's fine," he said with a smile. "I'm sure that'll be the only thing I try to teach you about how to do your job."

And it was, too, which was a good thing, because I never really mastered it. Hard as I tried, I was never able to completely assimilate what he tried to teach me that evening, even though it was the very same thing I'd tried to teach myself that morning. Which was this: There's a time and place to say what you really think, and do what your gut tells you to, no matter what your boss or your neighbors or the authorities or society as a whole might expect. But this wasn't it.

That was what Judge Evans was telling the people seated in his courtroom at that most anxious moment. But looking back on it, I wonder if his warning to the gallery wasn't really a plea to the jury, asking them one last time to base their verdicts on facts and not feelings, on the law and not their own sense of right and wrong, on the evidence and not their prejudices.

If it was, they didn't listen.

TWENTY-FOUR

THE DEATH OF MY
GREENWOOD

*H*andy Campbell looked down at his lap and jiggled his shackled leg.
Lanardo Myrick put his shackled hands on his big red Bible and closed his
eyes. Lee Jones scowled. Willie Perkins pursed his lips. Cheryl Griffin sat
up straight. Everyone in the gallery stayed very still. The bailiff instructed
the defendants to stand. Judge Evans took the verdicts from the jury foreman and read them aloud.

Handy Campbell's knees buckled.

Lanardo Myrick turned his face toward the ceiling and whispered: "Yes!"

Willie Perkins nodded.

Lee Jones laughed out loud and slapped his client on the back, then
turned around, grinned at me, and winked.

Cheryl Griffin quietly looked down and zipped up her briefcase, then
turned around, grinned at me, and shrugged.

Frank Carlton was not even there.

Iola Williams cried out, then crammed her fist into her mouth and bit it
hard.

Hattie Campbell let out a deep breath and slid down in her seat.

I felt sick.

Judge Evans banged his gavel once, twice, and ordered the courtroom sealed while the bailiffs escorted the jurors out to their cars.

The jurors drove home.

The bailiffs opened the courtroom doors.

The spectators filed out, murmuring relief or dismay.

Judge Evans called me over and said: "I don't know what you planned to do here, but you're not to contact any of those jurors, not now, not ever, y'understand?"

I said: "Yes."

The Leflore County deputies who had transported the two prisoners from Greenwood to Batesville every day now helped them out of their chairs and led them out through a side door and into the parking lot, where they unshackled them for the last time and released them to their families. Handy rubbed his wrists. Lanardo let out something approximating a rebel yell.

I held my breath for a moment, afraid I was going to throw up. When I was pretty sure I wouldn't, I approached Handy Campbell. "Congratulations," I said.

He smiled. "Thanks."

"I'd like to meet with you again, sometime soon," I said. "One last interview."

"All right," he said. "Come by my house tomorrow for lunch."

"Let's go," Hattie Campbell said and grabbed her son's arm. As she hustled him toward her car, Lanardo Myrick broke away from his own mother and walked over to me, his grin so large and manic it was almost blinding. Before I knew it, he had snatched my hand from my side and was pumping it frenetically. "I *told* you!" he said. "Didn't I tell you? I told you it would work out. Didn't I tell you? I told you!"

"Yes," I said, retrieving, with some effort, my own hand. "You did. But were you just being hopeful, or did you really believe it?"

For a second, no more, his smile dropped and he looked offended; but then it returned, even broader than before, and he raised his other hand, in which he still grasped his Bible, and held it up next to his head. "You *know* I did," he said. "You know I *did!*"

Somehow, though, I didn't believe him.

༄༅

"Man," Jack said, "you are one crazy Yankee sumbitch!"

I put my fork back down on my plate. "Excuse me?"

Jack raised his own fork and pointed it at my face. We were having supper at his house; his wife and son were out of town for the day, and he'd cooked up something himself, something special. "Pork and beans," he'd explained with a smile while setting the casserole dish down on his kitchen table, "in honor of my *Jewish* friend."

"Lemme get this straight," he said. "Your boy committed murder and then got away with it. You know it. He knows you know it. And you're gon' go over to his house—in Snowden Jones—*alone?*"

"He's not *my boy*," I said. "And why not?"

"Why not? I'll tell you why not: 'Cause he's liable to shoot your Yankee ass next!"

I laughed, not sure as I was doing so whether I was really amused or just nervous. "Right," I said. "He's going to kill me, a day after he's set free? There were two deputies there who heard him invite me to his house. He'd never get away with it."

"Maybe he will and maybe he won't, but you'll still be dead and gone to hell," Jack said with a laugh. Then something came over him; his smile faded until it was gone, and his voice grew soft. "Besides," he said, "he done got away with it once, now."

I raised my hand to my face and rubbed it hard, as if he had just slapped me. "That he did," I said. "That he did."

"I tell you what," Jack said, and shook his head. "If that had been a white man they killed, them sumbitches'd be hangin' from the courthouse roof right now."

I drew back in my chair, stunned and embarrassed, glad that his son wasn't there to hear him. But then I realized that he was just saying what Margaret had already said to me, only in different words. Jack knew as well as I did how things worked in Greenwood; he knew better than I did. He *was* Greenwood, as much as anyone I'd ever met, and more than most. He had seen it every day of his life, had seen it so much that most of the time he couldn't really see it anymore, unless, like now, it was so large and brazen and outrageous that nothing could camouflage it. Still, like Margaret, Jack didn't sound terribly outraged about it—just resigned, and a bit disgusted, and a little surprised, not much but enough that he let his usual cover, that layer of cool and amused detachment, slip for the briefest moment.

I did what any good friend would do at a moment like that. I changed the subject.

"All right," I said. "So I'll take him out for lunch instead. But where?"

His jaded smirk returned. "I wouldn't recommend the Crystal Club."

✒✒

His mother answered the phone, and handed it off to him.

"Hey, Handy," I said. "What time do you want to get together this afternoon?"

"I guess about twelve-thirty," he answered.

"Great!" I said, mustering all the fake enthusiasm I could. "Great. And hey, listen, how about I take you to Shoney's?"

The phone went dead for a moment. Or so it seemed.

"Uh, Handy?"

The voice was quiet, but not soft—a low growl. I'd never heard it before. "I invited you to my *house*."

"I know, but—"

"I invited you *to my house*."

"Okay, I just thought it might be nice for you—"

"Are you gonna come here, or not?"

My face grew hot. Ever since that conversation with Jack, the night before, I'd been thinking about how I was going to get out of going to Snowden Jones. And yet, I hadn't really been worried about going there until I saw—or heard, anyway—how adamant Handy was about my doing so. Still, I had to meet with him one more time, to ask him a few more questions, and if this was the only way I could do it, I had no choice.

"I—yes, of course," I said. "Twelve-thirty, right?"

"Right," he said, and hung up.

✒✒

It's a cliché to say that a life can change forever in a single moment, and an unusual cliché, at that, because it's rarely true. With very few exceptions—birth, marriage, accidents, death—the really big changes in our lives happen slowly, imperceptibly, without discrete watersheds. Most days, the nature of our existence is almost exactly the same as it was the day before, with no reason to suspect that tomorrow will be any different; and if, a year hence, we look back and see that we are no longer the person we were a year before, we will not, in all likelihood, be able to pinpoint one or two or even a dozen specific milestones that marked the road between there and here.

That is not true for Handy Campbell. He awoke the morning of August 2, 1995, on a thin, fetid mattress in an overcrowded jail cell, knowing that there was an excellent chance that by the end of the day he would be on his way to Parchman, where he would spend the rest of his life and die. Yet that night, he lay down and went to sleep in his own bed, the same bed he had slept in as a child, the same bed he had returned to after his college football career disintegrated. He had spent eleven months and two days as a prisoner, a man suspected of murder, a man indicted for murder, a man on trial for murder; and then, in the space of a few minutes, he was declared not guilty, led outside, unshackled and released, free to rub his wrists and get in his mother's car and drive on home and eat what he pleased and sleep where he wished and go to the bathroom without asking permission and drink and smoke and stay out all night and stay out for days and get a job and not get a job and vote. In a single moment, his life had changed as much as any man's can. And yet, as another cliché holds, he was still the same person he had been the day before.

Only that wasn't true, either, because when I rang the bell outside apartment 3-G at precisely 12:30 on the afternoon of August 3, 1995, the man who opened the door was a man I did not recognize, a man I had never seen before.

He didn't look any different, of course—in fact, he seemed to be wearing the same t-shirt and shorts he'd had on the first time I visited him in jail. But this was very clearly a different Handy Campbell standing before me now. This Handy Campbell didn't slouch or hunch his shoulders forward as if he were trying to fold himself up into himself. He didn't mumble, or cast his eyes down at the ground when he spoke. He didn't say things like "sir" or "thank you." He wasn't humble or shy. He wasn't depressed. There was nothing even remotely passive about him. This wasn't the Handy Campbell who had been on trial for his life, or the Handy Campbell who had moldered in jail awaiting that trial, or who had been kicked off the team at Ole Miss, or who had been relegated to the bench at Ole Miss, or who had been plucked out of Snowden Jones and given the chance to shine on the gridiron. This wasn't the Handy Campbell I related to, the one whose fortunes would climb in a parallel arc to mine; that Handy Campbell was gone. I was starting to doubt he had ever really existed.

This Handy Campbell was a man I did not know. He stood up straight, used his height to stare down and glower and intimidate. He looked me dead in the eye, and spoke loud and clear in a voice that wasn't confident so much as it was authoritative. This Handy Campbell wasn't content to sit and answer questions for an hour or two; he wanted to ask them. His objective was no longer merely to be heard. He had demands.

"Come on," he said, and led me silently to the kitchen. His mother was there, sitting at the table. She eyed me suspiciously for a moment, then pointed to a chair across from her. I took it.

"We're having macaroni," Handy said as he walked over to the kitchen counter. "With meat sauce."

"Great," I chirped, and tried to figure out if there was a way I could just ask my questions and leave. "So, uh, Handy," I said, attempting to do just that, "what are you going to do now?"

He turned around and looked at me for a moment. "First thing," he said, immediately making eye contact, "I need to get some money."

Okay, I thought. What am I supposed to say now? Should I ask him why? Or how? Or does he want me to tell him how to do it? Or to just offer it to him myself?

"You and me, both," I said.

He didn't laugh, or smile. "Maybe I'll sell cars or something," he said.

I wondered what local auto dealership would hire him to sell their cars, when everyone in town now knew him as both a failed football player *and* a man who got away with murder. "And—okay, and, uh, after that?" I asked.

"I need to finish my education," he replied, in a tone more grimly determined than hopeful. "I want to be a nurse. Maybe I'll be a lawyer." He raised his arm and rubbed the back of his neck, a gesture that was vaguely, oddly menacing. "I really want to coach."

I opened my mouth to speak; it seemed an appropriate moment to say *something*. But what could I say? That I thought the prospect of him coaching somewhere was even more absurd than that of selling cars? Why didn't he just run for mayor? What school did he expect to hire him—Ole Miss?

He seemed to read my mind. "I don't want you to print that stuff about race at Ole Miss," he said, then glanced at his mother and left it at that. She nodded sternly.

"Handy," I said, "you can't ask me not to print that. It's a true story."

He turned away from me and back to the counter, where there sat a large, unopened can of tomato paste and, right next to it, a can opener. He looked at both for a second, then opened a drawer, pulled out a large butcher's knife, and plunged it into the lid of the can. He knew how to make a point.

I turned to his mother, hoping, expecting, her to tell her son to stop clowning around, or at least tell *me* he was just clowning around. But she didn't say a word. Like her son, she seemed to have transformed into an entirely new person, a woman who would do anything—*anything*—to protect and support that son, a woman who seemed utterly incapable of anxiously saying something like "What do you think will happen to my child?" Now she seemed much more concerned with what would happen to me, and not in a good way.

It was a tense and silent lunch.

But at least it was mercifully brief. We all ate pretty quickly, and soon (if not quite soon enough) I was thanking them and rising to leave. Handy collected the dirty plates; his hands full, I decided it was safe to ask him one final question:

"What really happened that night?"

His mother narrowed her eyes and looked about ready to pitch me out a window without even opening it first; but Handy, to my surprise—and relief—remained calm.

"I don't want to talk about it," he said, continuing to clear the table. "I want to put that behind me."

"But Handy," I said, emboldened by the calm in his voice, "I'm just asking, because, uh, there *were* parts of your story that didn't—"

"I didn't have to prove my story was true," he said. "They had to prove it wasn't."

What could I say? He was right. And they didn't.

Now his mother looked ready to act on that urge. She stood up, and gestured, unmistakably, for me to do the same. As soon as I did, she firmly ushered me to the door. We were just about there when Handy called out from the kitchen, "Wait a minute!"

I tried to mask my excitement. Was this it? Was he going to tell me after all? Did he feel some sort of obligation to me, perhaps some gratitude for my coming to see him in jail, for sitting through his entire trial? Or was it for old times' sake, for all the Friday nights I came out to watch him play, and all the inches I gave him in the Sunday sports section? Had he once felt, like I had, that our lives were proceeding in parallel trajectories, that fate had placed us both in Greenwood, Mississippi in the fall of 1988 to fuel each other's ambitions, and that for the sake of karma, or the cosmos, or God, or closure, he would now tell me everything? Or was it simply that, knowing the prohibition against double jeopardy, he figured he had no particular reason *not* to tell me?

"Hey," he said, trotting over to the door, which his mother had already opened. "You gonna write about this?"

"I don't know," I said warily. "I might."

His lips slowly seeped into a smile. "What's my share?" he asked. "Fifty-fifty?"

I just stared at him, dumb. It had occurred to me, the minute he'd opened the door that day, that I no longer knew who he was; now I realized that, truly, I never had. Never.

Slowly, very slowly, I turned around and started walking down the steps. It was only when I heard the door close behind me that I started to breathe again.

I had three days to kill before my flight back to New York. I spent two of them visiting old friends in Jackson and Oxford and Greenville and Clarksdale and Indianola and Itta Bena and Vaiden and Carrollton and Greenwood. On the evening of the second day, just as the sun was beginning to set, I drove out Grand Boulevard and over the Tallahatchie and up to Money and parked across the road from the dilapidated old edifice that had once been Bryant's Grocery and Meat Market, the place where Emmett Till had said and done whatever it was that cost him his life. It was exactly forty years to the month from that fatal encounter, I realized, forty years since a jury deliberated just a half hour before finding the men who killed young Till not guilty. Some things had changed since then; a half hour was much less time than three hours and forty minutes. But in the end, Freddie Williams was no better off than Emmett Till. A black man's life, it seemed, still wasn't worth much in Mississippi.

That reality, though, had given Handy Campbell a perverse kind of justice. Call it the mixed blessing of being a black man in Mississippi: On the one hand, the state can't allow you to succeed, can't allow you to call the plays for white running backs and receivers, to throw the ball in front of white fans and alumni, to break out and make money, get famous, do *something,* be *somebody.* On the other hand, the state can't really be bothered to convict you for killing another black man, especially if he's also a "flashy dresser" and a "frequent outgoing socializer" and a homosexual or bisexual or some kind of queer, anyway. In the end it's a trade-off, a trade-off that left Handy Campbell no richer or poorer than he had been that afternoon eight years before when he first set foot on the gridiron at Greenwood High School.

On the morning of the third day—Saturday—I walked downtown. It was CROP day.

Cotton Row On Parade was another Greenwood festival that, like the Christmas parade, had degenerated a great deal over the years. It had once been something to see, I was told, an oasis of festivity in the middle of the oppressive Delta summer, a celebration of local culture and crafts, energetic and well-organized and centered around a huge parade and the elaborate Miss CROP Day pageant. Now, though, it was just a tired old street fair, sparse and forced and pocked by the empty storefronts that now held a controlling stake of the downtown. I made my way down Howard Street, past the darkened plate glass windows of Morris Office Machines, where I'd once attended a Christmas party with half the town, and turned onto Front Street. The proud old avenue of cotton brokerages was littered with ramshackle booths hawking knockoff watches and knockoff hair care products and bootleg cassettes, and hard as I tried not to I couldn't help thinking about the time I'd stood there in the December chill with Vic and Jack and Karen and watched the withered Christmas parade stumble by so pathetically it made Vic cry to think of how grand it had been when he was a child, and now I understood, because now my Greenwood was gone too, and my Greenwood had been as special to me as Vic's had been to him, and maybe we all get only one special Greenwood in a lifetime, and that by nature it has to be frail and fleeting and when it's gone nothing else can ever measure up to it again, and as we continue to live in the void left by its passing we are constantly reminded of that fact. Things change.

And I turned away from Front Street and walked back up Howard Street until I came to Goldberg's shoe store, and I went inside and chatted a while with Mrs. Goldberg and her son Mike and her daughter-in-law Gail, and we smiled and wished each other well and then I turned to leave and found myself not twelve inches away from and staring into the face of Lanardo Myrick.

Immediately he broke out that enormous grin of his and nodded and said: "I *bet* you didn't expect to run into *me* here!"

"No," I said, startled, "I sure didn't."

I walked on out of the store and he followed me into the street, so I turned and asked him the same question I had asked Handy: Did he want to tell me what really happened that night? And he just smiled and wagged his finger at me and said that there were people here in Greenwood who had said this strange thing or done that mysterious thing, and there was sure enough something very funny going on, but he couldn't say for sure what it was and that probably nobody would ever know the *real* truth, and then he laughed loud and said, "I told you it would work out! Didn't I tell you?"

"Yes, you did," I said. "So what will you do now?"

"I might go back to Houston," he said, "run some with Carl Lewis, or maybe I'll go back up to Ole Miss, run there. But that's just my short-term plans."

"Oh, yeah?" I said. "What do you have planned for the long-term?"

He looked right at me and winked. "You *know* I want to go into politics!"

I had to laugh, but not because I thought him absurd; just the opposite. I thought it a perfect fit, and much more likely than Lanardo Myrick sprinting at the Olympics or Ole Miss. This guy, I thought, really could be mayor of Greenwood someday. He was a survivor, an adapter, a conniver, consistent only in his confidence and his ability to get past, one way or another, anything life would throw at him. When Handy Campbell had succumbed to despair and broke down and confessed, Lanardo Myrick, who had dwelt in Handy's shadow for most of their lives, remained confident, almost cocky, that things would work out for *him.* I suspect that, no matter how he acted, Handy considered himself lucky to have beaten the rap; but I'm positive Lanardo believed that luck had nothing to do with it. Much as I despised the thought, it seemed to me that people like Lanardo Myrick represented Greenwood's future.

Handy Campbell represented its past. And more than anything else, his fall marked the death of my Greenwood.

❧

That night, I took Jack, his wife and son to dinner at the Crystal. We all had salad, a main course (mine was chicken fried steak), iced tea and dessert. As I recall, the check came to a little less than twenty dollars.

As we left, Jack and I lagged behind while his wife and son ran off to fetch their car.

"Say, Richit," Jack said, "you ever gon' write about this place?"

"I don't know," I said, wondering what share Jack was going to demand. "I might."

Jack grimaced, turned his head and spat some chew out on the sidewalk. "I tell you what," he said. "You make us all look bad, now, and I'll kick your Ivy League Yankee Jew ass!"

I was moved. "Just between you and me," I said, "the year I lived here was one of the best of my life."

He turned away, spat again. We walked on for a few seconds in silence, and then he said: "You ain't gon' put in there how I called you an ol' Yankee Jew now, are you?"

And I told him: No, indeed.

ACKNOWLEDGMENTS

I am greatly indebted to all of the people who graciously allowed me to interview them on the record for his book, despite the fact that, in almost every case, they stood to gain absolutely nothing by doing so. That's just how Mississippians are, at least in my expereince, and I am most grateful for having had that experience.

I am grateful, too, for all of the people in Mississippi who helped me plug the holes in my knowledge and memory, including Ruth Belcher, Phil Cohen, Reginald "Dean" Dean, Alita DeBarry, Harry Diamond, Celia Emmerich, Joe Martin Erber, Jennifer Flautt, Ilse Goldberg, Gail Goldberg, David Jordan, Tim Kalich, Gert Kornfeld, Leslie Kornfeld, Murray "Bubba" Kornfeld, Vic Laurent, Marshall Levitt, Susan Montgomery, Janie Mortimer, Frances Shivel, Erik Werner, and Jerry Wexler. And special thanks to Margaret Dean, Jack Henderson, Karen Freeman, and Frances "Bud" Welch, great friends who all did so much more than their share.

Many non-Mississippians have also helped this book along its way by reading part or all of it at one time or another or otherwise offering guidance, assistance, and support, including Leslie Epstein, Deborah Harris, Martha Hunt Huie, Dina Klugman, Rick Klugman, and Roberta Lehrman; Kathy Kappenburg Astor, Amanda Ayers, Joanna Goddard, Penny Haynes, Felice Javit, and Paolo Pepe at Atria Books; and Jud Laghi and John De Laney at ICM. Speical thanks to Steven Malk, who sold this book back when it was just a proposal; Emily Heckman, who bought it; The New York Public Library, which furnishes, at no cost, the finest writing space in existence, and where nearly every word of this book was written (and rewritten); Heather Morse, who with patience and care and to my great benefit read every word of every draft; Mitchell Ivers, my editor at

Atria, whose wisdom and experience left their mark on every page; and Kris Dahl, my agent, who somehow managed to keep me calm and focused most of the time.

Finally, I would like to thank two people without whom this book would not exist in any form. Anything of any import that I have written in the past decade—from emails on up—has been vetted by Kim Bartlett Koster; she is the best editor any writer could have, and the best friend any human being could have. John Oliver Emmerich, Jr. (1929–1995) hired me over the telephone to come down and work at his daily newspaper in Greenwood, Mississippi, despite the fact that I knew nothing and thought I knew everything. I only hope he didn't regret it every day.